The Road to *Wicked*

Kent Drummond · Susan Aronstein
Terri L. Rittenburg

The Road to *Wicked*

The Marketing and Consumption of Oz
from L. Frank Baum to Broadway

For Devin,
With all my love,
Terri

palgrave
macmillan

Kent Drummond
Department of Management
and Marketing
University of Wyoming
Laramie, WY, USA

Terri L. Rittenburg
Department of Management
and Marketing
University of Wyoming
Laramie, WY, USA

Susan Aronstein
Department of English
University of Wyoming
Laramie, WY, USA

ISBN 978-3-319-93105-0   ISBN 978-3-319-93106-7   (eBook)
https://doi.org/10.1007/978-3-319-93106-7

Library of Congress Control Number: 2018945490

Cover credit: Charoen pattarapitak/Alamy Stock Photo, Ger Bosma/Moment Open/ Getty Images
Cover design by Henry Petrides

Printed on acid-free paper

This Palgrave Macmillan imprint is published by the registered company Springer International Publishing AG part of Springer Nature
The registered company address is: Gewerbestrasse 11, 6330 Cham, Switzerland

We dedicate this book to our mothers—Evalyn, Evelyn, and Janet—who introduced us to The Wizard of Oz *and to the joys of musical theater.*

ACKNOWLEDGEMENTS

This book is the culmination of the work of its co-authors, but the final product is due to the help and support of so many others.

Our dear friends and colleagues at the University of Wyoming, including those in the Honors College and the Departments of Management and Marketing and English, sustained us intellectually and emotionally, and for that, we will always be grateful. We are also indebted to our graduate students who, in classes and hallways, were always willing to take a moment to talk about Oz and Cultural Sustainability. The Wyoming Institute for the Humanities, and the College of Business's Sustainable Business Practices Fund provided valuable financial support to kick-start this project. We especially thank President Laurie Nichols, "First Gent" Tim Nichols, and Provost Kate Miller for their unwavering belief in our Oz-Odyssey.

We also appreciate our professional Associations—the Macromarketing Society, the International Arthurian Society, and the Consumer Culture Theory Consortium—whose members helped us refine earlier versions of this work. Additionally, the producers and consumers who participated in our research proved invaluable; their experiences and insights definitively shaped this study. Convention organizers, festival volunteers and museum staff graciously welcomed us into their spaces and places, and for that, we are truly grateful. We would like to offer special thanks to John Fricke, Oz historian extraordinaire, who generously shared with us his vast knowledge and insights into all things Oz. His unique combination of brains, heart, and courage continues to inspire.

Samantha Velez, our exemplary research assistant quickly and cheerfully tracked down obscure references, organized research files, and aided in data analysis. Thank you, Sam! We also thank Shawn Vigil, Glenn Ramirez, and the staff at Palgrave Macmillan for their steadfast support, patience, and assistance as we traveled the road to *Wicked*.

CONTENTS

LIST OF FIGURES

CHAPTER 1

We're Off to See the Wizard: In Search of Cultural Sustainability

This book was born on a balmy summer night in New York City, in 2013. We were passing the Gershwin Theatre at almost 11 o'clock, when its doors suddenly swung open, disgorging 1900 patrons. As they poured out onto the plaza in front of the Gershwin, we noticed that some were wearing tiaras, some were sporting sparkly red shoes, and many were dressed in green. Talking excitedly, they began to wend their way down 51st Street and climb into cabs, Ubers, subways, and high-rise hotels. The sheer volume of the excited crowd flooding out of the theater, the buzz they created as they walked down the street, and their animation as they discussed—even reenacted—specific scenes and songs from the show they'd just seen suggested to us that a hot new blockbuster was playing at the Gershwin, the largest theater on Broadway. Instead, these patrons had just experienced *Wicked: The Untold Story of the Witches of Oz*, ten years into its run and still drawing standing room-only crowds. How, we asked each other, does this musical, a decade after its premiere, continue to draw consumers to its doors, not only in the major cities of New York and London, but also in more far-flung American cities such as Schenectady, East Lansing, Providence, and Appleton? And what can possibly explain its success in such non-American locations such as India, Norway, and Singapore?

Panned by nearly every critic who attended its 2003 premiere, *Wicked* remains a cultural phenomenon. By May of 2016, *Wicked* had grossed $4 billion worldwide, having played to 50 million people in 14 countries, including the UK, Germany, Brazil, and Japan.[1] It reached the $1 billion

© The Author(s) 2018
K. Drummond et al., *The Road to Wicked*,
https://doi.org/10.1007/978-3-319-93106-7_1

milestone on Broadway faster than any other show in history, according to *Variety*.[2] The *Wicked* soundtrack has been certified double-platinum. *Wicked* merchandise, ranging from golf balls to tote bags, at one point generated at least $300,000 per week—more than most Broadway plays.[3] A movie version of the show is promised in December 2019. Only *The Phantom of the Opera* and *The Lion King*, both much older musicals, exceed these performance figures. *Wicked*'s unprecedented success—its ability to sustain itself over time—poses a fascinating question for those of us who work at the intersection of consumer research and cultural studies.

The problem is that answering the question of why—and how—*Wicked* has been so successful for so long is like joining a game of Jenga in the middle of a round. Suddenly, it's your turn. You gently pull on a piece, and you immediately become aware that the piece you've chosen is critically connected to all the other pieces in the tower. But some pieces feel more "pressing" than others. And some pieces appear to be completely unaffected by what you're doing—until you move your piece just *this* way and watch the entire tower sway precariously.

To extend the metaphor: We soon learned that any attempt to precisely extract the *Wicked* piece on its own—without considering its relationship to *all* the other pieces in the tower that is the Oz complex—would not only be insufficient; it could annihilate the very tower we were trying to preserve. For *Wicked* is but one of *hundreds* of pieces—or, what we refer to as re-consumptions—of the Oz monolith, dating back almost 120 years. That's how long Oz has occupied a unique space in America's cultural landscape. For it turns out that before *Wicked*—and, for that matter, before Hogwarts and Middle Earth—there was L. Frank Baum's original story, *The Wonderful Wizard of Oz*, published in 1900. An immediate bestseller, the story inspired sequels, Broadway musicals, theme park attractions, and, ultimately, the famous MGM musical, *The Wizard of Oz*, debuting in 1939. In the '50s and '60s, this film became an annual, ritualized television event, weaving Oz into the cultural landscape of the baby-boomer generation. Even *Wicked*, the musical, is based on Gregory Maguire's 1995 novel, *Wicked: The Life and Times of the Wicked Witch of the West*, which is itself based on a combination of the MGM film and Baum's books.

Thus, *Wicked*'s sensational reception extends well beyond its fifteen years on Broadway; Oz has long been a place where authors and composers can tell an old tale in a new way, marketing their creations across space, time, and media. And consumers have long responded with equal engagement, eager to see, hear, and experience a new version of Oz—the latest sequel, the newest adaptation, and the untold story. So in order to answer our question about *Wicked*'s success, we need to expand our query: How has *Oz itself* remained culturally sustainable? More specifically, how does Oz keep reinventing itself, such that it becomes newly relevant to new groups of consumers, without losing its established consumer base?

In *The Road to Wicked*, we seek to answer these questions about Oz in general, and *Wicked* in particular, by examining the production and consumption of America's classic fairy tale, standing as it does at the intersection of narrative, marketing, media, and technological forces. Our study of the road to *Wicked*, then, is a study in cultural sustainability. On the one hand, we examine the capacity of artists, narratives, art forms, and genres to remain artistically viable over time; and on the other, we examine the marketing machinery and consumption patterns that make such viability possible. Drawing on the fields of consumer behavior, literary and cultural studies, and theories of adaption and remediation, we bring an interdisciplinary approach to the history of Oz that allows us to examine that history as an ongoing dialogue between producers and consumers.

As with many cultural artifacts, Oz is provoked by a seemingly-simple need-based exchange: consumers desire "more Oz," as one of Baum's early fans pleaded, and producers satisfy that desire by bringing to market new adaptations of Oz. The reality, of course, is far more complex than that. From Baum's 1900 novel, through the original Oz craze, the MGM film and its television afterlife, *Wicked* and its extensions, to the current post-*Wicked* years (including *Oz the Great and Powerful*, *Emerald City*, and young adult novels), cultural sustainability is born of a complicated interchange of multiple parties, spanning decades. Artists, producers, and distributors must continually make Oz marketable, in theme and form, to new audiences, all the while satisfying older audiences who wish to return to the Oz they once knew. And consumers must maintain their interest in an Oz myth that is now over 100 years old—in a marketplace full of so many younger, flashier alternatives (including *Star Wars*, *Harry Potter*, and Marvel action heroes). In the age of social media, Oz offerings must now be presented as *consumption experiences* that can be shared globally and instantaneously. Critics and bloggers, eager for wider readership and greater influence, must assess the value of these offerings in a way that sparks consumer interest. And prosumers, always eager to take matters into their own hands, must create home-grown variations of such offerings in a way that captures the admiration of online consumers while avoiding the legalistic gaze of producers. Compared to this complex interaction of moving parts and parties, the seminal art production framework offered by Howard Becker almost thirty years ago looks Spartan.[4]

THERE'S NO PLACE LIKE HOME:
OZ AND CULTURAL SUSTAINABILITY

But what does it mean to study Oz through the lens of cultural sustainability? That depends on what is meant by the latter term. Here, we take a somewhat different perspective from that of more conventional scholars in this area, such as cultural activist and promoter Jon Hawkes. For Hawkes, culture becomes the fourth leg added to John Elkington's well-known three-legged model of sustainability, in which the economic, social, and environmental aspects (i.e., profit/people/planet) of a business entity are assessed.[5] According to this view, cultural sustainability is essential to public policy and planning, and for the critical role it plays in a number of disparate functions, including the preservation of indigenous cultures, the artistic vitality of urban landscapes, and the conservation of heritage sites that promote cultural tourism. Culture, here, is about making and doing, as opposed to the examination of cultural artifacts.

Our take on cultural sustainability differs from Hawkes's because of the data we examine; Oz, in all its forms, is a collection of cultural artifacts. To study those artifacts is to acknowledge a reflexive relationship between the artifactual collection and the culture from which it comes and to which it continually returns for renewal. Thus it is that, in everyday conversation, we can deploy phrases such as "There's no place like home," "I guess we're not in Kansas anymore," and "Lions and tigers and bears – oh my!" and be reasonably assured that those around us will understand our cultural referent. And thus it was that in 2013, conservative commentator Glenn Beck was able to perform a ten-minute political parody of *The Wizard of Oz*, complete with the American people as Dorothy, then-President Obama as Professor Marvel, and various government agencies as the Wicked Witch of the West.[6] This in itself quotes a much earlier and more famous interpretation of Baum's worldview, which claimed that Oz was an elaborate metaphor for the Populist movement, a rising political force in the 1890s.[7]

The point is that people in America have been drawing on the cultural storehouse that is Oz for over a century. The fact that they can do so without having to explain very much speaks to Oz's cultural ubiquity—as well as its cultural capital, for almost everyone regards Oz fondly. At the micro-level, use or perform a reference to Oz adroitly in everyday conversation, and your interactional stock is bound to go up, if only momentarily. At the macro-level, put a new twist on an existing Oz tale (e.g., *Oz, The Great and Powerful*), and you could make literally hundreds of millions of dollars in a matter of months. Oz is not only a storehouse; it is a treasure house, waiting for the next creative entrepreneur to repurpose a share of its contents.

That is why, in our study of Oz and *Wicked*, it is more appropriate and more important to ask: How does this cache of cultural artifacts *sustain itself* within a culture? How does it stay relevant to that culture, so that it remains part of the complex of rituals, symbols, and utterances through which people convey meaning to one another and define themselves as a group? As we shall see in our examination of the Oz narrative, a symbiotic relationship is in play here: In order for an *artifact* to sustain itself, it must help sustain the *culture*; and in order for a *culture* to sustain itself, it requires a set of cultural *artifacts*—myths, narratives, artworks, and symbols—to circumscribe its community and communicate its values. That is why our approach operates at the meso-level, midway between micro- and macro-perspectives. Only from this vantage point can we appropriately collect and analyze data that reveals the complex interaction of forces we wish to capture.

Furthermore, in order to understand how Oz has sustained itself from Baum to *Wicked* and beyond, we build a theoretical framework that accounts for both its *narrative vitality* and its *commercial vitality*. By narrative vitality, we mean those aspects of a story that make it available to being adapted over time. To assess this, we draw on theories from literary and new media studies, including adaptation, remediation, transmedia storytelling, and fan and convergence culture. By commercial vitality, we mean the consideration of the economic, social, and environmental contexts that bring a text to market. In order to assess this, we draw on theories of macromarketing, Consumer Culture Theory (CCT), and experiential marketing (EM).

"There's No Place Like Oz:"
Meditations on Baum's Fairy Land

We are, of course, not the first to recognize the fact that Oz has woven itself into our cultural fabric. Nor are we the first to query what it is about Oz that has allowed the narrative to sustain itself for over a century. Indeed, as we will show, each iteration of the Oz myth inspires critics and reviewers to first recount the narrative's history to date and then to speculate on its enduring popularity—a move echoed in almost every academic study of Baum and his fantasyland. While a detailed examination of these speculations lies outside of our study of the marketing and consumption of Oz, since a *story* lies at the heart of the narrative's sustainability, it makes sense to at least begin our discussion of the ways in which Oz has extended and adapted itself over time with a speculative overview. As Ray Bradbury queries in his preface to *The Kansas Centennial Edition* of *The Wizard of Oz*: "And what, you may ask, are the reasons why?/ *The Wizard of Oz* will never die?"[8]

In his introduction to the 2013 collection, *Oz Reimagined: New Tales from Emerald City*, Gregory Maguire offers his take on the narrative's enduring power:

> Oz comes to us early in our lives ... It has no name way back then, just 'the other place.' It's the unspecified site of adventures of the fledgling hero, the battleground for the working out of early dilemmas, and the garden of future delights yet unnamed....We know our childhood through the living of it. And for a century or so, in America we have called [it] by the name of Oz ... as vast as Middle Earth and as moral as Camelot. This is to say, of course, that Oz is a mirror.[9]

Maguire's meditation on Oz speaks to the power of the marvelous "other place" to invoke and satisfy desire, to provide a testing ground for heroism and identities, and to offer those who journey there truths to carry back into their more mundane "Kansas" worlds. In other words, the power of Oz is the power of, to quote J. R. R. Tolkien, "Faerie," a realm "wide and deep and filled with many things: all manner of beasts and birds...; shoreless seas and stars uncounted; beauty that is an enchantment and ever-present peril."[10]

As the "other place" of adventures, Oz fulfills all of Tolkien's functions of the fairy tale. First, Oz offers a believable *fantasy* realm, a world that satisfies what Tolkien argues are primal desires for communion with other living things, including witches and dragons—a world in which choices matter and heroism is possible. Second, the fantasy *escape* from the gray of Kansas to the vibrancy of Oz provides a chance of *recovery*, as Tolkien terms it, "a re-gaining of a clear view." In this process, the memories and lessons from Oz are brought back to Kansas, providing the *consolation* of the happy ending.[11]

As almost every gatekeeper of Oz has noted—from the first reviews of *The Wonderful Wizard of Oz* to the most recent work on the myth—Oz's fantasyland has been coded as peculiarly American. Give or take the Cowardly Lion and the Hungry Tiger, its talking animals are domesticated farm beasts: horses, cows, chickens, and a cat or two. Friendly Scarecrows replace unicorns; and while there are dark forests, there are also farmlands and cities. Moreover, in the beginning at least, bravery and heroism in Oz meant very different things than they did in Grimm—or Tolkien. Self-reliance, friendship, loyalty, pragmatism, and ingenuity (exemplified by brains, heart, and courage) displaced swords and battles. The consolation of the happy ending was a homey one: friends reunited, order restored, a party in the Emerald City. For gatekeepers and consumers alike, the power of Oz lies in its basic, universal truths of heroism and the simple consolations that flow from it: a kindly philosophy, an essential optimism. As Bradbury, contrasting the "bakery air" of Oz with the winter landscape of Wonderland, observes: The traveler in Oz is "an impossible optimist, the happy warrior, the convivial far-traveler ... If the wicked witch is truly dead, it is because L. Frank Baum landed on her with his Boy's-Life-Forever-Sunkist-Philosophy."[12]

With its eternal American optimism, this is the Oz that carried the narrative through its first seventy years, mapping the childhood of so many writers who began as Oz-consumers and became Oz-producers. In addition to Bradbury and Maguire, these include Gore Vidal, Harlan Ellison, and Salman Rushdie. "I have a precise, tactile memory of the first Oz book that came into my hands," Vidal recounts, "It was the original 1910 edition of *The Emerald City*. I still remember the look and feel of those dark green covers, the evocative smell of dust and old ink.... In some mysterious way, I was translating myself to Oz, a place which I was to inhabit for many years."[13]

Today's Oz, at times darkly political (*Emerald City*), and at others bright and nostalgic (*Lost in Oz*), differs greatly from the Oz that Vidal inhabited in his childhood. That's because, as Maguire explains, "standards … vary from person to person. Oz is nonsense. Oz is musical. Oz is satire. Oz is fantasy. Oz is brilliant. Oz is vaudeville. Oz is obvious. Oz is secret."[14] For Maguire, these multiple Ozes stem from multiple childhoods, the Oz souvenirs each child has acquired along the way:

> Yours might be the set derived from those hardcovers in your grand-mother's attic, the ones with the John R. Neill drawings…Or your souvenir cards may be the popular MGM set starring Margaret Hamilton…. Or your souvenirs might be more like mine: memories of being a kid and reenacting (and expanding upon) the adventures of Dorothy using the terrain at hand … Perhaps my souvenirs of Oz are darker than yours. I can't help that, life gives what it will.[15]

Since the first Oz craze at the beginning of the twentieth-century to the most recent Oz-offering, gatekeepers have offered a range of explanations for the myth's enduring popularity, from its fantasy world of adventures, through its peculiarly American pragmatism, populism, and optimism, to its enduring hold on our childhood imagination and memories. What these explanations have in common is that they all posit an *ur*-Oz: a myth that stands outside of history, independent of any individual text or product. Yet as Salman Rushdie asserts, "No single author can claim Oz… not even the author of the original book…[it] is as close as you can get to that will-o'-the wisp of modern critical theory, the authorless text."[16] Yet this very quality renders Oz *adaptable* and *flexible*; if no one owns it, it can freely evolve to fit new times, new audiences, and new desires.

A YELLOW BRICK ROAD BUILT TO LAST: OZ AND THEORIES OF NARRATIVE VITALITY

Adaptation: Making Oz Suitable

In order to explore how and why the Oz narrative has been able to remain culturally sustainable, we examine its history through the lens of a number of theories. Studies of adaptation and fanfiction allow us to address the narrative *content* and the ways in which the story has adapted and expanded over time; Henry Jenkin's and Richard Bolter and David Grusin's discussions of new media, combined with more recent work on transmedia storytelling, provide us with a framework for the *mechanisms* of sustainability, which offer consumers narrative content across a variety of platforms, and both Jenkins and fanfiction scholars give insight into the ways in which consumers become producers to play a vital role in any narrative's cultural sustainability.[17]

As we seek to understand all of the factors that have contributed to Oz's longevity, Linda Hutcheon's groundbreaking work on adaptation theory provides us with a framework within which to examine over a century of Oz-adaptations, beginning with Baum's 1902 staging of *The Wizard of Oz* and concluding with NBC's 2016 televised *Emerald City*. Hutcheon argues that the first step to understanding the role adaptation plays in the production and reception of narrative is to abandon what she calls *fidelity criticism*. Fidelity criticism begins with a *source*, usually (but not always) a written source, that is assumed to have *priority* and *authority*, and measures adaptations in terms of how "faithful" they are to their original. Thus, the adaptation is always seen as somehow "secondary," and "derivative," and any deviation from the source text is coded as "'tampering,' 'interference,' 'violation'....'betrayal,' 'deformation,' 'perversion,' 'infidelity,' and 'desecration.'"[18] For fidelity critics, the best adaptation is one that deviates as little as possible from its original, and, at best, it serves as a kind of a gateway drug, leading consumers back to the source text. While Hutcheon's discussion of fidelity criticism focuses mainly on the reception of popular adaptations of high-cultural literary artifacts, such as cinematic versions of the works of William Shakespeare, James Joyce, and E. M. Forster, her observations apply equally to the reception of adaptations of more popular texts, such as Oz and Harry Potter.

This attachment to the priority of the source, with its accompanying suspicion of the adaptation, Hutcheon argues, fails to take into account the dynamic role adaptation plays in the cultural life of narratives. "An adaptation is not vampiric," she asserts, "It does not draw the lifeblood from its source and leave it dying or dead....It may, on the contrary, keep that prior work alive, giving it an afterlife it would never have had otherwise." The dictionary definition of "to adapt," she reminds us, is "to adjust, to alter, to make suitable."[19] As such, she suggests we think of adaptation not in vampiric but in Darwinian terms:

> To think of narrative adaptation in terms of a story's fit and its process of mutation or adjustment, through adaptation, to a particular cultural environment is something I find suggestive. Stories also evolve by adaptation

and are not immutable over time. Sometimes, like biological adaptation, cultural adaptation involves migration to favorable conditions: stories travel to different cultures and different media. In short, stories adapt as they are adapted.[20]

In other words, the ongoing process of adaptation is a process of making a narrative *suitable* to new contexts, new generations, and new consumers. As Leo Braudy observes in his discussion of film remakes, adaptations often address "unfinished cultural business" as they explore the "continuing historical relevance…of a particular narrative."[21] Without such explorations, narratives become fixed, outmoded, and outdated; if lucky, they are relegated to the classroom and classics shelf, along with Chaucer and George Elliot, and occasionally given a "prestige" film treatment. If not, they simply pass out of the cultural consciousness. In order to achieve and maintain long-term cultural sustainability, a narrative must adapt and be adapted.

Not all narratives, however, enter into the chain of adaptation. As Hutcheon reminds us, "marketability is key." Stories do not just spontaneously adapt themselves to new environments and new mediums.[22] Instead, adaptation takes place within a context of producers, consumers, and medium. No story gets adapted to film unless there is something in it for the producers/studios paying for that adaptation, and, while a text's "cultural capital" will occasionally compensate for less-than-stellar box office potential, in general, "the money" wants to make more money; a tale is considered fit for adaptation only if it has the potential both to deliver a preexisting audience and to attract a new one. Producers, whether they live in 1902 or 2018, tend to back a tried and trusted commodity in a new form, as opposed to a new product offering altogether. They want name—if not brand—recognition, an established base of consumers, and the potential for franchising and brand extensions, spin-offs, and repurposing. At the very least, they want cultural capital. For these reasons, producers tend to greenlight adaptations of narratives with high name-recognition (*Oz*), current bestsellers (*Harry Potter*), and literary icons (Shakespeare and Dickens). Most desirable of all, of course, is a popular work in the public domain, which comes free and brings with it the potential for high profits. Furthermore, the fact that the adaptation *is* an adaptation is central to its marketability; hence, adaptations aggressively tie themselves to their source text, building on the "preconstructed and preselected audience" of the original.[23] At the same time, however, adaptations seek to attract new consumers by offering them the narrative in a new form.

As they do so, adaptations depend on consumers' "horizon of expectations" in two distinct ways: they can appeal to the already-established expectations held by one segment of consumers familiar with the narrative; and they can establish new expectations for that segment of consumers experiencing the narrative for the first time. In fact, Hutcheon argues, once a narrative has entered into the chain of adaptation, there is no such thing as a singular original text. Since consumers can enter into that chain at any point, *that* point, for *them*, becomes the[ir] original text. Indeed, Oz perfectly supports Hutcheon's argument that versions of a narrative exist "laterally," not "vertically." Most consumers first encounter Oz through the 1939 MGM film, *The Wizard of Oz*, not Baum's novels, so the film sets their expectations. Then, they may read several of Baum's books, then watch *Tin Man*. Regardless of the scenario, adaptations become "palimpsestous," as each newly encountered adaptation writes over its predecessors, and each is "haunted at all times by its adapted texts."[24] This means that consumers cannot watch or read a new Oz—say *Wicked*—without recognizing and remembering other Ozes they have visited. And each new Oz may affect, in retrospect, their reading of the old Ozes, altering their horizon of expectations. Adaptations, then, are in "ongoing dialogue with the past, creat[ing] the double pleasure of the palimpsest: more than one text is experienced:" repetition with variation, recognition, and surprise.[25]

In their process of making—and keeping—texts suitable for new contexts and new consumers, adaptations seek to critique and replace as often as they replicate. In fact, narratives whose adaptations merely replicate themselves run the danger of becoming ossified and parodic, no longer living—or *sustainable*. In order for a narrative to survive, its adaptations need to offer consumers something *new*: a different take on plot or characters, a new perspective, an altered world, a different point of entry into the narrative, a new media, and a new genre. For example, *She's the Man*, the teen-adaptation of Shakespeare's *Twelfth Night*, replaces Shakespeare's aristocratic elite with teenage soccer players; *Wide Sargasso Sea*, a re-telling of *Jane Eyre*, begins in Bermuda and takes the perspective of Rochester's first wife; *Bride and Prejudice* translates Jane Austen's early nineteenth-century British society to modern-day Indian culture; and *Spamalot* "lovingly rips-off" *Monty Python and the Holy Grail*'s postmodern film to put on a Broadway musical.

"By their very existence," Hutcheon asserts, "adaptations remind us that there is no such thing as an autonomous text or an original genius that can transcend history."[26] In other words, to attract new audiences and stay relevant, texts must adapt. Shakespeare's *Taming of the Shrew*, for instance, with its retrograde gender politics, has had a history of being made more palatable. As a film starring Elizabeth Taylor and Richard Burton, it could be seen as art imitating life, a fictional version of the couple's notoriously dramatic and publicly contentious relationship. As the backstage musical, *Kiss Me Kate*, the off-stage story provided a commentary on the onstage relationship. As *Ten Things I Hate About You*, it became an exploration of high-school romance.

Fanfiction and Convergence: Opening Up the Oz Text

Adaptation theory focuses on the urge "to retell the same story;" Oz's vitality, however, also lies in consumers who "never want [the] story to end."[27] Let's go back to Maguire's souvenirs of Oz: his memory of "reenacting (and *expanding upon*) the adventures of Dorothy, using the terrain at hand." Maguire and his baby sister were not content to merely recapitulate Dorothy's journey down the yellow brick road; they added to it.[28] And they were far from the first to do so. From its very beginning, Oz begat consumers demanding more Oz. In the words of a fanfiction blogger, they wanted "to know what happened before, what happened after, what happened in between."[29] Over its long history, Oz tales and adaptations have not merely retold the same story; they have responded to consumers' "craving for further adventures, [to] explore new territories [and] develop characters and relationships."[30]

In *Fan Fiction: A Democratic Genre*, Sheenagh Pugh begins her discussion with a vignette that echoes Maguire's childhood memories:

> When my children were young, they had a set of Robin Hood figures. We would set them out on the floor, with plastic trees to represent Sherwood Forest, build Nottingham Castle out of Lego, and I would act out the stories I recalled from my childhood. When I ran out of stories, I and my audience would invent new ones.[31]

Here, Pugh argues, is the essence of fanfiction: stories "based on a situation or characters originally created by someone else," driven by the desire for more stories.[32] It seems simple. But as with any attempt to define a literary genre or phenomenon, it's more complex than that. For example, what distinguishes fanfiction (usually seen as a marginal, unofficial production) from adaptation and sanctioned continuations—Spock and Kirk on the internet from CBS's *Star Trek: Discovery*? Isn't "all literature, highbrow or low, from the *Aeneid* onward," as Michael Chabon asserts, "fanfiction?"[33] Virgil gives us more Homer, Chaucer more Virgil, Shakespeare more Chaucer, and the movie *Troy* ... more of all of them.

In their introduction to *Fan Fictions and Fan Communities in the Age of the Internet*, Kristine Busse and Karen Hellekson, referencing Roland Barthes, distinguish between a "closed text," what Barthes would call a readerly text, "whose interpretation is solidified with little room for the readers to enter into," and an open or writerly text, which is an "always ongoing, always renegotiated work in progress."[34] An open text, they assert, "invites responses, permits shared authorship, and enjoins communities."[35] In some ways, open and closed, writerly and readerly, are inherent in the narrative itself. Serial narratives, like *Star Trek* and *Buffy the Vampire Slayer*, which are premised on "next week's episode," lend themselves to continuation.[36] So do fantasy or science fiction narratives, as Chabon muses, with their maps of invented worlds: "Readers of Tolkien often recall the strange narrative engendered by those marginal regions and labeled on the books' endpaper maps, yet never visited or even referred to by the characters in *Lord of the Rings*. All enduring popular literature," he concludes, "has this open-ended quality, and extends this invitation to the reader to continue, on his or her own, the adventure."[37]

A narrative that sustains itself "rarely sits still. It's like a living, evolving thing, taking on its own life, one story building on another."[38] In more academic terms, it needs to be what Abigail Derecho, working from Jacques Derrida, calls "archontic," part of an archive "ever open to new entries, new artifacts, new contents." "An archontic text allows, or even invites, writers to enter into it, select specific items they find useful, make new artifacts using these found objects, and deposit the newly made work back into the source text's archive." "The archive is never closed. It opens out into the future."[39]

In order to achieve cultural sustainability, a narrative, like Jane Austen's *Pride and Prejudice*, needs not only to be adapted—to be made suitable to new contexts and new consumers, but it also needs to be part of an open, expanding archive, one from which consumers can draw "such usable artifacts as Elizabeth Bennet, Fitzwilliam Darcy, the sprawling estate of Pemberley, and Austen's peculiar version of English manners," and to which they can contribute: *Bridget Jones' Diary, The Other Bennett Girl, Pride and Prejudice and Zombies,* among others. This concept of text and archive will help us understand the history of Oz, from Baum's novels through the latest post-*Wicked* explosion.[40]

Whether or not a narrative is available to continuation, to living in a "perpetual present," however, sometimes lies beyond the control of the text itself. Corporate-driven concepts of authorship, ownership, and expertise mean that texts really *can* be owned. In a world where "definitive versions are produced, authorized and regulated," in the words of Henry Jenkins, "by some media conglomerate," narratives can be seen as "a limited good" rather than as "shareware" that "accrues value as it moves across different contexts, gets retold in various ways, attracts multiple audiences, and opens itself to a proliferation of meanings."[41] Additionally, narratives can be "closed" by cultural gatekeepers who subscribe to what Jenkins, building on Peter Walsh, calls the "expert paradigm," a paradigm that insists on a closed, bounded body of knowledge that can be mastered, an "interior" and an "exterior" of "people who know things and others who don't." Between the "owners" and the "experts," a closed narrative is only officially available to certain kinds of production and consumption.[42] While this may serve the best interest of the text's owners—say J. K. Rowling and Warner Brothers, or the Baum family and MGM—in the end, it may be that this attitude toward a narrative may not be in the best interest of its cultural sustainability, as our examination of the history of Oz will demonstrate.

Theories of adaptation and fanfiction provide us insight into the *content* of narrative vitality. But Henry Jenkins provides a model for the *mechanism* of cultural sustainability in what he has famously termed "convergence culture:" "where old and new media collide, where grassroots and corporate media intersect, where the power of the media producer and the power of the media consumer interact in unpredictable ways."[43] Examining "the flow of content across multiple media platforms, the cooperation between multiple media industries, and the migratory behavior of media audiences who will go almost anywhere in search of the kinds of entertainment experiences they want," Jenkins argues that "every important story gets sold, and every consumer gets courted across multiple media platforms."[44] In other words, it's no longer about the primary media product, say the film, or novelizations, or the games that are a "means of stamping the franchise logo on some ancillary product." Rather, every media experience offers consumers "a means of expanding the story telling experience."[45] The *Harry Potter* novels tell us one "piece" of the story, and continuation films, such as *Fantastic Beasts and Where to Find Them*, give us another piece, still more pieces are to be found in various interactive games and on the official *Pottermore* site. Media convergence allows corporations to coopt, then monetize, consumers' desire for more by offering them multiple experiences of the narrative—each one reaching consumers where they live, play, and seek entertainment.

This extension of the narrative across multiple platforms, Jenkins observes, responds to a new kind of consumer. "Old consumers," he writes, "were predictable and stayed where you told them to stay...New consumers are migratory, showing a declining loyalty to networks or media.....If the work of media consumers was once silent and invisible, the new consumers are now noisy and public."[46] They are willing "to take media into their own hands," and, if they don't get what they want, they are not unwilling to produce it themselves.[47] No longer isolated individuals, but digitally connected communities, consumers now seek to participate in the production of content, blurring the line between producer and consumer into a new role: the prosumer. Within this evolving consumer culture, the entertainment industry seeks to reach and satisfy multiple markets "by moving content across different delivery systems," where new media and technology coexist with older media, each offering different pleasures and experiences.[48] The result is additive rather than substitutive, Jenkins maintains, because "printed words did not kill spoken words. Cinema did not kill theater. Television did not kill radio [and] each old medium was forced to coexist with the emerging media." New media and technology, and the ability to take advantage of them, are also key to the process of narrative cultural sustainability.[49]

In the early twentieth century as well as the early twenty-first, remediation—defined by theorists David Bolter and Richard Grusin as the movement of content from one media to another, from print to stage, from stage to film, from film to game, from 8 byte games to virtual reality—promises consumers *immediacy*, "experience without mediation." Purporting to provide a real, less-mediated access to the materials, new technologies claim to place consumers "there" in the story in ways that the old technology cannot.[50] As they do so, according to Bolter and Grusin, they also deploy *hypermediacy*, inscribing the earlier technology within the new, in a move that both references it and displaces it.

Consider computer interfaces, for example: We click on an icon of a file, or an address book. DVD players have us click on a reel of film. Our Kindles have us select books by their covers. However, the best—and most time-honored—example of remediations' twin poles of *immediacy* and *hypermediacy* (the calling of attention to the media and its technology) is the transition from book to film, where the stilted print of the book fades away into the immediacy of the film—placing the viewer "right there" in the tale, watching the characters come to life and experiencing events not as they are "told" in retrospect, but as they unfold on the screen before them.

Remediation targets established consumers by offering them a new and more immediate experience of the narrative product; but it also reaches new consumers who may not normally consume products in the old media. Furthermore, as Hutcheon observes, remediations offer consumers different modes of narrative engagement, ranging from *telling* (print) which is "gradual and sequential," and requires "conceptual work" to imagine and visualize a world from "black marks...on a white page," through *showing* (stage, film, and television), or "simultaneous seeing," which depends on "perceptual decoding," to *interacting* (games) in which instead of just interpreting, a player kinetically intervenes in the narrative, "at once, protagonist and director."[51] A narrative that is able to provide consumers multiple modes of engagement is able to both satisfy old consumers with a different way of experiencing the tale and reach multiple market segments: readers, movie goers, theater lovers, and gamers.

Bringing Oz to Market: Commercial Vitality

Yet narrative vitality, by itself, is not enough to afford the kind of sustainability Oz has enjoyed for over a century. Commercial vitality also plays a critical role in sustaining Oz. In order to conceptualize commercial vitality, we draw on several sub-disciplines within the field of marketing, including macromarketing, Consumer Culture Theory, and experiential marketing. Taken together, they explain the marketplace forces that keep Oz artifacts in the forefront of consumers' perceptions, emotions, and experiences.

Just as narrative vitality depends upon a work's ability to adapt itself over time to new audiences, commercial vitality depends upon an artifact's ability to adapt itself over time to new markets. As such, our analysis of Oz's cultural sustainability depends on macromarketing. Standing at the intersection of markets, marketing, and society, macromarketing focuses on *systems* to examine the impact of marketing on society, and vice versa.[52] Encompassing such diverse topics as marketing and development, global policy and sustainability, ethics, critical marketing, quality of life, and marketing and the arts, this sub-discipline is well-positioned to explain Oz's sustainability as it relates to societal forces and marketplace dynamics. Of particular value is Wroe Alderson's concept of *assortments*, which he defines as "a set of separable or distinguishable products, services, experiences, or ideas ... assembled in response to or in anticipation of consumer demand."[53]

Drawing on Alderson's assortment framework, we maintain that insofar as Oz provides the marketplace with literally hundreds of assortments, it is able to satisfy highly specialized markets for Oz, thus enhancing its sustainability. In fact, as we show in our concluding chapter—and as Oz expert John Fricke observes—the future of Oz may lie not in rallying large segments of consumers around a few monolithic Oz touchpoints (e.g., *The Wizard of Oz, The Wiz, Wicked*) but in providing niche Oz experiences to niche Oz markets. In macromarketing terms, as long as consumers deem these assortments beneficial to their quality of life, the probability of Oz sustaining itself remains high.

If macromarketing emphasizes the societal implications of marketing systems, Consumer Culture Theory focuses on what Eric Arnould and Craig Thompson describe in their field-founding article as "the dynamic relationships between consumer actions, the marketplace, and cultural meanings."[54] Consumer Culture Theory provides consumer researchers with a series of analytical tools to better understand consumer identity projects. Like macromarketing, Consumer Culture Theory contrasts with the rational-actor paradigms found in such long-standing research traditions as microeconomics.[55] Although rooted in specific contexts, Consumer Culture Theory research expands beyond these contexts to characterize broader consumer predicaments and opportunities, "generat[ing] new constructs and ... extend[ing] existing theoretical foundations."[56] Thus, the plight of plus-sized consumers frustrated by the lack of clothing options manufactured by mainstream fashion designers becomes a more generalizable examination of how marginalized consumers mobilize to create more choice and inclusion.[57] Likewise, a study of women's flat track roller derby is exemplified as one instance of how ideological edgework serves to resolve the tensions between re-signifying performances of femininity and naturalized gender constraints.[58] The best examples of Consumer Cuture Theory research are at once emblematic, dramatic, and pragmatic.

For these reasons, Consumer Culture Theory is ideally suited to our study of Oz and cultural sustainability. Not only does it align with our focus on sociohistorical patterning of consumption as it relates to all Oz experiences—our emphasis in the first half of this book—but it accommodates our focus on consumer identity projects that enable us to reveal precisely what, and how, *Wicked* "means" to consumers from both personal (micro) and cultural (macro) perspectives—our focus in the second half of this volume.

Additionally, our study answers several recent calls for future research identified by leaders in the field. As Linda Price noted at a recent roundtable on the future of Consumer Culture Theory, the sub-discipline needs to embrace a portfolio of approaches.[59] While work in the field is usually nested in the micro, she argued, researchers should take it to the macro. Our in-depth analysis of hundreds of Oz experiences does precisely that, bridging the gap between micro and macro. At the same time, we make no apology for context, as Craig Thompson urged at the same roundtable, but rather analytically induce an incipient model of cultural sustainability based on a single (extensive) case analysis.

Additionally, we find that *consumption experiences*, as researched by Bernd Schmitt, Joseph Pine, David Gilmore, Clinton Lanier, and Scott Rader, are also key to understanding the marketing and consumption of Oz.[60] Their sub-discipline, experiential marketing, emphasizes the lived experience of consumers set within a dramatistic framework. While the domains of Consumer Culture Theory and experiential marketing often overlap, the former ultimately generates fresh theoretical constructs based in and through the interaction of consumers and culture, whereas the latter generates managerial insights into how to provide consumers with new experiences of already-existing products, or new experiences of new products, bearing in mind their prior experiences with related products. Thus, presenting *Paramour*, a Cirque-du-Soleil-based show, on Broadway becomes a managerial challenge of how to reconcile the often-conflicting expectations of a Cirque-style show with what consumers expect from a Broadway experience.[61]

On the one hand, due to its focus on the everyday lifeworld, the roots of experiential marketing can be traced to the development of phenomenology, whose early adherents included the philosophers Heidegger, Husserl, and Merleau-Ponty. On the other, the concepts of staging, ritual, and performance align with the works of Goffman, Shechner, and

Turner. With its focus on looking and discovering as opposed to assuming and deducing, phenomenology provides a fitting foreground for experiential marketing, whose major concern lies in how, at any given moment, the consumer is experiencing a given product or service. Yet because it draws on the findings of dramatistic theorists as well, experiential marketing also speaks to the producer side of the marketing exchange, enabling it to advise producers on how to engineer particular aesthetic and performative elements of an experience in order to achieve a particular effect.

What are the key elements of experiential marketing? Drawing from a number of sources—but focusing on Pine and Gilmore's 2011 study, *The Experience Economy*—we offer these six defining principles:

- **Immerse consumers**: Experiential marketing endorses enveloping consumers in a cocoon of physical sensation, shutting out the distractions of the external world in order to focus on the taste, smell, touch, sight, and sound of the product at hand. For example, when Patron launched Roca Patron, its new line of ultra-premium tequilas, the company hosted "Roca on the Rails," an event that offered food-and-tequila pairings served aboard the Patron Tequila Express, an exquisitely appointed 1927 Pullman car, festooned with satin wallpaper, oriental rugs, and crystal chandeliers. Consumers were invited to board the train and "Experience Roca Patron."
- **Educate consumers**: Once consumers enter the sensual world of the brand in question, they also become a happily captive audience, eager to listen to whatever message the marketer may offer about how the product is made, what differentiates it from its competitors, and what inspired the producers to create the product in the first place. The highly successful sales staff at Murray's Cheese, the famous cheese deli in Greenwich Village, are masters of this technique. When customers sample cheese at Murray's, the cheese-monger tastes the cheese with them, guiding them through their sensations and explaining why (and how) they are unfolding as they are. This provides a common experience through which producers and consumers interact, allowing producers to "teach connoisseurship" to consumers, deepening their appreciation of the product and providing them with the vocabulary to discuss it.
- **Create buzz**: When done properly, experiential marketing creates excitement, prompting consumers to feel a sense of immediacy—as well as exclusivity. "Right here, right now ... this is the place to be!"

For instance, Adidas built "D Rose Jump Store" for an event featuring Chicago Bulls star Derrick Rose; while hundreds of bystanders looked on, participants got to meet Derrick Rose and then qualified to win a free pair of shoes if they could jump 10 feet in the air (the height of an NBA basketball hoop).

- **Encourage sharing**: In the past, marketers organized exclusive promotional events whose privacy was guaranteed. Now, the opposite is true: Marketers actively encourage consumers to share their experiences of an event, in real time, with as many "friends" as possible. Social media outlets such as Facebook, Twitter, Instagram, and Snapchat comprise a vast array of instantaneous heraldry, announcing to select others what is happening *now*. If marketers have become facilitators of this process, consumers have become curators of the same, capturing, and captioning images that express what an experience is meaning to them as it happens. Friends respond immediately with comments such as "So cool" or "Envious!", and they in turn share the event with others. Experiential marketing provides the genesis for this ripple effect; when done properly, the event impacts consumers far beyond those experiencing it directly.

- **Facilitate synergy**: At its best, the total impact of experiential marketing is greater than the sum of its parts. Promoters of brands usually create several ways in which consumers can "experience" their brands, but the impressions formed should be consistent across experiences, and they should also be consistent with the overall (intended) experience of the product or service itself. In other words, they should reinforce, rather than contradict, each other and the core product. Red Bull, for instance, conveys the adrenalin-fueled excitement consumers associate with its brand across multiple experiences: Air Race, F1 Team, Extreme Sports Events, and the famous Stratos jump—in which Felix Baumgartner jumped from Las Vegas' Stratosphere, breaking the sound barrier with his body, while millions of viewers watched a point-of-view video of the event.

- **Foster emotional connection**: The overarching goal of experiential marketing is to inspire a deep and memorable emotional connection with the brand at hand. Consumers should remember this brand and attach to it a particular affect—because of the direct encounter they had with it. Doc McStuffins, a children's show on the Disney Channel about a 6-year-old girl who heals toys in her imaginary clinic, is a case in point. To promote the show, as well as to increase merchandise sales, Disney recreated Doc's Clinic in selected grocery and toy stores across the UK. Children experienced a 10-minute immersion in Doc's Clinic, culminating in a role-play in which they diagnosed what was wrong with Big Ted, a giant teddy bear. As they waited for their turn in the role-play, children played with merchandise and watched clips from the TV show. Almost 8000 children took part in the experience.

Like macromarketing and Consumer Culture Theory, the concerns of experiential marketing dovetail nicely with the research agenda of this volume. Not only does experiential marketing focus on new ways for consumers to experience a particular brand over the long term, it also, deploys both phenomenological and theatrical frameworks to do so. As we show in the following chapters, the producers of Oz's key cultural touchpoints—from original author L. Frank Baum to *Wicked* creators Schwartz, Holzman, and Platt—deeply understood and deftly applied experiential marketing's twin theoretical foundations. We maintain that these account, in large measure, for Oz's cultural sustainability.

Following the Yellow Brick Road

Thus, our examination of the ways in which Oz has sustained itself over time is a study in texts, but one with a special focus on the marketing and consumption of those texts. Part I: *The Road* offers a sociohistorical study of the production and consumption of Oz from Baum to Maguire; it opens before Oz, in a rapidly changing late nineteenth- and early twentieth-century America. Chapter 2, "The Wonderful Wizard of Marketing: L. Frank Baum as Producer and Promoter," discusses how this period's shifts in national production and consumption patterns—including the rise of consumer culture, and the birth of the marketing profession—shaped both Baum and his famous narrative. We then examine Baum's early and influential career in sales and marketing—as a poultry breeder, axle-oil entrepreneur, theater producer, department store owner, and show window designer, a career that uniquely prepared him to market and manage Oz, before turning to his later career as Oz's creator, chief marketer, and brand manager, in which he launched a national Oz craze and successfully sustained his product on page, stage, and screen, for nearly two decades. We conclude the chapter with an analysis of how and why Oz resonated so strongly with its original consumers.

In Chapter 3, "Extending the Yellow Brick Road: More Books and a Technicolor Rainbow," we examine the circumstances, strategies, texts, and events that allowed Oz to continue on in the decades immediately following Baum's death. It begins with Baum's publishers and heirs, who hired Ruth Plumly Thompson to continue the series, and then assiduously marketed Oz through contests, clubs, promotional plays, and radio productions. From here, we discuss the legal battle between Baum's oldest son, Frank Joslyn Baum, and his publishers, Reilly & Lee, over the ownership (and the future) of Oz, before focusing in on the production, marketing, and consumption of the Oz-event that ensured that future, MGM's 1939 Technicolor musical spectacle, *The Wizard of Oz*.

Chapter 4, "Of Living Rooms and Libraries: Oz's Journey from Fairy Tale to Myth," opens in 1956, with two events that assured Oz's sustainability throughout the second half of the twentieth century: CBS's television broadcast of MGM's film and Columbia Library's exhibition of Baum's works. We place CBS's historic broadcast in the complex relationship between Cold War America, television, and corporate sponsorship, a relationship that produced and marketed the annual telecast and led to the ritualized viewings of *The Wizard of Oz* that shaped a generation and embedded Oz in the cultural imaginary. We then turn to the concurrent fight between librarians and educators and fans over Baum and Oz's literary heritage, as librarians sought to pull the Oz books from the shelves, while Oz-fans, many of whom belonged to The Wizard of Oz Club, founded in 1957, researched, preserved, and defended Baum and his works. The chapter ends with a discussion of the ways in which Baum himself became an American mythic figure in printed and televised biographies—a Horatio Alger of the imagination, whose persistence and dreams finally brought him fame and fortune.

In Chapter 5, "Expanding the Map: Oz in the Public Domain," we analyze the ways in which the diversification and reimagining of Oz, once the narrative began passing into the public domain in 1960, met with resistance from cultural gatekeepers and audiences at the same time that it kept the narrative vital for a new generation. We begin with the multiple productions that sought to capitalize on *The Wizard of Oz* during the broadcast years (1956–1998), before moving to an analysis of the role marketing and promotion played in *The Wiz*'s unlikely journey from flop to hit, and how the musical's success changed the ways in which it was consumed by both gatekeepers and mainstream audiences. We conclude with an examination of the revisionist Ozes produced at the end of this era by consumers who had grown up on Oz: Walter Murch's *Return to Oz* (1985), Phillip Jose Farmer's *A Barnstormer in Oz*, Geoff Ryman's *Was*, and, finally, Gregory Maguire's novel, *Wicked: The Life and Times of the Wicked Witch of the West*.

Part II: *Wicked* builds on an examination of the initial production, marketing, and reception of *Wicked: The Untold Story of the Witches of Oz* to present a real time, ethnographic-based study of the blockbuster musical that continues to play to 97% capacity in Broadway's largest theater 15 years after its debut. This study uses depth interviews with consumers and theater professionals and extends to an examination of the beyond-the-stage *Wicked* experiences that influence an audience's relationship to the musical. We begin with a prologue to this single-case study, in Chapter 6, "Telling and Selling: The Untold Story of the Witches of Oz," which investigates the process by which Stephen Schwartz and Winnie Holzman made Maguire's dark political novel into a Broadway musical; the critics' largely negative reception of that musical; and the ways in which producer Marc Platt and his marketing team built on consumer enthusiasm to save the show from a precarious beginning and create an unqualified hit. Chapter 7, "'My Entire Body was Shaking': Consumers Respond to *Wicked*," turns to the consumers themselves, drawing on hundreds of hours of in-depth interviews to discern what, exactly, it was about *Wicked* that spoke so powerfully to so many. Fully one quarter of the consumers we interviewed were nestled within *Wicked*'s purported target market (females, aged 15 to 25), and the other three quarters were drawn from a range of ages, genders, and occupations, allowing us to gauge both the extent to which *Wicked* actually met its target market and how well it succeeded in extending that market. In Chapter 8, "The Audience Unites in One Big *Yes!*": "Theater Professionals Reflect on *Wicked*," we ask theater professionals—people who make their living in and around Broadway and the West End—to assess the strengths and weaknesses of the show from their expert perspectives. Their ruminations help explain the chasm between critical and consumer reactions to the show. We conclude our in-depth analysis of the marketing and consumption of *Wicked* with Chapter 9, "Drawing Back the Curtain: *Wicked* Experiences," which focuses on the tours, exhibits, nights-out, special appearances, and social justice campaigns that deploy experiential marketing tactics to foster an emotional connection between consumers and the show and to keep audiences coming through its doors, thus ensuring that both *Wicked* and Oz retain their commercial vitality.

Part III: *Beyond Wicked* combines the methods and perspectives of the first two sections—the sociohistorical and the ethnographic—to speculate on Oz's post-*Wicked* future in a highly mobile, mediated, and volatile narrative marketplace. "Whither Oz?" asks Chapter 10, beginning with an overview of Oz's renewed post-*Wicked* life, examining the flurry of new Ozes that seek to capitalize on the musical's success. Ranging from the dark Ozes of *Tin Man* and *Emerald City*, through a series of girl-power young adult novels, to Disney's Technicolor return in *Oz the Great and Powerful*, these Ozes occasion a discussion of ownership and cultural sustainability as producers, gatekeepers, and consumers clash over what is and isn't Oz, with fans often taking matters into their own hands. We end this chapter with a more detailed analysis of fan-engagement, fan communities, and fan spaces as we analyze the work that fans do—on the internet, in museums, at conferences, and in festivals—to keep Oz alive and sustainable for both themselves and more casual, perhaps new, consumers.

We conclude with Chapter 11, "At the Gates of the Emerald City: Towards a New Theory of Cultural Sustainability," where we offer a foundational framework that draws on our study of nearly one hundred and twenty years of Oz history to conduct what Franco Moretti calls a "distant reading" of Oz. We then generalize our observations to propose a set of explanatory conditions under which any artistic experience might achieve cultural sustainability.[62]

Oz and Beyond: Contributing to the Conversation

The Road to Wicked's focus on cultural sustainability sets it apart from the numerous historical and analytical studies of Baum and the Oz narrative in several respects. First, we explain how major re-consumptions of Oz were marketed and consumed at the time of their creation and reception. Our examination of marketing strategies, consumer reactions, and commercial forces reveals a complex patterning of interaction among producers, texts, and consumers. We find that Oz's cultural sustainability stems from an intricate web of narrative suitability, opportunity, strategic exploitation, and—dare we say it?—the luck of offering up the right story to the right people at the right time.

Second, as we focus on patterns of production and reception, we build on the invaluable work done by Oz historians such as John Fricke, Michael Hearn, Joe Scarfone and William Stillman, and Mark Swartz

(to name only a few), complement the impressive body of literary criticism on Oz, and add a marketing and consumption focus to more
text- and media-based studies of transmedia storytelling.[63] We draw on
archival research, a database of over 500 Oz products, and an in-depth
examination of historical and modern producers' perceptions and consumers' reactions. Thus, we supplement their vital narrative histories
with a cultural analysis of the marketing and consumption of Oz, but-
tressed by archival research on one hand and literary studies on the
other. This approach allows us to read Oz texts as they were "read" by
their original consumers, gaining insight into what each Oz item meant
to and in its particular cultural moment. We also examine how producers
and marketers played with and on those meanings to ensure their products' commercial viability. This more targeted reading of the narratives
allows us to distinguish between the multiple kinds and functions of
Oz—the assortments that keep the narrative sustainable over time.

Third, our approach to the Broadway musical *Wicked* makes a different contribution to existing research, due to the opportunity presented
by this still-running show and the preponderance of consumers who
have seen it. Rich accounts detailing *Wicked*'s arduous journey from page
to stage, such as David Cote's *The Grimmerie*, Paul Laird's *Wicked: A
Musical Biography*, and Carol Di Giere's *Defying Gravity*, abound, and
they are related, justifiably, from its creators' and adaptors' points of
view.[64] Yet virtually no account is taken of how consumers have received
Wicked for the past 15 years. *The Grimmerie* and *Defying Gravity* quote a
handful of fan letters about the show and some brief consumer reactions
regarding the cast recording. By contrast, we systematically collect and
analyze 75 in-depth interviews of consumers who have seen a production of *Wicked*, and we do the same with an additional 25 theater professionals. The resulting data enables us to describe and analyze an array
of perceptions orbiting around the show 15 years after its debut, from
both producers' and consumers' perspectives. Such real-time sense-mak-
ing is a consequence of the often-contentious decision-making present at
Wicked's conception 20 years earlier. Thus, while prior research emphasized authorial intent, our approach to *Wicked* captures both audience
reception and professional assessment, exploring the role that actual consumers play in a cultural artifact's continuing sustainability.

Finally, as we travel the road to *Wicked* (and beyond), we will also
contribute to larger conversations about marketing and consumption.
The study of how Oz has been marketed over time brings a historical

perspective closely aligned with macromarketing's concerns, particularly as it relates to the development of experiential marketing, a strategy that—as we shall see—dates back to at least the mid-nineteenth century. Additionally, we will build on Consumer Culture Theory—which serves as both foundation and springboard for our own cultural sustainability theory-building agenda—extending the field's central consumer research tenets to explain how a single artistic event that took place over 100 years ago morphs its way through a multiplicity of marketplace forces, spawning literally hundreds of re-consumptions as it evolves. Tracking, explaining, and conceptualizing that evolution allows us to begin building a foundational model for a new theory of cultural sustainability, particularly as it relates to artistic artifacts. Arts-based corpuses that have enjoyed long-term cultural sustainability—such as Jane Austen's novels, Caravaggio's paintings, and Tchaikovsky's ballets—can now be examined using this transdisciplinary model, which is the ultimate aim of this book.

Notes

1. Michael Paulson and David Gelles, "'Hamilton Inc': The Path to a Billion-Dollar Broadway Show," *New York Times*, June 8, 2016, https://www.nytimes.com/2016/06/12/theater/hamilton-inc-the-path-to-a-billion-dollar-show.html.
2. Gordon Cox, "'Wicked' Hits $1 Billion on Broadway Faster than Any Other Show," *Variety*, March 15, 2016, http://variety.com/2016/legit/news/wicked-broadway-sales-1-billion.
3. Brooks Barnes, "How Wicked Cast Its Spell," *The Wall Street Journal*, October 22, 2005, https://www.wsj.com/articles/SB112994038461876413.
4. Howard Becker, *Art Worlds* (Berkeley: University of California Press, 2008).
5. Jon Hawkes, *The Fourth Pillar of Sustainability: Culture's Essential Role in Public Planning* (Melbourne: Common Ground Publishing Pty Ltd, 2001); John Elkington, "Towards the Sustainable Corporation: Win-Win-Win Business Strategies for Sustainable Development," *California Management Review* 36, no. 2 (1994): 90–100.
6. "Glenn Beck Ties the Wizard of Oz to Today's Problems," YouTube Video, 10:07, posted by TheBlaze, November 7, 2013, https://www.youtube.com/watch?v=iPXYWhZlj0g.
7. Henry M. Littlefield, "The Wizard of Oz: Parable on Populism," *American Quarterly* 16, no. 1 (1964): 47–58.

8. Ray Bradbury, "Foreword," in *The Wonderful Wizard of Oz: The Kansas Centennial Edition*, ed. L. Frank Baum (Lawrence, KS: University of Kansas Press, 1999), xiii–xvii, xiii.

9. Gregory Maguire, "Foreword: Oz and Ourselves," in *Oz Reimagined: New Tales from the Emerald City and Beyond*, ed. John Adams and Douglas Cohen (Las Vegas: 47 North, 2013), 1–5, 1, 4.

10. J. R. R. Tolkien, "On Faerie Stories," in *Tree and Leaf* (New York, Houghton Mifflin, 1964), 3–73, 3.

11. Ibid., 57.

12. Bradbury, "Foreword," xiv, xvii.

13. Gore Vidal, "On Rereading the Oz Books," *The New York Review of Books*, October 3, 1977, ProQuest.

14. Maguire, "Foreword," 1.

15. Ibid., 1, 4.

16. Salman Rushdie, "Out of Kansas," *New Yorker*, May 11, 1992, https://www.newyorker.com/magazine/1992/05/11/out-of-kansas.

17. Henry Jenkins, *Convergence Culture: Where Old and New Media Collide* (New York: New York University Press, 2006); David Bolter and Richard Grusin, *Remediation: Understanding New Media* (Boston: MIT Press, Reprint edition, 2008). For recent examples of studies on transmedia storytelling see: Kelly McErlean, *Interactive Narratives and Transmedia Storytelling* (New York: Routledge, 2018); Matthew Freeman, *Historicizing Transmedia Storytelling: Early Twentieth Century Transmedia Story Worlds* (New York: Routledge, 2016).

18. Linda Hutcheon, *A Theory of Adaptation* (New York: Routledge, 2012), 2–3.

19. Ibid., 176.

20. Ibid., 31.

21. Qtd. in Hutcheon, *Adaptation*, 116.

22. Ibid., 5.

23. Ibid., 128.

24. Ibid., 5.

25. Ibid., 4

26. Ibid., 67.

27. Ibid., 9.

28. Maguire, "Foreword," 2.

29. Qtd. in Sheenagh Pugh, *The Democratic Genre: Fan Fiction in a Literary Context* (Bridgend, Wales: Seren, 2006), 218.

30. Pugh, *Democratic Genre*.

31. Ibid., 9.

32. Ibid.

33. Michael Chabon, *Maps and Legends: Reading and Writing Along the Borderlands* (New York: Harper Collins, 2009), 56.
34. Kristina Busse and Karen Hellekson, "Introduction: Work in Progress," in *Fan Fiction and Fan Communities in the Age of the Internet*, ed. Kristina Busse and Karen Hellekson (Jefferson, NC: McFarland, 2006), Kindle.
35. Ibid.
36. Frank Kelleter, "'Toto, I Think We're in Oz Again' (and Again and Again): Remakes and Popular Seriality," in *Film Remakes: Adaptations and Fan Productions*, ed. Kathleen Loock and Constantine Verevis (New York: Palgrave Macmillan, 2012), 19–44. Kelleter speculates that the narrative's seriality plays opens it up to adaptation, a theory which plays into Chabon's map and Derecho's archive.
37. Chabon, *Maps*, 56.
38. Qtd. in Pugh, *Democratic Genre*, 267.
39. Abigail Derecho, "Archontic Literature: A Definition, A History, and Several Theories of Fan Fiction," in *Fan Fiction*, ed. Busse and Hellekson.
40. Ibid.
41. Jenkins, *Convergence*, 266.
42. Ibid., 53.
43. Ibid., 2.
44. Ibid., 2–3.
45. Ibid., 8.
46. Ibid., 19.
47. Ibid., 17.
48. Ibid., 19.
49. Ibid., 14.
50. Bolter and Grusin, *Remediation*, 23.
51. Hutcheon, *Adaptation*, 23, 130, 135.
52. Terry Witkowski, "Round Table on the Commonalities Between Macromarketing and Consumer Culture Theory," at the Consumer Culture Theory Consortium, Anaheim, CA, July 2017.
53. Wroe Alderson, *Dynamic Marketing Behavior* (Homewood, IL: Richard D. Irwin Press, 1965); Roger A. Layton and Zhirong Duan, "Diversity and Marketing System Assortments," *The Journal of Macromarketing* 35, no. 3 (May 2014): 320–323.
54. Eric J. Arnould and Craig J. Thompson, "Consumer Culture Theory (CCT): Twenty Years of Research," *Journal of Consumer Research* 31, no 4 (March 2005): 868–882, 868. The roots of Consumer Culture Theory stretch back to Levy's ground-breaking semiotics-of-brands research, see Burleigh B. Gardner and Sidney J. Levy, "The Product and the Brand," *Harvard Business Review* 33, no. 2 (1955): 33–40.

Other important moments in CCT include Morris B. Holbrook and Elizabeth C. Hirschman, "The Experiential Aspects of Consumption: Consumer Fantasies, Feeling and Fun," *Journal of Consumer Research* 9 (September 1982): 132–140; Russell W. Belk, "The Role of the Odyssey in Consumer Behavior and Consumer Research," *Advances in Consumer Research* 14 (1987): 357–361; and Grant McCracken "Culture and Consumption: A Theoretical Account of the Structure and Movement of the Cultural Meaning of Consumer Goods," *Journal of Consumer Research* 13 (June 1986): 71–84.

55. Craig Thompson, Round Table, 2017.
56. Arnould and Thompson, "Twenty Years," 869.
57. Daiane Scaraboto and Eileen Fischer, "Frustrated Fatshoinistas: An Institutional Theory Perspective on Consumer Quests for Greater Choice in Mainstream Markets," *Journal of Consumer Research* 39 (April 2013): 1234–1257.
58. Craig J. Thompson and Tuba Ustuner, "Women Skating on the Edge: Marketplace Performances as Ideological Edgework," *Journal of Consumer Research* 42 (2015): 235–265.
59. Linda Price, "Round Table Discussion of the Future of CCT," Consumer Culture Theory Consortium, Anaheim, CA, July 2017.
60. Joseph Pine and James Gilmore, *The Experience Economy* (Boston: Harvard Business Review Press, Updated edition, 2011), Bernd H. Schmitt, *Experiential Marketing* (New York: Free Press, 1999); Clinton Lanier and C. Scott Rader, "Consumption Experience: An Expanded View," *Marketing Theory* 14, no. 4 (2015): 487–508.
61. Scott Zeiger, "Keynote Address on The Consumer Experience in Arts and Culture," Leadership Nouveau Conference, New York, 2016.
62. Franco Moretti, *Distant Reading* (London: Verso, 2013).
63. Historical studies of Oz include John Fricke, Jay Scarfone, and William Stillman, *The Wizard of Oz: The Official 50th Anniversary Pictorial History* (New York: Warner Books, 1989); John Fricke, *The Wonderful World of Oz: An Illustrated History of the American Classic* (Camden, ME: Down East Books, 2013); Michael Hearn's Introduction to *The Annotated Wizard of Oz* (New York: W. W. Norton, 1973); and Mark Swartz, *Oz Before the Rainbow: L. Frank Baum's The Wonderful Wizard of Oz on Stage and Screen to 1939* (New York: Johns Hopkins Press, 2000). For a selection of book-length literary discussions of Oz, see, Michael O. Riley, *Oz and Beyond: The Fantasy Worlds of L. Frank Baum* (Lawrence, KS: University of Kansas Press, 1997); Allissa Burger, *The Wizard of Oz as American Myth* (Jefferson, NC: McFarland, 2012); and Evan L. Schwartz, *Finding Oz: How L. Frank Baum Discovered the Great American Story* (New York: Houghton Mifflin, 2009).

64. David Cote, *Wicked: The Grimmerie, A Behind-the-Scenes Look at the Hit Broadway Musical* (New York: Hatchette Books, 2005); Carol di Giere, *Defying Gravity, The Creative Career of Stephen Schwartz from Godspell to Wicked* (New York: Applause Books, 2008); and Paul Laird, *Wicked: A Musical Biography* (Lanham, MD: Scarecrow Press, 2011).

PART I

The Road

CHAPTER 2

The Wonderful Wizard of Marketing:
L. Frank Baum as Producer and Promoter

Most of us know L. Frank Baum, the Dreamer of Oz; fewer know Baum, the astute marketer and savvy brand manager. It's this latter Baum who assured Oz's initial success by carefully positioning his products in the competitive marketplace, and set the stage for its longevity by cultivating a long-term relationship with his audience, fostering what would later be called brand loyalty. *The Wonderful Wizard of Oz* may have initially sold well because it offered consumers a good product: a well-written story that spoke to them, written by an author they recognized. But Oz became a *sustainable brand* because its author, over a period of decades, provided consumers with a succession of products that enabled him to achieve brand recognition across a variety of market segments and delivery platforms. Baum also had the marketing savvy to leverage that recognition into new, uncharted *experiences* of Oz. He adapted Oz through what we now call line and product extensions—new books, Broadway musicals, newspaper stories, picture books, traveling productions, and motion pictures—providing consumers with unique, immersive, and multi-sensory ways in which to experience Oz. In so doing, he anticipated Pine and Gilmore's advice in *The Experience Economy* by nearly 100 years.[1] The result was an *Ozmania* that lasted well beyond his death in 1919; it solidified Baum's place as America's preeminent teller of tales—and Oz's place as quintessential American fairy tale.

© The Author(s) 2018
K. Drummond et al., *The Road to Wicked*,
https://doi.org/10.1007/978-3-319-93106-7_2

SETTING THE CULTURAL STAGE

Baum and Oz came of age as America's markets and consumption patterns shifted, and examining the production and marketing of Oz in the context of these larger cultural trends provides an interesting window into advertising and consumption in late-nineteenth and early-twentieth-century America. It also illuminates both the nation's emerging consumer culture and Oz's initial reception and early cultural sustainability. In *Fables of Abundance: A Cultural History of Advertising in America*, Jackson Lears argues that this national shift in consumption patterns occurred at the end of the nineteenth century with a growth in markets, an increased access to commodities, and the development of professional marketing.[2] During this period, he asserts, Puritan-based scarcity models–which assumed that limited resources of money, goods and energy must be carefully conserved, were replaced by new models of industrial abundance—epitomized in the neoclassical buildings of Chicago's 1893 White City (often seen as inspiration for the Emerald City) which, "by accumulating and displaying tons of stuff," celebrated American corporations' "imperial ambitions and achievements, [and] their place at the cutting edge of progress."[3]

The corporate impulse to accumulate and display as a celebration of achievement and identity shaped the American marketplace. There, the emergent consumer culture was inflamed by the rise of scientific management techniques pioneered by William Taylor and Henry Ford. As work became tedious and regulated, a shorter work week offered increased leisure time. Higher wages and the rise of credit meant increased buying power, enabling workers to "compensate" for the tedium of their work week "by seeking satisfaction off the job, with the pleasures and comforts money could buy."[4] At the same time, mass production allowed for the proliferation of affordable products, from "fine art" prints and games, to clothing and household appliances. Imperial expansion in Panama, Cuba, and Hawaii opened new markets for American goods, while lowering the prices of "exotic" goods, such as sugar and bananas, at home. As they became more available, goods such as electric irons and toasters, knickknacks and chromolithographs, as well as exotic fruits and spices, all became "markers of economic and cultural ascent."[5] Soon, not only were goods more available and more affordable, but they were also easier to come by. The rise of the retailer, in the form of department and five and dime stores, meant that consumers had access to a stunning array of new products, provided they had money to buy them—and the time to shop for them. Woolworths, founded in 1879, was firmly enshrined in the American landscape by 1913, when President Wilson himself turned on the lights of the new Woolworth tower from a switch in the White House.

Woolworths, according to Lears, "epitomized the democracy and accessibility of goods." And goods promised "regeneration through purchase."[6] As such, consumption, Lears argues, stood at the center of Americans' quest for "magical self-transformation through market exchange," "animating the endless renewal of consumer desire."[7] Furthermore, material products were not the only transformative commodity offered for purchase; this period also saw the rise of mass entertainment and the commodification of "experience." As the century progressed, amusement parks, vaudeville shows, Broadway theaters, and touring spectacles, such as Buffalo Bills' Wild West Show and Barnum and Bailey's three-ring circus, competed with the developing motion picture industry for the growing consumer market. Professional sports also entered the entertainment marketplace, as did commodified wilderness experiences, from guided tours in the Adirondacks to explorations of the nation's newly established national parks.[8] These entertainments offered "regeneration," an alternative to disenchanted, fragmented ways of being in the world, a way of getting in touch with "real life." "Everyone," psychologist Stanley Hall opined, "especially those who lead the drab life of the modern toiler, needs and craves an occasional good time. Indeed, we all need to glow, tingle, and feel life intensely now and then."[9] This magical self-transformation of "glow" and "tingle" were available for purchase at a variety of venues, all of which promised to take their consumers away from the monotony of their daily lives as surely as the cyclone transported Dorothy out of the gray world of Kansas into the magical land of Oz. During this time, hedonic consumption grew from idle frivolity to bona fide consumer need.

The challenge then became: how to get one's own product noticed among all of the hedonic consumption experiences jostling for consumers' attention. How to convince them that *this product* was the key to magical self-transformation—to glow, to tingle, and feel life intensely? How did shop owners persuade consumers to "create a sense of individuality by buying (and continuing to buy) things that were essentially the same"?[10]

EARLY MAD MEN

The solution came in the form of a new profession. By the late 1860s, a fledgling advertising profession was evolving whose aim was to create marketing campaigns that would "surround mass-produced goods with an aura of uniqueness." As the nineteenth century drew to a close, early pioneers, such as Frances Ayers and George P. Rowell, established New York ad firms and launched a series of trade journals dedicated to the new "science of marketing." In 1879, Ayer's firm conducted the first marketing survey, and in 1888, Rowell's journal, *Printer's Ink*, defined the parameters of the new profession: "calculating an advertising budget, promoting new methods of packaging and promoting products that would reach a remote and scattered buying audience...(and) shorten and standardize the distance between producer and consumer."[11]

These new ad professionals faced a difficult task: They sought to make marketing respectable, to remove it from the realm of the carnival barker, the peddler, and the confidence man, all who purportedly used trickery and guile to dupe naive consumers. By positioning advertising as a science, ad executives argued that they served the needs of both the producer and the consumer—an argument clearly bought by no less a personage than former US President, William Howard Taft, who, in 1919, introduced Ayer with these words: "We are honoring today a man who has made advertising a science.... We owe a debt of gratitude to Mr. Ayer, for having rendered a form of publicity useful and elevating, which might have been vicious and deplorable."[12]

This new "useful" science claimed to inform and educate America's consumers, using plain speech and mimetic illustrations to provide "facts," presented "brightly, imaginatively, magnetically," about new products. But even as they sought to educate consumers on the one hand, they strove to entice them on the other. Early trade journals instructed marketers to:

- **"Excite the imagination:"**[13] The more consumers' imaginations were stimulated, it was reasoned, the more likely they were to set foot in a store. Printed advertisements, often engaging in memorable wordplay, enticed customers to drop in and check out what the shops had to offer. An 1895 Montgomery Ward & Co ad, echoing Longfellow's popular poem "Hiawatha," illustrates this technique: "In the city of Chicago, By Lake Michigan the Windy....

Stands a large, imposing structure. Stores nine and numbers seven...And from the roof down into the basement, Merchandise to please the people."[14] The echo of Longfellow's well-known poem catches the reader's eye, while the vision of seven stores, crammed with merchandise, fires their imaginations. Then, as now, the subtext was "Come inside and see for yourselves!"

Similarly, in-store displays and show windows worked to catch the eye, play into the imagination, and encourage consumption, as in this tale related by marketing guru James Collins: "A retail hardware dealer... had some hunter's axes he couldn't move, so he put them in his front window. While he was at lunch, those baby axes were all sold, being carried away by the noonday [business] crowd ....They were bright, touched with red paint, and sharp. They made office men feel like they wanted to chop something."[15]

- **Invite consumers into a narrative**: This era saw the rise of the copywriter, tasked with "using words and images to entice the audience into the agreeable scenes being created."[16] If the axes in the window inspired the businessmen who bought them to imagine a narrative about hunters or lumberjacks, copywriters provided one ready-made, such as a 1903 Quaker Oats ad that linked oatmeal, "the Work Food," to a vigorous workday and future prosperity: "It puts its whole strength straight into your system [providing] Will to Do—Power to Do it—Spirit and Energy, parents of Success."[17]

- **Imbue products with symbolic value**: In 1901—long before Barthes and Baudrillard wrote treatises on semiotics and systems of objects—James Collins urged advertisers to "learn to participate" in "the economy of symbolism," by "surround[ing] the product with condensed clusters of words and symbols that gave it symbolic as well as utilitarian value."[18] Quaker Oats not only offered a narrative of success and productivity, but also "the fires of youth" and "life and laughter."[19] In 1900, Ivory Soap offered a disturbing narrative of purification and assimilation, as Plains Indians extolled the virtues of the product: "Ivory Soap came like a ray of light across our darkened way. And now we're civil, kind and good....We wear our linen, lawn and lace, As well as folks with paler face."[20] Taking their cues from such print ads, show windows surrounded products with scenes of high living and domestic harmony.

- **Foster a connection between the consumer and the product**: In an increasingly crowded market, advertisers became "more and more preoccupied with casting a haze of pseudo-intimacy over the relations between the producer and the consumer."[21] One way of doing this was to tell the manufacturer's story, generally casting him as a self-made man who rose from rags to riches. Another tactic was, as *Everybody's Magazine* advised in 1910, to endow products with "personality:" "Every machine, every enterprise, every product has its personality.... It is a tangible asset when capitalized."[22] In addition, by inviting consumers to imagine themselves in a narrative, advertising companies could create narratives about characters and products, often casting the products themselves as characters. An influential 1915 article, "What Copy-writers Can Learn from Story-writers," argued, "If you have a rather high-priced alarm clock to sell you had better look for something humanly interesting. Naming the clock Big Bill endows it with personality....And people will actually pay the big new price because you tell them that 'he,' not 'it' is a big, fine jolly fellow with a brave, cheerful voice."[23]

- **Weave the product into the fabric of daily life**: Consistent, repetitive, ubiquitous advertising created brand recognition and developed brand loyalty. It connected the nation, serving, as Collins argued in 1902, as a "'space annihilator' like the trolley, the train, and the telephone."[24] "The Folk of Ad-land," Samuel Hopkins Adams observed in 1909, had become an integral part of American life, "Think how much duller your ride to business would be if the car hoardings were blank instead of being filled with color and print. They are decent and companionable myths these folk of Ad-land; the smiling chef of Cream of Wheat, the frolicky Gold Dust Twins, the gaily youthful, toothful Sozodont girl, the round-eyed chubs who fatten to bursting on Campbell's soup, the hale old friend of Quaker Oats."[25]

Adams' litany of recognizable advertising characters testifies to their creators' effectiveness in imbuing them with both personality and symbolic value. These are not just any cereals, washing powder, toothpaste, or soups; they all have "companionable" spokesmen whose benefits go beyond clean clothes, white teeth and robust nutrition. Cream of Wheat is brought to you by a smiling chef; Gold Dust is associated with "frolick;" Sozodont with youth; Campbell's with thriving children; and Quaker Oats with general well-being.

Baum the Entrepreneur

Just as Quaker Oats, Sozodont and Campbell's strove to stand out from competition, so Oz needed to find a way to distinguish itself from the hundreds of other juvenile titles on offer. And it faced an additional challenge that these other products did not: while soup cans and cereal boxes "ask" to be replenished as soon as they are empty, a book can simply be read again, without re-purchase. Thus, if Baum were to sustain his brand, he needed not only to employ all of the marketing strategies discussed above, but also to create new pathways to Oz. Part entrepreneur, part showman, Baum was ideally suited to this challenge; as he had proved again and again in his pre-Oz years, he understood, seemingly instinctively, how to drop his product strategically into America's burgeoning consumer culture.

Baum's early career, often portrayed as a series of impractical dreams and failed enterprises, actually prepared him uniquely for success as the marketer of Oz. Before Oz, Baum had founded four businesses and marketed everything from fancy poultry and machine oil to exotic goods and plays.[26] During these years, he developed what his son would recall as an "instinctive" sales sense, often incorporating what would later become the central tenets of the fledgling marketing profession. To these, Baum added lessons learned from his stints as an actor and theatrical manager: the use of the "event" to stimulate excitement and curiosity, the deployment of special effects and spectacle, and the creation of his own persona as an extension of the product.

This last technique played a central role in Baum's first foray into marketing his own product, B. W. Baum and Sons, sellers of fancy poultry. Baum built a network around his Hamburg Poultry: creating a community of consumers, providing that community with a forum for the exchange of knowledge, and establishing his own expert-status. First, he founded the Empire State Poultry Association, which provided him with consumers and a sales platform for his boutique chickens; next he established *The Poultry Record*, a trade journal that allowed him to distinguish his product from those of rival breeders; and, finally, through a series of articles written for *Poultry World*, which would be later collected and published as *The Book of Hamburgs, A Brief Treatise on the Mating, Rearing and Management of Different Varieties of Hamburgs*, Baum confirmed himself as the "expert" on Hamburgs, using his authority to assert the superiority of his product. Admittedly, B. W. Baum and

Sons was a small operation aimed at a niche audience, but in a period of four years, Baum had taken that business from a start-up to the top of its category. His marketing techniques, which relied on the creation of an insider community overseen by himself as the "expert," might not have been traditional, but they were undeniably effective.

Baum moved on from the poultry business in 1882 to focus on Baum's Castorine Oil (founded with his brother in 1883, and still in business), which marketed a newly patented axle and machinery oil. Baum ran sales for the company, working as a salesman and window designer. He also created marketing materials aimed at educating his audience and distinguishing the product from its competitors. Some of these materials stress that the company is "Pantentees and sole Manufacturers" of the "Great Axle Oil," warning consumers about "unscrupulous imitators" selling "cheap and worthless so-called axle oils."[27] Others feature endorsements "by all express co's cartmen and hackmen," proclaiming it "the only practical axle oil ever manufactured." Baum also sold Castorine with humorous narratives. One 1884 trade card features a series of vignettes in which hapless consumers learn that they need to choose different axle oil. A dandy in a fancy carriage is outstripped by children in a farm wagon, taunting, "Why don't yet catch us Mr.? We uses Castorine on our axels we does."[28] With his poultry business, Baum marketed himself and his expertise to consumers; with Castorine, he used bright colors, eye-catching illustrations and comic vignettes to establish his unique patented product in the market.

While it may seem that Baum's fledgling theatrical career directly competed with this early business career, these two seemingly incompatible ventures actually informed each other. When in 1882, his company, a moderately successful purveyor of touring Shakespeare productions, gained recognition in with *The Maid of Arran*, Baum's musical adaptation of William Black's popular 1874 melodrama, *A Princess of Thule*, Baum's marketing skills kept the play going. As the production toured, he traded on its name-recognition, "fine mechanical scene effects," exuberant musical numbers, and *himself*, Louis F. Baum, a "brilliant young author-actor," with "a fine presence, a handsome countenance and withal an ease of grace in his stage movements."[29] Marketing for the *Maid of Arran* also worked to excite the consumers' imagination and create buzz. Baum commissioned twelve cast-cards to advertise upcoming performances, and newspaper ads trumpeted *Arran's* previous success performing to "a succession of crowded houses and delighted audiences."[30]

Of all these promotions, an 1883 pamphlet, designed by Baum to be sold in the theater lobbies, is the most predictive of the techniques he would later use to market Oz. The cover featured cameo drawings of Baum and his co-star, Agnes Hallock. Text, blazoned across an atmospheric gothic castle, announced: "Louis F. Baum's Popular Songs, as Sung with Immense Success in his Great 5 Act Irish Drama, The Maid of Arran," and the bottom of the pamphlet warned audiences not to miss the event: "Positively the only appearance of this renowned company in this city this season."[31] While its elaborate cover and equally elaborate claims reinforced *The Maid of Arran's* brand, and sought to attract future consumers, the pamphlet also encouraged current consumers to take a little bit of their experience home by purchasing the music and lyrics for six of the play's songs. With this pamphlet, Baum sought to sustain the play's success; as the six songs left the theater to enter consumers' homes, they would be replayed, reaching new consumers, and reminding established ones how much they enjoyed the performance. If *The Maid of Arran*—or something like it—returned to town, both new and established audiences would be eager to hear those songs again.

The Aberdeen Experience

In spite of the success of these marketing campaigns, Baum's axle oil and theatrical enterprises came to an end after suffering a series of setbacks between 1883 and 1888. None of these setbacks, however, can be blamed on Baum's business acumen. A gambling bookkeeper destroyed Castorine's finances, and a fire brought down the theatrical company. Baum moved west, to Aberdeen, South Dakota in 1888, where, ever the entrepreneur, he purchased Baum's Bazaar and, drawing on his earlier experiences in sales and theater, settled in to market Aberdeen's first fancy dry-goods store. Advertising campaigns for Baum's Bazaar fancifully piqued consumers' curiosity. He heralded new arrivals in newspaper ads using clever wordplay and ingenious conceits, such as when he announced the store had received a "poetry grinder," printing samples of its poetic output: clever ditties that advertised the store's latest products.[32] Others demonstrated Baum's unique theatricality, his sense of the event—and the promotion. An advertisement for the store's first holiday season appeared as an invitation: "Mr. Baum announces his first annual

Holiday Opening…and requests the pleasure of your presence on that day to examine and criticize his magnificent collection of articles suitable for Christmas and New Year's gifts."[33] This invitation creates an immediate, personal relationship between Baum and his consumers, who are invited to *his* home to view *his* magnificent collection and pass judgment on it. This is an event not to be missed because: "On the same day occurs the Annual Prize Drawing for costumers, and the promised distribution of gifts to all ladies present."[34] Note that the image presented here is strangely prescient of the Wizard of Oz handing out "the promised gifts" to everyone present. Note also that, aside from the reference to costumers, no mention of an exchange is made; rather, consumers are invited to a party. Following marketing's best practices, Baum focuses on the *relationship* between host and guest, from which exchanges will naturally and unobtrusively follow.

One memorable ad from Baum's Bazaar demonstrates Baum's remarkable copywriting skills, especially his ability to both invite consumers into a narrative, and to imbue products (or in this case, the very act of consumption) with symbolic value. Appearing in the April 19, 1889 edition of *The Aberdeen Daily*, as "glorious Easter is about dawning upon us," the ad paints the following scene:

Aberdeen stands upon the threshold of the grandest era in her history. About her are millions of acres covered with ambitious shoots of infant grain e'en now thrusting their tender heads above the generous soil to bring our city wealth and prosperity. The tinkle and buzz in our ears of hundreds of hammers and saws—wealded (sic) by lusty arms—assure her greatness and extent.

The kindly smiles and elastic steps of our merchants, lawyers, bankers, real estate brokers, and citizens of every grade are the prediction of peace and plenty in our midst.

The sun of Aberdeen is rising; its powerful and all-reaching beams shall shed its glory over the length and breadth of the continent and draw the wondering eyes of all nations to our beautiful hub (city).[35]

This elaborate—and of course, overblown—introduction reads like a script for a political advertisement. In fact, it strongly brings to mind Reagan's "It's Morning in America" campaign. It connects Aberdeen with spring, which connects to Easter, which suggests renewal and prosperity. Like the sun—and the Son—Aberdeen is on the rise, as the world watches.

The ad then uses clever wordplay to connect this prosperity with an obligation to consumption:

> And that reminds us that hubs—or hubbies rather—should see their wives and families are provided on Easter day with some of those delicious Flowers and Plants we have. Easter is the season of flowers—don't neglect it.[36]

Here, Plants and Flowers acquire symbolic value—associated strongly with being a good husband and providing a festive Easter household. The last paragraph of Baum's scene turns to the ladies, establishing a personal relationship between them and the store. "We would like to show every lady in Aberdeen our beautiful Easter novelties," before inviting them to a gift event. "To show our feeling of good will at this joyous season…we shall present each of our customers on Saturday with a beautiful potted plant."[37] By the end of this narrative ad, which predates all of the marketing manuals we discussed above, Baum has employed many of these manuals most sophisticated techniques; he has invited consumers into an attractive narrative, imbued his goods with symbolic value, established a personal relationship with them, and excited their imagination.

Baum may have been a skilled marketer, but his picture of Aberdeen on the threshold of greatness was, unfortunately, as fictional as Oz itself. His expansive vision for Baum's Bazaar was incompatible with droughts, failed crops, and financial recession. Eventually, he was forced to sell the store and move his family to Chicago, where he worked first as a department store buyer for Siegel, Cooper, and Company, and, later, as a traveling salesman for Pitkin and Brooks, a manufacturer of china and glass wear.

WINDOW DRESSING

It was during these years that Baum, always an instinctual salesman, made a certified mark on the marketing profession. It began, as son Harry recounts, with Pitkin and Brooks. "Years before the modern marketing principle of 're-sale' had been founded…he knew he should…

help buyers resell the goods to users. He therefore made it a practice...
to arrange the merchandise in an attractive attention-getting display that
would move the various items into consumers' homes more quickly."[38]
In his career as a china salesman, Baum employed the same techniques
that Collins described a decade later in the story of the red hunters' axes.
In short, his success at using theatrical displays to sell china established
Baum as a window dresser, or more precisely, as an expert authority
in the developing show window profession. He served as the founding editor of, and frequent contributor to, the trade journal, *The Show
Window*. And he authored what was, for years, the definitive manual for
the field, *The Art of Decorating Dry Goods Windows and Interiors*, published in 1900. This manual, "designed as an educator in all the details of
the art according to the best modern methods," covered topics ranging
from the artistic ("How to plan show windows;" "How to create perfect backgrounds;" and "How to decorate for all the national holidays")
to the practical and technological ("How to build stands and fixtures;"
"How to wire a window for electricity;" and "How to apply a motor to
mechanical displays").[39]

Show windows, as pioneered by Baum, perfectly met the objectives
of early marketing professionals. Their cunning displays and technological wizardry excited the imagination; their elaborate scene-setting invited
consumers into a narrative, imbuing products with symbolic value; and
they fostered deep connections between consumers and products by
weaving those products into everyday life. A successful show window,
Baum emphasized, served as a "frame to the picture or setting to a
gem."[40] In 1899, shamelessly using his position as editor of *The Show
Window*, he was given a unique opportunity to practice these principles
on his own product, *Father Goose: His Book*, publishing detailed directions for a promotional window. Brilliantly drawing the consumer into a
narrative of domestic harmony and maternal care, the window featured
a mother fondly watching one child read Baum's book, while another,
at her knee, leafs through its pages. Oversized copies of Denslow's illustrations rest on easels scattered around "the nursery" and a centered
placard reads "For the children: Father Goose his Book."[41] A decorative
arch, composed of more illustrations, frames the scene. Several department store window designers adopted Baum's ready-made design for
their store's displays, ensuring that *Father Goose* was very much in the
public eye. These displays may well have been one of the reasons that the
book "made a hit," as Baum told his brother, "and sold plenteously."[42]

The Father Goose window indicates that Baum's pre-Oz marketing career had prepared him to be an extremely effective marketer of his own books. When the time came, he fully understood the connection between his career as a marketer and his career as a writer. From self-marketing and the creation of an insider community, through clever narrative ads, promotions, and events, to the use of staging and technology in the creation of eye-catching windows, he knew how to drive the sale. Thus, when *The Wonderful Wizard of Oz* unexpectedly launched a brand, Baum was well-positioned to manage it.

INTRODUCING OZ

By the time *The Wonderful Wizard of Oz* was published in 1900, the success Baum's first juvenile offering, *Mother Goose in Prose* (1897), followed quickly by that of *Father Goose his Book*, had established Baum's reputation as a children's author. L. Frank Baum was, in a sense, already becoming a brand, able to sell books *because* they were by "the author of..." His pre-*Wizard* letters to his siblings demonstrate that Baum was both very much aware of the power of author (or brand) recognition, and that he fully expected his new book to help build his author brand, an expectation at odds with popular depictions of Baum as "the dreamer of Oz." These depictions work to separate Oz from the world of commerce, presenting *The Wonderful Wizard of Oz* not as a product, but as an offering, and its consumption not as a market exchange, but as a magical connection between story and audience. Baum's account of Oz's origins, however, shows that, for him, Oz was, first and foremost, a product—and that he had high expectations for its sales success. Writing to his brother in April 1900, he discusses his prospects for the coming year:

> The financial success of my books is yet undetermined and will only be positively settled after the coming fall season. We only had three months sales of "Father Goose" and tho it made a hit and sold plenteously, we cannot tell what its future might be....My work is now sought by publishers who once scorned my contributions....But I shall make no contracts with anyone until January....Then there is this other book, the best thing I've ever written, they tell me, "The Wonderful Wizard of Oz."...If [the publisher] is right, that book alone solves my problems.[43]

For Baum here, *The Wonderful Wizard of Oz* is but one in a series of products he has lined up for the following year, including spin-offs from the recently released *Father Goose* collection. In fact, if he expects anything to carry-over, it is the volume's beautiful binding and innovative use of tipped-in color illustrations. *The Wonderful Wizard of Oz's* packaging features both in this letter to his brother, which praises Denslow's "profuse illustrations," that will make the book "glow with color," and one to his sister. "I expect [Oz] to make a success, for it is beautifully printed and bound," he writes, before quickly moving on to his other projects, telling his sister, "The same publishers will produce my Phunniland book next year."[44]

Even though Baum never expected Oz itself to become *the* brand, he expected it to sell well and to increase his overall brand. In his quest to differentiate his product from the myriad of other holiday offerings competing for the juvenile audience, he had done his market research. First, there was the book's use of color. As his son, Harry recalled, "although it was contrary to all standards of publishing and an utterly impractical idea, [my father] knew within himself that color was absolutely necessary and would make all the difference in the appeal and use of the book."[45] Second, there was the narrative itself, a fairy tale adapted for the modern American child. "Every healthy youngster," Baum explains in his introduction to *The Wonderful Wizard of Oz*, "has a wholesome and instinctive love for stories fantastic, marvelous, and manifestly unreal. The winged fairies of Grimm and Andersen have brought more happiness to childish hearts than all other human creations."[46] Having identified a desire, and a previous product, Baum goes on to offer a new product, a way to meet changing needs:

> The time has come for a series of newer 'wonder tales' in which the stereotyped genie, dwarf and fairy are eliminated, together with all the horrible and blood-curdling incident devised by their authors to point to a fearsome moral to each tale. Modern education includes morality; therefore the modern child seeks only entertainment in his wonder tales.... Having this thought in mind, the story of "The Wonderful Wizard of Oz" was written solely to pleasure the children of today. It aspires to be a modernized fairy tale, in which the wonderment and joy are retained and the heart-aches and nightmares are left out.[47]

This new product, with its beautiful packaging and modern take on wonder tales, was, as Baum had predicted, a success with both critics and consumers. Critics, on the whole, responded enthusiastically to Baum's modern fairy tale, praising both Denslow's whimsical drawings and Baum's narrative, "ingeniously woven out of commonplace material," with "delightful humor and rare philosophy on every page," and comparing the tale favorably to Aesop's *Fables* and Carroll's *Alice in Wonderland*.[48] Within two months of its publication, the book had nearly sold out of its first two printings, establishing *The Wonderful Wizard of Oz* as the season's—and the new century's—hot-seller.

What Baum didn't predict, or perhaps even envision, was that his musical adaptation of *The Wonderful Wizard of Oz*—penned with musician Paul Tietjens in 1901, and substantially revised by Julian Mitchell— would be a runaway success, shattering box-office records, reaching a new audience, keeping Oz in the public eye, and stimulating consumers' desire for more Oz experiences. Indeed, as his son Frank later observed, it was in all likelihood the musical Oz, which "appealed to adults" that "made the book so famous."[49] The show's success, as we shall see, is certainly what led Baum to launch the Oz brand. The process by which the book moved from page to stage, his initial resistance to it, and the show's ultimate success taught Baum valuable lessons about adaptation, media, genre, and audiences, lessons that he would later put to good use as he extended the Oz brand.

Baum wrote a script for a show that loosely followed the original plot of his book. But by the time the show premiered onstage, *The Wizard of Oz* had mutated into a vaudeville-style spectacle that, according to some sources, dismayed and bewildered Baum. In an early interview with the *Chicago Tribune*, he recalls, "I was told that what constituted fun in a book would be missed by the average audience, which is accustomed to regular gatling-gun discharge of wit—or what stands for wit." As adapted by Julian Mitchell for this average audience, Baum observes "the original story" was practically ignored, "the dialogue rehashed, the situations transposed, my Nebraska wizard into an Irishman, and several other characters forced to conform to the requirements of the new schedule.... I was filled with amazement indeed, and took occasion to protest against several innovations I did not like, but Mr. Mitchell listened to the plaudits of a big audiences and turned a deaf ear to my complaints." "The people" Baum concludes, "will have what pleases them and not what the author happens to favor, and I believe that one of the reasons Julian Mitchell is recognized as a great producer is that he faithfully tries to serve the great mass of playgoers—and usually succeeds."[50]

Mitchell—and the show he produced—succeeded spectacularly. *The Wizard of Oz* opened in Chicago, on June 16, 1902, to a house "packed with people standing in the aisles at the rear and behind the last row of seats," and an enthusiastic audience. "It was after midnight when the final curtain fell," one attendee recalled, "but the audience stayed til the close, delighting in the performance."[51] Reviews, on the whole, were equally enthusiastic; the *Chicago Daily News* gushed: "The most superbly arrayed, beautifully set, and humorously played spectacular burlesque ever given at any time in this summer show town...Money fairly drips from the gorgeous walls and skies of the Emerald City, and from the costly robes of the pretty girls and amazing atmospheres of silver mists and golden lights."[52] And if some reviewers, such as Abraham L. Erlanger, predicted that the "show would never go in New York because it was primarily a fairy tale," they proved to be dead wrong.[53] As Mark Swartz observes in his study *Oz Before the Rainbow*, "the show sold out, week after week. On some nights as many people were turned away for lack of tickets as were admitted"—even in New York. "No matter how uncomfortably hot the weather, standing room was at a premium and encores for favorite songs and favorite performances were numerous."[54] Repeat viewers sang along, society matrons hosted elaborate theme dinners, and David Montgomery and Fred Stone, who played the Tin Woodman and the Scarecrow, became stars.

In short, *The Wizard of Oz* was the most successful musical of its day. Foreshadowing blockbusters such as *The Lion King, Wicked* and *Hamilton*, it enjoyed an unprecedented eight-year run, that at one time included multiple touring companies. It also influenced theater for the next decade, much to the dismay of *Theater Magazine*, which lamented the rise of "that formless, vacuous kind of stage entertainment known as musical comedy," "received by a large class of the paying theater goers" "with great favor." Constituted of "entertainment agreeable to the senses...as welcome to the weary man of business as to those parasites of society whose sluggish brain-cells discourage work at any time," and made of "noise, tinsel, and calcium," these shows, alas, cannot "be ignored by the practical manager, whom no one else can blame for giving the public what it seems to want."[55] And what the audience seemed to want was the "glow" and "tingle" they found in Oz's glittering, expensive, all-out spectacle—an experience that could compensate for the dull life of the "modern toiler."

EXTENDING OZ

Fresh from this success, Baum showed his pragmatic side. "Should," he told the *Chicago Tribune*, "I ever attempt another extravaganza, I mean to profit by the lesson Mr. Mitchell has taught me, and sacrifice personal preference to the demands of those I expect to purchase the tickets."[56] Indeed, as the show continued its runaway success, Baum's critiques of Mitchell and consumers' demand for "what pleases them," morphed into a whole-hearted embrace of Oz's new medium, as he trumpeted the stage's potential for providing what the page could not. "To describe [characters] with pen and ink," he told the *Chicago Sunday Record*, "is very different from seeing them actually live. When the Scarecrow came to life on the first night of the *Wizard of Oz*, I experienced strange sensations of wonder and awe; the appearance of the Tin Woodman made me catch my breath spasmodically, and when the gorgeous poppy field, with its human flowers burst into view—more real than my fondest dreams had ever conceived—a big lump came to my throat and a wave of gratitude swept over me that I had lived to see the sight."[57] Ever the marketer, Baum turned this approval into an endorsement, exhorting all fans of the book to come see Oz in a new, *more real* way. This marks Baum's first articulation of what would become a central tenet in his creation and marketing of Oz: the use of new technologies and new media to deploy remediation's promise of immediacy—to enable consumers to "experience strange sensations of wonder and awe" in an Oz "more real than (their) fondest dreams."

While Baum may initially have seen adapting Oz for the stage as a one-off—or as a chance to return to his abandoned theatrical career—he quickly moved to capitalize on the musical's success, creating and sustaining, in his words, "the Oz line." Over the next seventeen years, he drew on his earlier marketing experience to pioneer many of the techniques we now associate with experiential marketing. He began by striking while the iron was hot, rolling out the next Oz product over several platforms and with as much fanfare as possible. It started with a new Oz book; Baum and his publisher, Reilly & Britton, explicitly positioned *The Marvelous Land of Oz*, published in June 1904, as an Oz *product*, "a sequel... superbly illustrated," that featured "characters already famous the country over."[58] Furthermore, Baum avows in his introduction, this sequel was only written in response to the consumer demand evidenced by an initial onslaught of letters asking him "to write something more" about the Scarecrow and the Tin Woodman that only increased after "the success of the stage production of the Wizard of Oz" made "new friends for the story."[59] He further ties his Oz products—the original book, the stage production, *The Marvelous Land of Oz*—together in the book's dedication to Stone and Montgomery, featured in their stage-costumes, "whose presentations of the Tin Woodman and Scarecrow have delighted thousands of children throughout this land."[60] Although the promotional strategies collectively known as Integrated Marketing Communications (IMC) would not be developed until some 75 years later, Baum instinctively practiced them at the turn of the twentieth century.

Baum clearly saw *The Marvelous Land of Oz* as the first offering in the carefully orchestrated launch of his brand extension; its June publication was followed in August by a weekly newspaper serial, *Queer Visitors from the Land of Oz*. "From the Land of Oz to the United States Here They Come!" the *Sunday Record Herald* trumpeted, "They are in their first vacation away from the Land of Oz and the Emerald City. They want to romp with the children of the US."[61] The weekly installments were accompanied by a "children's guessing contest," "What did the Woggle-Bug Say," sponsored by the newspapers, who collected the answer cards and distributed $500 a month in prizes.[62] As the series was winding down (the last installment was published on February 26, 1905), Baum published *The Woggle-Bug Book*, an elaborate color picture book chronicling the further adventures of the "highly-magnified and thoroughly educated" bug. Reilly & Britton distributed Woggle-Bug buttons and copies of the *Ozmapolitan*, a four-page fully realized mock newspaper from "The Emerald City—Land of Oz," complete with Ozian classified ads, society notices and letters to the editor, and featuring articles on the Scarecrow's and company's upcoming trip to the USA, along with a review of "our official historian," "L. Frank Baum's new history of our country."[63]

The Woggle-Bug promotion, which presented Baum's new book across a variety of platforms and provided consumers with multiple ways to experience Oz, proved to wildly successful; in addition to Woggle-Bug posters, cards, and buttons, Parker Brothers produced, *The Woggle-Bug Game of Conundrums*, and Baum and Tietjens penned a new song, "What did the Woggle-Bug Say?," available in sheet music for purchase. Within six months of its publication, *The Marvelous Land of Oz* was in its third printing, and Reilly & Britton's trade advertisement could rightly boast that it was "the most extensively advertised book ever put on the American market." "What did the Woggle-Bug Say?," the ad began. "It's worth your money to know, because thousands of children are guessing, thousands are wearing Woggle-Bug buttons and 3,000,000 newspapers are asking the question every day."[64] All of this boded well for the success of the final product tie-in, *The Woggle-Bug*, a musical extravaganza, that premiered at Chicago's Garrick Theater on June 18. Baum seeking to sustain the Oz line and its income had, as the *Cleveland Leader's* review of *The Marvelous Land of Oz* noted, written the book with this finale in view. Whereas *The Wizard of Oz* had had to be substantially rewritten for the stage, its sequel was written with an eye to performance. "Mr. Baum," the reviewer asserts, "as we have said, has the child heart. But he has the business head as well. Part of his book…has been written with a view to the stage. General Jinjur and her soldiers are only shapely chorus girls. The observant reader can see their tights and ogling glances."[65] Baum, taking a page from Julian Mitchell, seemed determine to give the stage audiences what pleased them.

On the morning of *Woggle-Bug's* premiere, the *Chicago Record Herald* printed Baum's article "Fairy Tales on Stage." In this article, as he had back when he was a marketer of chickens and axle oil, Baum establishes himself as *the* expert on American fairy tales, and distinguishes the Oz stage brand from its competitors. *The Wizard of Oz*, Baum asserts, is "distinguished as the first fairy extravaganza to be founded on a fairy tale written by an American. Its success brought me many propositions from managers to utilize other stories of mine in the same way, but I have not allowed them to rush me into any premature propositions…notwithstanding the fact that 'The Wizard of Oz' has many imitators, 'The Woggle-Bug' will be its first legitimate successor."[66] Here, Baum guarantees both the quality of this product—he has not allowed himself to be "rushed into premature propositions," and *The Woggle-Bug* as a genuine Oz product. Alas, this genuine product, written to please, "those [Baum] expect[ed] to purchase tickets" was not a success. Reviewers panned its banal libretto and stage excesses, its "electric lights of all colors and in all sorts of places and…stage full of girls…[who] always have something and generally it lights up."[67]

The Woggle-Bug closed less than a month after it opened. In some ways, this extravaganza's fate is puzzling; negative reviews from New

York critics had certainly not doomed *The Wizard of Oz*, and Baum's and Oz's brands were still very strong. It may simply be that the play, for all of its pretty girls and electric lights, was not very good. But two other factors must also be considered. First, Baum's original plan, as he indicated by dedicating *The Marvelous Land of Oz* to Stone and Montgomery, had been for them to star in the production, thus ensuring continuity between the two productions, and the success of the new play as it featured the popular stars of the old. Stone and Montgomery, however, fearing that another stint as the Scarecrow and Tin Woodman would irrevocably typecast them, declined. Second, the original, better-known play was still touring and thus in direct competition with *The Woggle-Bug*, and, indeed, one critic savaged the show as "only a shabby and dull repetition of a cheapened *Wizard of Oz*."[68] Directly competing with his own product, Baum may well have saturated the theater-going market. *The Woggle-Bug's* poor reception, however, while disappointing, did not tarnish Baum's brand. *The Wizard of Oz* continued to play for enthusiastic audiences; both Oz books continued to sell well; and Oz increasingly became part of America's cultural landscape. Oz characters began to appear in political cartoons, California's Chutes Amusement Park's featured a "Fairies of Oz" attraction, and a *Wizard of Oz* float traveled down the streets of New Orleans in the city's famous Mardi Gras parade.

During this period, Baum worked to consolidate his own brand as America's teller of fairy tales. We have already seen a glimpse of Baum's plans to brand himself in the letter he wrote to his brother just before the publication of *The Wonderful Wizard of Oz*. As *The Woggle-Bug* premiered, Baum staked his claim as "the only American writer whose fairy tales have become popularly known and some one of my sixteen published books may be found in nearly every home in the country where there are children and young hearts that love wonder tales." At this point in his career, Baum saw Oz as a part of his larger brand and, while he embraced his role as "The Royal Historian of Oz," he hoped to use that role to sell his other tales. In the three years between *The Wonderful Wizard of Oz* and the third book in the series, *Ozma of Oz* (1907) Baum published five novel-length non-Oz fairy tales, *The Life and Adventures of Santa Claus*, *The Master Key*, *The Enchanted Isle of Yew*, *Queen Xixi of Ix* and *The Adventures of John Dough and the Cherub*, all branded as Baum products.

A Spectacular Venture

In 1908, following on the publication of his fourth Oz book, *Dorothy and the Wizard of Oz*, Baum again sought to both capitalize on his brand and provide his consumers with a new way to experience Oz through visual spectacle. He produced, wrote, and starred in *Fairylogue and Radio Plays*, a traveling show providing a clever twist on the popular travelogue: lectures supported by slides from travel abroad.[69] Baum's version of this genre, however, was quite elaborate. It entailed Baum himself as narrator, a full orchestra, 114 colored slides, and 23 *colored* film clips. *Fairylogue's* marketing traded on Baum's status as "America's Author of Fairy Tales." The promotional program included a carefully crafted biography of the man "generally considered the greatest living author of Fairy Tales," whose "books have sold in the millions and (whose) name today is a household word," extolling his "creative genius," that, first, inaugurated an "epoch in juvenile publishing when he issued his gorgeously colored fairy tale, *The Wizard of Oz*" and, then, "creat[ed] another epoch" with a stage adaptation, which "set the pace for...extravaganza and musical comedies" and "is still delighting thousands." "Today," the biography concluded, "Mr. Baum is again a creator—an originator. This time he has invented the RADIO PLAY, a form of entertainment as different from the extravaganza as the extravaganza is from the fairy tale." Once again the stage has been set for a new Oz experience.

Baum's long history as a pioneer in entertainment assured consumers that his latest product would be well-worth their time and money. Yet, as with any truly new product—the Discman and MP3 player come to mind—advertisers must educate consumers even as they persuade them to try it. Thus, both the marketing campaign and reviewers heralded the *Fairylogues* as an "entirely new" form of entertainment: "Nothing more amazing than these acting pictures has ever been seen in America." It was an extravaganza, they assured audiences, "a curious and novel entertainment." "Quite and delightfully different from anything yet seen on stage," the *Fairylogue* also offered consumers a perhaps once-in-a-lifetime opportunity to see Baum himself. "Every child," newspaper advertisements asserted "should meet personally America's greatest Fairy Tale author." And Baum did not disappoint. Appearing on stage, "garbed in a lovely white frock coat," (in a clear, and, we are pretty certain, deliberate, visual reference to Mark Twain), he "won the affections of a good size audience of children and grown-ups."[70]

The Fairylogue and Radio Plays employed new media and technologies to produce a visual spectacle that brought Oz's narrative to life. Not only was film still a novelty, but also the color-process, purchased by Baum from France, offered an entirely new technology to American consumers, one that, much like MGM's technicolor Oz, inspired wonder and awe. Taken together, the elements of the *Fairylogue and Radio Plays* provided audiences with an immersive experience, which in turn fostered a lasting emotional connection to Baum's world. This was true for consumers already familiar with Baum's other Oz creations as well as for consumers new to the Oz experience. Additionally, the show's *Fairylogue* educated both sets of consumers, providing them with new information about Baum's Fairyland, including the first map of Oz.

In its multi-media remediation of Oz, the experience of the *Fairylogue and Radio Plays* offered consumers both "more"—more stories, more characters, more spectacle—and, as Baum himself promised in an interview with the *New York Herald* about the production's use of film, *immediacy*:

> My little characters step from the pages of an Oz book. A closed book is shown, which the faeries open. On the first page is disclosed a black and white picture of Dorothy. I beckon and she straightaway steps out of its pages, becomes imbued with the colors of life and moves about. The fairies then close the book, which opens again and again until the tinman, the scarecrow, and all of the others step out of the pages of the book, and come, colored to life, where they move and group themselves together to the side[71]

From black and white to color, from stationary to active, from the page to life, from the fictive to the "real": *Fairylogue and Radio Plays* provided consumers with a new and memorable experience of Oz. Ads for the show emphasized its visual spectacle and immediacy, "SEE!" they urged, "Dorothy shipwrecked," "the Gump soar" "the Wooden Sawhorse kick and prance," "the live…Hungry Tiger and Cowardly Lion."[72]

From his days at Baum's Bazaar, Baum understood the power of the event to draw consumers through the door, and he made sure that *Fairylogue and Radio-Plays* carried with it the festive feel of a traveling carnival. Newspaper stories and ads generated buzz: "Playing for three nights only!" "Oz comes to town!" At some shows, the great author himself would sign books at intermission, and at "Souvenir Matinees" he gave out illustrated books.[73] Other shows included surprise appearances, as one Thursday matinee in Chicago, where the child who played Dorothy in the films, was instructed by Baum to "come down dressed in her Dorothy suit and be introduced to the audience."[74]

For consumers looking for an event, for an experience that would make them glow and tingle, Baum's show certainly fit the bill, and the *Fairylogue and Radio Plays* provides a fascinating example of an extended, immersive Oz experience. Reviewers may have praised the show's "use science to aid (Baum) in simulating the things which faeries really achieve," carrying "the record of illusions in the motion picture field as far as it would seem possible to go," but the audiences' reactions were more visceral, they "squealed with delight," and "warmly applauded" "when the more familiar characters...stepped out of the pages of the huge book."[75] Baum and his publishers clearly hoped that this Oz experience would inspire consumers to buy more books, to re-experience the story in a different medium. Bracing for a massive cross-sell, publishers Reilly & Britton urged booksellers to "order plenty" of *Ozma of Oz*, *Dorothy and the Wizard of Oz*, and *John Dough and the Cherub*, which "form the basis for the merry, whimsical and distinctly original...theatrical novelty, staged at the cost of many thousands of dollars." "In every city," they assured their buyers, "elaborate advertising will be done, insuring large audiences and a tremendous demand for the BAUM BOOKS mentioned above."[76]

The show, which opened in September and toured for three months before closing in New York City, was a critical and box-office success— spectacular, popular, and extremely expensive. This "foolish" venture, however, is often blamed for plunging Baum into bankruptcy, and, indeed, he did file for protection from his *Fairylogue* debts on June 3, 1911. But, we would argue, we need to rethink the myth about the destitute Dreamer of Oz this bankruptcy filing might seem to suggest. In it, Baum lists his assets as a used typewriter, two suits of clothes, and eleven reference books, and while it is true that he had already sold both his Chicago home and "The Sign of the Goose" to meet creditors demands, and that Ozcot, his recently built California residence, was built with his wife's inheritance, Baum was surely not reduced to the penury this filing implies. In addition to five Oz books, there were Baum's other fairy-tale novels, which may not have sold as well as the Oz books, but they did still sell respectably. Furthermore, Baum was also the author of four popular serials, *The Daring Twins*, published under his own name, *Aunt Jane's Nieces* (as Edith Van Dyne), *Sam Steele's Adventures* (as Captain Hugh Fitzgerald), and *The Boy Fortune Hunters* (as Floyd Akers). Thus, while Baum may have been temporarily overextended—something that the bankruptcy filing took care of—his brand was still sound.

ROYAL HISTORIAN OF OZ

And it was that brand, carefully shepherded by Baum, that sustained Oz. In an August 1909 interview with *Theater Magazine*, Baum boasted of his first extravaganza's amazing success, even as its unprecedented run was reaching an end: "I would like to say a word for 'The Wizard of Oz.' It never grows old. It is just as bright and fresh and popular today as it was at its first performance 8 years ago. The 'Wizard' is an extraordinary thing. It is the only musical comedy that has lived for 8 years." However, he quickly moved on to remind readers of his larger brand:

> It isn't through opera...that I base any hopes I may have of having my name written in bronze. My important work I consider to be my fairy tales, not my plays. The 'Wizard' was written as a children's book three years before it was put on as a play. My books have been translated into almost every language including Japanese, and in my travels abroad, I have found them cherished by children from Egypt, in Nubia on the edge of darkest Africa, to the interior of the Philippines, and a friend said he saw one at a house at Hongkong China. The children are all friends of ...all my queer people, and I am a friend of the children.[77]

Here, Baum recognizes that his brand, his "hope of having (his) name written in bronze," depends upon the children who are his primary consumers. As such, he carefully cultivated a relationship with his young readers, personally answering the thousands of letters they wrote to him, and carrying on an ongoing dialogue with them in his introductions to the Oz books. In that sense, Baum's fans were his *clients*, not his customers. He cared about—thought about—each one, as much as was humanly possible in the early days of mass-mediated fandom. They responded in kind.

Throughout the introductions to the Oz books, Baum works to foster an emotional connection between himself and his primary market. He positions the books as direct responses to consumer demand and presents them as products of a partnership between the author and his readers. Baum consistently addresses his readers as "my dears" and "my little friends," emotionally thanking them for their letters:

> I believe my dears that I am the proudest story teller that ever lived. Many a time tears of pride and joy stood in my eyes while I read the tender, loving and appealing letters that come to me...from my little readers. To have pleased you, to have interested you, to have won your friendship and perhaps your love is to my mind as great an achievement as to become President of the United States.... You have helped me to fulfill my life's ambition, and I am more grateful to you, my dears, than I can express in words.[78]

Baum here powerfully describes the affect that his "little readers'" letters have had on him and assures them that his relationship with them has helped him "to fulfill his life's ambition," identified as precisely that relationship, "to have pleased you." Each book is offered as the fulfillment of a promise to his friends, and those friends are encouraged to continue to write to him, which "more than repay(s) me for the pleasant task of preparing these books."

The letters not only repay Baum for writing the last book; they also produce the next one. Without children who want "something more," Baum implies, there would be no more tales from Oz: "My friends the children are responsible for this new Oz book as they were for the last one.... Their sweet letters plead to know 'more about Dorothy'"; and they ask "What became of the Cowardly Lion?" "Indeed, could I do all that my little friends ask, I would be obliged to write dozens of books to satisfy their demand." "Well, my dears, here is what you asked for: another Oz book."[79] Furthermore, Baum encouraged his readers to see themselves as having an active stake in the story—as co-creators of Oz—anticipating and capitalizing on Henry Jenkin's "convergence culture" by nearly one hundred years. In the introduction to *Ozma of Oz*, Baum states he tried to please his correspondents by including their suggestions—"Please have Dorothy go to the land of Oz again," or "Why don't you make Dorothy and Ozma meet up and have a good time together?"[80] By his next book, however, he acknowledges them as co-authors: "This is our book—mine and the children's. For they have flooded me with thousands of suggestions in regard to it, and I have honestly tried to adopt as many of these suggestions as could be fitted into one story," and he continues to do so throughout the series. As he introduces *The Emerald City*, Baum writes[81]:

> Perhaps I should admit on the title page of this book that it is "By L Frank Baum and his correspondents," for I have used many suggestions conveyed to me in letters from children. Once on a while, I imagined myself "an author of fairy tales" but now I am merely an editor or private secretary for a host of youngsters whose ideas I am requested to weave into the thread of my stories. I am proud of this alliance. Children love these stories because children helped create them…. I hope it will be a long time before we are obliged to dissolve the partnership.[82]

In other words, as the series goes on, Baum increasingly presents Oz as "shareware," an ever-expanding archontic text, and this "partnership" with his consumers sustained the Oz brand for nearly twenty years.

Consumers' demand for more Oz eventually subsumed Baum himself within that brand, in spite of his continued efforts to use his relationship with his readers to introduce new products. "I know lots of other stories," Baum tells his readers, "and I hope to tell them some time or another." But "It's no use– no use at all. The children won't let me stop telling tales of the Land of Oz. My loving tyrants… cry 'Oz!—More about Oz Mr. Baum!' And what can I do but obey them?"[83] In one last effort to move on from Oz, Baum ended 1910's *The Emerald City of Oz* with a telegram from Dorothy, announcing that Ozma had cut Oz off from the outside world; there would be no more stories from Oz. "This seemed to me to be too bad at first," Baum tells his readers, "for Oz is a very interesting fairyland. Still, we have no right to be grieved for we have had enough of the history of Oz to fill six story books."[84] His consumers, like today's *Star Trek* and *Harry Potter* fans, were not convinced, and, in the end, Baum accepted that his future products would all need to be issued as part of the Oz brand.

Beginning with 1913's *The Patchwork Girl of Oz*, published three years after Ozma closed Oz's borders, Baum gave up on introducing new lines; instead, he incorporated his non-Oz narratives an ever-expanding "Oz-verse" and concentrated on, as he wrote to Reilly & Britton in 1915, giving "new impetus to the Oz line."[85] He penned *The Little Wizard* books, six short picture books designed to introduce the narrative to a new generation of younger readers, to accompany the release of *The Patchwork Girl*. And, in the same year, Oz returned to the stage, with *The Tik-Tok Man*. The show—which attempted to lure fans to the theater with an original Oz narrative, rather than merely adapting an existing book—was trumpeted as "the most costly, novel, and up-to-date extravaganza the American stage his ever known,"[86] and Baum toured with it, calling on the relationship he had fostered with his consumers, to help sell tickets. *Tik-Tok* did well in Los Angeles, less well with the critics elsewhere, and decently at the touring box office. Ultimately, however, the extravaganza proved too costly to sustain, and the producer closed it while it was still in the black.

Hollywood Calling

The Little Wizard Series and the *Tic-Tok Man of Oz* sought both to expand Oz's market to younger children and adults and to provide consumers with new ways to experience Oz. With his next enterprise, the Oz Film Manufacturing Company, Baum offered his consumers an even more novel visit to Oz. When asked by *The New York Dramatic Mirror*, why he "left the paths of contentment in middle age, to desert his garden and fireside desk and to take on care and worries in new form, when health, wealth and contentment bade him frolic instead of labor," to enter the film business, Baum replied:

> As you know, my books are rather high-priced because of the colored plates. Many children see them, but a multitude do not. This has always been... of regret to me. One night I was passing a suburban theater and saw a crowd of poor children entering the door or crowded around the box office of a motion picture theater.... The idea came to me—here is the opportunity to solve the problem; to accomplish that which I have been unrestful over. I will put all my books into film that every child in the whole country may see them. A whole book for a nickel. That is the reason for the Oz Film Company.[87]

Stripped of its almost-Dickensian dramatic sentimentality, Baum's vignette points to his awareness of film medium's potential to bring Oz to consumers from a new socioeconomic sector, to reach "every child in the whole country." Furthermore, as films, these Oz experiences would appeal to multiple generations of consumers. Grandparents, who remembered Stone and Montgomery, could relive Oz with their grandkids; children who adored the books could take Mom and Dad to the show. *The Patchwork Girl of Oz*, *The Magic Cloak of Oz*, and *The Scarecrow of Oz* had it all: affordability, availability, cutting-edge technology, and wide-spread consumer appeal; as such, they seemed poised to launch a new branch of the Oz line. Baum, writing to his wife, Maud, on company letterhead, was certainly optimistic about his latest venture:

> In Philadelphia, the Stanley Theatre turned crowds away (and) Philadelphia papers declare it the most moral and delightful picture of the year. At other places, it was a big success. In a few it fell down.... We are going ahead with a strong advertising campaign and expect to create a demand for "Patchwork" and make money out of it yet.[88]

Knowing that the success of his new enterprise depended upon its connection to Oz, Baum carefully marketed the Oz Film Manufacturing Company as possessing "Exclusive Control of the Works of L. Frank Baum in Motion Pictures." A portrait of Ozma, wearing a crown emblazoned with a jeweled "OZ," served as the studio's logo, branding all marketing, correspondence and films. The studio's trade newsletter led with Baum's successful multi-media career to assure exhibitors and theater managers of its films' market potential:

> L. Frank Baum....is famous the world over.... The ten Oz books have sold over four million copies during the last 6 years....Believing that there was a field for a new line of motion picture plays, Mr. Baum organized the Oz Film Manufacturing Company.... The work is all done under Mr. Baum's personal direction and supervision, and he has shown a capacity for making just as successful motion pictures as he did books and musical shows.[89]

Baum explicitly positioned these new "Special Features in Fairy Extravaganzas" as a chance to revisit and relive his previous books and musical shows. Marketing tied cast and crew to earlier Baum productions, and Baum promised "the thousands—yes millions—of people who saw and enjoyed the *Wizard of Oz* during the 8 years that it ran on the legitimate stage that all of their old favorites may be seen once more in motion pictures."[90]

By inviting consumers to remember and re-experience Oz, marketing for *The Patchwork Girl* sought to expand its audience. The studio lauded the film as a children's picture, perfect for "solving the matinee problem," at the same time that it targeted parents and grandparents. The advertising newsletter featured several reviewers who put their "stamp of approval" on this "cleanest and most fascinating of this class of pictures." One mother observed, "Finest photoplay I ever saw, and my son and daughter were simply crazy about it...To think of the children of Topeka who were not taken to see it makes my heart ache." Additionally, the paper reported, "a large percentage of parents who (had) seen the first of the Oz series," took "the children to the second one...merely to 'please the youngsters,'" "without admitting that we really want to see it ourselves."[91]

The Oz Film Manufacturing Company's marketing department, supported by reviews and consumer's letters, predicted that the films would replay the success of their "operatic sisters" at the cinema. *The Patchwork Girl of Oz*, it assured potential exhibitors, "has jammed the houses every afternoon (with) enthusiastic kiddies and their mothers, and the more 'grown up' audiences at night have been just as enthusiastic." The film "will surely pack every theater that shows it to capacity afternoon and night."[92] The *Topeka Capital* agreed: "The Standing Room Only sign will have to be used today."[93] Both marketers and reviewers praised the film's expensive use of sets and effects to transport their audiences, particularly their adult audiences, to "a place so full of whimsical abandonment that adults will give themselves up to its fairy land with as much absorption as children." "The Never-Never Land of quaint fancy," *The Motion Picture News* observed, "is a place of delightful retirement from the harsh realities of the workaday world. This realm of poesy and odd conceits... has been explored by L. Frank Baum with pleasing results." "Older people," the reviewer asserted, "will say to each other, 'Forget a while the cares and turmoil of our busy lives, and hie us back to childhood.'"

In spite of this film's relative success and aggressive marketing campaign, *The Patchwork Girl of Oz* was the only Oz film to receive wide release, as the studio had difficulty finding a distributor for other Oz projects. Taken together, a patent violation lawsuit brought by Edison's lawyers, an unwillingness on the part of studios to give up "theater space" for a non-studio product, and the difficulty of booking "kiddie films," doomed Baum's venture into filmmaking. The studio folded in

1915, but Oz continued as Baum turned his attention once again to writing. He began by adapting *The Tik-Tok Man of Oz* and *The Scarecrow of Oz* from stage and screen to page, reversing the more usual direction of adaptation (*The Scarecrow of Oz* is actually the first novelization of a film). Baum, however, was careful in the prefaces to these books to distinguish them from the stage/screen products, assuring readers of 1914's *Tik-Tok of Oz* that the play "is not like this story…although some of the adventures recorded in this book are included in the play…. Those who have seen the play and those who have read the other Oz books will find in this story a lot of strange characters and adventures that they have never heard of before."[94] In short, the book provides a new experience of Oz. As the film version of *The Scarecrow of Oz* (1915) had never been widely distributed, Baum was able to present that tale, as he had so many others, as a response to "The Army of Children, which besieged the Post Office, conquered the Postmen and delivered to me its imperious commands." "It takes more and more Oz Books every year," he concludes, "to satisfy the demands of old and new readers and there have been formed many 'Oz Reading Societies' where the Oz books owned by different members are read aloud. All this is very gratifying to me and encourages me to write more stories."[95]

This active community of consumers—the result of years of effort of Baum's part—attests to Baum's success as not just the Dreamer of Oz, but also as its chief marketing officer and brand manager. His forays into new technologies and new media may not have always been successful. But his assiduous marketing efforts—branding himself as "America's Teller of Fairy Tales," cultivating an abiding emotional connection between himself and his consumers, designing integrated marketing campaigns, and creating novel buzz-worthy consumption experiences—proved indispensable in setting Oz on the path to cultural sustainability in its formative years.

Oz Affordances

Baum was clearly a wizard of marketing, but despite our emphasis on the marketing and consumption of Oz, we readily acknowledge that even the most astute marketing strategies cannot sustain a product that consumers do not want. The Oz story itself—its content, style, and the values it conveyed—was critical to its success. Thus, before we move on to discussing the ways in which the narrative was adapted, remediated, and marketed to sustain itself over time, we need to examine why and how the narrative itself connected—and continued to connect—so powerfully with its initial readers.

Oz was born in a rapidly changing America, a time that spanned from the Gilded Age through World War I. On the one hand, this was a period of amazing technological advances: the transcontinental railroad, the electric light, the telephone, and the movie camera. On the other, it was a period of constant upheaval: labor riots, Wounded Knee, economic depressions, and the rise of crony capitalism. America in Baum's lifetime was a nation poised between optimism and anxiety. On optimism's side were America's twin myths: democratic opportunity epitomized in Horatio Algers' quintessential "rags to riches" American dream-tale, *Ragged Dick*, which ran as a serial when Baum was ten; and Progressivism, which trumpeted technological advances in factory and farm equipment generating more productivity, mass production increasing access to goods, and new domestic technologies transforming American homes—all of which promised to raise the standard of living and provide new opportunities for leisure. On anxiety's side, was the lived experience of rapid urbanization, immigration, economic crises, and industrialization that left many Americans reeling, and called these myths into question. Oz's first audiences, thus, lived in a divided America; for some, it was a nation that had lived up to its promise of social mobility and prosperity; for others, it was a nation plagued with self-doubt, in which the gap between the haves and the have-nots widened daily, and where, in spite of the promise of national prosperity, people lost their homes and their livelihood.

Both of these Americas contributed to Oz's conception, reception and marketability, and given this context, let us return to Baum's original market analysis as laid out in the introduction to *The Wonderful Wizard of Oz*. Here, Baum offers Oz as a tale of the "fantastic, marvelous and manifestly unreal," *without fear*. Instead of "horrible and blood-curdling incident," inanimate objects come delightfully to life—the Scarecrow, the Patchwork Girl, and Jack Pumpkinhead. Instead of rampaging dragons, Animals converse—the Cowardly Lion, the Pink Kitten, Bellina the Hen, and, eventually, even Toto. Here, children are not, like Hansel and Gretel, endangered by starvation. Trees bear buns, and cream puffs, and three-course nuts (soup in the top, meat, potatoes and a "fine salad" in the middle, and multiple desserts on the bottom). And heartaches and nightmares are indeed left out; there is just enough danger for the plot to advance, and no predicament lasts longer than a short chapter. Most of the "villains" aren't really evil at all, just selfish or misguided, and those who are (like the Wicked Witch of the West) are quickly disposed of. Oz is a *safe* world. What problems cannot be solved by ingenuity, optimism, and friendship are resolved—*dea ex machina*—by Ozma and Glinda, who monitor all that happens in either Ozma's Magic Mirror or Glinda's Magic Book. In a period marked by upheaval and crisis, Baum's Oz offered readers a gentle, optimistic fairyland, one in which the very American traits embodied in Horatio Algers' heroes prevail over all adversity. In some ways, as many have argued, Oz embodies the possibility of an ideal America, and to those who were living in that America, Baum's magic land mirrored their national myths.[96]

Ironically, however, by the end of the series, this most American of all fairy stories offered its consumers an alternative to America, a fairyland that provided refuge to those who, like the Gales, had suffered severe reversals of fortune in the primary world. Each Oz book that starts in the real world begins with juxtaposition between the USA and Oz. In *The Wonderful Wizard of Oz* (1900), it's that between the gray, sunbaked joyless prairie and the "stately trees bearing rich and luscious fruits." Later books continue this contrast between a lush Oz and joyless and gray America; in *Ozma of Oz* (1907), Dorothy and Uncle Henry are on their way to Australia, seeking a rest cure for Uncle Henry, who "was not very well, because he had been working so hard on his Kansas farm that his health had given way and left him weak and nervous," when their ship goes down at sea. An earthquake sends Dorothy and Zeb and an emaciated ranch horse to Oz in *Dorothy and the Wizard in Oz* (1908), and *The Road to Oz* (1909) opens up before Dorothy and a "Shaggy Man," dressed in rags, without money (or any desire for it, for "money makes people proud and haughty)," but also without love.[97]

Each of these books present Oz as a temporary escape from circumstances; in each, Dorothy returns to Kansas, and the gray farm that she defends in the first Oz adventure, "no matter how dreary and gray our homes are, we…would rather live in them than in any other country, be it ever so beautiful. There is no place like home."[98] However, in *The Emerald City of Oz* (1910), home becomes untenable: "Uncle Henry grew poorer every year, and the crops raised on the farm only brought food for the family. Therefore the mortgage could not be paid."[99] Faced with dispossession, Uncle Henry and Aunt Em urge Dorothy to flee to

Oz and prepare to spend their waning years in the workhouse. Instead, they live out their days in the utopian commonwealth of Oz:

> Every inhabitant of that favored country was happy and prosperous.... No disease of any sort was ever known among Ozites...There were no poor people in the Land of Oz, because there was no such thing as money, and all property of every sort belonged to the Ruler... Each person was given freely by his neighbors whatever he required for use, which is as much as anyone may reasonably desire....Each man and woman, no matter what he or she produced for the good of the community, was supplied with food and clothing and a house and furniture and ornaments and games.... Everyone worked half the time and played half the time, and the people enjoyed the work as much as they did the play. There were all sorts of queer creatures among them, but not a single one who was evil, or who possessed a selfish and violent nature....the reason that most people are bad is because they do not try to be good.[100]

From *The Emerald City* on, the traffic to Oz is one way, and, by the end of Baum's series, Dorothy, Uncle Henry, Aunt Em, and a host of others have become permanent residents, escaping poverty and deprivation in an America where they cannot thrive. Thus, for its original audiences, in a time of cultural and economic upheaval, Oz provided a reassuring escape to safety, plenitude, and happiness. In contemporary marketing terms, Baum's Oz was a mecca of hedonic consumption, in which the inhabitants, even though they toiled half of the time, enjoyed themselves all of the time. Under such circumstances, according to consumer researchers, Morris Holbrook and Elizabeth Hirschman, fantasies, feelings, and fun are bound to follow.[101]

In their depiction of a benevolent land where nothing truly bad could ever happen, the Oz stories offered their readers a reassuring world of plenty and harmony. And their formulaic predictability reinforced this feeling of safety and promised happy endings. Each novel follows essentially the same quest pattern, comprised of short episodes and leading to the Emerald City, where, after *The Land of Oz* (1904), Ozma will greet the questers, grant their requests, and preside over a magnificent feast. Each offers its readers the pleasures of repetition and recognition; old stories are recounted (previously in Oz....) and familiar friends make at least a cameo appearance. Much of Oz's appeal to consumers lay in this continuity, in Baum's creation of a familiar, homey, ideal fairyland—an *other-where* without fear or lack.

Oz-Mosis

Indeed, consumers attested to Oz's therapeutic value, circulating anecdotes in which Oz supplemented or replaced more conventional medicine. "During the scourge of Infantile Paralysis," a New York doctor recalled, "when little bodies were pain-wracked, arms or legs had to be stretched, the children were told if they did their best a nurse would read an Oz book to them." Another doctor reportedly added, "The Oz stories, read to the children invalids, has done more to mitigate their suffering than all other remedial measures combined."[102] The story of a dying child in East Lynn, New York, encapsulates early-twentieth-century depictions of Oz's therapeutic powers:

> Some years ago, a little girl lay distraught with a fatal nervous disease. She was so delicate and so sensitive that the physicians dare not give sedatives of any kind. As she lay, prey to physical ailment, her spirit wandered in Fairy Land. Pictures of the Land of Oz came into her mind and she asked Mama to read to her from *The Wizard of Oz*....During the reading the little face lighted up with pleasure and interest. The delirium stayed, and the suffering made bearable... the early part of the third night, the fading voice murmured, 'Princess of Oz' and her life passed out in that Fairyland that made a beautiful world for her.[103]

Here, Oz both becomes medicine, the sedative drugs that the physicians dared not give, and functions as a mirror of and gateway to heaven. And indeed, this sense of "Oz" as the heaven beyond became part of the narrative's myth. Purportedly, Baum's own final words pointed to Oz: "Now I can cross the shifting sands," the deadly sands that, in the books, separate Oz from the real world of pain, loss, and deprivation.[104]

The numerous tributes published after Baum's death in 1919 support our speculations about why Oz was so popular in its original market. In a time of rapid change, economic and social upheavals, strikes, riots, and wars, they argue, Baum, offered "realms of joy, safe charted for boys and girls of earth where no sting poisoned," "and led [them] into the laughing fields of the New Fairyland of Love-without-fear."[105] "He never pictured cruelties or told a tale that excited fear. This was the reason children could doze off to pleasant dreams in a darkened room."[106] These tributes, appearing in newspapers across the country, also attest to the strength of Baum's brand. "L. Frank Baum is dead," the *New York Times* solemnly announced, "and the children, if they knew it would mourn.

That endless procession of Oz books, coming out just before Christmas is to cease.... And the children have suffered a loss they do not know."[107] The *NYT*'s obituary to Oz, however, was premature; Baum's marketing experience and talents, his forays into new forms and technologies, and the relationship he carefully crafted between himself and his consumers, assured that that endless procession of Oz books (and films and shows and toys and collectibles) would continue long after his death.

CONCLUSION

Our examination of Baum's marketing career, in which he helped to shape the fledgling profession, sheds light on the circuit of production, marketing, and consumption that sustained Oz for nearly twenty years during his lifetime. From this first phase of Oz's life, we can deduce a set of strategies that Baum used to position his narrative for long-term cultural sustainability:

- **Distinguish the product**: Baum learned this lesson early with Castorine Oil. Consumers need to be convinced that the product they are buying is a uniquely superior instance of its kind, not to be confused with other, inferior imitation products. He carefully packaged Oz. Not only was the original Oz product, *The Wonderful Wizard of Oz*, elaborately unique, designed to catch consumer's eyes with its lavish use of color and illustrations, but also he explicitly positioned its narrative as something new, a timely response to the needs of "modern children." As more Oz products appeared, Baum assured consumers that *these* products (the spectacles, musicals, and films) were exclusively and authentically Oz, warning them away from lesser imitations.
- **Create an insider community**: Starting with his foray into exotic poultry, Baum recognized that an insider community drove sales. As the Oz phenomenon grew, he offered his consumers multiple chances to "participate" in Oz. Baum encouraged community involvement through contests and events and provided gathering places for engagement with his touring shows. He used his book prefaces to posit a virtual community of readers connected by their love for Oz and to recognize them as co-creators of the ongoing story. All of these attempts to create community paid off as his avid

young fans formed their own Oz reading clubs, to read, discuss and exchange books, while waiting for the next Oz story or event.

- **Fashion a compelling persona**: From the moment *Mother Goose in Prose* earned Baum name-recognition, he carefully managed his brand; the success of Oz, however, inspired him to create *himself* as a celebrity author. If, as the proprietor of B. W. Baum and Sons, Baum had established himself as an expert in Hamburg hens, as the Royal Historian of Oz, be fashioned himself as the America's best-beloved purveyor of fairy tales, weaving himself into the everyday life of American consumers to become one of the "companionable spokesmen of Ad Land." From his published conversations with his little friends and white-suited appearances in the *Fairylogue*, through his home at "Ozcot," and photographed sessions of him reading Oz stories to children, to his numerous public interviews, Baum carefully presented and marketed himself as the friend and champion of childhood imagination, imbuing his Oz product with the symbolic value associated with childhood and wonder.

- **Provide a festive context for consumption**: From his theatrical career, Baum understood the power of the performance and the event. He knew how to stir up excitement and pique the consumer's imagination. As the proprietor of Baum's Bazaar, he used event-marketing to entice customers through his doors, and as the Royal Historian of Oz, he used similar tactics to lure them to Oz. The extravaganzas themselves were merely the most obvious of Baum's event-marketing. He also deployed special events within the runs, such as souvenir matinees of *Fairylogue* and gala commemorative performances of *The Wizard of Oz*.

- **Emphasize an experiential rather than transactional relationship between the product and the consumer**: Baum understood the importance of the experience. From his early Baum's Bazaar promotions, which invited guests to an event rather than advertised products, through the films of the Oz Film Manufacturing Company, he promised consumers not a product but an emotional, spectacular experience, and full of magic and wonder. If these experiences drove the demand for products, those products were offered as souvenirs of the event. Even the Oz books were marketed and promoted not as products, but based on the *experience* they offered, not only in their fantastic narratives but also in their rich colors and presentation.

- **Offer consumers multiple points of entry**: Baum adopted this principal with *The Maid of Arran*, selling souvenir song sheets so consumers could re-experience the show's songs and fully developed it with Oz. By the time of his death, consumers could visit Oz on screen and stage, in the Oz and *Little Wizard* books, in the pages of magazines and newspapers, and in the comic section. Each of these entry points appealed to a different market segment, from the very young readers of the *Little Wizard* books to the more adult audiences for the stage extravaganzas, while potentially drawing consumers from all of these market segments.

- **Use new technologies to promise consumers an updated and more immediate experience**: Baum was the king of the theatrical spectacle, using new technologies to dazzle his viewers and make his works come to life; as early as 1883, he had earned accolades for *The Maid of Arran's* mechanical effects, and he and his producers received similar praise for the stage version of *The Wizard of Oz*. Not only did each subsequent stage spectacle update its effects, but also Baum was an early adopter of film, and he marketed his cinematic products by lauding their ability to bring Oz to life. In remediating his work, Baum attracted both his established consumers, and consumers interested in experiencing these new technologies.

NOTES

1. Joseph Pine and James Gilmore, *The Experience Economy* (Updated Edition, Cambridge: Harvard Business Review Press, 2011).
2. Jackson Lears, *Fables of Abundance: A Cultural History of Advertising in America* (New York: Hatchette Book Group, 1995).
3. Jackson Lears, *Rebirth of a Nation: The Making of Modern America, 1877–1921* (New York: Harper Perennial, 2010), 167.
4. Lears, *Rebirth*, 263.
5. Lears, *Fables*, 14.
6. Lears, *Rebirth*, 322.
7. Ibid., 7.
8. Lears, *Fables*, 273.
9. Qtd in Lears, *Fables*, 179.
10. Ibid., 270.

11. Ibid., 192.
12. Ibid., 94.
13. *Fame Magazine*, 1892, qtd. In Lears, *Fables*, 282.
14. Qtd in Lears, *Fables*, 283.
15. Ibid., 210–211.
16. Ibid., 217.
17. Ibid., 158.
18. Ibid., 289.
19. Ibid., 158.
20. Ibid., 163.
21. Ibid., 273.
22. Ibid., 291.
23. Ibid.
24. Ibid., 205.
25. Ibid., 293.
26. Our biographical information on Baum is drawn from several sources, including the archival materials from the L. Frank Baum Collection at Syracuse University, Frank Joslyn Baum and Russell McFall, *To Please a Child: A Biography of L. Frank Baum, Royal Historian of Oz* (Chicago: Reilly & Lee, 1961), Michael Hearn's "Introduction" to *The Annotated Wizard of Oz* (New York: W.W. Norton, 1973), and Katherine M. Rogers, *L. Frank Baum: Creator of Oz* (New York: St. Martins Press, 2007).
27. Image reproduced on "Baum's Castorine," Hagley Digital Archives, http://digital.hagley.org/islandora/object/islandora:2307008#page/1/mode/1up, accessed October 20, 2017.
28. Castorine Oil Advertisement, 1888, Box 1, Folder 1, Baum Papers. Image reproduced on "Oil in the Land of Oz," Energy Education Resources, https://aoghs.org/energy-education-resources/oil-in-the-land-of-oz/, accessed October 20, 2017.
29. *Oil Echo*, June 3, 1882, Box 2, Folder 1, Baum Papers.
30. "Maid of Arran Review," 1882, Box 2, Folder 1, Baum Papers.
31. Case exhibit, All Things Oz Museum, Chittenango, NY.
32. *Aberdeen Daily News*, 1889, Box 1, Folder 11, Baum Papers.
33. *Aberdeen Daily News*, November 26, 1888, Box 1, Folder 1, Baum Papers.
34. Ibid.
35. *Aberdeen Daily News*, April 19, 1889, Box 1, Folder 2, Baum Papers.
36. Ibid.
37. Ibid.
38. Harry Neal Baum, "My Father was the Wizard of Oz," Box 1, Folder 1, Baum Papers.

39. Advertisement, *Show Window Magazine*, Box 1, Folder 9, Baum Papers.
40. Letter from Baum, *Show Window Magazine*, Box 1, Folder 9, Baum Papers.
41. Ibid.
42. Letter from Baum to His Brother, April 8, 1900, Box 1, Folder 11, Baum Papers.
43. Ibid.
44. Ibid.; Letter from Baum to His Sister, October 3, 1897, Box 1, Folder 11, Baum Papers.
45. Harry Baum, "My Father."
46. L. Frank Baum, *The Wonderful Wizard of Oz* (Chicago: George M. Hill, 1900), Introduction, Kindle.
47. Ibid.
48. *New York Times*, September 8, 1900; *Kindergarten Magazine*, October 1900, qtd. in Michael Patrick Hearn, "Introduction," in *The Annotated Wizard of Oz*, ed. Michael Patrick Hearn (New York: Norton, 1973, 2000), xliv.
49. Letter from Frank Joslyn Baum to Russel MacFall, Box 2, Folder 3, Baum Papers.
50. Typescript, *Chicago Tribune*, June 26, 1904, Box 2, Folder 3, Baum Papers.
51. Letter Frank Joslyn Baum to Russel MacFall, 1957; Herma Clark, "When Chicago Was Young," Box 2, Folder 3, Baum Papers.
52. *Chicago Daily News*, June 17, 1902, Box 2, Folder 3, Baum Papers.
53. Letter, Baum to MacFall.
54. Mark Swartz, *Oz Before the Rainbow: L. Frank Baum's The Wonderful Wizard of Oz on Stage and Screen to 1939* (New York: Johns Hopkins Press, 2000), 66; Scrapbook Clipping, Box 2, Folder 3, Baum Papers.
55. *Theater Magazine*, 1903, Box 2, Folder 3, Baum Papers.
56. *Chicago Tribune*, June 26, 1904, ibid.
57. *Chicago Sunday Record*, June 29, 1902, ibid.
58. Advertisement for *The Scarecrow and Tin Woodman*, Box 2, Folder 5, Baum Papers.
59. Baum, *The Marvelous Land of Oz* (Chicago: Reilly & Britton, 1904), Author's Note, Kindle.
60. Ibid.
61. *Queer Visitors, Sunday Record Herald*, Oversize Folder 10, Baum Papers.
62. Ibid.
63. *The Ozmapolitan*, Hungry Tiger Press, http://www.hungrytigerpress.com/tigertreats/ozmapolitan_1904.pdf, accessed September 2, 2017.
64. Advertisement for *The Land of Oz*, Box 2, Folder 5, Baum Papers.

65. *Cleveland Leader*, qtd. in Michael O. Riley, *Oz and Beyond: The Fantasy Worlds of L. Frank Baum* (Kansas: University of Kansas Press, 1997), 108.
66. "Fairy Tales on Stage," Box 1, Folder 10, Baum Papers.
67. Burns Mantle, "Review of 'The Wogglebug,'" *Chicago Inner Ocean*, Box 2, Folder 6, Baum Papers.
68. Qtd. in Riley, *Oz and Beyond*, 111.
69. For more detailed discussions of Baum's remediations of Oz see Hearne, *Annotated*, Swartz, *Before the Rainbow*, and Matthew Freeman, *Historicizing Transmedia Storytelling* (New York: Routledge, 2017).
70. Chicago Tribune 10/2/1908, Box 2, Folder 7, Baum Papers.
71. "In the Fairy Land of Motion Pictures, L Frank Baum Explains How his Modern Fairies Work, Aided by Ingenuity and the Camera, and Tells of the Wonderful Illusions Process," *New York Herald*, September 26, 1909, Box 2, Folder 7, Baum Papers.
72. *Fairylogue and Radio Plays*, Program, 1908, Box 2, Folder 7, Baum Papers.
73. Ibid.
74. Letter from Baum, 1908, Box 2, Folder 8, Baum Papers.
75. "Fairy Land of Motion Pictures;" Burns Mantle, *Record Herald*, October 10, 1908, Box 2, Folder 7, Baum Papers.
76. Advertisement, Reilly & Britton, ibid.
77. *Theatre Magazine*, August 1909, 62–83, Box 1, Folder 3, Baum Papers.
78. L. Frank Baum, *Dorothy and the Wizard in Oz* (Chicago: Reilly & Britton, 1908), To My Readers, Kindle.
79. L. Frank Baum, *Ozma of Oz* (Chicago: Reilly & Britton, 1907), Author's Note, Kindle; L. Frank Baum, *The Road to Oz* (Chicago: Reilly & Britton, 1909), To My Readers, Kindle.
80. Baum, *Ozma*, Author's Note.
81. Baum, *Dorothy*, To My Readers.
82. L. Frank Baum, *The Emerald City of Oz* (Chicago: Reilly & Britton, 1910), Author's Note, Kindle.
83. Ibid.
84. Baum, *Emerald City*, How the Story of Oz Came to an End.
85. Qtd in Rogers, *Creator of Oz*, 210.
86. Advertisement, *Tik Tok* premiere, Box 2, Folder 6, Baum Papers.
87. W. E. Wing, *New York Dramatic Mirror*, October 7, 1914, Box 2, Folder 9, Baum Papers.
88. Letter from Baum to Maud, October 12, 1913, Box 1, Folder 11, Baum Papers.
89. Oz Film Manufacturing Newsletter, Box 2, Folder 9, Baum Papers.
90. Ibid.

91. Ibid.
92. Ibid.
93. Ibid.
94. L. Frank Baum, *Tik Tok of Oz* (Chicago: Reilly & Britton, 1914), "To my readers," Kindle.
95. L. Frank Baum, *The Scarecrow of Oz* (Chicago: Reilly & Britton, 1915), "Twixt you and me," Kindle.
96. Readers interested in textual studies of Oz should see Riley, *Oz and Beyond*; Allissa Burger, *The Wizard of Oz as American Myth* (North Carolina: McFarland, 2012); Evan L. Schwartz, *Finding Oz: How L. Frank Baum Discovered the Great American Story* (New York: Houghton Mifflin, 2009); Ranjit DIghe, ed., *The Historian's Wizard of Oz: Reading L. Frank Baum's Classic as a Political and Monetary Allegory* (New York: Praeger, 2002); and Tison Pugh, "'Are We Cannibals, Let Me Ask? Or Are We Faithful Friends?': Food, Interspecies Cannibalism, and the Limits of Utopia in L. Frank Baum's Oz Books," *Lion & The Unicorn* 32, no. 3 (September 2008): 324–343, and "'There Lived in the Land of Oz Two Queerly Made Men': Queer Utopianism and Antisocial Eroticism in L. Frank Baum's Oz Series," *Marvels and Tales* 22, no. 2 (2008): 217–239.
97. L. Frank Baum, *The Road to Oz* (1909), Kindle, Chapter 1.
98. Baum, *Wizard* (1900). Kindle, Chapter 4.
99. L. Frank Baum, Chapter 2.
100. Ibid., Chapter 11.
101. Morris Holbrook and Elizabeth Hirschman, "The Experiential Aspects of Consumption: Consumer Fantasies, Feeling and Fun," *Journal of Consumer Research* 9 (September 1982): 132–140.
102. Box 1, Folder 2, Baum Papers.
103. Typescript, "Hall of Fame" Speech, Box 1, Folder 14, Baum Papers.
104. Joseph Haas, *Chicago Daily News*, 1963, Box 1, Folder 3, Baum Papers.
105. Guy Bogert, *Publisher's Weekly*, June 14, 1919, Box 1. Folder 14, Baum Papers.
106. Hall of Fame, Baum Papers.
107. *New York Times*, May 11, 1919, Box 1, Folder 14, Baum Papers.

CHAPTER 3

Extending the Yellow Brick Road: More Books and a Technicolor Rainbow

When Baum died in 1919, Oz was part of both the American cultural landscape and the global world of childhood. Ozmania, however,
could easily have ended with Baum, with the Oz books relegated to an
"Illustrated Classics of Children's Literature" series as the decades passed
and their cultural relevance faded. But Baum's publishers, his widow, and
his son took up the mantle as marketers of Oz. Its vast marketability had
already been proven. The challenge now was to usher the narrative further down the road.

Baum left his heirs and publishers a two-generation community of
engaged consumers—all of whom had fond memories of Oz experiences
and extravaganzas, thirteen published books, one complete manuscript,
and, purportedly, a set of unfinished notes. He also left them with Oz
itself, ready to be peopled with new characters and available for new
narratives. Reilly & Lee, initially with the support of Maud Baum, were
quick to capitalize on these assets. When Baum's final novel *Glinda of Oz*
appeared in 1920, "The Publishers" addressed Baum's readers, reminding them of their relationship with "Mr. Baum (who) did his best to
answer all the letters from his small earth-friends before he had to leave
them…to take his stories to the little child-souls who had lived here too
long ago to read the Oz stories for themselves. We are sorry he could
not stay here and we are sad to tell you this is his last complete story."
Moving on from this sentimental picture of Baum telling Oz stories to
cherubic children in heaven, the preface assures earthly children that Oz
itself will continue: "He left some unfinished notes about the Princess

Ozma and Dorothy and the Oz people and we promise that some day we will put them all together like a picture puzzle and give you more stories of the wonderful Land of Oz."[1]

As promised, in 1921, Reilly & Lee released *The Royal Book of Oz*, "enlarged and edited by Ruth Plumly Thompson." In the introduction to this book, Maud Baum took great pains to authenticate the product and establish the new author's Ozian credentials. She assures consumers that Ruth Plumly Thompson, "who has known and loved the Oz stories ever since she was a little girl," has transformed "Mr. Baum's...unfinished notes about the Princess Ozma and Dorothy and the jolly people of the Wonderful land of Oz," into an authentic "new Oz story, with all the Oz folks in it and true to life." "I am sure," she declares, "Mr. Baum would be pleased." She concludes by reminding readers of their special relationship with Baum—and, through him, with Oz: "This note is intended for all the children of America, who knew and loved Mr. Baum, and it goes to each of you with his love and mine."[2]

The Royal Book of Oz could well have been the last new Oz story, and Reilly & Lee could have continued simply to market and sell the existing Oz books. However, the book sold well, confirming that the market for Oz survived beyond its original author, and the publishers retained Thompson to continue the series. It was a calculated gamble, but, as Reilly wrote to Maud in a 1922 letter, one that had every chance of success: "I read every line of the Thompson manuscript, and am satisfied that she has the true Oz book spirit. There's no possible way of telling how an Oz book by any other author than L. Frank Baum is going to catch on, except to judge by advance orders, which are very satisfactory. The great thing for both you and us is that a new Oz book will help a lot in selling the older ones."[3] Maud agreed, "I am sure the children will like it.... I trust this will be a good book year for us all."[4] Note that, for Reilly, his continuation of the Oz line was as much about the market sustainability of the older books as it was about the new book. New books, he opined, sell old books—a philosophy embraced by today's entertainment marketers, regardless of the media outlet in which they work.

Reilly & Lee's gamble paid off. *Kabumpo in Oz*, "founded on and continuing the famous Oz stories by L. Frank Baum, 'Royal Historian of Oz,'" marked the beginning of a post-Baum Oz that bolstered the publishers' holiday line for over twenty years. It also marked a transition of "Oz" from a personal brand to a corporate brand. Thompson's preface to *Kabumpo* signals a shift in the relationship between the producers and consumers of Oz in the post-Baum era. She abandons Baum's careful cultivation of a bond between himself and his co-producing consumers, focusing instead on the new product: "Do you love all the jolly people of the Wonderful Land of Oz?" she asks, "Well then you'll want to hear about the latest happenings in this delightful Kingdom." While Baum was always careful to point out the ways in which his "dear readers" had participated in creating the new adventure, Thompson merely promises her readers an authentic product, "set forth in true Oz fashion," with all of their "old friends" "alive and well in the new book."[5]

Thompson's preface was in keeping with Reilly & Lee's goals: to capitalize on Oz and to sell books. As such, the publishers focused on a marketplace transaction (the exchange of cash for books) rather than a long-term, personal relationship (the experience of Oz). To that end, they devised marketing campaigns to exploit Oz and get consumers through the doors of retail stores, borrowing several of Baum's techniques: tie-ins, remediations, and Oz events. However, they deployed them very differently. For Baum, each new remediation of Oz—the newspaper stories, the Broadway extravaganzas, the *Fairylogue and Radio Plays*, the *Ozmapolitan*, the films—was a new *experience* of Oz, an artistic product in its own right, meant to foster an ongoing, long-term relationship between consumers and his fairyland. But for Reilly & Lee, it was all about the sales, as is evident in the publicity for and response to performances of *A Day in Oz*, a promotional "playlet" penned by Thompson. *A Day in Oz* is, quite frankly, dreadful, a tired recycling of characters and tropes. It isn't an extravaganza; it doesn't take advantage of new technologies or offer consumers Oz in a new way. Rather, it exists merely to provide an "event" and drive sales.[6] Indeed, Reilly & Lee marketed the play not to consumers but to bookstores—the middlemen in this all-important supply chain—advertising in *Publishers Weekly* that "copies of the play and music are obtainable from the Oz publishers, as well as souvenirs to be distributed at the end of the play," along with "window and interior display materials" "to make the play a complete success."[7]

And the play *was* a complete success—at least in the terms that Reilly & Lee had promised. Foreshadowing today's mall events (including The World of *Wicked*, which we discuss in Chapter 9), *A Day in Oz* attracted shoppers and drove sales, attesting to Oz's continued marketability six years after Baum's death. Store and book-department managers across the country reported unexpected crowds and strong sales—both for Oz books, and for traffic and sales throughout the store. From San Francisco, Weinstocks, Lubin &Company wrote, "We do not know whether to report it as a huge success or a gigantic failure. We expected 200 children at the most, and provided seating capacity for that number. Instead we had about 1500...and our entire floor was literally mobbed."[8] Rhodes Brothers in Tacoma experienced similar crowds: "our attendance was greater than our accommodations could take care of." So did Frederick and Nelson in Seattle, which "was obliged to exclude grown-ups" while their auditorium was "crowded to the doors for every performance."[9] Store after store reported "tremendous crowds" and "an unnatural influx of children." Mothers shopped the store, Oz books were sold, books in general were sold, children's merchandise was sold. In St Louis, the enterprising manager of Scrubbs, Vandervoort & Barney partnered with "one of the best-known schools for dramatic expression," in their production, casting the "sons and daughters of our very best patrons (who) attend(ed) this school" in the play bringing the children's "fathers and mothers and friends down in great numbers."[10] Proving that there really is nothing new under the sun, these retailers were planning and marketing personalized experiences in their stores ninety years before *Wicked*'s promoters did the same.

In order to enhance their marketing efforts, Reilly & Lee revived the *Ozmapolitan* in 1926. This iteration of the Oz newspaper, however, was much more focused on marketing new Oz products than it was on providing readers with more Oz. Its centerpiece was the announcement of "Ozmite clubs": publisher-sponsored events that sought to harness and capitalize on the Oz book groups Baum praises in *The Scarecrow of Oz.* "The boys and girls are going to have OZ CLUBS!" the first issue of the new *Ozmapolitan* proclaims. "And besides there's going to be a real Oz magazine called the OZMAPOLITAN...for fun and to tell all of the Oz news that happens in between books." At club meetings, the newsletter enthused, consumers will "play Oz games and have Oz puzzles and parties and shows and badges and picnics and secret signs."[11] However, unlike the original Oz clubs, which had arisen from a deeply felt relationship with Oz and created a spontaneous community of consumers, Reilly & Lee's producer-oriented "Ozmite" clubs were highly intentional, designed to convince bookstore managers to feature the Oz books, and bring consumers into the store to consume them. The *Ozmapolitan* breathlessly announced, "OZ CLUBS FORM ALL OVER USA...nearly every city is to have an Ozmite Club," and enlisted children to help market the clubs (and hence the books) to their local stores—"if you don't have one, ask your bookstore to get one, Reilly & Lee will supply all of the materials for free."[12]

The clubs kept Oz in the consumer's consciousness between books and created "buzz" for new products. Members were promised a "special Ozmite club pin to wear" and "Oz secrets, parties, games, picnics etc."[13] They also encouraged engagement with Oz, but—much like Rowling's *Pottermore* site—under corporate auspices. Rather than being co-creators, co-discoverers of Oz, as Baum had consistently figured them in his prefaces, consumers now participated in corporate "contests." Furthermore, in order to produce these corporatized Oz products, club members first had to consume existing ones. One contest featured the call to revise the map of Oz. Booksellers provided consumers with a blank map for an "Ozzy prize contest that is fun," and contestants were directed to "color (it) with the proper color (each country has its own color you know!). Make corrections in the locations of the cities, places, etc., that you think necessary, and also locate new countries and places."[14] These corrections and locations, however, were not an invitation to participate in the creation of Oz. Instead, they required a re-reading of the earlier books. "All information needed," the rules assured contestants, "can be obtained from your Oz books."[15] In other words, successful mapmakers will own *all* of the Oz books; if they do not, well then, their local bookstore will be happy to help.

The Oz clubs and the *Ozmapolitan* provided Reilly & Lee with a forum in which to pass over the mantel of "the Royal Historian of Oz" from Baum to Thompson. The newspaper awarded Thompson the official title (which the books still reserved for Baum) and featured her Oz promotions and tie-ins, such as a 1926 Chicago radio program. This transfer, along with other attempts to capitalize on a post-Baum Oz, led to legal wrangling between Baum's heirs and Reilly & Lee over control and ownership of the Oz brand. Maud, for instance, objected to both Thompson's recording of Oz readings for a 1929 NBC radio promotion—"I don't like this...she has no rights in the Wizard except in the books she has written,"[16] and the Junior League's production of an Oz play penned by one of its leaders. Reilly & Lee, in turn, continually sought to assure her that the productions, promotions, and spin-offs all contributed to sales and brand recognition. In a 1928 letter to Maud, Reilly wrote, "we cooperated on the basis of what we thought was good advertising for the books on which you get a royalty," concluding

"I am… of the opinion that productions of the 'Land of Oz' by the Junior League…would be mighty good publicity for the Oz books."[17] On April 4, Maud tartly replied: "I feel that the advertising would be just as great for the Oz books whether the league paid a small royalty or not."[18] Maud's concerns seem to have primarily centered around royalty rights, fearing that Reilly & Lee "could get some outsider to write an Oz book and pay me no royalty on it," and concluding, with some dismay, "anyone could write an Oz book."[19]

It was Frank Joslyn Baum's concerns, however, that eventually landed Oz in court. Frank seems to have fancied himself his father's literary as well as financial heir, and sought not only to profit from Oz, but also to extend its commercial reach. His first foray into production, 1924's "Oz Dolls," earned the cooperation of Reilly & Lee. Here, Frank merely sought to capitalize on Oz, selling the characters "beloved by many children." The dolls, each "bear[ing] the Fac-simile Signature of L Frank Baum the Famous Author of the Oz books,"[20] were a tie-in product, their "sales more than half-made by the tremendous sales of the Oz books." As such, they could only help Reilly & Lee sell more books. Like the Oz Clubs, department store productions, and the Parker Brothers game, they kept Oz in the consumer's view. In the 1930s, however, Frank tried to take on the mantel of Royal Historian; when Reilly & Lee refused to publish his Oz stories, the younger Baum, who had trademarked "Oz" in 1924, published *The Laughing Dragon of Oz* with Whitman. When Reilly & Lee responded with a cease-and-desist letter, Whitman withdrew *The Laughing Dragon* and cancelled production on a second Baum Jr. book, resulting in the "The Trademark Cancellation Case: Reilly & Lee vs Frank J. Baum."[21]

The legal battle over the ownership of Oz raised issues directly related to the narrative's long-term cultural sustainability. Who is allowed to produce new Oz narratives and products, and who is allowed to benefit from them? In the case in question, Frank argued that Reilly & Lee, who owned the copyrights to all of Baum's books except *The Wonderful Wizard of Oz*, had essentially hijacked Oz, forcing his mother (who sided with Reilly & Lee in the case) "to consent to the appropriation of said original characters and continuing to use the word 'Oz' as part of the title thereof." But "Oz," Frank argued was not part of the deal. Reilly & Lee may own thirteen books by Baum about Oz, but they did not own Oz. Reilly & Lee responded that the books are known as "the Famous Oz books," and that "the wide popularity of the…books" and, thus Oz itself, was "due in large part" to *marketing*, "the heavy expenditures of time, effort and money which (had) been made by them."[22] Frank disagreed, asserting that "the books and…musical did more to popularize Oz then Reilly & Lee."[23]

Although neither side could have characterized their battle in these terms, both understood that to own Oz is not only to *control* the brand—dictating what new products can be offered in the marketplace—but to *protect* the brand—ensuring that inferior knockoffs will not flood the marketplace, confuse the consumer, and cheapen the brand. Then, as now, authenticity was the critical factor. Using this logic, Reilly & Lee argued that Frank's stories were "fake" Oz products, including as evidence a letter from Lieutenant Colonel Ralph Wilson, warning the publisher that "market is being flooded with a 10-cent book…which has somewhat disillusioned the followers of your authentic Oz stories."[24] Frank, they argued, was being confused with the *real* Baum, thus cheapening the brand. Reilly & Lee won. The trademark was cancelled, and the publishers retained the rights to control the production of new Oz narratives—at least until the books went out of copyright, beginning in the late 1950s. Even though Thompson retired from Oz with 1939's *Ozoplaning with the Wizard of Oz,* the publishers found new Royal Historians to pen six additional stories. By doing so, Reilly & Lee sustained Oz for thirty-two years after Baum's death.

Oz was a writerly text; its fantastical map, margins, and unnamed regions invited readers to explore the terrain beyond the established stories suggesting that there were so many more stories to tell—and its creator had certainly treated Oz as an ever-expanding archive. Yet that very writerly map raised questions of ownership and control. Could anyone, as Maud fretted, write an Oz story? Or was Oz owned? And if so, who owned it? The copyright case decided these questions in favor of the publisher. For the time being, anyway, Reilly & Lee owned future extensions of Oz.

MAKING AND MARKETING THE RAINBOW

Frank, however, still held the copyright to *The Wonderful Wizard of Oz* and its film adaptations. This meant, ironically, that he controlled both the narrative and the media that would ultimately ensure Oz's cultural sustainability. While Reilly & Lee focused on the production and sales of new books, Baum's son sought to capitalize on the brand's first products: the original Oz book and its dramatic remediations. He explicitly tied his Oz Dolls to the stage extravaganza, reminding merchandisers that the "Wizard of Oz show played in New York and Chicago" for eight years, and linking his Scarecrow figure and his Tin Woodman to that production's stars.[25] He also continually sought to trade on the family name to exploit *The Wizard of Oz* on film. For instance, director Larry Semon marketed Frank's first foray into film production, Chadwick Studio's 1925 *The Wizard of Oz* (featuring Oliver Hardy as the Tin Man), as Frank Joslyn Baum's adaptation of "the play by L. Frank Baum." Baum Jr. was not Baum Sr., however, and the film failed to realize enough profits to keep the studio afloat. Undaunted, Frank continued to try his hand at remediating Oz. In 1933, he partnered with Ted Eshbaugh, and writing as Col. Frank Baum, produced an animated short, in which Dorothy was transported from the gray Kansas prairie to the technicolor world of Oz. This transition from gray to color, suggested by both Baum's book and his use of color in the *Radio Play* films, however, depended on technicolor's new three-color process, which unfortunately Eshbaugh failed to license from the company. As a result, the animated short languished in legal limbo before eventually being released in black and white.

Following this latest cinematic Oz disappointment, Frank Joslyn Baum sold the film-rights for *Wizard* to Samuel Goldwyn. That project languished in development—perhaps because the dismal track record of previous film versions of the book—from *Fairylogue and Radio Plays*, through the Oz Film Manufacturing Company, to Semon and Eshbaugh—gave the producers pause. Indeed, *The Wizard of Oz*, despite the continuing popularity of the books, may never have been green-lit for another film attempt had it not been for the success of Disney's *Snow White* in 1937, which sent studios scrambling for their own "fairy tale properties." MGM put an extravagant $75,000 on the table for Oz, and on June 3, 1938, the studio concluded a deal with Goldwyn for the rights to Baum's book and all of its previous adaptations.

It's hard to predict what Oz's fate would have been without the MGM purchase. Reilly & Lee had clearly sustained the brand, but there had not been a major Oz event since Baum's death two decades prior. Without a major event to revive Oz in the public eye and bring it to new consumers, Baum's fairy land may well have failed to achieve wide-spread, long-term cultural sustainability; it would, most likely, have passed out of public consciousness as its original consumers aged.

In 1938, however, *The Wizard of Oz* was still extremely marketable—a known property with a ready-made audience. Thus, it was a natural fit for a studio that needed a fairy tale property to showcase its technological wonders (including the new magic of technicolor) as well as to capitalize on America's *Snow-White*-fueled desire for fantasy films.

MGM's executives realized, however, that narrative popularity and technological wizardry alone would not necessarily ensure that their cinematic Oz would thrive in the marketplace. They knew that, in order to succeed where other studios had failed, their film needed to appeal across generations, reaching a new audience without alienating established consumers. Paying careful attention to the narrative's adaptation, they focused on making the story suitable to 1939, while still satisfying a nostalgia for 1900. At the same time, recognizing that *The Wizard of Oz* was a three-million-dollar gamble, the studio designed an unprecedented promotional campaign to "Ozify!" the nation.[26] Promising Oz "brought to thrilling life," and providing consumers with multiple ways of entering into the Oz experience, MGM urged America to "follow the yellow brick road to OZ!"[27]

MGM's promotional campaign targeted both the business-to-business market and the end consumer. On one hand, the studio worked to educate and engage the theater owners and managers responsible for the film's distribution and local marketing. And on the other, its national marketing efforts enticed and excited potential audiences across the country. The studio courted distributors with what *Film Daily* called "one the most comprehensive exhibitor aids ever issued on a production...an encyclopedia of contests, bally-hoos, stunts and displays...to assure highly effective promotion."[28] At the center of MGM's promise of record crowds and profits lay Oz's proven record of sustainability, which assured a ready-made audience of consumers eager to see a film based on "a book famous in fiction"—one that already proven itself as "a play celebrated on the American stage."[29] "The magic tale spun by L. Frank Baum," the studio reminded distributors, has been "read the world over by millions." Based on "the greatest best seller of modern fiction," the film, they promised, was "truly a triumph for exploitation."[30] And the elaborate campaign book provided distributors with multiple ways to "Exploit Oz!" "Advertise Oz!" "Publicize Oz! for record business."[31] It also promised theater owners that they would be working hand-in-hand with the studio, which had committed considerable resources of its own "to bring [consumers] into your theatre!"[32] MGM unabashedly courted these marketing intermediaries by shouldering the lion's share of the film's marketing costs and promising distributors a win-win outcome: more business for the film meant more business for the theater.

The studio's end-user strategy also played to Oz's proven sustainability; here, however, the campaign invoked consumers' nostalgia for beloved childhood memories. Consumer-directed ads and publicity spreads, such as *The Wizard of Oz* edition of the fan magazine *Modern Screen*, spurred memories of earlier Ozes—from Baum's beloved book, through the Broadway extravaganza, to 1930's radio broadcasts.[33] Additionally, studio publicity presented the film's artistic team as themselves nostalgic consumers of Oz. Producer Mervyn LeRoy told interviewers, "I've wanted to do this story since I was fifteen years old."[34] Roy Bolger acknowledged that not only was he a lifetime fan of the Oz books, but that Fred Stone had inspired his performing career. Margaret Hamilton fondly recalled her mother reading the Oz books to her, and Gilbert Adrian, the film's costume designer, proclaimed Baum's books the "favorite stories of his youth," confiding that he had sent home for his schoolbooks because "he had sketched Oz characters in their margins twenty years earlier."[35] A story circulated by the publicity department brought together these themes of nostalgia and continuity, Baum and MGM, claiming an amazing serendipity: "When the crew found the initials LFB in the lining" of the used topcoat purchased for the Scarecrow's costume, "they took the coat to check with Mrs. Baum. She authenticated both the coat and its initials. She said the coat had been her husband's thirty years before."[36]

MGM was not as anxious to remind consumers or distributors of Oz's previous film history, which was completely elided in both the business-to-business and business-to-consumer campaigns. This elision served two purposes: distributors were not reminded that Oz had indeed failed to turn profits in the past; and the studio was able to position its Oz as an entirely new cinematic experience. "Movies," LeRoy rationalized, "weren't equipped to make such fantasies until recent years."[37] But now "daring what has never been dared before," as a full-page studio ad declared, "MGM has brought to life the story book that has long defied filming!"[38] In this strand of its promotion, the studio complemented its nostalgic "looking-back" to Oz campaign with a focus on innovation and novelty that sought to attract new consumers to the Oz narrative. The company's *Studio News* offered owners and managers suggested ads for local distribution heralding the film as "Celebrating the

GOLDEN JUBILEE of Motion Pictures. Climaxing a half-century of Entertainment Progress...*the* Miracle in Celluloid."[39] These press-book ads focused on the film's breakthrough achievements, trading in superlatives: "Greatest magic film ever to be made," "the screen's most spectacular musical," the "biggest show."[40] Often, these superlatives explicitly invoked *Snow White*—"the biggest screen sensation since *Snow White*"; "unmatched since the wonders of famed *Snow White*"—comparisons to Disney's 1937 animated sensation that aimed at (and promised to deliver) an audience of younger consumers who may have never heard of Oz.[41]

MGM used this direct-comparison advertising technique both to appeal to *Snow White's* consumers and to establish the studio's superior brand identity. If, LeRoy observed, "Disney can reproduce humans with cartoons," MGM "can reproduce cartoons with humans."[42] The studio's promotional newsletter, *The Lion's Roar*, placed Oz in a longline of studio products—*Ben Hur, The Good Earth, Mutiny on the Bounty, David Copperfield*—proclaiming "*The Wizard of Oz* tops them all."[43] Only MGM had the "magnificent courage" to take on this best-seller that "long remained untouched by producers."[44] Only MGM had the "well-nigh unlimited facilities" "to translate the mythic land of Oz into vivid screen entertainment."[45] Publicity for both distributors and consumers emphasized the extravagant resources that went into the film's making. In order to bring consumers "one hundred minutes of fascinating, scintillating entertainment," the studio "built 64 separate sets," "gathered together hundreds of midgets," "built a city of 22,000 separate glass objects," "made 40,000 poppies bloom" "created 212,180 separate sound effects" "introduced...120 musicians," and "a chorus of 300," "employed 9200 actors," and "took two years" to produce "100 miles of footage, a quarter of a million feet of sound track, and one half of a million feet of technicolor footage."[46] Furthermore, MGM solved "engineering and photographing problems never before encountered": "Trees had to dance. Monkeys had to fly. A tornado had to sweep down from the heavens and bear a real Dorothy away to a land of her imagining that was as real as life itself–yet utterly unlike anything seen on earth!"[47]

This last quote exemplifies MGM's exploitation of remediation's promise of immediacy in order to attract consumers. To new consumers of Oz, the studio's "sheer wizardry" promises a fantasy "given realism throughout."[48] These consumers can delight in a fantasy "as real as life itself."[49] To Oz fans, it offers something more: "wonders of [Oz] come true," "*The Wizard of Oz* filmed as L. Frank Baum himself would have wished it."[50] Indeed, the film's marketing campaigns worked visually to co-opt Baum's book in the service of the film, displacing Denslow's illustrations with MGM's characters. Advance publicity stills featured a larger-than-life volume of "*The Wizard of Oz*, by L. Frank Baum," but the illustration on the cover is of Garland, Bolger, Haley, and Lahr (and Toto, too) in costume, and the "real" actors themselves have emerged from its cover. Similarly, print ads for the film evoked the book, often deploying the yellow brick road as a story-strip, illustrated with sketches based on the film, to relate its major plot points. A full-page "comic" translated the plot to multi-panel strips.[51] But even words and pictures based on the film were stand-ins, poor substitutes meant to be displaced by the experience of the film itself. Both the text ribbon down the yellow brick road and the panel captions employ imperative active verbs to invite consumers into the world of the film, promising them immersion in MGM's Oz brought-to-life: "*Whirl* from the everyday on the black wings of a tornado;" "*Don* magic red slippers;" "*Dance* down the Yellow Brick road"; "*Join* the harum-scarum Scarecrow"; "*Meet* the Tin Man"; "*Coax along* the Cowardly Lion"; and "*Sing* and *whistle* these gay, tuneful song hits."[52]

In these print ads and newspaper tie-ins, MGM capitalized on consumers' previous experience of Oz, promising them a new, better, more exciting experience. The film's much-lauded technicolor trailer intensified this promise.[53] Over two minutes of carefully selected spectacular scenes and songs, the trailer visually displaces Baum's books with MGM's film, trumpeting both Baum's classic creation and the studio's unprecedented accomplishment. The narrator, speaking over a slow-pan into the technicolor wonders of Munchkinland, sets the stage, "Many, many miles east of nowhere, lies the amazing land of Oz, a magnificent empire created in the mind of a man who wrote a great book about it. Like wildfire in a wheat field the fabulous tale of the *Wizard of Oz* spread from town to city, to nation, to the entire world." As the narrator tells us the story of Oz's initial spectacular appeal, scenes from the film play out across the screen before a fade-shot transitions from the film to a shelf of Oz books. "Although the *Wizard of Oz*," the narrator continues, "has captivated the children of four generations and fired the imagination of youthful adults who have never grown old; although ten million copies have reached eager hands and hearts"—shots of Baum's books floating off the shelf and falling slowly out of the frame—"no one has dared the towering task of giving life and reality to the land of Oz and its people."

On "no one has dared," *The Wonderful Wizard of Oz* stays in frame, and the cover opens to the first page, with its famous illustration of Dorothy gazing out on the flat fields of Kansas. Then the pages of the book start to flip, and, as the narrator proclaims, "every delightful character of L. Frank Baum's classic is now reborn," another fade-shot transitions the viewers back into the world of the film, which now completely displaces the printed page. "Every glorious adventure has been recaptured," the narrator assures us, "and painted with a rainbow." Just as Baum had promised with his *Fairylogue and Radio Plays*, MGM, through technicolor and technology, promises consumers a cinematic experience of an Oz reborn and recaptured—an Oz brought to life.

If Baum's technological remediations sought to sustain Oz as a brand, and Reilly & Lee's promotional plays and events were designed to sell more books, the studio had no desire either to promote Oz as a brand or to sell more Oz books. For MGM, it was all about MGM. The studio merely wanted to book its film in more theaters, sell more tickets, attract more merchandising tie-ins, and promote its other cinematic products. Therefore, in addition to its unprecedented print campaign, the studio orchestrated a series of experiences designed to generate buzz and whip consumers and gatekeepers into a frenzy of expectation. In January of 1939, Culver City's float in the Rose Parade treated onlookers to a glimpse of MGM's characters; in June, the studio premiered the film's songs on its *Good News Radio Program*, an event that "for once," *Variety* observed "may have left radio listeners with an urge to see the screen vehicle."[54] By August, orchestra leaders across the USA included Oz segments in their programs. Meanwhile, MGM prepared for not one, but two, gala premieres. Ella Wickersham observed in the *Los Angeles* Times that the first of these galas, at Grauman's theater on August 15th, managed to "out Hollywood-Hollywood."[55] Stars and celebrities came out in force, filling the theater's two thousand seats.[56] Furthermore, seeking to create as much buzz as possible, MGM had extended the premiere into the streets, with the first instance of "grandstand bleacher seats for the fans" at a premiere, which transformed Hollywood Boulevard into its own gala party. Under klieg lights and the eyes of a mounted police force, fans crammed into five thousand seats and overflowed onto the pavement, windows and rooftops.[57] The event was a smash success; as the *Hollywood Reporter* observed: audiences at a premiere "are important ambassadors of good will," and MGM "cashed in on this potential good will mine," by including fans.[58]

The LA premiere was designed to appeal to audiences' nostalgia for the "Oz" of their youth, while it offered them a chance to share Baum's magical land with a new generation. Many stars came with their young daughters in tow; "Harold Lloyd arrived with a pretty daughter on each arm, Eddie Cantor brought his youngest daughter, and Joan Bennett had Diana and Melinda along with her."[59] Perhaps not surprisingly, given their longtime association with Southern California and the film business, MGM also featured the Baums, as well as the original Broadway play, at the West Coast premiere. Invited guests included Fred Stone, David Montgomery's niece, and Ashton Stevens, who had reviewed the 1902 Broadway opening. Most importantly, Maud Baum would be there with her granddaughter, Ozma—to introduce the film and bestow the original Royal Historian's stamp of approval. Fans listening to the premiere on the radio heard Emcee Whitlock observe that Maud would "dedicate this premiere to [her] husband and to the books he wrote—and to the happiness he brought to millions of children."[60] And Maud, echoing MGM's marketing taglines, enthusiastically endorsed the film, "One of the greatest thrills of my life will be to see the land of Oz, with all its queer people that Mr. Baum created, come to life under the magic of MGM in their marvelous production of *The Wizard of Oz*."[61]

As the klieg lights played across Hollywood Boulevard, a very different extravaganza was ramping up in Manhattan. If the Hollywood premiere appealed to established consumers, to nostalgia, to cross-generational transmission, the New York City premiere was aimed at an entirely different consumer base, one that did not necessarily know or care about Oz per se. In a ploy to draw teenagers into the theater, the hype was all about Judy Garland and Mickey Rooney, who, *Variety* reported, gave "Oz a rousing b.o. send off" while "serving as a swell trailer for *Babes in Arms*."[62] Seeking to whip up as much buzz as possible, the publicity department kicked off the event with a contest, inviting fans to apply to be one of 150 lucky teens selected to meet the duo at Grand Central and lunch with them at the Waldorf Astoria. This ploy was wildly—perhaps too wildly—successful. 250,000 teenagers entered, and ten thousand joined the official welcoming party. By 5:30 a.m. on premiere day, August 17, consumers started to line up at Loew's Capital Theater, where Judy and Mickey were putting on live performances between screenings; an estimated 15,000 were there by the time the theater opened at 8, and the line continued to stretch around the block as the day went on. For two weeks of multiple live shows a day, Judy and Mickey drew teenage crowds to Oz. While Maud played on nostalgia on the West Coast—her husband's creation brought to life—MGM's teenage stars updated Oz through humor and fads on the East Coast. The press office, for instance, announced that Judy and Mickey were "empowered to issue and legalize membership in the Merry Munchkins of Oz": "To be a Munchkin you greet people by putting your thumbs in your ears and wiggling your fingers and exclaiming 'Oz about it pal?'"[63] Baum would surely have been appalled, but the draw of Garland and Rooney clearly created buzz. The two helped sell-out the Capital, breaking attendance records in the first week alone.

MGM's massive pre-release publicity drive, culminating in bi-coastal gala premieres, set its cinematic Oz firmly on the road to commercial success. However, as *Variety* observed, the work of attracting consumers to the theaters was not yet done. While there should be "a market for Oz wherever there's a projection machine and a screen," "'Oz' is aimed for the masses and will require a heavy advance buildup at all spots and out of routine approach."[64] Indeed, the magazine continued, MGM's return of profit was "wholly dependent on the breadth of its appeal and the effective showmanship of its handling."[65] Deciding against a road show rollout, with more expensive seats and advance bookings, in favor of the industry's largest saturation booking to date, MGM opened the film across the nation on August 25th, paving the way for its success by working with local distributors on advance buzz and community-based buzz-events, called "ballyhoos."

The most extravagant of these was the studio's "Wizard of Oz Tour," touted in the press book as "unique in the annals of exploitation."[66] Featuring "the original two black ponies....along with the phaeton that transported Dorothy and her pals," this ballyhoo promised an experience—*right here, right now*—that would generate excitement in both children and adults. Its uniqueness, MGM assured its business-to-business consumers, lay "in the sense that it allows youngsters to actually participate and play the roles of characters." "The ponies and phaeton are used to transport the passengers lucky enough to be chosen to impersonate [the characters]...off on a gay party starting from the theater, visiting patients convalescing in hospitals, shut-ins etc." "It," the press book assured distributors, has "great local tie-ins and merchandising angles." The press book did not exaggerate. "The Wizard of Oz" tour began in Hartford in August and successfully traveled the country through October, drawing communities so far into "Ozmania" that many towns closed schools to allow children to attend the event.

The studio also urged distributors to host ballyhoos and contests of their own, providing theater managers with multiple suggestions for increasing attendance and profits. Like The *Wizard of Oz* Tour, these suggestions, ranging from letter-writing and costume contests to hiring locals to play principal characters, sought to create hype, to provide consumers with an opportunity to experience Oz, and to partner with local businesses and communities. "Organize a Wizard of Oz Club," MGM urged, providing numbered "Oz Club" buttons for purchase. "Kids are magnetized by buttons....Your theater sidewalk and lobby will be jammed with them."[67] Oz buttons, the studio suggested, could be used in a variety of ways: a lucky number drawing for free tickets, in partnership with local newspapers as a prize for selling subscriptions, working with local schools to reward good grades. Across the country, theaters, communities, and businesses jumped on the Oz bandwagon. The *Chicago Daily Tribune* held a letter-writing contest, promising to take 100 lucky, eloquent children to see *The Wizard of Oz*.[68] In Boston, children in costume "tramp[ed] over Back Bay streets, reminding the citizenry that the picture was in town."[69] "Atlanta become the Merry Old land of Oz...as series of boys and girls attended...[an] unusual masquerade" that "transformed" a local hotel ballroom "into a land of a different color" for a contest hosted by "the Wonderful Wizard of Oz" and co-sponsored by Loew's Grand Theater and the *Atlanta Constitution*.[70] Cities and park services put on costume parties and coloring contests, department stores featured windows and promotions. "The whole nation," MGM crowed in 1939, "is Oz-conscious."[71] Young consumers had themselves become marketers.

CONSUMING THE FILM

Once the ballyhoos were over and the lights dimmed in the theaters, the fate of *The Wizard of Oz* lay in the hands of the consumers and critics. One of the enduring myths about the film is that, in spite of its hyped-up and expensive promotional campaign, *The Wizard of Oz* was a disappointment both at the box office and with the critics. However, while it is true that MGM did not quite recoup its original investment in 1939, the film reliably packed theaters. As Fricke, Scarfone, and Stillman observe, "Variety pulled out its powerhouse adjectives to report the grosses" and *Film Daily* consistently estimated that the film was performing well-above box office across the country.[72]

Indifferent or absent consumers were not the reason that *The Wizard of Oz* initially failed to earn back its investment. Rather, between acquisition, production, and promotion, it was an extremely expensive film to make and market. It was targeted to a family audience, which meant that a larger percentage of tickets than usual were sold at discounted prices (the one consumer we interviewed who saw the film in theaters in 1939 paid 25 cents to do so). Furthermore, in an era where films moved in and out of studio-run theaters quickly, *Oz* needed to leave the theaters in order make way for other MGM products—a far cry from today's blockbusters, which can sometimes stay on multiple screens in multiple theaters for months.

In spite of these factors, *The Wizard of Oz* was the ninth-highest grossing film of 1939. Myths about the film's initial critical reception are similarly misleading. Critics named it to their "Best 10 List" that year, and it was nominated for six academy awards, including best picture, taking home best score, best song, and an honorary "Juvenile Award" for Garland. Furthermore, MGM clearly delivered a product that spoke to both established and new consumers of Oz, gatekeepers and fans, critics and the public. As the *Los Angeles Times* observed "Nearly 10,000 people stood in line to see *The Wizard of Oz* on the day it opened at the Capitol. ...in the face of such public response, critical praise is beggared....Perhaps part of the Capitol's tremendous business is accounted for by the fame of the book, a wide-spread publicity campaign, and personal appearances by Judy Garland and Mickey Rooney. These factors, however, have little to do with the satisfaction felt by patrons who enter the theater expecting a lot for their money."[73]

Contemporary accounts of consumer-reactions to the film attest to this satisfaction. On August 16th, the Associated Press reported, "Oz was unveiled to the public last night, bringing 'ohs' and 'ahs' from the colony's upper-crust and an almost unheard-of outburst of raves from usually blasé critics."[74] After the New York premier, the *New York Telegram* wrote that the first audience "wept, howled with glee, and trembled with fear"; the *Washington Post* observed "the universal glee of audiences leaving the theater."[75] A reviewer for the *Austin American* reported being "practically inundated in gasps and cheers," concluding "the kids were having a wonderful time."[76] Indeed, across America, the audience was "joining in as it seldom does," causing many critics to conclude "there is wholly a quality of magic in the triumph of this picture, which succeeds where so many fantasy films have heavily failed."[77]

Figuring out what accounted for that "magic" is key to understanding both the triumph of MGM's film and the path that led from Baum to *Wicked*. MGM's gamble on Oz—its counting on a ready-made audience of current consumers and nostalgic adults—clearly paid off. A large majority of reviews and articles invoke nostalgic memories of the book, celebrating a chance to look back and reconnect with their lost childhood. One notable article takes us back to 1900, and a wood filled "with all the fall glory of trees," where a "rural mail carrier...jogging along in his two-wheeled cart," carries a present from a small boy's aunt: *The Wonderful Wizard of Oz*, "beautiful, enticing, not only to the child but to his parents as well."[78] Others fondly remember the Broadway play, and MGM scriptwriter, Jane Hall, writing in the August issue of *Good Housekeeping*, recalls, "When I first read the Whiz of Oz, these many, many years ago, it ran as a Sunday serial. My brother and I used to spread it out on the floor, to water color the illustrations."[79] From a young boy in rural America leafing through one of the first copies of Baum's book, through audiences at the historic Broadway extravaganza, to a girl coloring-in newspaper illustrations with her brother, memories of Oz spanned generations and transcended media and genre. To all of these consumers, addressed in the film's dedication as "those of you who have been faithful" to "this story," MGM promised "*The Wizard of Oz* as L. Frank Baum himself would have wished it."[80] "You," Jane Hall assured her readers "are going to like the way my studio has brought your favorite fairy tale to life."[81]

The critics, on the whole, agreed. If one is nostalgic for what one has lost—childhood, innocence, wonder—*The Wizard of Oz*, many argued, could at least temporarily restore these losses. "There is no better cure for a troubled heart, or a troubled world," Sara Hamilton asserted in the *Los Angeles Examiner*, "than a journey back to a cherished childhood memory. And MGM's Oz is just that, a memory glorified on the screen."[82] As such, the film provided a product that adult consumers needed—whether they knew it or not. Not only would it *satisfy* the "young in heart," it would *create* them. "Maybe," the *Boston Globe* told its readers, "you don't like such fare today, or maybe you just think you don't and will regain all of the earlier thrills when you take your youngsters to see the film."[83] In fact, the article concludes that, watching *The Wizard of Oz*, "it's almost impossible to keep from feeling yourself back in the fairy tale days."[84] The *Hartford Courant* told readers, "If you have a youngster, you'll be going anyway, but if you haven't, we suggest here and now that you borrow one and take him to the Land of Oz." Not only do you owe it to the child, since Oz "belongs to each child's life as much as his ABCs" but you also owe yourself a "charming escape from the grim reality of worldly cares."[85]

These gatekeepers' responses to the film confirmed its symbolic capital. Its association with childhood, fairytales, and wonder made it, quintessentially, a *family* film: one that not only crossed generations, but also transcended them—as *Wicked* would do much later. "This picture will spell enchantment for children," the *Los Angeles Times* promised. "It will also have the virtue of taking grown-ups to Never Never Land."[86] "Youngster, oldsters, all the young in heart will go wild," *Commonweal* asserted. Jack Moffat told the readers of the *Kansas City Star* that "Three generations will see their gayest dreams come true in Oz"[87] And Mary Harris confirmed "Oz is a picture for the whole family. You'll feel guilty if you see it and don't take Junior."[88]

Crucially, the published record shows that, as they celebrated the film, a large percentage of consumers and reviewers reacted to it precisely as they had been instructed to do by MGM's promotional campaign. They even echoed the themes and language provided to them by the studio. With this movie, promotional intent and consumer reception aligned beautifully. The marketing of *The Wizard of Oz* seamlessly educated gatekeepers and consumers alike, while deftly directing their consumption of the film. Reviewers raved that MGM had delivered on its promises, lauding the studio's extravagant deployment of technology and resources to produce a breakthrough film. They hailed *The Wizard of Oz* as "a triumph of showmanship," in which "all of the technical resources of the movie medium are put at the service of fantasy," a "gorgeous, fantastic, radiant with technicolor filmmusical extravaganza." The "inventiveness of the technical forces that were employed without stint of effort or cost," they enthused, had brought to the screen "scenic passages...so beautiful in design and composition as to stir the audiences by their sheer unfoldment."[89] Here, the gatekeepers promised potential audiences, was something truly new, a turning point in film history. "Fantasy," Ed Schellart wrote in the *Los Angeles Times*, "is at last brought to success in a full-fledged form...Oz may well be described as epochal."[90] When *The Wizard of Oz* switched to color, Frances Crow agreed, "the history-making character of the film struck this reviewer most forcibly. For surely her first sight of the Land of Oz could have been no more wonderful to Dorothy than the sight of this photoplay itself would have been to the eyes of film fans twenty years ago."[91]

Crow's observation confirms LeRoy's assertion that "movies weren't equipped to make such fantasies until recent years"; *now* however, "this picture brings Oz to life beyond one's happiest expectations."[92] Here, enchantment trumps effects, and some reviewers urged audiences to "pay no attention to the man behind the curtain": "Never," said Clark Rodenbach in the *Chicago Daily News*, "did we hope some day to have these delightful characters come to life in colors as bright and gay as those in our book and speak to us.... How the effects were produced, don't ask. Just sit and look back in wide-mouthed astonishment," a sentiment echoed by Hall: "The Publicity Department has waylaid me at every corner with great sheaves of statistics about how many million-watt lights and how many thousands of magicians and how many dozen make-up experts went into this whole creation, but I would rather just tell you that you haven't even dreamed of fairyland until you have seen 'The Wizard of Oz.'"[93]

The Heart of the Matter

Interestingly enough, many critics—and one presumes, many consumers—equated the film's ability to "bring to the screen what has hitherto existed only in the minds of little girls and boys," with narrative fidelity, taking the trailer's claim that "every glorious adventure has been recaptured" at face value.[94] *The Wizard of Oz's* producers, however, fully knew that the publicity department's claims of fidelity were merely a marketing ploy—a sleight of hand—much like the fade shots that in the trailer superimposed footage of the film over the disappearing pages of Baum's books. They also fully understood that, in order to make Oz not only work on film but also to speak to new audiences, it would have to be "made suitable" for its media and time.

But what did that mean, in terms of adaptation? As they adapted Baum's work, MGM's team had before it the three *Wizard of Ozes* purchased along with the rights to the novel; much could be learned from each of these failed attempts to bring *The Wizard of Oz* to screen. For instance, the Selig film completely abandoned Baum's plot in favor of a cobbled-together sequence of gags and dance routines; replaced character motivation with chorus girls, elephants and camels;

and blurred the line between Kansas and Oz by having Dorothy meet the "magical Scarecrow" *before* a cyclone carries the two of them, Toto, her horse and her cow to Kansas.[95] The result was a film that lacked coherence, emotional connection, and "magic," satisfying neither existing nor new consumers. Semon's film is arguably worse, despite the fact that it was penned by Baum's son. In this puzzling combination of melodrama and slapstick, a coquettish Dorothy, her evil uncle and her rival farmhand beaus don't arrive in Oz until half way through the film. Magic has been replaced by treachery, shenanigans, canons, and airplanes; the famous trio of the Scarecrow, Cowardly Lion, and the Tin Woodsman are merely the buffoonish farmhands in disguise.[96] As for the animated cartoon: it can hardly be called an Oz adaptation at all. It merely uses Dorothy's trip to Oz to showcase the animator's art—including the switch from black and white to color as Dorothy falls into Oz.[97] In that respect, Eshbaugh's short owes more to Disney than to Baum.

It is possible—perhaps even likely—that MGM's creative team took two key ideas from these earlier films: the doubling of the farmhands as Oz characters; and the use of color to mark the transition between Kansas and Baum's fairyland. However, they completely integrated them into a very different adaptation of *The Wizard of Oz*. Interviews with the film's producers indicate that they understood they could not simply reproduce the book or musical on screen. Their goal in writing, designing, and directing the adaptation was to "get away from any precedents to create Oz, its characters, and its events like nothing in existence," and yet remain true to the spirit of what LeRoy, in a letter to Maud, called "Mr. Baum's kindly philosophy" and "wonderful imagination."[98] An early plan to present "Oz as a fairyland of 1938, not 1900 was quickly abandoned" (one can't but wonder if watching Semon's flapper Dorothy might have convinced the writers that this was a bad idea), in favor of a focus on the story's emotional foundation.[99] The film's assistant producer, Arthur Freed, outlined this approach in a 1939 memo, insisting on "the urgent necessity of getting a real emotional and dramatic quality through the Oz sequences, so that when the picture is over, besides our laughs and our novelty, we will have had a real assault on our hearts."[100] The focus, Freed continued, should be on Dorothy, who has "a heart full of love," "but no one to love," and her "escape in her dream of Oz." The film's success, Freed concluded, depended on the "soundness of the sentimental and emotional foundation of this story, because it is only against such a canvas the novelty and music of our venture can mean anything."[101]

While a detailed point-by-point comparison of the film to Baum's book lies beyond the purview of this study, it is worth outlining a few of the ways in which Oz's writers followed Freed's advice. First, they situated Dorothy firmly in Kansas, establishing an empathic relationship between the audience and the vexed girl whom nobody has time to listen to. Second, once Dorothy arrives in Oz, Baum's episodic narrative is given a villain and a clear through-line that simplifies the literary Dorothy's multiple adventures, heightens the suspense, and solidifies the links between Oz and Kansas. In Baum, the Wicked Witch of the West plays a comparatively minor role; she doesn't even appear until the Wizard demands her death in exchange for helping the companions. By contrast, the film not only presents her as the double of the Toto-threatening Elmira Gulch, but also uses her as the threat that ties Dorothy's adventures together. The film also heightens the threat level. In the book, Dorothy is never in any real danger; even when she is briefly a prisoner of the Witch, she sneaks out at night to feed the Cowardly Lion, and when she flings the bucket of deadly water at the Witch, it is in a fit of temper because the Witch tripped Dorothy and stole one of her silver shoes. But in the film, as the sands of the hour glass run out, Dorothy faces almost certain death at the Witch's hands. The producers and creators complemented this streamlining of Baum's plot for narrative effect by avoiding the temptation to recycle the songs from the Broadway hit. Instead, Arlen and Yarburg wrote new songs to advance the plot, clarify character motivation, and create a richly textured emotional connection with the audience. "Over the Rainbow" is the most famous, of course, but all of the film's songs—from the triumphant "Ding, Dong the Wicked Witch is Dead" through the wistful iterations of "If I Only Had …" and the jaunty "We're off to see the Wizard," to Burt Lahr's tour de force, "If I Were King of the Forest"—work to advance the plot and carry the audience with them—the very qualities our theater professionals praise Stephen Schwartz for seventy-five years later.

Not all critics were fooled by MGM's claims to fidelity. As *Variety* observed, "liberties were taken with the original story," but even many of these gatekeepers were won over by the film's adaptation. Some, like Hall, opined that those liberties had resulted in a tighter and more coherent tale. "I think it's superior to the original story as a movie vehicle in that [it]...makes a very amusing and logical tie-up between Dorothy's farm life in Kansas and the later sequences in Oz."[102] Others celebrated it as a "new Oz," "as much an individual achievement in its own right as its literary original." John Alden of the *Minneapolis Morning Tribune* admitted to having overcome his initial skepticism, "Sure, this wasn't strictly the Oz I knew," he writes, "It was a wonderful Oziological adventure of its own... I'm for it. It was a splendid adventure for me."[103]

Whether they saw the film as a new "Oziological adventure," or as a faithful rendition of Baum's tale, many gatekeepers argued that MGM's film transcended its technical medium to become more than the sum of its visual effects, technological wizardry, and a cast of thousands. In the final analysis, they attested to the adaptation's successful achievement of Freed's emotional punch. Reviewers across the country testified that *The Wizard of Oz* was a "warmly human, deeply emotional film."[104] They verified that it was "much more than a visual treat, ... a really human document," whose "entertainment value [was] due not only to its clever handling of fantasy, but also to the heartwarming aspects of its story."[105] Francis Crow's account of the Los Angeles film critics' preview on August 9th, provides a narrative summation of these consumer responses, "When the lights went up, many of the critics still had tears in their eyes. They had been crying with the young star, Judy Garland, at her farewell to the wonderful people of Oz."[106]

While we could offer our own reading of the film—and present those of other scholars—what matters here is how MGM marketed *The Wizard of Oz* in 1939, and how its original audiences consumed it. "Fairy stories," *Variety* asserted, "must teach simple truths."[107] Some consumers took the film at its word, as a tale in which Dorothy learns the simple truth, "there is no place like home," "that the land beyond the rainbow is not all she had thought it would be."[108] As a perceptive eight-year-old guest reviewer summed it up, "She wants to go home. The good witch tells her all she has to do is think she is happy in her own back yard and then she will be home again. And she is."[109] Others saw in it "the theme of conquest of fear," as Dorothy and her companions repeatedly overcome their fear—of witches, of fire, of the Wizard himself—to achieve both safety and their hearts' desire.[110]

These readings of *The Wizard of Oz* responded to a fairy tale particularly suited to 1939. Indeed, MGM's Oz proffered "a message well-timed to current events."[111] "It could scarcely have been released at a more propitious hour," the *Austin American* affirmed, "*The Wizard of Oz* is a timely escape from reality. Earth-bound adults may be able to summon a childish wistfulness to catch Dorothy's cyclone express to the land of Oz, where nothing more dreadful than a green-faced, black-hearted witch cackles grotesquely."[112] In that respect, MGM's film, like Baum's book before it, offered consumers a therapeutic narrative fit for its time. To a country hobbled by ten years of the Great Depression, Oz's assertion that your heart's desire can be found in your own back-yard, despite its apparent trials and deprivations, urged Americans to be content with the black-and-white world they had, and not to clamor for the glitzy technicolor promises of the land over the rainbow—which, however alluring, could not provide the true satisfactions of home and family. And, as Europe plunged into World War II (it would "officially" begin one week after *The Wizard of Oz's* nationwide release), the story of a group of plucky allies who defeated a wicked tyrant became unexpectedly relevant. Indeed, one of the first political cartoons ever to deploy MGM's characters cast Hitler as the Wicked Witch of the West and the allies as the Scarecrow, the Tin Woodman, and a Not-So-Cowardly British Lion.

CONCLUSION

By successfully translating Oz to the medium of film, MGM's *The Wizard of Oz* made Baum's narrative available to new consumers who, while they may well had heard of the books, had never read them, at the same time that it provided established consumers with a new experience of Oz. Furthermore, by providing the nation with a highly visible Oz event, MGM brought Oz back into fashion, reaching a mass-audience through marketing, promotions, merchandising and the film. While MGM may have been uninterested in Oz's sustainability apart from how it affected the studio's profits and prestige, its film was crucial to Oz's cultural sustainability, in both senses of the concept, as a narrative that sustained American culture and as a narrative that sustains itself. Furthermore, the studio's re-consumption, production and marketing of the *Wizard of Oz*, along with consumers' consumption of the film, provides us with further insights into the mechanisms by which individual re-consumptions enable a narrative to achieve this long-term cultural sustainability.

- **Tap into an unbroken chain of memory**: If the original "Ozmania" stretched from the publication of *The Wonderful Wizard of Oz* in 1900 to Baum's death in 1919, by 1939 most of Oz's original consumers were well into middle-age. While Reilly & Lee's continuations and promotions, and "Jello's" 1930 broadcasts, had kept Oz going, MGM's film was the first major "Oz-event" in twenty years. Released just on the cusp of the passing of the generation that had first encountered Oz, the film gave these older consumers a chance to re-experience Oz and to share it with younger consumers, who would then be able, in their turn, to re-experience and share new re-consumptions of Oz with new generations.
- **Reach a large pool of new consumers**: While the continuing Reilly & Lee series offered existing consumers "another Oz book," it is unlikely that it extended the brand far beyond the children's book market. MGM, on the other hand, deployed mass-marketing and mass-distribution to attract mass audiences. It also cross-branded *The Wizard of Oz* with the studio's other films and products, most notably its star-power—Judy Garland and Mickey Rooney for the teenagers, and Roy Bolger, Burt Lahr, Jack Haley and Frank Morgan, for the adults—to bring in new consumers.
- **Go beyond repetition and imitation to offer something new**: While remediation ensures that a re-consumption reaches new consumers, such as adult film audiences, a re-consumption needs to do more than simply slavishly remediate original content. An adaptation needs to be "made suitable" to both new audiences and new media. MGM's *The Wizard of Oz* took full advantage of new film technologies to create a new and vivid Oz, at the same time that its adaptation shifted the narrative's genre, recasting it as an integrated musical.
- **Welcome new consumers, standing on their own merit**: While knowing audiences should be able to engage in the pleasures of recognition, new consumers should be able to enjoy this instance of the narrative without any previous knowledge. Furthermore, as we saw in the critics' response, a re-consumption must be a good product—a good film, a good musical, a good book—apart from its originary narrative.
- *Mean something* **beyond their re-presentation of the narrative but that something must be malleable**: Narratives that achieve cultural sustainability have a moral and ethical valence. Baum's meditations on

a utopian society without evil or want, MGM's celebration of home and hearth and, as we shall see, many other iterations Oz teach "simple" (or not so simple) truths. Those truths, however, are not fixed, and can be re-read and re-interpreted by consumers.

- **Resonate emotionally with consumers**: Freed's memo to Oz's production team encapsulates this principle. Narratives that achieve cultural sustainability connect with consumers' emotions. Furthermore, the emotional resonances available must be able to reach consumers where they are, both individually and culturally.

NOTES

1. L. Frank Baum, *Glinda of Oz* (Chicago: Reilly & Lee, 1920), Preface, Kindle.
2. Maud Baum, "Dear Children," Preface to L. Frank Baum and Ruth Plumly Thompson, *The Royal Book of Oz* (Chicago, Reilly & Lee, 1921), Kindle.
3. Letter from Reilly to Maud Baum, 1922, Box 3, Folder 6, L. Frank Baum Papers, Syracuse University Libraries Special Collections Research Center, Syracuse University Library.
4. Maud Baum to Reilly, May 15, 1922, Baum Papers.
5. Ruth Plumly Thompson, *Kabumbo in Oz* (Chicago: Reilly & Lee, 1922), Preface, Kindle.
6. Ruth Plumly Thompson, "A Day in Oz," 1925, Box 3, Folder 13, Baum Papers.
7. Promotional Advertisement, *Publisher's Weekly*, November 7, 1925, ibid.
8. Box 3, Folder 13, Baum Papers.
9. Ibid.
10. Ibid.
11. *Ozmapolitan*, 1925, Hungry Tiger Press, http://www.hungrytigerpress.com/tigertreats/ozmapolitan_1926.pdf, accessed November 11, 2017.
12. Ibid.
13. Ibid.
14. Reilly & Lee, Contest Map, 1925, Oversized Folder 1, Baum Papers.
15. Ibid.
16. Letter from Maud Baum to Reilly, 1924, Box 3, Folder 6, Baum Papers.
17. Letter from Reilly to Baum, March 20, 1928, ibid.
18. Letter from Baum to Reilly, April 4, 1928, ibid.
19. Ibid.; Letter from Baum to Reilly, 1924, Box 3, Folder 6, Baum Papers.
20. Advertisement, 1924, Box 6, Folder 4, Baum Papers.
21. Trademark Case, 1937, Box 3, Folder 7, Baum Papers.

22. Ibid., 76.
23. Ibid.
24. Ibid., 37.
25. Advertisement, 1924, Baum Papers.
26. Jay Scarfone and William Stillman, *The Wizardry of Oz: The Artistry and Magic of the 1939 MGM Classic* (New York: Applause Books, 2004), 175. We are indebted to this book, as well as to John Fricke, Jay Scarfone, and William Stillman, *The Wizard of Oz: The Official 50th Anniversary Pictorial History* (New York: Warner Books, 1989), for much of the historical information and images discussed in this chapter.
27. "Oz Advertisement," *Ladies' Home Journal*, September 1939, 3.
28. Qtd. in Fricke et al., *Anniversary*, 138.
29. "MGM Campaign Book," Image Reproduced in Scarfone and Stillman, *Wizardry*, 176–177.
30. "Lion's Roar," October 1939, Image Reproduced in Fricke et al., *50th Anniversary*, 125; "Campaign Book."
31. Ibid.
32. Ibid.
33. "A Star is Born and Made," *Modern Screen*, August 1939, 72.
34. Jane Hall, "The Wizard of Oz," *Good Housekeeping*, August 1939, 40.
35. Fricke et al., *Anniversary*, 45.
36. Hall, "Wizard," 139.
37. Ibid., 40.
38. *Modern Screen*, 31–32.
39. MGM *Studio News*, Image Reproduced in Scarfone et al., *Wizardry*, 178.
40. MGM Promotional Flyer, Image Reproduced in Fricke et al., *Anniversary*, 90–91.
41. Ibid.
42. Qtd. in Scarfone et al., *Wizardry*, 17.
43. "Lion's Roar."
44. Ibid.
45. Ibid.
46. *Modern Screen*, 31–32.
47. "Lion's Roar."
48. MGM Promotional Flyer and Postcard, Images Reproduced in Fricke et al., *Anniversary*, 90–91
49. "Lion's Roar."
50. "Campaign Book;" "Lion's Roar."
51. "Comic Strip Promotion," Image Reproduced in Fricke et al., *Anniversary*, 130–131.
52. Ibid.
53. "The Wizard of Oz Original Trailer [1939]," YouTube Video, 2:11, posted November 26, 2013, https://www.youtube.com/watch?v=_AtOEMlOahg.

54. Qtd. in Fricke et al., *Anniversary*, 126.
55. Ibid., 141.
56. Ibid., Image Reproduced on 133.
57. Ibid., 140.
58. Ibid., 145.
59. *Modern Screen*, 31–32.
60. Fricke et al., *Anniversary*, 144.
61. Ibid.
62. Ibid., 162.
63. Ibid., 160.
64. Fith, "Film Reviews: The Wizard of Oz," *Variety*, August 16, 1939, 14.
65. Ibid.
66. MGM Press Book, Image Reproduced in Scarfone et al., *Wizardry*, 180.
67. MGM Campaign Book, Image Reproduced in Fricke et al., *50th Anniversary*, 139.
68. Sally Joy Brown, "A Good Letter is Passport to 'Wizard of Oz,'" *Chicago Daily Tribune*, August 22, 1939, 15.
69. "Youngsters Do Own 'Wizard of Oz,'" *The Christian Science Monitor*, August 18, 1939, 10.
70. "Oz Dress Prized Awarded to Children," *Atlanta Constitution*, August 19, 1939, 6.
71. Qtd. in Scarfone et al., *Wizardry*, 174.
72. Fricke et al., *Anniversary*, 165.
73. "Wizard of Oz Smash Hit," *Los Angeles Times*, August 29, 1939, 11.
74. AP Press Release, August 16, 1939, Fricke et al., *Anniversary*, 183.
75. Mary Harris, "Wizard of Oz Begins Second Palace Week," *Washington Post*, September 9, 1939, 11.
76. Ruth Lewis, "The Wizard of Oz," *Austin American*, August 27, 1939, 18.
77. "Smash Hit."
78. "The Wizard of Oz—Early Edition," *Christian Science Monitor*, October 23, 1939, 10.
79. Hall, "Wizard," 137.
80. "Lion's Roar."
81. Hall, "Wizard," 139.
82. Sara Hamilton, *Los Angeles Examiner*, August 20, 1939, qtd. in Fricke et al., *Anniversary*.
83. "New Films: State and Orpheum," *Daily Boston Globe*, August 18, 1939, 9.
84. Ibid.
85. "The Wizard of Oz," *Hartford Courant*, August 25, 1939, 9.
86. Harris, "Second Week."
87. Qtd. in Fricke et al. *Anniversary*, 186.

88. Harris, "Second Week."
89. "Smash Hit," 11; "'Wizard of Oz' is Well Done," *Chicago Daily Tribune*, August 26, 1939. 13; "The Wizard of Oz," *Variety*, August 16, 1939, 14.
90. Edwin Schallert, "'Wizard of Oz' Epochal as Fantasy," *Los Angeles Times* August 10, 1939, 9.
91. Frances Crow, *Hollywood Citizen News*, August 10 1939, qtd. in Fricke et al., *Anniversary*, 172.
92. Archer Winsten, *New York Post*, August 18, 1939, qtd. in ibid., 184.
93. Clark Rodenbach, *Chicago Daily News*, August 25, 1939, qtd. ibid., 185; Hall, "Wizard," 41.
94. "New Films," 9.
95. *The Wonderful Wizard of Oz*, Directed by Otis Turner (1910: Selig Polyscope Company); YouTube, 13:30, posted January 18, 2011, https://www.youtube.com/watch?v=jpV29YZ7Ksw.
96. *The Wizard of Oz*, Directed by Larry Semon (1925: Chadwick Pictures Corporation); YouTube, 124:56, posted on May 24, 2015, https://www.youtube.com/watch?v=uDiXIgfQSu0.
97. *The Wizard of Oz*, Directed by Ted Eshbaugh (1933: Ted Eshbaugh Studios); YouTube, 7:45, posted on January 15, 2014, https://www.youtube.com/watch?v=QlcivMXxXPk.
98. Fricke et al., *Anniversary*, 42, 147.
99. Ibid., 26.
100. Ibid., 29.
101. Ibid., 30.
102. *Variety*, "Review of the 'Wizard of Oz,'"; Hall, "Wizard."
103. John Alder, *Minneapolis Morning Tribune*, August 25, 1939, qtd. in Fricke et al. *Anniversary*, 186.
104. Crow, *Hollywood Citizen*.
105. *Hollywood Spectator*, September 2 1939, qtd. in Scarfone et al., 199; *Modern Screen*.
106. Crow, *Hollywood Citizen*.
107. *Variety*, "Review of 'The Wizard of Oz.'"
108. R.W.D. "Wizard of Oz Opens Today," *New York Herald Tribune*, August 17, 1939, 12.
109. "Eight-Year-Old Previews Wizard of Oz," *Washington Post*, August 20, 1939, AM1.
110. Lewis, "Wizard of Oz."
111. *Variety*, "Review of the Wizard of Oz."
112. Lewis, "Wizard of Oz."

CHAPTER 4

Of Living Rooms and Libraries:
Oz's Journey from Fairy Tale to Myth

As Baum's books fell out of fashion and Reilly & Lee ceased to publish new Oz tales, MGM's cinematic triumph, *The Wizard of Oz*, adapted to a new genre and a new medium, kept the narrative alive.[1] The studio re-released the film in 1949 and again in 1955, billing it as "brought back in response to more requests than any other picture."[2] However, in a pre-VHS, pre-DVD, pre-digital era, even popular theatrical films were transitory; with each new film released, an older film's chances of wide-screen re-release dwindled. Thus, Oz stood again at the crossroads, at risk of being relegated to history: its written narratives out of fashion, its visual spectacle only sporadically available.

Then, in 1956, two events kept Oz on the road to enduring cultural sustainability: CBS and *Ford Star Jubilee* featured *The Wizard of Oz* as a television event, and Columbia University hosted the exhibit "L. Frank Baum, the Wonderful Wizard of Oz, in commemoration of the centenary of his birth." The first inaugurated *The Wizard of Oz's* television afterlife, assuring Oz's status as an icon whose events, characters, lines, and images became firmly embedded in the cultural imaginary. The second marked the beginning of an archival movement, keeping Baum and his books in the public eye through recovering, celebrating, and extending his work. The television showings created a generation of Ozzites, while Baum fan's and scholars enriched the experience, expanding Oz beyond the borders of MGM's fantasy. For nearly seventy-five years, these two strands have assured Oz's status as a living narrative, one with

© The Author(s) 2018
K. Drummond et al., *The Road to Wicked*,
https://doi.org/10.1007/978-3-319-93106-7_4

an established consumer base, that is at the same time available to new adaptations and new markets.

'A HAPPY NIGHT FOR ALL OF YOU'

We begin with the annual television broadcasts, which, if they did not create the interest in Baum and his works, created the circumstances for their expansion. For many baby boomers, the annual, ritualized event of watching Oz on TV stands as their first introduction to the narrative. In this, as with the film, the tale's remediation—its movement from one media platform to another—plays a key role in its long-term sustainability. As such, it's worth taking a moment to consider that medium, exploring the role television played as a source of entertainment and culture, a creator of markets and consumers, and, as Anna McCarthy terms it, a "citizen machine." In Oz's early broadcast years, all these factors contributed to Oz's place in our cultural imaginary, as the narrative worked to create and sustain American national identity during the Cold War.[3]

The TV played an integral part in what *McCall's* editor and publisher Otis Lee Weise coined in 1954 as "togetherness." "Men, women and children," he observed in his rebranded "Magazine of Togetherness," "are creating [a] new and warmer way of life not as women *alone*, or men *alone*, isolated from one another, but as a *family* sharing a common experience."[4] "Togetherness" became, as Betty Friedan later observed, "a national purpose." The family, in its suburban home, surrounded by its suburban appliances, ensured the nation's democratic future.[5] And, situated in the literal and symbolic center of that home, was the television. American television ownership—bringing with it a continuous stream of entertainment, most of it suitable for the entire family, delivered straight into their living rooms—increased steadily throughout the 1950s—rising from a mere 9% of households in 1950, to 55.7% in 1954. It was at 71.8% in 1956 for the first broadcast of *The Wizard of Oz*, then 87.1% in 1960.

"Television's mass audience," McCarthy asserts, "provided…powerful people with opportunities to talk about…culture and economy in a democratic society." In other words, carefully considered programming could "disperse ideas and automate perception," shape "conduct and attitudes," and "give form to the amorphous collectivity of the nation."[6] By "spreading education, morality, and happiness among the citizenry" television could help produce ideal Cold War citizens: a "safeguard against" communism and "the spectral apocalypse of class, race and nuclear war."[7] Reaching across geographic—and, to a lesser extent, socioeconomic—boundaries, TV shows, Alan Nadel observes, offered "a set of experiences and narratives...solidifying what we would call a 'national imaginary'": "a set of common imagery and narratives that people shared when they thought of America as a nation and themselves as citizens."[8] This national imaginary presented an America grounded in "citizens governed by concepts of self-regulation, voluntarism and entrepreneurial initiative"; individuals were the "part" that stood for the national "whole."[9] In this equation, "belonging and responsibility" were opposed to comradeship, and "individuals and their everyday actions" to the communist state.

As program sponsors, America's major corporations played a significant part in television's citizen-machine. They had a vested interest in making sure that the content of programs conveyed the appropriate cultural messages. After all, corporate profits depended on properly constructed Cold War citizens, and television could play a critical role in building self-regulated workers who contributed to the good of the company.[10] Furthermore, sponsorship was good institutional marketing, allowing corporations to position themselves as "community institutions bringing culture and learning to mass audiences."[11] The right sponsorship could foster good will, and, if the sponsored program "[left] a nice taste in your mouth," it could also generate cultural capital for the company, transferring that nice taste from the program to the corporation itself.[12]

Sponsored programming could come in many forms, from historical series, such as Dupont's *Cavalcade*, that connected "the heroic pursuit of freedom [or knowledge, or technology] in past centuries to the domestic and geopolitical challenges of the day," to anthology series, "in which Americans might routinely encounter the corporation in its guise as a public servant or citizen."[13] While historical series offered run-of-the-mill programming, anthologies featured prestige productions that prided themselves on their aesthetic quality. As an executive associated with Ford's *Producers' Showcase* explained, "We wanted to reflect the tremendous prestige of the Ford Motor Company to present something new, different and spectacular to the American Public."[14] Statements such as these "fostered the impression that...sponsors were patrons of the arts...donating cultural goods to viewers and asking only their good will in return."[15]

All of these factors—the ethos of togetherness, television's role in the creation of American Cold War citizens, and the culture of corporate sponsorship—contributed to Oz's translation into a television product and framed its marketing and consumption. *The Wizard of Oz* was the first MGM film to make the move from the large to small screen, and CBS paid a then-staggering fee of $225,000 for the rights to two showings of what the network billed as a "motion picture classic." Its decision to air *The Wizard of Oz* as the final installment of the award-winning *Ford Star Jubilee* positioned the film as a prestige product, a gift from Ford to the American people. This "classic entertainment for the entire family" would be the first film on television to be "seen in its entirety," "a two hour presentation" uninterrupted by commercial breaks.[16] A narrative voice-over during the closing credits of the October 6th show, *You're the Top*, set the stage for the buzz that would surround *The Wizard of Oz's* television premiere: "Four weeks from tonight, your entire family, children and adults of all ages, is in for one of the most enviable experiences entertainment has ever offered, an introduction to the wonderful land of Oz.... It will be a happy night for all of you."[17]

There couldn't have been a better film to cater to a market that prized togetherness, and CBS consistently highlighted *The Wizard of Oz's* cross-generational magic, playing up both Oz's long pedigree and its family appeal. The *Ford Star Jubilee* ad in *TV Guide* tied the television showing to both the books—"In 1900 L. Frank Baum wrote his fantasy for children, *The Wizard of Oz*, and it proved so popular that he wrote a whole series of Oz books"—and the "original performance in which Judy Garland enchanted millions."[18] On the night of the big event, the announcer reiterated these themes:

> From New York, in color and black and white, *Ford Star Jubilee* presents the motion picture classic, *The Wizard of Oz*... Now...we mean [classic] only in the most popular sense of the word. For not only as a main feature film but as a masterpiece of literature which has fascinated children and adults for years, *The Wizard of Oz* ranks with the great works of all time... Those of you sitting here with your families tonight, will find a special pleasure in being acquainted with the stories, characters, and familiar music which has timeless appeal.[19]

Not only was *Ford Star Jubilee's* presentation of *The Wizard of Oz* a family event, it also provided the older generation with the means of passing down this iconic American experience to the younger generation. This was suggested by a dynamic setup in the live segment that proceeded the first showing. Judy Garland's daughter, Liza, settled into watch the film with Burt Lahr (Judy, on stage in New York, was not available). Together with their mothers and fathers, and perhaps their grandparents, the *Los Angeles Times* observed, "a new generation (will) see *The Wizard of Oz* tonight."[20]

And see it they did. *Variety* reported that "*The Wizard of Oz* outwizarded its competition over a two hour span on Saturday night...more than doubling the ratings of its competitors...(and capturing) a 51.2% share of the viewing audience."[21] Its review was positively ecstatic, gushing that CBS and *Ford Star Jubilee* "couldn't have picked a grander swansong than 'Over the Rainbow'....In fact they couldn't have picked a grander show than Oz, which defies both time and diminution to the small screen."[22] The program was so successful that it sparked off a debate about the future of television programming, as *The New York Times* observed that the showing "may prove to be an event of more than passing significance." Could film-come-to-television be the wave of the future, with "the whole potential of TV and broadcasting ...add(ing) up to one small adjustment, moving the motion picture theater from downtown into the living room?" Although the writer hopes not, asserting that "television is and must remain far more than a revision in the method of distributing Hollywood's wares," he recognizes the appeal of such a move to the consumer: "When sitting at home under the most modern of electronic conditions...a viewer was bound to be aware of the implications of 'Oz.' Watching such a film in glorious color, in one's own home, with the entire family sharing in the laughs, without paying a box-office admission."[23] *The Wizard of Oz* showed what television could do with movies; as Phillip Scheuer observed in the *Los Angeles Times*, movies may well "win the battle with TV—but in the home."[24]

Distribution systems matter, and by placing *The Wizard of Oz* on television, CBS and Ford reached millions of Americans, all across the country, at the same time, creating a virtual community of consumers brought together through their television screens. If this had been a one-off event, or even a sporadic one, Oz may have still passed into relative cultural obscurity. But CBS (and later NBC and Turner Broadcasting) heeded *Variety*'s advice—"The network should make provisions for an annual out of it, preferably at an earlier time period and closer to the holiday season in the future"—and Oz became enshrined in the American national imaginary—a fact powerfully illustrated by Norman Rockwell's portrait of Judy Garland as Dorothy, commissioned by Singer in conjunction with its sponsorship of the annual broadcast the year after Garland's death.[25] As a prestige film that could be targeted to a family audience, *The Wizard of Oz* was a natural fit for Ford, CBS, and the Cold War market. An *American* fairy tale, penned by an American author, filmed by an American studio, and brought to you by a series of American corporations, Oz—particularly as it was adapted in the MGM film—was ideally suited to the construction of good Cold War citizens. From Dorothy's acceptance of home and "her own backyard" as the site of her "heart's desire," through the depiction of the Scarecrow, Tin Woodsman and Cowardly Lion as characters who embrace "belonging and responsibility," and whose individual actions save Dorothy and free the Winkies, to the film's ultimate message of self-reliance, wave after wave of young viewers, watching with their families, learned its lessons.

In an era of unlimited streaming and programmable DVRs, it's hard to remember that once-upon-a-time television was on the producers' schedule, not the consumers'. But, from its first showing in 1956 until its VHS and Betamax release in 1980, *The Wizard of Oz* was a television *event*, a once-in-a-year opportunity, and it was marketed as such. Newspapers, advertisements and on-air and announcements created buzz, urging viewers not to miss the experience, to be right there, right then, in their living rooms with their sets tuned in ready to meet the year's celebrity host (Red Skelton, Dick Van Dyke, Danny Kaye) and his children, and again experience together the wonders of Oz. The years passed, the broadcast moved from CBS, to NBC, and back to CBS, and the tradition wove itself into the fabric of American culture, as consumers eagerly anticipated their annual visit to Oz. When a Milwaukee CBS affiliate decided in 1961 that football was more important than Dorothy, they endured the wrath of disappointed consumers, and wrangled permission to show the film at a later date; that was the last time an affiliate messed with the people's Oz, and, with two exceptions (1963 and 1977), the film showed annually until 1998. As the years went on, consumers continued to enjoy the annual broadcast; even after the film was released in video cassette in 1980, viewers still tuned in. In 1982, CBS reported that the annual showing had drawn "14,780,000 children— some 49% of the children in the United States between the ages of 2 and 11, along with more than 12 million men, and a few million teenagers."

Seven years later, a 50th anniversary documentary on the making of *The Wizard of Oz* settled for a less precise "more people have seen this movie than any other movie, over a billion of them."[26]

John Fricke, longtime chronicler of Oz and Garland, assesses the critical role these "teleshowings" played in the cultural sustainability of Oz itself:

> You can't overstate the impact of these annual teleshowings on CBS. Starting in '56, then from '59 on ... this movie came to the American public at home. So you can't talk to anybody of a certain age who grew up in the United States between 1956 and the mid-80s who doesn't remember sitting down to watch this film with their families. You'll hear people recall those evenings, and they'll say things like,'It was the one night of the year when were allowed to stay up late.' Or, 'I got to sleep in the den and have popcorn and orange soda.' Or 'The neighbors had a color tv so we went over there.' Today, nothing really commands that kind of cross-generational, inspirational moment. Now it's the sporting event, the awards ceremony. That's legitimate too, but to have three generations plopped down in front of the tv set – that's extraordinary.[27]

It's hard to pin down the range of the long line of consumers who participated in this annual ritual, but it is certainly safe to say that the ritual viewing of *The Wizard of Oz* profoundly affected those born in the eighteen years of the baby boom. As we will see in Chapter 7, this ritual, dubbed the "Oz Bowl" by *Time* in 1965, is indelibly inscribed in their memory. *Time's* description sets the stage for these later interviews: "Parents are again preparing for the occasion.... The children with a special restlessness will collect around the television set in much the same way their fathers do for the professional football championships. The children will know the names and styles of the players they are going to see, for the program has become a modern institution and a red letter day in the calendar of childhood. It is the **Oz Bowl game**."[28] Looking back from the perspective of 2015, a Solano newspaper columnist recalls, "Growing up we never missed it. By the time the black and white beginning of the film started, me and my brothers were 'becouched' with our bladders empty and our snack bowls full of Jiffy Pop Popcorn. The following day at school me and my friends would talk about our favorite parts...and sometimes neighborhood kids and I would even act out the movie—skipping along and singing the irresistibly catchy songs from the show."[29]

This account—the eager boys on the sofa, the schoolyard rundown, the sidewalk reenactment—speaks to *The Wizard of Oz's* continuing consumability; more than a viewing, even more than an event, the film resonated beyond the final credits; for this generation, it provided a common narrative, a set of shared images, and a series of ready-made phrases. As one of the guests "contentedly munching on lion-shaped cookies and munchkin-sized crudites, while smiling at table settings of straw baskets, sunflowers, rainbow-striped ribbons and oil cans" at the Museum of Modern Art's 50th Anniversary screening of the film observed:

> It's amazing how much a part of people's lives "The Wizard of Oz" has become...I find myself using lines from the movie all the time...There are many situations when I say "Pay no attention to that man behind the curtain" or "What a world! What a world!" Of course there aren't too many occasions to use "Surrender Dorothy," but whenever anyone says, "And Toto, too," everyone else smiles.[30]

Add to these some of the most recognizable lines in movie history: "I'm melting!"; "I've a feeling were not in Kansas anymore," and "There's no place like home." *The Wizard of Oz* has provided a shared vocabulary, an emotional and narrative shorthand, endlessly available for appropriation in comedy, satire, political cartoons and memes, that now exists apart from the original text. In 2018, this narrative, these images, this vocabulary—Oz itself—is part of our cultural memory, recognized and used even by a generation that may well have never seen the MGM film, read an Oz book, or attended a production of *Wicked*.

TROUBLE IN OZ

For many—if not most—baby boomers, MGM's *The Wizard of Oz* fulfilled the promise it made in the studio's 1939 promotion campaign. It had become THE Oz, consumers' first encounter with Baum's fantasy land and characters; however, if Oz's cultural sustainability had had to rely on the ritual viewing of the film alone, Oz, fixed into a single narrative, unable to expand or adapt, would have been in danger of becoming merely an artifact to be either reverenced or parodied. Fortunately for Oz, the years between 1956 and 1998 also saw a flurry of scholars and fans working to recover, promote, expand, and celebrate Baum and his Oz. On January 16, 1956, a little less than 10 months before

CBS's historic broadcast, Columbia University opened its commemorative exhibit, "L. Frank Baum, the Wonderful Wizard of Oz." Roland Baugham's, Head of Columbia Library's Special Collections, introduction to the exhibit's catalog sets the tone and themes for this recovery and celebration of a more literary, Baum-centric Oz. Baugham begins with unabashed nostalgia for a world which regularly produced new Oz adventures: "There was a time, not too long past for some of us to hold in vivid recollection, when Christmas could not come soon enough. For then, as surely as the sun rose over the frosty rooftops, there was a new 'Oz' book under The Tree, and the wonder of untried fantasy waited to unfold before us." Moving on from his childhood memories of the Oz books, Baugham asserts their value, as certified by an older generation of scholars, "Even now...those stories are still new and deathless. I know a distinguished professor who takes unabashed delight in having his successive offspring reach the 'story age'—for that gives him a solid reason for re-reading the Oz books by L. Frank Baum."

As Baugham concludes his introduction, he sets consumers—both established and new—in opposition to "certain teachers and children's librarians" who allowed the "Oz stories" to fall "into some neglect." "Fortunately not even the fiats of educators and librarians are timeless and the land of Oz and its whimsical creations and denizens are very much current today. Those of us who knew the series, and so eagerly awaited each new addition during its creator's lifetime, may well have reason to regret the passing years—until we recall that we are the elect for whom the Oz books were first written."[31] And indeed, the story of Baum and Oz in these years is the story of consumers and fans fighting back against the gatekeepers to ensure both Baum's place in American letters and the cultural sustainability of his magic land.

Baugham's cryptic mention of educators and librarians refers to a growing sense among educational experts that the Oz books were, at best, outdated and badly written, and at worst, downright dangerous for children. An Oz consumer from the late twenties recalls, "When my son was small, every time I asked for an Oz book at the library, they always acted like it wasn't proper reading for a child."[32] In 1928, the Chicago Public Library simply pulled the books from the shelves, deciding, as Frances Meusel, who worked there as a children's librarian, writes, *The Wonderful Wizard of Oz* "was NOT literature, but somehow, rather evil fare for children and, in addition, sinned the terrible sin of leading little library patrons on to other Baum enchantments."[33] This hostility to Baum's work—and, indeed, to fantasy literature in general, ironically, came to a head in the years immediately following Columbia's exhibit—and as "the Oz bowl" became an American tradition. In 1957, the Detroit Public Library followed Chicago in banning the books not just because they were "of no value," but also for "preaching negativism," and "dragging young minds down to a cowardly level."[34] The Toronto Public Library, according to columnist Pierre Berton, concurred, "Has the Oz era ended? Up at the Boys and Girls House at the Toronto Public Library, they tell me it has. There are no Oz books on the shelves....the librarians found an old copy of *The Wizard* in a back room. They don't think much of it here. It isn't good literature, they told me. It's had its day....No they don't consider it a classic."[35] Herb Caen had a similar experience in San Francisco, where the coordinator of the public libraries informed him, "We allow *The Wizard of Oz*, but the others have been consigned to the historical section. Badly written you know."[36] In 1959 Florida State librarian, Dorothy Dodd, passed judgment on the entire series as "poorly written, untrue to life, sensational, foolishly sentimental, and consequently unwholesome for the children in your community," and urged all Florida public libraries to withdraw it from circulation.[37] Several Florida librarians agreed with Dodd; Frank B. Sessa, chairman of the Miami Public Library, stated that the books "were outdated and poorly written by modern standards. Kids don't like that fanciful stuff anymore. They want books about missiles and atomic submarines."[38] His children's librarian, May Edmonds, concurred condemning Oz as "very, very, outdated" and without "real value."[39]

Again and again, librarians blamed the demand for the Oz books on sentimental adults. In Toronto, they told Berton that "the chief reason for its survival is in the memories of adults," creating a "demand," that Edmonds asserted was "strictly nostalgic."[40] Nostalgia, however, as *Life Magazine* observed in a 1959 editorial, "Dorothy the Librarian," is a powerful thing, and the banning of Oz in Detroit and Florida mobilized a vocal cadre of nostalgic editors, writers, and critics, who marshalled their memories of Oz to launch a spirited defense of Baum and his books.[41] This battle for Oz's sustainability was played out between the "experts" and gatekeepers: on one side, the librarians and educators, who controlled public access to the books, and on the other, consumers, readers, and writers whose cultural capital *as* readers and writers both lent them the authority with which to speak and provided them with a platform on which to do so. The defense of Oz took three primary forms: a valorization of childhood and the child-like, a vindication of fantasy literature, and a celebration of Baum's "kindly philosophy." Columnists Berton and Caen juxtaposed the librarians' dictates with their own childhood memories. While Caen settles for an ironic "I must have had lousy taste as a child," Berton recalls "devouring" *The Land of Oz*—along with bread and cheese—when he was nine and, after his visit to the library, concludes, "Who am I to judge? Whenever I travel to the land of Oz, I cease to be a critic. Once again, I am a small boy, crouched over the kitchen table, longing for bread and cheese."[42] Other writers, such as Shirley Jackson and Ray Bradbury, railed against "grave folks who believe that reading and learning should be inseparable."[43] In Bradbury's "The Exiles," this attitude leads to a bleak world, "dedicated firmly to science and progress," in which all books of fantasy and the supernatural have been banished, the last copies burnt, the Emerald City fallen; Jackson's article, "The Lost Kingdom of Oz," argues that "our children are being brutally cheated....No doubt these children are capable of doing the week's marketing or putting together a steam engine by the time they are twelve," but "they have never heard of the four countries of Oz."[44] Books about missiles and atomic submarines are all very well, as is putting together a steam engine, but in the four countries of Oz, children learn "the message," as Professor Russel Nye of Michigan State University observed in his spirited defense of the Oz books, "that love, kindness and unselfishness makes the world a better place." And if, Nye concluded, that message "seems of no value today," it is time "to reassess a good many other things besides the Detroit Library's approved list of children's reading."[45]

Ironically, Oz owes some of its cultural sustainability to the librarians' attempts to exile it. The controversies in Detroit and Florida brought the books back into the public eye, not only enlisting, as we have just seen, a battalion of critics and writers in its defense, but also inspiring new "Oz" output and increasing sales. Russel Nye and Martin Gardner's 1957 *The Wizard of Oz and Who He Was*—one of the first, serious critical evaluations of Baum and his works—published together with a facsimile of the 1900 edition of *The Wonderful Wizard of Oz*, was a direct response to the Detroit Library's edict on Oz. *The Detroit Times* ran a serial publication of the story, introducing each section by stating that the book had been banned by the city's libraries. In 1957, there were seven editions in print—all selling briskly, and Reilly & Lee were preparing to issue a new edition, with new illustrations. Oz, it seems, was set to outlive the "fiats of librarians and educators." And indeed, in 1961, *The Wizard of Oz* was included in the Children's Literature Catalogue, and in 1968, the *Chicago Daily News* identified it as the "all-time favorite children's book," and, *Time Magazine*, as the 11th best-selling juvenile, and the 20th best-selling fiction book of all time.

Even after the initial controversy died down, the Oz books were slow to be restored to library shelves and classrooms, and still faced occasional challenges from religious groups and parents, objecting to everything from the books' portrayals of non-traditional gender roles to their suggestion that there could be such a thing as a good witch. Each new objection, however, actually contributed to the narrative's cultural sustainability, bringing the series new visibility and spurring a new round of defenses, including a growing library of academic evaluations of Baum and his books, all proclaiming Oz's status as an *American* classic, one not only worthy of reverence and preservation but also key to America's own cultural sustainability. In 1946, *Colliers Magazine*, writing on the occasion of *The Wizard's* 45th anniversary, opined:

> This particular (book), which critics and serious thinkers never did value much, goes on seemingly forever. Why? Our theory is that it survives because it is a fairy tale of a strictly American kind, with a deep appeal to the best of American characteristics...What the story says, then, is: Don't believe in the big bad wolf...don't be overawed by people who talk big... don't depend on hearsay and propaganda.... The latest achievement to its credit was that it kept us from being intimidated by Messers. Hitler and Tojo..and inspired us in due time to step up and contribute heavily to the slapping of them down...Let us just hang on to that realistic, inquiring, skeptical and fearless attitude of mind. It is a priceless national asset.[46]

As if responding to the series undervaluing of by "critics and serious thinkers," when Henry Regnery Company (which had bought Reilly & Lee) reissued the books in 1959, flyleaves on the dust jackets featured academic endorsements, assuring consumers that "Oz fans range all the way from learned college professors to tiny children...Literary students, collectors of juvenilia, and Americana express increasing interest in the Oz books."[47] As the body of critical work on Baum grew, so did the series respectability in the academy. If the Oz books were classics, if they taught good morals, if they were peculiarly American, then their place in American literary history—and on the bookshelves of libraries—should be assured.

Club Beginnings

Over the same years that these public "Oz-eruptions" were bringing the books back into the cultural discourse, some of the growing Oz fans identified by Henry Regnery—dedicated readers, teachers, collectors, booksellers, and, yes, librarians—formed The Wizard of Oz Club (1957); over the next several decades, the Club flourished, playing a crucial role in Oz's long-term cultural sustainability. While the writers and editors who rallied around Oz did so in defense of its *consumption*, the Wizard of Oz Club provided a site for *production*—of community, of knowledge, of archives, of "more Oz." Fittingly, the Oz Club's founder, Justin Schiller, participated in both the Columbia Commemorative Exhibition and the inaugural television broadcast. At twelve years old, he contributed several of his own items, as noted in an addendum, to the exhibit, and his contribution brought Justin to the attention of CBS's team; he was there, with his first-edition of *The Wonderful Wizard of Oz*, "watching" the original broadcast with Liza Minnelli and Burt Lahr. The following year, working from the mailing lists of Jack Snow, one of the last Royal Historians of Oz, Justin invited people to join "The Wizard of Oz Club." From a handful of members in the late 1950s, the Club grew in both membership and impact, providing "Oz fans" with, at first, a virtual community (through the old-fashioned technology of mail and newsletters), and, then, beginning with 1960's "Ozcot" convention, a chance, as John Fricke observed in his 2017 talk on the history of the Oz Club, to convene "in the name of Oz," to raise "toasts to Oz," "face-to-face, glass-to-glass."[48]

As the Oz Club raised their glasses, the media noticed, and public interest stories on the group, and their interest in Oz, appeared in local and national newspapers, introducing "Oz fans...as gloriously varied as Dorothy's friends who people the Oz tales. They call themselves Ozmapolitans, or Ozophiles or Ozmaniacs," and discussing their activities, ranging from the Ozcot conferences to screenings of forgotten or lost films, such as Oz Film Manufacturing Company's 1914 *Scarecrow of Oz*. These articles raised the profile of the club, placed Oz and Baum in the public eye, attracted new members, and created new consumers.[49]

As such, the Oz Club and their annual gatherings provided a site for consumption of all things Oz. The membership list supplied sellers with a trove of potential consumers, and the Oz conferences became a mecca for Oz consumption, a chance for rare booksellers, and artisans to sell their wares. In this alone, the Oz Club played an important role in Oz's cultural sustainability as it provided a market for Oz. The club's function as a center of production, however, was even more crucial to ensuring Oz's future. Members of the Oz Club worked to recover lost and rare texts and artifacts and revived historic productions, such as the Jello-sponsored radio shows, at the annual conventions. The club's magazines, *The Baum Bugle*, founded in 1957, and *Oziana*, founded in 1971, offered venues for Oz publications, from articles on history and production in the *Bugle* to new stories in *Oziana*. In 1972, the club went into the book business, bringing out previously unpublished books by Ruth Plumly Thompson and Rachel Cosgrove, and books by "new" Royal Historians, Dick Martin, and Gina Wikwar. Oz illustrators Dick Martin and award-winning graphic novelist, Eric Shanower, published with the Oz Club, which also provided them with a community in which to hone their "Oz-skills." Club member Michael Hearn authored the comprehensive annotated edition of *The Wizard of Oz* in 1971. And in the 1980s, an informal partnership with New York's Books of Wonder bookstore kept the original Oz books in beautiful, facsimile print and continued to produce new Oz narratives.

John Fricke speaks to the synergy between the Oz movie and the Oz books at the Oz Club level:

> You have to remember that when the move started showing at home, the books were all still in print! And because of the biography, there was a lot of interest in Baum. So all of a sudden, you had this perfect storm: the books, the film, and the biography. Everything was fair game, and this was not lost on the Oz Club, or in the *Baum Bugle*. We wrote about all of it. What started as a snowball became an avalanche.[50]

In addition to the club's contributions to the "Oz-canon," founding members Russell MacFall and Frank Joslyn Baum were instrumental in recovering and popularizing Oz's creator, providing the foundation for the mythic Baum we discussed in Chapter 2. Working in the late 1950s, MacFall and Baum conducted extensive biographical research, tracking down newspaper articles, fliers, firsthand accounts, personal recollections, public records, and photographs, creating the extensive collection on Baum now housed in the Syracuse University Library. Among the correspondence MacFall conducted at this time, is a letter from Pierre Couderc, an employee at Baum Film Manufacturing Company, who provided the authors with some photographs and anecdotes, but queried the project "One thing I am curious about," he wrote, "Who's going to publish such a biography? And why? Who's going to buy the book?"[51] Couderc's query indicates that, by 1960, Baum himself was in danger of being forgotten, not marketable.

The annual television broadcast, however, supplied the why: consumers' love of the film spurred an interest in the creator of Oz. The biography found a publisher, and *To Please A Child: A Biography of L. Frank Baum, Royal Historian of Oz*, published in 1961, found a market.[52] This book combined archival research and family recollections in the first comprehensive overview of Baum's life and works; part chronicle, part anecdote, part plot-summary and thematic analysis, the work contributed to Oz's cultural sustainability in three important ways. First, as it was widely (and mostly favorably) reviewed, it brought Baum and Oz back into public discourse, with many newspapers offering short articles on Baum's life. Second, the revival of interest in Baum's life inspired towns and cities with a "Baum-connection"—Chicago, Aberdeen, Syracuse, Chittenango, Coronado and Los Angeles, Macatawa—to capitalize on that connection through Oz festivals and dedicated public spaces, such as Chicago's Oz Park and L. Frank Baum School, and Chittenango's Yellow Brick Road. Finally, the biography's account of Baum's life became available for romanticizing, and the next decades codified the myth of the Dreamer of Oz, casting Baum as an American hero, a Horatio Alger of the imagination.

Early reviewers of the biography were the first to give the tale this spin. *The Chicago Sun Times* concludes its review with what was to become the standard take on Baum's life: "A fascinating, thrilling story about a lad, a dreamer who evidently did not know the possibility of failure, who loved children and looked with confidence on the world he lived in as a place where all things turned out right, particularly in that area he called the land of Oz."[53] This reading of the biography quickly became codified as myth. In 1964, *American Heritage* featured Daniel P. Mannix's article, "The Father of the Wizard of Oz," which begins: "At the turn of the century, a disillusioned man who had failed at almost everything he had ever attempted, wrote to his sister, 'When I was young, I longed to write a great novel that should win me fame. Now that I am getting old, my first book is written to amuse children....To please a child is a sweet and lovely thing.'"[54] Mannix proceeds to chronicle the story of a "shy, sickly child," who had a "nervous breakdown" while in school, and, as an adult, told tales to "escape from his miserable existence," but who, finally, found success and happiness in Oz.[55]

This version of Baum was highly consumable, particularly in Cold War America. It cast the Dreamer of Oz as an American-type, the self-made man who, through persistence, achieves his dreams. *The Wizard of Aberdeen*, a 1970 episode of the popular anthology series, *Death Valley Days* ("Where Western History Comes Alive") exemplifies the very-marketable connection between Baum, Oz, and American identity. Host Dale Robertson, who had achieved television fame playing Western heroes, framed the segment as a story "of the Old West...of hardship, of dreams, of courage...(of) an American pioneer...part of our past, our heritage." This particular pioneer, Robertson continued, traveled West to find his fortune, and while he "didn't find his fortune...he did find a treasure of ideas that later made him the Wizard of Aberdeen." The episode itself focuses on an incident reported in *To Please a Child* where a typo in Frank's newspaper forces him into a duel with an outraged husband/father, but places this incident in the context of Frank's inability to succeed as a businessman, and his failure to recognize that "Aberdeen operates on money...Not on nonsense and fairy tales." A desolate Frank, presenting a litany of his failures to his wife, agrees. "You sure picked a dilly of a husband," he laments. Maud disagrees, citing his wonderful imagination, and Frank responds, "Imagination won't pay the bills. How long am I going to chase rainbows?" "You will find your rainbow someday," Maud insists. The episode ends with Frank and his family leaving Aberdeen for Chicago, and Robertson returns to assure the audience "Not long after he left South Dakota, Frank put his notes together and found his rainbow in a book about a little girl named Dorothy and her friends the Scarecrow, the Cowardly Lion, and the Tin Woodsman."[56]

This romanticized version of Baum reached its fullest cinematic treatment in NBC's 1990 *The Dreamer of Oz*, starring John Ritter as L. Frank Baum. This made for-tv biopic perfectly captures the myth of Baum and Oz, at the same time that it authenticates that myth by having the film told, in flashback, by Maud Baum on the eve of *The Wizard of Oz's* gala 1939 premiere. Her story begins with the young Baum, fresh off the stage, arriving late to his sister's party. His sister responds to his excuse— "there is nothing more important to me than being an actor"—with a long list of Frank's other, abandoned, "important" vocations, setting young Frank up as an impractical dreamer, flitting from one obsession to another. As the film progresses, we watch Frank fail again and again, moving his long-suffering family from city to city, job to job, ever-supported by his long-suffering wife. The only thing he seems to be good at is fantasy, and scenes of his failures are crosscut with scenes of story-telling, with Baum spinning fables (come to life through the magic of cinema) for an audience of enraptured children. His "Magic Land" offers escape from sickness and poverty; it transforms reality into fairy tale, making the real world bearable for a man who seems incapable of succeeding in it. But, in the end, the film assures us, dreams do come true, and it turns out that everyone needs a little fantasy in their lives. Baum's success proves that there is more to America than the commercial world of buying and selling, that a man who was an utter failure as a business man can live the American dream. In this film, Oz succeeds simply because it is *Oz*. It's not a product; it doesn't need to be marketed. As Maud finishes Frank's tale, a montage shows Baum's book literally flying off the shelves and into the eager hands of children. The film switches back 1939, and Maud walks into Grauman's theater to attend the premiere of MGM's *The Wizard of Oz*. The film begins to play; the "Dreamer of Oz's" dream lives on.[57]

This switch from Baum's life to MGM's film, along with *The Wizard of Aberdeen's* deployment of the rainbow as the central image for both Baum's dreams and his success, illustrates the ways in which the various strands of the "Oz brand" came together in the television broadcast years, producing a symbiotic relationship between the annual viewing ritual and the recovery and promotion of Baum and his works. Authors, journalists, illustrators, editors, and members of the Oz Club built on the film's enduring popularity to expand Oz beyond the borders of MGM's yellow brick road—and the popularity of the film ensured that there would be a market for their work. This market, in turn, attracted the attention of studios, marketers, and production managers.

CONCLUSION

The television broadcast years illuminate the attributes that made the narrative suitable to sustaining American cultural identity during the Cold War years:

- **Suitability**: MGM's *The Wizard of Oz*, as we have seen, conveyed values in-keeping with those of the culture: the Wizard's inability to give the companions anything that they didn't already possess, stems from an American populist suspicion of institutions; the companions triumph through self-reliance and combining their individual strengths (in keeping with the ideal of "togetherness"); and, in the end, Dorothy affirms the values of home and family.

- **Ritual**: The annual viewing of Oz functioned as a ritual, bringing America together in both actual living rooms and the virtual space of television, to partake of a narrative that confirmed their values and beliefs. Repeated ritual viewing renewed the community and its values over a period of more than thirty years.

- **Shared symbols and common vocabulary**: Oz provided Americans with a shared set of resonant symbols and characters—the rainbow, poppies, flying monkeys, the yellow brick road, the Wicked Witch of the West, Dorothy and her companions. Additionally the film supplied a common vocabulary of songs and dialogue. All of these functioned metonymically: from the "part" (for instance, "There's no place like home"), Americans could supply the whole (the story of Dorothy and her companions, as well as the film's message).

- **Mythic figures**: Not only did the film provide such figures in Dorothy and the Oz characters she meets along the way, but also, this period saw Baum himself mythologized as an American icon. In biographies, children's stories, newspaper articles, and television shows, Baum was cast as the "Dreamer of Oz," an artistic version of a Horatio Alger's hero, whose persistence and imagination brought him from rags to riches.

- **Believers**: A community committed to preserving the texts, values, and beliefs of the culture. In Oz's case, this community ranged from the American citizens, who embraced the dominant reading of the film's central messages, through the writers and scholars, who defended Baum's books, to the members of the International Wizard of Oz Club, who preserved Baum's work and provided a community for Oz fans.

Deriving meaning from the "culturally constituted world" of Cold War America, Oz, through MGM's *Wizard of Oz*, mythologized stories of L. Frank Baum, and Baum's original stories, transferred, to repeat Nadel's formation, the "'national imaginary'...a set of common imagery and narratives that people shared when they thought of America as a nation and themselves as citizens" to consumers. This transfer, however, was not, as

McCracken's Meaning Transfer Model suggests, a one-way street. Not only did Cold War consumers, through Oz, transfer meaning back to the culturally constituted world, but also, as we shall see in the next chapter, consumers came to use Oz to challenge the values and meanings of that world.

NOTES

1. Rachel Cosgrove's (1951) *The Hidden Valley of Oz* was the last in Reilly & Lee's regular "Oz" series; the press attempted to return to Oz in 1963 with Eloise Jarvis McGraw and Louise Lynn McGraw's *Merry Go Round in Oz*, but decided not to continue the series.
2. "The Wizard of Oz Trailer," YouTube 2:32, posted by YouTube Trailers, May 24, 2016, https://www.youtube.com/watch?v=c_Ne5g5F-WY.
3. Anna McCarthy, *The Citizen Machine: Governing by Television in 1950s America* (New York: New Press, 2010).
4. *McCall's Magazine*, May 1954, qtd. in Mary Jezer, *The Dark Ages: Life in the United States, 1945–1960* (Cambridge, MA: South End Press, 1982), 223.
5. Alan Nadel, *Television in Black and White America: Race and National Identity* (Lawrence, KS: University Press of Kansas, 2005), 16.
6. McCarthy, *Citizen Machine*, 3, 8, 10.
7. Ibid., 2.
8. Nadel, *Television*, 6.
9. McCarthy, *Citizen Machine*, 31, 21.
10. Ibid., 11.
11. Ibid., 25.
12. Ibid., 38, 41.
13. Ibid., 15, 39.
14. Ibid., 38.
15. Ibid., 39.
16. "Liza Minelli and Burt Lahr Debut of THE WIZARD OF OZ," YouTube Video, 2:29, posted by Buzz Stephens, November 2, 2015, https://www.youtube.com/watch?v=BwubJJgRLRI.
17. "Closing Credits for *Ford Star Jubilee* (1956)," YouTube Video, 2:01, posted by MattTheSaiyan, August 3, 2016, https://www.youtube.com/results?search_query=ford+star+jubilee+closing+credits.
18. Image Reproduced on ozmuseum.com, https://ozmuseum.com/blogs/news/15727188-is-this-the-road-to-iconic, accessed November 2, 2017.
19. "Minelli and Lahr."
20. Walter Aims, "A New Generation to See 'Wizard of Oz' Tonight," *Los Angeles Times*, November 3, 1956, B5.

21. "Radio-Television: The Weekend Trendex," *Variety*, November 7, 1956, 23.
22. Ibid.
23. Jack Gould, "Program Crisis," *New York Times*, November 11, 1956, 151.
24. Phillip Scheuer, "A Town Called Hollywood," *Los Angeles Times*, November 25, 1956, F2.
25. "'Wizard of Oz,'" *Variety*.
26. Aljean Harmetz, "'A Wizard of Oz': A TV Success Story," *New York Times*, March 16, 1983, C21.
27. John Fricke, Interview by Kent Drummond, February 2, 2018. See also, Fricke, "Timeless Appeal: The 'Wizard of Oz' Comes to Television Sixty Years Ago," *Baum Bugle* 60, no. 2 (August 2016): 8–15.
28. "The Oz Bowl Game," *Time*, January 1965, 86.
29. Tony Wade, "The 'Wizard of Oz' Used to Be an Annual Television Event," *Daily Republic*, November 26, 2015, http://www.dailyrepublic. com/solano-news/local-features/local-lifestyle-columns/the-wizard-of- oz-used-to-be-an-annual-television-event/, accessed October 20, 2017.
30. Ron Alexander, "A Celebration to Touch the Heart of a Tin Man," *New York Times*, August 20, 1989, 46.
31. Roland Baugham, *L. Frank Baum: The Wonderful Wizard of Oz, an Exhibition of His Published Writings in Commemoration of the Centenary of His Birth* (New York: Columbia University Libraries, 1956), 1.
32. Letter from "Oz Fan" to Russell MacFall, 1961, Box 6, Folder 1, L. Frank Baum Papers, Syracuse University Libraries Special Collections Research Center, Syracuse University Library.
33. Letter from Frances Meusel to Russell MacFall, September 26, 1961, ibid.
34. Vincent Starrett, "'The Wizard of Oz,'" *Chicago Sunday Tribune Magazine*, May 2, 1954, 225.
35. Pierre Berton, *Toronto Star*, 1957, Box 3, Folder 8, Baum Papers.
36. Herb Cain, Typescript, Box 6, Folder 1, Baum Papers.
37. *Miami Herald*, Typescript, 1958, Box 6, Folder 1, Baum Papers.
38. Ibid.
39. Ibid.
40. Berton.
41. "Dorothy the Librarian," *Life Magazine*, February 16, 1949, 47.
42. Caen; Berton.
43. Shirley Jackson, "The Lost Kingdom of Oz," *The Reporter*, December 10, 1959, 42.
44. Ibid.
45. Russell Nye, Press Conference, 1957, qtd. in *The Wizard of Oz and Who He Was*, eds. Russell Nye and Martin Gardner (East Lansing: Michigan State Press, 1957, 1994), 2.

46. *Colliers Magazine*, February 9, 1946, Box 3, Folder 8, Baum Papers.
47. Oz-Book Dust-Jackets, Oversized Folder 6, Baum Papers.
48. John Fricke, "History of the Oz Club," Paper Presented at Oz-Con, Portland, OR, June 2017.
49. *Chicago Tribune*, 1963, Baum Papers, Box 2, Folder 7.
50. John Fricke, Interview by Kent Drummond, August 17, 2017.
51. Letter Pierre Couderc to Russell MacFall, 1960, Baum Papers, Box 2, Folder 9.
52. Frank Joslyn Baum and Russell MacFall, *To Please a Child: A Biography of L. Frank Baum, Royal Historian of Oz* (Chicago: Reilly & Lee, 1961).
53. *Chicago Sun Times*, September 24, 1961, Oversized Folder 8, Baum Papers.
54. Daniel P. Mannix, "The Father of *The Wizard of Oz*," *American Heritage*, December 1964, 36.
55. Ibid., 41, 43.
56. "Death Valley Days S18 E14 The Wizard of Aberdeen," YouTube Video, 25:41, posted by This Is Invader, February 20, 2017, https://www.youtube.com/watch?v=2RJZjkAK1xg.
57. *The Dreamer of Oz*, Directed by Jack Bender, Bedrock Productions, 1990; YouTube Video, 131:15, posted by Steve Klimetti, January 29, 2018, https://www.youtube.com/watch?v=T1wveL698Ig.

CHAPTER 5

Expanding the Map:
Oz in the Public Domain

Not surprisingly, Disney was the first studio that sought to capitalize on the success of CBS's *Wizard of Oz* broadcast. Walt himself must have been fuming over the fact that MGM had beaten him to the Oz goldmine—not once, but twice, and less than a year after CBS's first screening of *The Wizard of Oz*, an episode of the studio's popular Mickey Mouse Club featured the Mouseketeers pitching a new Disney-Oz product, *The Rainbow Road to Oz*. They begin by staking the studio's claim on Oz, reminding the audience that Disney—with the exception of *The Wonderful Wizard of Oz*—owned the rights to all of Baum's Oz books.[1] They then move to position and sell their new Oz story to Baum's and MGM's established consumers, promising them that they will see old friends—Dorothy, the Scarecrow, and the Cowardly Lion—and meet new ones, including the Patchwork Girl and Ozma, and offering this new tale as a continuation of *The Wizard of Oz* in which Dorothy and her friends travel to the Emerald City to set things right and get a heart for the Patchwork Girl. Finally, and perhaps most significantly for a study of Oz's sustainability, the Mouseketeers' sample scenes build on audiences' attachment to and memory of the MGM film. Numbers such as "Patches," in which the Patchwork Girl and the Scarecrow sing and dance down the yellow brick road, and the episode's finale, "Rainbow Road to Oz," a song that draws heavily on both "Follow the Yellow Brick Road," and "Over the Rainbow," strongly echo the older film's narrative structure, choreography, and musical style.

© The Author(s) 2018
K. Drummond et al., *The Road to Wicked*,
https://doi.org/10.1007/978-3-319-93106-7_5

OPEN TEXT, OPEN SEASON

Despite the Mouseketeers' fervent pitch, *The Rainbow Road to Oz* never materialized, for reasons known only to Walt Disney himself. What we do know is that when Disney lost his monopoly on Oz in 1960 (as Baum's second Oz book, *The Land of Oz*, entered the public domain), other studios were ready to provide consumers with "more Oz," and many of them deployed the Mouseketeers' marketing tactics in their own campaigns. As more and more Baum books passed into public domain—the last, *The Magic of Oz*, lost its copyright status in 1995— the "liberation" of new Oz characters and adventures enabled producers to introduce a flurry of new Oz products to an eager American public. Once in the public domain, Oz truly became an "open" text, an ever-expanding site of continuing adventures. Between 1960 and 1998, six feature-length films, two short specials, and seven seasons of cartoon series, aimed at children and the family audience, played on America's screens, while various marionette shows and stage versions of Oz toured the country. Providing consumers with a steady stream of "Oz experiences," these shows depended on viewers' previous loyalty to and knowledge of Oz, marketing themselves as supplements to the annual broadcast ritual. Each of these brand extensions held out the promise of more—infinitely more—Oz.

Shirley Temple's Storybook Hour was the first to take advantage of public domain access to Baum's work, and in *The Land of Oz* (1960), the child star introduced the show by invoking the expansiveness of Baum's creation. "In just a moment," Temple promised viewers, "a magic word will transform your television set into the marvelous land created by L. Frank Baum, the land of talking flowers, and flying furniture, that happy land where no one can die and everyone enjoys himself forever. The magic word is Oz."[2] Host Michael Gross introduced 1987's *Dorothy Meets Ozma of Oz* in a similar fashion, "Now those of you who saw the movie *The Wizard of Oz* have probably wondered, as I did, 'Did Dorothy ever return to Oz?' Well, believe it or not, there are over forty different stories about Dorothy's adventures in the magical place of Munchkins and witches, and I am happy to be able to share one of them with you."[3] The fact that Oz was a "marvelous land" full of infinite wonders—one that had already inspired "over forty stories"—assured consumers that there was more to the tale than MGM had told, and that these continuations would offer them an authentic Oz experience.

These productions authenticated their tales by explicitly connecting them to *The Wizard of Oz*. A generation brought up on the MGM film expected specific features from this magical land, and a new adventure needed to extend from the old. The theme of "rejoining old friends," and "meeting delightful new characters," as Shirley Temple puts it, is carried over from the Baum and Thompson prefaces. These shows promise that viewers will "meet old friends and new." In addition to incorporating established characters, these productions often contain a recap connecting the new tale to the old. Sometimes the host explicitly invokes the familiar tale, as does Bobby McFerrin in 1996's televised version of *The Wizard of Oz on Ice*, when he tells the audience, "You remember how it began. It was summer, Kansas;" sometimes, as does Shirley Temple, they nudge the audience's memory; they will join "the Scarecrow, still as proud as ever of his great brains, and the Tin Woodman with his gentle, tender heart."[4] Sometimes, it's Dorothy who recounts the story. In 1964's *Return to Oz*, she asks Toto, "Do you remember Oz? That wonderful land we went to?" and in the opening sequence to 1974's *Journey Back to Oz*, she observes, on "a day just like this I was swept away to Oz."[5] And the Oz that Dorothy, her friends, and the audience returns to conforms to what the consumers expect from Oz by deploying a visual and narrative vocabulary established by the MGM film: the flat plains and farmhouses of Kansas, the art-deco Emerald City, Glinda's glittery pink gown, green sparkles, and ubiquitous rainbows, meeting the Scarecrow, traveling down the yellow brick road, Toto chasing chickens or cats, a version of the "Over the Rainbow" song—to both appropriate and authenticate the Oz experience.

Journey Back to Oz, the most elaborate of the broadcast-era's line-extensions, exemplifies these productions' desire to exploit consumers' attachment to the film. "Remember," the trailer asks, "Judy Garland and the yellow brick road? Now Liza Minnelli recreates the role of Dorothy." The film also featured the voices of MGM-alums, Margaret Hamilton and Mickey Rooney; the casting of Minnelli, Hamilton, and Rooney indicates a deliberate invocation of nostalgia, one that extends this film's audience beyond the "kiddies" targeted in many of the other productions. "Bring the kids, bring yourself, bring the whole family," the trailer urged, "and journey back to Oz."[6] In these early post-MGM magical Ozes, Oz functions, mostly lackadaisically, as a conveyor of ethics and values; like any family-oriented show or children's cartoon, the specials modeled appropriate (and inappropriate) behavior, from the gentle early schoolyard lessons of 1996–1997's *Oz Kids*, through dealing with some pre-teen angst in Turner's 1990 animated series, to the slightly more advanced explorations of good and evil in *Journey Back to Oz*.

Over the years, MGM, and later Turner Broadcasting, also mined their own product, re-releasing, re-packaging, and remediating the film. In 1970 and 1972, the studio sent it to theaters again as a children's matinee; in 1987, a Royal Shakespeare Company stage production appeared; in 1989, they accompanied all of the hoopla surrounding the film's 50th anniversary with a touring production of *The Wizard of Oz, Live!*, and 1995 saw a children's benefit concert production. In 1994, *The Wizard of Oz on Ice* toured, before premiering as a television broadcast in 1996. In 1998, the last of the broadcast years, a remastered version of the film was released for the home market. And in 1991, Oz provided the theme for the MGM Grand Hotel in Las Vegas as the casino sought to attract baby-boomer tourists to an adult theme park that allowed them to relive their childhood memories. The studio also licensed a growing range of products and merchandise, ranging from lunchboxes and happy meal toys, through dolls and collectibles, to real ruby slippers.

The majority of these offerings were not interested in adding a new dimension to the myth, and none, by themselves, were particularly notable. Taken together, however, they contributed significantly to the narrative's cultural sustainability; the MGM remediations offered consumers the chance to re-experience the film, and the products allowed them to bring it into their homes and wardrobes. The films, television shows, and stage productions provided audiences with new experiences of Oz to accompany the ritual annual viewing of the MGM film. As the repeated consumption of *The Wizard of Oz* wove its narrative, images, characters, and dialogue into the fabric of American culture, these line-extensions added depth and breadth to Oz, ensuring that the myth did not become ossified, available only to quotation and parody. Furthermore, the new narratives "kept up" with visual and musical styles, added contemporary humor, and translated Oz into new media forms. Television specials and traveling shows added "events" and created buzz. Cartoon series, airing daily or weekly, provided ongoing Oz touch points. By continuing Oz, they both met and created consumer demand; but they did not engage with Oz beyond appropriating and extending it. Instead, they targeted established, nostalgic consumers who by now had children of their own—children parked in front of the television set or at a children's matinee.

CORPORATE, CORPOREAL, AND COMEDIC OZ

With Oz so firmly established in America's cultural landscape, America's corporations came calling, appropriating Oz and its characters in an onslaught of commercials. Glinda and the Wizard feasted the hungry companions on Crispy Wheats and Raisins; the Scarecrow hawked Lily White Cornmeal, Club Biscuits sent the characters down the yellow brick road; the Energizer Bunny battled the Wicked Witch of the West; and the Tin Man worked for both Esso Oil and the American Heart Association.[7] For the next 20 years, Oz also lured consumers to new Oz-themed experiences. Ice Capades, Ringling Brothers, and Weeki Wachi Springs all offered Oz attractions in the 1960s, with Mardi Gras and the Rose Parade following suit. From theme parks to educational programming, Oz was never far from America's corporate consciousness. Even Seattle became the Emerald City in 1980. Towns and cities capitalized on their Oz connections—or created them—to boost local tourism. These included Chittenango, New York's Yellow Brick Road; Chesterton, Indiana's Oz Festival; Liberal, Kansas's Dorothy's House and the Land of Oz Museum; and Chicago's Oz Park, to name a few.

While these real-life locations may have been constructed as tourist opportunities, they also provided consumers with a chance to become *embodied* in a new version of Oz, to view authentic Oz artifacts, and purchase a little bit of Oz to take home with them. Here, consumers could *immerse* themselves in their own Oz experience. The most sophisticated example of this type of opportunistic Oz, The Land of Oz theme park, constructed by the Carolina Caribbean Corporation, opened to the public in 1970. CCC's development team clearly saw Oz as a commercial opportunity and, thus, spent five million dollars building an elaborate and unique Oz experience, branded by the slogan, "You don't just see it! You live it!" The Land of Oz was an immediate success, drawing consumers from areas well beyond the local market. The park garnered widespread publicity, winning Washington DC's *Daily News'* "Outstanding Tourist Attraction" award in 1970, and its first season attracted over 400,000 visitors, including several celebrities.

The park's success stemmed from its appeal to consumers who wanted an embodied Oz experience. The Land of Oz, the attraction's website observes, "wasn't about roller coasters; it was about creating an emotional experience" by allowing visitors to experience MGM's version of the tale through a form of participatory cinema.[8] Upon entering the park, consumers passed through Dorothy's house, trod down a road paved with 44,000 custom-glazed yellow bricks, and met all of the companions along the way before arriving at the Emerald City, where they could dine, shop, explore the Oz museum, and view one of the half-hourly "Magic Moment" shows before riding in the Wizard's Balloon. Unfortunately, 1975 was a disastrous year for the attraction: a fire destroyed many of its exhibits, and key artifacts were stolen from its museum. The parent company did not reinvest in the park, and it fell into decay and disuse. Although the park officially closed in 1980, it continues to host festivals and special events.

Deserted, over-grown, its houses listing and its magical trees weathered—yet hauntingly beautiful—the bare, ruined Land of Oz provides an apt image for what might have happened to the Oz narrative had it been confined to the types of product extensions we have discussed thus far in this chapter. The family shows and ads seeking merely to capitalize on the success of the MGM film, rather than expanding the narrative, would not have been enough to ensure the narrative's cultural sustainability beyond the broadcast years. The Wizard of Oz Club would have continued its work, and true fans of Oz would have continued to find and explore Oz, but Oz itself might have ceased to be a part of a living cultural tradition. Furthermore, as we observed earlier, when a narrative becomes fixed into a single artifact that sets expectations for all other instances of it, it risks losing its ability to adapt to new audiences, contexts, media, and technologies—the very things that assure its cultural sustainability. Thus, the MGM film and its ritual repetition were both a blessing and a curse. It wove Oz into the cultural fabric and implanted it in the memories of a generation. But by so doing, it also made it available for allegory and parody, modes that, as Hans Robert Jauss observed, often signal that a narrative or genre has lost its cultural relevance.[9]

The first parodic use of Oz occurs relatively early in the broadcast years with Rankin and Bass's 1961 animated series, *Tales of the Wizard of Oz*. In the tradition of *The Rocky and Bullwinkle Show's* "Fractured Fairy Tales," then in its last season, *Tales of the Wizard of Oz* retells the film's narrative with its tongue firmly in its cheek. The series' theme song sets the tone: "Three sad souls—Oh me! Oh my!—no brains, no heart and rather shy. The wizard will fix it in that funny old place, the land of Oz."[10] *Tales of the Wizard of Oz* expects viewers to recognize echoes of the musical film and revel in the show's send-up of MGM's spectacle. In the first episode, the ironic narrator reveals that the wizard is a card shark, and ruby slippers become ruby red rutabaga seeds—which produce Munchkins instead of rutabagas. As the companions meet up and Dorothy joins them, the point of the narrative remains the parody, an Oz exposed as not magical and enchanting but quaint, anachronistic—"a funny old place." As the broadcast years continued, Oz increasingly provided subject matter for parody: Jerry Lewis become the *Wizard of Ooze; Mad Magazine* visited Oz multiple times; and the characters and situations became favorite vehicles for political satire.

The use of Oz in political satire also signals the narrative's turn to allegory. While the fact that a tale is available for allegory speaks to its cultural significance, the act of allegory attempts to fix a story's meaning outside of the tale itself. Oz had always had what J. R. R. Tolkien calls "applicability:" the ability to speak profoundly about cultural and personal issues. Yet once Oz is allegorized, its meaning lies not in what Tolkien termed the "freedom of the reader" but in "the tyranny of the author."[11] As if they had read this dictum, authors of self-help and religious guidebooks turned to the Oz books as an almost-Biblical text, explicating them as a road map to emotional and spiritual health. Oz was offered as an allegory of office relationships. It even served to relay public health messages: *Trouble in Oz* was a cautionary drug tale; and *The Wizard of A.I.D.s.* killed the Wicked Witch with a giant condom.

While these parodies and allegories are very amusing, they speak to a narrative in danger of becoming fixed. They rely on consumers' knowledge of a single instance of the narrative, the MGM film; the fact that *The Wizard of Oz* was available to allegory and parody shows both that it was part of the cultural vocabulary and that consumers had achieved distance from it. However, as long as the film remained *the* Oz, any producer who tried to re-envision or re-consume Oz, to engage with it, encountered what Jeff Silverman called in the *Chicago Tribune* a "yellow-brick-road-block" that had "clicked its heels in a way that seemed to make the route to the Emerald City forever impassable to the filmmakers who tried to follow it."[12] As the baby boomers grew up and sought to recreate Oz for a new generation, they predictably encountered this anti-re-consumption barrier. The tale of Oz from 1975 to 2018 is, in effect, the tale of a tug-of-war between MGM and Baum purists on the one side, and, on the other, the writers, directors, and producers who adapted and remediated Oz to new genres and media, often questioning the values and aesthetics of the narrative's founding texts. This latter group, however, beginning with *The Wiz*, is key to the narrative's cultural sustainability. In "making it new," they rescued Oz from allegory, parody, and the children's market, keeping the narrative alive after the broadcast years.

EASING ON DOWN THE ROAD

As numerous accounts reveal, *The Wiz* almost wasn't. This all-black *Wizard of Oz* was the brainchild of producer Ken Harper, who— unlike Mervyn LeRoy, for whom Oz was an end in itself—originally saw Oz as merely an opportunity, a vehicle for a "contemporary show with black music as its focus." "If you examine the charts today," he told *Black Enterprise's* Peter Bailey, "four of five of the top ten songs are black. So, I felt that if we had a show with good black music, it would go over. I ended up using *The Wizard of Oz* because it is in the public domain and hadn't been revived since the 1939 film."[13] In spite of this rather off-hand comment, Harper must have also taken into account the tale's popularity and brand recognition, as well as the fact that the MGM film was an established part of America's cultural furniture. He clearly had a good sense of what made a product marketable; in fact, he first thought of realizing his black *Wizard of Oz* as a television special, marketed with the star power of Flip Wilson, Bill Cosby, and Pearl Bailey. When the television show did not pan out, Harper brought in a different kind of star power: Julliard graduate and established musician Charlie Smalls to compose the music and lyrics, and rising playwright William F. Brown to write the book. After previewing in Chicago, *The Wiz* opened at the Majestic Theater on January 5, 1975. It posted a closing notice the next day.[14]

Harper's marketing concept—the decision to use a popular and established tale to remediate black music for a mainstream audience— may have been sound. But at least as far as New York's establishment critics were concerned, *The Wiz* slammed straight into the yellow brick roadblock. The ghost of Baum and MGM, race, and cultural ownership haunted all of these reviews, raising questions about whether or not Oz could or should be adapted into an entirely new context. How far from the "original" could a producer stray? And, if the answer is, "not far," in the end, how sustainable could the narrative be? *The Wiz* was immediately categorized as a "black musical," not only was it an all-black production, but also in its music, dialogue, and style, it translated its source material into black vernacular. Some critics saw this move as simply pointless. "William F. Brown's book," Douglas Watts observed, "has the primary purpose of couching the familiar story in jive talk, which allows for some easy jokes. It doesn't exactly twist the familiar story out of shape, but it doesn't enhance it either."[15] Others, such as Rex Reed, saw it "designed and delivered by people with larceny in their hearts.....Garbage is garbage no matter what color it is and this all-black sacrilege is at the top of the rubbish pile. Next to bombing the White House, I can't imagine a better way to start a race war then to denigrate *The Wizard of Oz* and everything it stands for in the minds and hearts of children of all ages. Descendants of L. Frank Baum should sue. Judy Garland fans should picket the theater where this monstrosity is playing."[16] Clive Barnes more subtly opined that "fantasy is only enthralling when it is rooted in experience," and the *Wiz* had failed to enthrall.[17]

At best, critics saw a production that had "vitality and a very evident and gorgeous sense of style," one that was "so enormously good natured, spectacular looking and slickly done that is (was) hard to resist," "vulgar" "in the word's primary definition... 'of or belonging to the common people or general public.'"[18] But, with the exception of *Cue Magazine's* Marilyn Stasio, they saw its re-consumption of Oz as either a gimmick or an abuse; Stasio alone seems to have recognized Oz's potential to be reimagined, adapted, and sustained: "When L. Frank Baum dreamed up his children's classic...he surely never had visions like the ones you'll see in this fantastic new musical. But Oz is whatever your imagination wants it to be, and a lot of talented, creative minds want it to be a trip to remember. All the essentials of the beloved story of Dorothy and her friends are retained," but "every character and situation has been given a sly, hip and very funny contemporary twist. Maybe this isn't exactly the Wiz that was, but it is the Wiz that is, and it's a wow."[19]

By the end of 1975, most of the critical establishment had come around to Stasio's point of view, and the story of how that happened demonstrates the essential role marketing plays in cultural sustainability. Harper reports that, in spite of the closing notice, the show's producers determined that *The Wiz* was worth fighting for: "We decided to bring in marketing techniques, perfected by films, to the legitimate theatre.

We knew what audience we were aiming for—blacks of all ages, moviegoers, young whites, chic whites, people who listen to the top 40 radio stations, families. We used heavy radio saturation and the black press, who gave us extensive coverage."[20] By so doing, *The Wiz* worked around Broadway's cultural gatekeepers to reach a new consumer base; "spurred on by a heavy response to the show by the black community" (by the sixth week, the show had more than doubled its box-office intake and could cover its weekly expenses), Fox "put up $120,000 to buy 101 commercial spots."[21] And then, on April 20, 1975, a little over three months after critics had nearly signed its death warrant, *The Wiz* dominated at the Tony Awards, garnering seven statues, including Best Musical and Best Director. Stamped with the American Theatre Wing's seal of approval, *The Wiz* "began to attract the established theatre-going, middle-class whites."[22] As a result, the show that almost closed as soon as it had opened enjoyed a four-year run on Broadway and a successful and lucrative national tour. Furthermore, the all-black *Wizard of Oz* that had so riled its original reviewers became the first major new Oz experience since the MGM's film—and a crucial cultural touchpoint in Oz's sustainability.

While "Oz" got in the way of *The Wiz's* original reception, Oz definitely sold it in its post-Tony career. "Somewhere over the rainbow," the *Chicago Tribune* observed in November 1976, "the man who wrote *The Wizard of Oz* should feel terrific about a Broadway transformation called *The Wiz*."[23] The show's translation of Baum and MGM into something new, modern, and edgy was lauded as "not a spoof of *The Wizard of Oz*, but a loving translation."[24] "A carnival of fun...it grins from the soul, sizzles with vitality, and flaunts the gaudy hues of an exploding rainbow."[25] "Part *Star Trek*, part black history, part urban blues, part Emerald City looking glass, and the rest is pure magic."[26] Additionally, as the show gained popularity, Oz translated *The Wiz* from all-black musical to universal fairy tale; the play's director, Geoffrey Holder continually played down—in fact, denied—the show's African American roots. "It's an old fairy tale about the Wizard of Oz.... The message is 'there's no place like home. It's just a nice fairy tale with a black cast.... It has nothing to do...with me black, you white." "It's a universal story of growing up—everyone, black, red or green goes through it."[27] Later critics agreed: "*The Wiz* ignores stereotypes and hair-splitting concerns," stated the *Chicago Tribune*, "concentrating on the obviously universal message—self-reliance."[28] As a fairy tale, as an Oz experience, *The Wiz* could then be marketed to the same cross-generational audience targeted by MGM in 1939, "a big audience of all ages and colors."[29] Promising to satisfy consumers' "cross-cultural, trans-familial urge for family entertainment," *The Wiz* became "one show you've got to see, and if you don't let the children see it, you belong with Evilene (the Wicked Witch)." [30]

From "dubious legit prospect to standing room only smash," *The Wiz* successfully hurtled MGM's yellow-brick-roadblock to invest Oz with new life and new excitement.[31] It was an *event* rather than a repeated ritual; it promised to add a new and flourishing branch to the Oz tree; its own film, its own merchandise, its own endorsements; perhaps even, Harper dreamed, its own television show. That branch, however, soon withered, when 1978's much-anticipated film version of the show flopped resoundingly. Despite a big budget, an all-star cast, and the creative talents of Sidney Lumet and Quincy Jones, the film is simply bad. While an argument can—and was—made that the film's box-office suffered from a racist distribution scheme, critical reception to the film indicates that it also suffered from both the miscasting of a thirty-something Diana Ross as Dorothy (referred to as "terminal bankability") and its attempt to "bleach out" the tale to appeal to a white audience.[32] While they may have been right about Diana Ross—after all, if Oz's perceived universality derives, in part, from its coming-of-age narrative, an adult Dorothy definitely stands in the way of that narrative—we would argue that the problem with the film version of *The Wiz* is not so much its "bleaching" of the Broadway show as it is the allegorizing of the tale. Screenwriter Joel Schumacher, who like Ross was a proponent of Erhard Seminar Training, transformed Brown's transformation of Baum into a textbook for the movement. As an allegory of EST, the film, in spite of its marvelous sets and spectacular production numbers, lost its wonder and magic. The Broadway show beckoned the imagination and invited identification. The film, from the first emergence of the Munchkins from playground graffiti, demanded decoding. As such, it ran straight back into the roadblock of both its Broadway original and MGM. "*The Wiz*," *The Globe and Mail* observed, "was street-smart, hip, urbane and sexy; it capitalized on all of the things *The Wizard of Oz* was not...the movie capitalizes on its capital."[33] After the film, *The Wiz's* moment pretty much ended; a 1984 Broadway revival lasted for a mere 20 performances (including previews), and, apart from sporadic school and community productions, the show remained out of the public eye, until *Wicked* revived interest in all things Oz, paving the way for 2015's *The Wiz, Live!*

RETURN TO OZ

It was seven years before there was another mass-market attempt to re-imagine and re-invigorate the Oz narrative, and as the original Oz generation grew up, and as the baby boomers increasingly questioned Cold War truths about America and its founding myths, there was a corresponding fear that Oz and all that it represented—childhood, innocence, wonder, magic—was in danger of being lost. In 1980, the same year that The Land of Oz closed its Oz-emblazoned gate to the public, an otherwise entirely forgettable Oz special, *Thanksgiving in Oz*, introduced what was to become a recurring theme of loss and return in post-70s Oz narratives. If MGM offered Oz *to* the young at heart, *Thanksgiving in Oz* used Oz to recall adults to their true selves: "Three magic words that each kid knows, Christmas, toys, and Oz...But kids grow up and soon forget those words of long-ago.... The child they were will not forget, Christmas, toys and Oz. You'll always have a child inside, with Christmas, toys and Oz."[34]

This desire to return to childlike innocence, wonder and belief characterizes many of the films and television shows produced the 1980s, dubbed by Andrew Britton as the era of Reaganite entertainment—perhaps best illustrated in the films of George Lucas and Stephen Spielberg—which also encompassed a revival of genre films, the return of heroes, clear-cut distinctions between right and wrong, and an emphasis on spectacle.[35] Given the popularity of these themes, the 1980s would seem to have been the perfect time for a mass-market, big screen return to Oz, and Disney Studios clearly thought so. In 1983, the studio began production on *Return to Oz*—more than twenty-five years after the Mouseketeers had promoted *The Rainbow Road to Oz* to Walt. They put the project in the hands of Lucas protégé Walter Murch. Like Mervin LeRoy before him, Murch chose the Oz project based on his own early attachment to Baum's books—and he was fully aware of the monumental roadblock standing in the way of his new Oz. "The '39 film," he told Sliverman, "is part of the mental furniture of everyone's life.... You can never hit the note of (that) film again." Instead, Murch said, "What we tried to do is to go further down and further up the piano and find another note."[36] In *Return to Oz*, then, Murch sought not a continuation but a variation: a chord that would satisfy consumers steeped in the MGM film, even as it revived Oz for a generation seeking a return to childlike wonder, and brought a new Oz to new consumers.

Disney Studios was also not unaware of the challenges any return to Oz would face in a market steeped in nearly 30 years of annual televised trips down the yellow brick road. "The most difficult marketing problem will be to get the audience to come with an open mind," studio president Richard Berger admitted.[37] Disney executive Jeffrey Katzenberg agreed: "The pitfall is expectations."[38] As such, advance marketing for the film sought to manage consumers' expectations—while still playing on their nostalgia for and attachment to the MGM film—and trade on the Disney brand as a guarantor of quality family entertainment. The trailer begins with music that echoes the tornado/witch themes from *The Wizard of Oz* and the announcement: "This summer, Walt Disney Pictures presents a motion picture fantasy adventure beyond your fondest imagination," promising, "you will be transported miraculously back to the enchanted land of Oz, that magical kingdom beloved by young and old for generations." The visual that accompanies this promise, however, is of Dorothy, played by nine-year-old Fairuza Balk—who is most definitely *not* Judy Garland—picking up fragments of a ruined yellow brick road. The narrator continues, "You'll share with Dorothy Gale the shock of finding everything changed." But, he assures us, "You'll delight in her discovery of four wonderful new friends." "This," we are told, "is the Oz you haven't seen before, and this is the Oz you will want to visit again and again."[39]

In spite of the studio's attempt to manage expectations, reviewer after reviewer started with the MGM film, and found Disney's Oz offering lacking. Jay Boyar, in the *Orlando Sentinel*, accused the studio of duping audiences, "All over America," he observed, "well-meaning parents will grab their kids by their hands and take them to see *Return to Oz*. These parents, fondly remembering *The Wizard of Oz* of 1939 will hope to relive their youthful fantasies and share them with their children. And the kids, many of whom have seen *The Wizard of Oz* on TV, will be anticipating pure enchantment: a joyous ride on a cinematic carpet. But the sad reality is that *Return to Oz* is a disappointment for kids of all ages."[40] Instead of enchantment, most reviewers found a "menacing world," "whose gritty realistic shades" compared poorly with MGM's vibrant technicolor—"a dour, leaden downright frightening film about

Dorothy's return to a post-nuclear Oz."[41] Reviewers also lamented the loss of MGM's beloved lesson, "there is no place like home," complaining either that the film had no lesson at all, or that it had the wrong lesson, that in fact the lesson was "it's dangerous to return to Oz," a lesson that perhaps, they opined, the filmmakers themselves should have heeded.[42]

Return to Oz is a complex touchpoint in the history of Oz's cultural sustainability. It was the first big-budget cinematic attempt to reimagine Oz rather than simply ride on the coattails of the MGM film. In 1985, this attempt was, on the whole, woefully unsuccessful. The original audiences seem to have agreed with the critics, at least if box-office receipts are any indication. Costing nearly 26 million to make, the film returned only just a little over 11 million of that investment on its initial US release; it was the biggest box-office disappointment of the summer. Consumers, it seems, were not ready to accept Murch's grim variation on Oz. What makes *Return to Oz* interesting in terms of cultural sustainability, however, is that not all consumers dismissed the film. In fact, some argued that this Oz was much more true to the "real" Oz than MGM's brighter, more musical fairyland. *Chicago Tribune* writer, Rachel Jones, asserted, "Anybody who criticizes 'Return to Oz' because it's not upbeat enough…could not have read the original Oz books. If they did, they must be to old to remember those books." I "would testify before a congressional subcommittee that those things could scare the eyeshadow off of Boy George."[43] A twelve-year-old Oz fan hoped that the film, truer to Baum, would help "readers and viewers rediscover the real story of Oz."[44] Other reviewers opined that the film was merely "ahead of its time," lost in the "harsh economics of a mass-market medium," destined to "be discovered in ten years" and "become a cult favorite."[45]

It turns out that this second group of consumers and critics were right: *Return to Oz* has been rediscovered and has become a cult favorite in the current market, and its darker Oz does look more "authentic" than MGMs bright-hued sound set. (Similarly, many consumers will respond that they prefer *Wicked* to *The Wizard of Oz* because the former is more "realistic".) When it was first released, *Return to Oz* may have looked like a dead-end, a film that crashed on the great yellow-brick-roadblock. Yet it became an important touchpoint in the narrative's sustainability. In fact, what the reviewers at the time seem to have missed in their condemnation of *Return to Oz's* post-nuclear, ruined Oz, is that the film itself actually centers on the question of Oz's cultural sustainability. *Return to Oz* begins with Dorothy back in Kansas, where all the adults around her insist that Oz "simply doesn't exist."[46] Aunt Em orders her "not to talk about Oz," forcing her to admit—if not believe, "it's just my imagination," and, when Dorothy persists in her fantasies, her aunt takes her to be cured by a doctor specializing in electro-therapy. Treatment is scheduled to "control the excess currents" in her brain, to get "unpleasant dreams out of your head. And when you wake up, you'll never be bothered by them again."

When Dorothy awakens in Oz, she, as the trailer proclaims, "is shocked to find everything changed;" but she still *recognizes* it, *remembers* it, and is able to read the clues to successfully navigate the Deadly Desert and follow the fragments of the yellow brick road to the ruined Emerald City. Here, Dorothy finds not a living city, but crumbling stone buildings and people turned to statues, including her companions the Tin Woodsman and the Cowardly Lion. Her beloved Scarecrow is missing. Captured by Mombi and confined to a tower until her head is big enough to be added to Mombi's collection of interchangeable heads, Dorothy finds fragments and abandoned pieces of Old Oz, including Jack Pumpkinhead and a Gump head; she assembles the flying Gump from these pieces and the companions escape to the Mountain of the Gnome King, intent on rescuing the Scarecrow.

The Gnome King has robbed the Emerald City and turned Oz into artifacts—statues and ornaments. Happy in his rule over an appropriated and ossified Oz, and fearing Dorothy, whose memories of Oz pose a threat to that rule, he offers to send her back to Kansas. "When you get back," he promises, "you will never think of Oz again.... There is no place like home." But, in *Return to Oz*, at least at this moment, home is the wrong place; if Dorothy goes back to Kansas, or if she fails to correctly identify which ornament is the Scarecrow in the Gnome King's guessing game, and becomes an ornament herself, "there will be no one left who remembers Oz." But Dorothy does not go home, and she does remember Oz, a memory that allows her to correctly read the ornaments in the Gnome King's gallery and rescue her friends.

Dorothy may arrive in a dour and gritty Oz, but she restores that Oz to vivid celebratory technicolor, revives her friends, and goes back to Kansas with the promise of endless returns to the land that she rescued from being lost to memory. With *Return to Oz*, "return" came to mean much more than "go back to," and audiences were asked to remember more than a tale. This return, despite the critics' dismayed reading of the film, actually resurrects a colorful, affirming, fully-revived Oz, if only for a few moments at the end of the film. Thus, although often identified with "Dark Oz," *Return to Oz* is not really in that tradition, although it reacts to the cultural environment that produced it.

Oz Grows Up

The first instance of Dark Oz is arguably Phillip Jose Farmer's 1982 novel, *A Barnstormer in Oz*, and Farmer's novel is a good place to begin an examination of the role authors and the written tradition played in Oz's continuing cultural sustainability.[47] While written versions of Oz generally lack the mass-market appeal and reach of film, television, or stage, they still represent a continuing engagement with the story, and they still contribute to its narrative growth. Furthermore, as we saw in our discussion of the Oz library wars, authors played a key part in Baum's defense, and Oz has clearly continued to influence writers and their works over the years. Prior to *Barnstormer*, Oz and its characters had been incorporated into non-Oz narratives, such as Bradbury's "The Exiles" and Robert Heinlein's *The Number of the Beast*, made guest-appearances in other universes, such as *Cycle Toon's* "Hogg in Oz" or DC Comics, Supergirl-"Oz" crossover, "The Mysterious Motr of Doov," and provided symbolic imagery and resonance for authors such as Keith Lamar, Poul Anderson, and Farmer himself. *Barnstormer*, however, marks the beginning of stand-alone, full-blown literary re-consumptions of Oz. Farmer—who read Baum's books in 1925, as a child of seven, was a young adult when the film premiered, and nearly forty at the beginning of the television broadcast years— clearly engages with Baum rather than MGM and definitely, as the reviews note, aims at an adult audience. His novel is neither for the young nor the young at heart. This return to Oz features not Dorothy, but her son, Hank Stover, and he is brought there not by magic, or Ozma, or even a random tornado, but by a shadowy government engaged in dubious experiments and military operations.

Farmer presents his Oz as the "real" Oz, and throughout the book, Stover is in dialogue with Baum, who, he claims, stole the story from his mother and fictionalized it. He constantly "corrects" Baum's false picture of Oz. Stover chronicles a sci-fi Oz: futuristic technology displaces magic, and politics take the place of adventure. This Oz is definitely not utopian; it features forced population control, a political big-brother system, exploitation, execution, and war. Glinda may be "good," but good is relative; she is certainly ruthless. If Oz is a place of happy endings, this happy ending is at best qualified; Glinda may triumph, but about the best thing you can say about her is that she is "better" than the Wicked Witch. Oz here—as flat as Kansas—is not an escape. In the end, little separates Oz and an equally problematic USA; both lands engage in dubious political and military maneuvers, both sets of leaders operate to protect themselves and their regimes, and both sides of the rainbow are riddled with treachery and violence.

As a writer in the *Baum Bugle* concluded, "Farmer's vision of Oz is definitely not ours," a sentiment echoed in *The Intergalactic Reporter*, "Baum's Oz was wondrous, fanciful, and sparkling with fun; Farmer's Oz has all the rocking jollity and elfin charm of *The Texas Chainsaw Massacre*."[48] Nevertheless, *A Barnstormer in Oz* introduced a strand of the Oz narrative that is crucial to the myth's cultural sustainability: revisionist Oz, an Oz that purports to offer consumers the "real Oz," the truth behind the myth. In addition to attracting those adults who are not interested in remaining young at heart to Oz, revisionist Oz also makes the narrative available for production and consumption as a high, rather than popular or mass culture, artifact. Revisionist Ozes can be taken seriously.

Before Geoff Ryman's 1992 novel *Was*, Oz books, from *The Wizard of Oz* to *A Barnstormer in Oz* had been categorized and reviewed as genre offerings—juveniles, fairy tales, science fiction, and fantasy; *Was* entered the market as literary fiction and was reviewed as such in prominent publications. Published near the end of the broadcast era, the novel, in Ryman's words "treat(s) a series of cultural icons—the Baum book, the film, and this television ritual of watching as historical facts within an historical novel."[49] As such, *Was* is both a meditation on Oz's cultural significance and a re-consumption of the narrative. If Farmer returned to Oz to give us the "real" Oz, Ryman provided consumers with the narrative's origins, the real-life Dorothy, whose escape from an unbearable Kansas into the Land of "Was," inspired Baum, inspired the film, and "gave millions of children …entrée to a magical realm where they might temporarily forget the harsh realities of daily life."[50] Ryman intertwines Dorothy's story with those of Judy Garland's early, also traumatic, childhood and Jonathan, an AIDS patient obsessed with the idea of Oz. Enriched with allusions to the book and the film, often echoing both in theme, tone, and style, *Was* is, in the words of Erin McLeod, "a culture bearing book," one that attests to and examines Oz's lasting imprint on the baby-boomer generation.[51] In it, Oz becomes the occasion for a "mythic meditation on the enduring power of fantasy and art and on the loss of innocence…a moving lament for lost childhoods."[52] Oz here— place, book, film—represents a haunting, a nostalgia for a lost past that never was, the quest to recover, "a now made tender."[53]

Just as Farmer gave consumers an adult, political "real" Oz, Ryman reimagined Baum's magic land for an adult audience uninterested in making the kind of sentimental return advocated by *Thanksgiving in Oz* and *Return to Oz*, but who, like Jonathan, were on their own quest for a "back then," for the "magic of healing and wholeness."[54] Both novels offered an Oz without green glasses. They served a cultural moment in which old myths and old truths were being questioned, deconstructed, and overturned, freeing Oz from technicolor and optimism and making it available for serious explorations of family, social, and religious structures, paving the way for what was to prove to be one of the most important texts in the ongoing history of Oz, Gregory Maguire's 1995 novel, *Wicked: The Life and Times of the Wicked Witch of the West.* Maguire, like Farmer and Ryman, had grown up with Oz; he returned there, he told *Variety* "because I was interested in the corrupt landscape of adulthood."[55]

While Farmer turned to science fiction and Ryman to magical realism in their revisionist Ozes, in *Wicked* Maguire would "use the material of children's fantasy to talk about the political world in which (he) found himself."[56] "Not such a surprise," he observed, as the thesis of his dissertation on children's fantasy had been that "far from being escapist (it) always has been a lot more attuned to the social and political realities of the twentieth-century than we would like to think."[57] For Maguire, Oz provided a landscape in which to explore "the nature of evil and the various ways people demonize their enemies," and, as a scholar and writer of children's literature, his turn to Oz to explore the question of evil seemed almost inevitable.[58] From a "childhood obsession with fairy tales, with telling stories and asking 'what if?,'" it's a short step to "start[ing] to think about what I knew about [the Wicked Witch]. In the original 'Wizard of Oz,' the Wizard tells Dorothy, 'Remember that the witch is wicked, tremendously wicked, and ought to be killed.' Well, I found the Wizard, hiding behind the curtain, sending children, effectively four children, off to kill somebody as scary as the witch."[59] Stemming from the premise that perhaps there is more to the Wicked Witch of the West than meets the MGM-blurred eye, and that the Wizard, a man we all know to be a "humbug," is perhaps a bad man as well as a bad Wizard, Maguire's novel presents a richly imagined, expanded, adult Oz, more indebted to Tolkien, as many reviewers observed, than to Baum. Maguire was fully aware that he "was playing around," as he told *Wired*, "with sacred material, but not in any way to disgrace the original material, just actually to make it seem richer and make its richness make more sense."[60]

The novel's eye-catching packaging was designed to intrigue the baby-boomer consumers who had grown up on MGM's film. Fairy-tale thorny vines, straight from the Witch's dark forest, framed a circular cutout, providing a peep-hole through which consumers could glimpse at the iconic pointed hat and green profile, made famous by Margaret Hamilton; the title, ringing the profile, promised readers new information about this most-well-known of fairy-tale witches, urging them to pick-up the book, open the cover, and see the true story revealed. Furthermore, by choosing to release the novel as literary fiction, rather than confining it to the genre-shelf, HarperCollins assured that the book would both be widely reviewed and have high-shelf-visibility, displayed at eye-level in the "new arrivals" stands at major bookstores around the country. Between the reviews and the shelf-placement, consumers were sure to see—and hopefully to buy—*Wicked*. In spite of all of these advantages, as Maguire recounts, *Wicked* was not an instant bestseller. At an early reading in Chicago, "seven people showed up. Four were homeless and had come into get out of the snow...two were friends of my brother's and the genuine book-buying public was reduced to one representative buyer who...bought one book. I thought: my life is over. My career has tanked before it started."[61]

Maguire's career was safe. *Wicked* caught on, fueled by a string of positive reviews and strong word-of-mouth. Not every reviewer—most notably *New York Times'* Michiko Kakutani, who dismissed the book as a "deadly dull" use of "Baum's most famous character as fodder for [Maguire's] own philosophizing," and lamented the novel's "politicizing Oz and investing it with a heavy dose of moral relativism"—embraced Maguire's expanded, adult Oz.[62] The majority, however, dismissed what they called the "Oz purists," who "may grump."[63] They were entranced by Maguire's audacious take on the fantasy land of their childhood, in which "the Wicked Witch of the West is a radical socialist...the Wizard is an evil autocrat, and Glinda the Good Witch is a dippy blond socialite looking for a rich husband."[64] They delighted in this new, expanded, rich, Oz that allowed them to revisit Munchkinland and the Emerald

City, and to re-meet, as adults, the companions of their youth. "We remember her," Susan Larson wrote in the *Times-Picayune*, "in a flurry of black, alighting from her broomstick and threatening Dorothy. We remember her frightening flying monkeys and her chilling laugh. Finally, we remember her melting away, done in by a single pail of water in a young girl's hand."[65] Throughout the reviews, critics ground their reading of *Wicked* in their childhood memories of Oz. "I was devoted to the Oz books when I was young," Robert Rodi writes, "and it's thrilling to see the familiar places and personages fleshed out with added literary depth."[66] From Baum's simple four-kingdom map, Maguire redrew Oz into a land with complex physical, social, and political geographies, as is evident from the Middle-Earth style map that proceeds our first introduction to the Witch. And indeed, many of the reviewers couch their appreciation of the novel in terms of this generic translation from child's tale to fully realized epic fantasy. They praise *Wicked* as a Tolkienesque "vividly imagined Oz, complete with detailed geography, creation myths, language, and even architecture," a novel whose "flap copy compares it favorably to both J. R. R. Tolkien and Gabriel Garcia Marquez, and, for once it's not P.R. lip-flap. Maguire fills in L. Frank Baum's broad outlines to create a fully-realized fantasy realm that coheres politically, culturally, sexually—and magically."[67] As such, *Wicked*, they concluded, "gives readers a very adult view of the land of Oz, making the classic American fantasy alive in a wonderfully new and powerful way."[68]

Wicked, the reviewers recognized, gave consumers "more Oz"—a more complex Oz, a more adult Oz—that spoke to those who had first visited Oz as children in the "clearly-delineated world" of either pre-World War II or Cold War America, "where no one questioned," Melanie Chandler remarked, "that Oz's skinny, cackling Margaret Hamilton character must be evil."[69] In 1995, "Governments we have learned, are quite as humbug as the phony Wizard, and for greed, not high principle, industry has eroded the ozone around the rainbow."[70] Chandler's observations, given MGM's *Wizard of Oz's* corporate-sponsored, Cold War broadcast history, are particularly apt; she concludes her analysis of *Wicked's* message with the novel's reimagined, fascist Wizard's position on social order and citizenship, "This is the prevailing order. Those who are good will maintain it, says the Wizard, echoing many another manipulative leader. Except we, as readers, know better. For political 'good,' prevailing orders have swept us into war; for corporate 'good,' they've destroyed the environment."[71] Still, if many of the

baby boomers who grew up on MGM's film had outgrown its technicolor fantasy and black-and-white morality, they yet harbored fond and
nostalgic memories of Oz. Maguire's complex reimagining of its realm
made it seem alive, new, and relevant.

HarperCollins—and Demi Moore and Universal Pictures who almost
immediately snapped up the film rights—realized, as an Oz product,
Maguire's novel had built-in consumer appeal. *Wicked* may have taken
a while to catch on, but in the wake of positive reviews and consumer
word-of-mouth, sales took off. By the time that Stephen Schwartz
and Winnie Holzman raised the curtain on what was soon-to-become
Broadway's biggest phenomenon, Maguire's ambitious and adult version
of Oz, "filled with truth about the real world—about religion and politics, identity and fate, good and evil, and of course, magic" had made a
respectable splash of its own, selling over 500,000 copies and transforming Maguire from a children's author to a major literary talent.[72]

The revisionists Ozes of the 1980s and 1990s did not offer consumers
an Ozzy-Oz; in fact, they deliberately countered all that Oz, at least as
Baum and MGM envisioned it, stood for. However, they still offered a
magic land, a space apart from our world, that asked us to explore what
it means to have passion, mind, and heart. And by questioning the myth,
they allowed it to evolve, making it relevant to consumers who had
themselves begun to question the truths about America and authority,
gender and sexuality, good and evil, and identity and home that had
framed their initial encounters along the yellow brick road.

CONCLUSION

The television broadcast years both ritualized and splintered Oz.
Memories of their annual trip down the yellow brick road shaped an
entire generation of American consumers. Not only did they remember
the film; they remembered *the conditions under which they watched it*.
Both acts provided the nation with a common narrative, imagery, and
vocabulary. Later, the passing of Oz into the public domain made the
myth widely available for production and re-consumption, adding a new
dimension to its cultural sustainability. Freed from the control of a small
group of heirs and producers, the narrative exploded: television shows
and specials, commercials, touring shows and festivals, comic books and
new stories: the One Oz became many Ozes.

This massive splintering of Oz significantly impacts our task as researchers. From the 1960s on, it becomes necessary to ask ourselves a series of questions in order to determine "which Oz" is being offered to consumers. Thus, we present the following taxonomy to clarify, and ultimately situate, each re-consumption of Oz under examination.

- What *kind* of Oz is offered? Not all Ozes are created equal, and not all of them are equally interested in Oz. Some are very close to Baum's vision; others turn that vision on its head. In some, Oz exists for itself; in others, it is a means to an end. Post-1960s Oz's fall into the following types:
  - **Magical Oz**: This is the Oz closest to Baum's vision, a "fairy-land" rife with magic, full of wondrous trees and flowers, and peopled with talking animals, animated Scarecrows and Pumpkinheads, Good and Wicked Witches, Princesses and Wizards. It is a real place, a land of marvelous adventures and great delight, of innocence and wonder. Right and wrong, good and evil are clearly delineated, and good always wins in the end. Although people from our world may—and usually do—find themselves there, Oz exists in its own right; it has a history and a purpose apart from what Baum calls the "civilized" world.
  - **Translated Oz**: These Ozes take Baum's characters and/or plot and translate them into another context. This translation takes many forms, from crossover narratives in which Oz characters find themselves in another imaginative universe (or characters from that universe find themselves in Oz), through casting the narrative into a different genre, such as science fiction, or moving the cast of characters into space, to playing out the narrative in a realistic landscape.
  - **Allegorical Oz**: Allegorical Oz does not exist in its own right, nor do its characters. Instead, Oz, like the world of *Pilgrim's Progress*, provides the setting, and the journey of characters who stand-in for abstract concepts exists solely to teach a moral. The correspondence between fiction and meaning is a simple one-to-one equation.
  - **Revisionist Oz**: Often referred to as "Dark Oz," revisionist Oz deconstructs magical Oz, often suggesting that Baum and the producers of the MGM film either did not have access to the "truth" about Oz, or that they deliberately misled their

audiences. Here, Oz may be magical, but it is also deeply political. This Oz exists in shades of gray (often literally as well as
metaphorically). Good and evil are not clearly delineated,
and no one is precisely as they seem—or as you, as consumers of Oz—have been taught to believe. Happy endings are not
guaranteed.
- **Parodic Oz**: Here, Oz exists as a site of parody or of ironic revisitation. This is Oz as an inside joke, to be enjoyed with an ironic
wink. It invites the kind of laughter that dismisses or undermines
the values, styles, and tastes of previous Ozes—most often the
MGM film—as old-fashioned, quaint, and out-of-touch with the
modern world.
- **Opportunistic Oz**: Oz is merely a pretext, or bait, providing producers with an opportunity to lure consumers in, but
the experience provided has little or nothing to do with Oz.
Opportunistic Ozes run the gamut from educational games,
through television and print advertisement, to peanut butter jars.
- **Archival Oz**: Oz is a *subject* for preservation, study, exhibition,
and analysis. Archival Oz ranges from museums, exhibitions, and
conventions, through studies of Baum and his works, through
reproductions of first-editions, restorations of early films, and special viewings of rare footage.
• How does Oz *function*? What is the purpose of Oz in this work?
What is the relationship between it and the real world? What values
does it teach? What is the consumer meant to "take-away" from this
visit to Oz? These functions are not necessarily mutually exclusive;
for instance, an individual Oz can function as both commentary and
a narrative of self-discovery.
- **As a conveyor of ethics and values**: Adventures in Oz model
values-based ethical behavior, emphasizing the role of the individual in the community. The narrative valorizes friendship, compassion, bravery, intelligence, self-reliance, and commitment—heart,
courage, and brains—as the center of Oz's utopian vision.
- **As a model of self-discovery**: The main character, almost always
Dorothy or another visitor from the "real" world, begins the
tale in a state of lack, not certain of who they are or where they
belong in the community. Their time in Oz teaches them who
they are and where they belong. In Oz, they learn to become
their "best self."

– **As a site of lost truth**: Oz has been forgotten, and with it essential truths and values; in these versions of Oz, both Oz and the real world have become a wasteland and the beloved characters are in crisis. Only by remembering Oz, returning to it and its values, can both worlds be restored and the characters be healed.
– **As a commentary on our world**: Oz, as either a utopia or a dystopia, serves as a foil to the contemporary world and lessons learned in Oz are meant to be applied to real-world situations. Ozes that function as commentaries tend to downplay individual adventures to center on Ozian political and social structures.
– **As a marketing device**: Oz does not exist in its own right, but rather as a way to sell a product, idea, or experience. The crossover appropriation of Oz into established storylines, such as *Passions* and *Spongebob*, where Oz is used merely to advance the plot and themes of the "host" show is also an example of Oz as a marketing device.

As we shall see in our final chapter, this taxonomy can be used to track a number of trends by decade, including the *types* of Ozes offered to consumers over time. These trends enable us to make pivotal observations about how Oz has achieved cultural sustainability.

NOTES

1. *Mickey Mouse Club*, Season 3, Episode 1, September 30, 1957; "Walt Disney's Wizard of Oz," YouTube Video, 10:21, posted by Freedogshampoo, August 4, 2007, https://www.youtube.com/watch?v=kJjhqBb3qGI.
2. *Shirley Temple's Story Book Hour*, "The Land of Oz," Season 2, Episode 1, September 18, 1969; YouTube Video, 51:22, posted by Gerald Hine, June 3, 2015, https://www.youtube.com/watch?v=H8mD5L7QQig.
3. *Dorothy Meets Ozma of Oz*, Directed by Myrna Bushman et al. (1987: Kushner-Locke Company); YouTube Video, 28:21, posted by Connor Hicks, May 14, 2916.
4. *Wizard of Oz on Ice*, Directed by Paul Miller (1996: CBS); YouTube Video, posted by WizardofOzfan39, August 20, 2008, https://www.youtube.com/watch?v=5gm55VXGZY4; Shirley Temple, "Land of Oz."
5. *Return to Oz*, Directed by F. R. Crawley et al. (1964: Rankin/Bass Productions); "Return to Oz Intro," YouTube Video, 5:05, posted by Martin Boyce, January 30, 2012, https://www.youtube.com/watch?v=2LHjhae98tQ; *Journey Back to Oz*, Directed by Hal Sutherland

(1972, 1974: Filmation Associates); YouTube Video, posted by Darthraner83, December 14, 2011, https://www.youtube.com/watch?v=FwQCfCSjOns.
6. "Original Journey Back to Oz Trailer 1," YouTube Video, 3:20, posted by VIdeoSam16, December 7, 2009, https://www.youtube.com/watch?v=IuY-Psc2n_0.
7. "Wizard of Oz Commercials," YouTube Playlist, Digital DG.
8. "History in the Making," *Land of Oz*, 2017, https://www.landofoznc.com/history, accessed December 15, 2017.
9. Hans Robert Jauss, *Towards an Aesthetic of Reception*, translated by Timothy Bahti (Minneapolis, MN: University of Minnesota Press, 1982), Chapter 3.
10. *Tales of the Wizard of Oz* (1961–1964: Rankin Bass); "Rankin/Bass's Tales of the Wizard of Oz," YouTube Video, 10:20, posted by Robby4000, December 20, 2006, https://www.youtube.com/watch?v=KS-K02xqV6w&list=PLy0mRMkCOQhPlBpVFemGy-Jl50T4TkWMWj.
11. J. R. R. Tolkien, "Forward," *The Fellowship of the Rings* (New York: Houghton Mifflin, 1965), 3.
12. Jeff Silverman, "One Man's Dream Brings a Different Sort of 'Oz' Story onto the Screen," *Chicago Tribune*, June 30, 1985, ProQuest.
13. Peter Bailey, "The Wiz," *Black Enterprise*, January 1976, 43–45, 44.
14. Advance and group sales had been slow, and weekly box-office takes looked to be about half of the show's weekly operational costs.
15. Douglas Watts, "Fine Cast and Splendid Look in Wiz," *New York Daily Review*, 1975, http://www.thewizthemusical.com/productions/original-broadway-production-1975/press-and-reviews/article/1024.
16. Rex Reed, "The Wiz," *New York Daily News*, January 6, 1975, http://www.thewizthemusical.com/productions/original-broadway-production-1975/press-and-reviews/article/1015.
17. Clive Barnes, "The Wiz, (of Oz)," *New York Times*, January 6, 1975, 32.
18. Michael Feingold, "Dorothy Plays the Palace," *Village Voice*, 1975, http://www.thewizthemusical.com/productions/original-broadway-production-1975/press-and-reviews/article/1004.
19. Marilyn Stasio, "Witty Wiz," *Cue Magazine*, 1975, http://www.thewizthemusical.com/productions/original-broadway-production-1975/press-and-reviews/article/1026.
20. Bailey, "The Wiz," 44.
21. Ibid., 45.
22. Ibid.
23. L. Winer, "Tempo the Arts," *Chicago Tribune*, November 13, 1976, Proquest.

24. D. Sullivan, "Stage Review," *Los Angeles Times*, June 20, 1977, Proquest.
25. "Jumping Jivernacular," *Time*, January 20, 1975, http://www.thew-izthemusical.com/productions/original-broadway-production-1975/press-and-reviews/article/1022.
26. Jay Scott, "Tripping Out in Oz," *The Globe and Mail*, February 1, 1978, A14.
27. P. Weingarten, "People," *Chicago Tribune*, December 24, 1976, ProQuest.
28. C. Childs, "The Wiz," *Chicago Tribune*, October 26, 1975, ProQuest.
29. Jack Kroll, "Oz with Soul," *Newsweek*, 1975, http://www.thewiz-themusical.com/productions/original-broadway-production-1975/press-and-reviews/article/1009.
30. Winer, "Tempo;" Sullivan, "Stage Review."
31. Tim Gray, "The Wiz: How TV Turned a Troubled Stage Show into a Smash," *Variety*, December 2, 2015, http://variety.com/2015/tv/news/the-wiz-broadway-tv-1201651417/.
32. Al Auster, "The Wiz," *Cineaste* 9, no. 2 (Winter 1978): 41–42, 41.
33. "Film Wiz Drops a Great Yellow Brick," *The Globe and Mail*, October 28, 1978, 29.
34. "Thanksgiving in Oz," Directed by Charles Swensen et al. (1980: Mueller-Rosen Productions); YouTube Video, 23:46, OTAKUMEDIATV, December 4, 2015, https://www.youtube.com/watch?v=pMDDqTv-JIrI&list=PL0R_avcBGqm6IbeQ9J5UNs_R3QfO-z2EJ.
35. Andrew Britton, "Blissing Out: The Politics of Reaganite Entertainment," in *Britton on Film: The Complete Film Criticism of Andrew Britton*, ed. Barry Grant (Ann Arbor: Wayne State Press, 2009), 97–154.
36. Silverman, "One Man's Dream."
37. Aljean Harmetz, "After 46 Years, Hollywood Revisits Oz," *New York Times*, June 16, 1985, ProQuest.
38. Ibid.
39. "Return to Oz (1985) Original Trailer," YouTube Video, 1:36, posted by SKYTV, August 1, 2011, https://www.youtube.com/watch?v=CklyKCKFtwE.
40. Jay Boyar, "Return Trip to Land of Oz is Grim Going," *Orlando Sentinel*, June 22, 1985, ProQuest.
41. Ibid.; Joe Baltake, "'Return to Oz'," *Philadelphia Daily News*, June 21, 1985, ProQuest; Jay Carr, "Summer Movies; The Winners and Losers," *Boston Globe*, August 29, 1985, ProQuest.
42. Carr, "Summer Movies."
43. Rachel Jones, "The Real Oz is a Slice of Life," *Chicago Tribune*, August 11, 1985, ProQuest.
44. "Letters to the Editor: Judy Lacked Punch," *Wall Street Journal*, July 12, 1985, ProQuest.

45. Baltake, "Return;" Desmond Ryan, "Sadly, Few Choose to 'Return to Oz'," *Philadelphia Inquirer*, July 16, 1985, ProQuest.
46. *Return to Oz*, Directed by Walter Murch (1985: Disney Studios), Amazon, Streaming.
47. Phillip Jose Farmer, *A Barnstormer in Oz* (New York: Berkley Press, 1982).
48. *Baum Bugle*, 76, 1983; *Intergalactic Reporter*, Both Reproduced on PJFarmer.com, http://www.pjfarmer.com/WRITTEN-ABOUT-reviews.html#barnstormer, accessed November 1, 2017.
49. John Crowley, "The Road to Hell Is Paved with Yellow Bricks," *New York Times*, July 5, 1992, ProQuest.
50. Michiko Kakutani, "Books of the Times; Using the Reality of Oz as the Basis for Fantasy," *New York Times*, June 9, 1992, ProQuest.
51. Erin McLeod, "From Oz to AIDS," *The Whig–Standard*, August 29, 1992, ProQuest.
52. Ibid.
53. Ryman, *Was* (Easthampton, MA: Small Beer Press, 1989, 2013), 359.
54. McLeod, "Oz to AIDS."
55. Sam Thielman, "Wicked Writer Explores Phenomenon," *Variety*, October 24, 2008, http://variety.com/2008/legit/news/wicked-writer-explores-phenomenon-1117994631/.
56. Alex Witchel, "Mr. Wicked," *New York Times Magazine*, March 11, 2007, http://www.nytimes.com/2007/03/11/magazine/11maguire.t.html.
57. Ibid.
58. Ibid.
59. Ibid.
60. "Wicked Author Gregory Maguire Is Headed Out of Oz," *Wired*, February 20, 2013, https://www.wired.com/2013/02/geeks-guide-gregory-maguire/.
61. Witchel, "Mr. Wicked."
62. Michiko Kakutani, "Let's Get This Straight: Glinda Was the Bad One," *New York Times*, October 24, 1995, ProQuest.
63. Melanie Chandler, "Wicked Puts Witch in a Kinder, Gentler Light," **The Vancouver Sun**, December 2, 1995: D.23, ProQuest.
64. Cathy Hainer, "Somewhere Over the Rainbow Lies a 'Wicked' Fable," *USA Today*, October 23, 1995, 5D.
65. Susan Larson, "Off to See the Wizard in a Whole New Light," *Times-Picayune*, October 29, 1995, E6.
66. Robert Rodi, "It's Not Easy Being Green: An Alternate History of the Wicked Witch of the West," *Los Angeles Times*, October 29, 1995, ProQuest.

67. Hainer, "Rainbow;" Rodi, "Green."
68. Larson, "New Light."
69. Chandler, "Gentler Light."
70. Ibid.
71. Ibid.
72. Larson, "New Light."

PART II

Wicked

CHAPTER 6

Telling and Selling: The Untold Story of the Witches of Oz

Maguire's *Wicked*, by providing baby boomers with a new and different experience of Oz that built upon their previous trips to Baum's and MGM's magic lands while adapting the narrative to their more-adult and contemporary experiences, sustained their engagement with the tale. Additionally, the novel's highly visible reviews and strong sales brought Oz once more to the attention of producers looking for a marketable property. "While writing the novel," Maguire recalls, "I could see its downstream potential."[1]

Maguire's suggestion that we look again at the Witch and see her not as a narrative function—the evil villain whom our heroes must defeat to find themselves and prove their worth—but as a fully realized character with a history of her own, proved to be conceptual gold. After Robert Rodi's positive review appeared on the front page of the *Los Angeles Times*, the movie studios came calling. Maguire quickly sold the film rights to Universal Studios, then headed by Marc Platt. "Part of what I loved initially," Platt remembers, "was the surprise of familiar characters in unexpected circumstances, undoing preconceived notions. These were the characters I grew up with, icons like the Wicked Witch, who struck terror in me."[2]

Both Stephen Schwartz and Winnie Holzman recount similar tales of immediate fascination with Maguire's novel. In his oft-repeated account, Schwartz credits folksinger and friend Holly Near with calling his attention to a book about Oz from the Witch's point of view during a Hawaiian snorkeling trip. "In an instant," his biographer Carol di

© The Author(s) 2018
K. Drummond et al., *The Road to Wicked*,
https://doi.org/10.1007/978-3-319-93106-7_6

Giere writes, "his imagination flashed through the implications of a back-story for *The Wizard of Oz* from the perspective of the unpopular witch. It was the best concept for a musical he had ever heard."[3] "Only a little ways into" the book, Schwartz told his lawyer to "start looking into the rights."[4] Holzman also found herself instantly captivated by Maguire's premise; when she came across the novel in 1996, she was drawn in by the "incredible cover of a green girl with her face hidden by the black hat…It really affected me….I bought the book, but didn't read it. I called my agent and said, 'How do I get the rights to this?'"[5]

Tellingly, both Holzman and Schwartz were not necessarily inter-ested in the rights to Maguire's novel; they wanted the rights to his *con-cept*—the intriguing possibilities offered up in the idea that perhaps the Witch was not so wicked after all. Schwartz, in particular, recounts an immediate recognition of the emotional power, the *potential*, of both the tale and Elphaba herself: "There were things I knew right away. I knew how it was going to begin. I knew how it was going to end. I knew who Elphaba was, and I knew why—on some strange level—this was autobiographical, even though I knew it was about a green girl from Oz."[6] For Schwartz, at the heart of the story was, as he asserted when he publicly announced the *Wicked* project on his fan website in 2000, the "extremely clever idea of telling the story of the Wicked Witch of the West—how a little green Oz girl grew up to be the greatest villain in the land… This is a story about how appearances can be deceiving and how life is more nuanced and complex than we would like to believe."[7]

As a nuanced and complex reading of Maguire's philosophical novel, Schwartz's summation of the book's meaning is simplistic at best; as the kernel of his next Broadway musical, it turned out to be—as theater his-tory has proven—nothing short of brilliant. The point is that *Wicked* the musical was never meant to be a simple remediation of *Wicked* the novel, and, thus, its adaptation from page to stage required that its origi-nal author allow the musical's creators free rein. Fortunately, Maguire—once he had been assured that "however the plot evolved to suit the stage, the grim themes of the novel would inform the show"—welcomed this play of re-consumption, trusting Schwartz to bring his "sprawling slice-of-Oz history" to a new medium and a new audience.[8] It probably helped that Maguire was himself a re-consumer of narratives. As such, he opined in an interview with the *Christian Science Monitor*, "it was only natural for him 'not to be too protective [of his own work] as if it were sacrosanct," finding it "rewarding…that other people might dream about [it]. Children might write alternate endings; composers might be inspired to set part of it to music."[9] Or a group of consumer-and-market-savvy-producers might bring it to the cinema—or to the Broadway stage.

Maguire's embrace of the idea of re-consumption may have made the adaptation process easier—as he himself later put it, "I made it my business to stay out of Stephen and Winnie's way so that they could answer the call of the project, without having to answer to me." Nevertheless, the translation was far from an easy one.[10] The yellow brick road from novel to stage was, to borrow a term from Robert Hurwitt, who reviewed the preview run in the *San Francisco Chronicle*, filled with "potholes."[11] "A thickly-plotted and densely populated novel," as another early reviewer observed, does not an easy "swift-moving mainstream musical make."[12] *Wicked*'s multiple plots, complex characters, lengthy disquisitions on religion, politics, and moral philosophy, all of these had to go. So, too, did the novel's tragic ending—in much the same way (Maguire argued) that Alan Jay Lerner and Frederick Loewe had discarded T. H. White's dark meditation on power, politics, and war while constructing their road to *Camelot*.

If Maguire, in his own terms, had been Mahler, Schwartz and Holzman needed to be Mozart. In order to be Mozart, what Schwartz refers to the novel's "so much plot...all over the place," needed to be more than "simply" cut; "it was a matter of taking the basic idea and re-examining it—of letting go of some of the pieces."[13] When Holzman finally read the book, she agreed: "I put it aside. I couldn't be too tied to what happened in it. So we sort of stole the things we just had to have...certain things that were brilliant in the novel wouldn't work in a musical."[14] Novel put aside, plot discarded, Schwartz and Holzman were left with the original concept, "what they stole" (most notably "the knockout idea" "that Glinda and Elphaba were roommates in college"), and the insistence that they had stayed "true" to the "spirit" and "essence" of Maguire's novel.[15]

From the moment Schwartz heard that Marc Platt and Universal owned the rights to *Wicked*, he sought to convince the producer that the Broadway musical was the best form in which to remediate Maguire's work; the novel, he argued, told Elphaba's internal story, and in order to portray that on film, screenwriters would have to resort to either a voice-over or a series of soliloquies, both of which would distance the audience from the tale's emotional impact. A musical, however, would place these emotions in the spotlight, in songs that would connect with audiences. Furthermore, since MGM owned the "look" of the characters that audiences expected to see on a screen, any cinematic Oz risked audiences' refusing to "accept characters who looked different." "The abstractness of the theater [would] mitigate that [risk]."[16] Platt, himself a veteran of Broadway and already disappointed with his studio's attempts to produce a workable screenplay for the novel, eventually relented. Schwartz and his team went to work on bringing *Wicked* to the musical stage.

Two Witches Instead of One

Schwartz may have been drawn to his "green Oz girl" as an "autobiographical story" about prejudice and exclusion, but he knew from the very beginning that successfully adapting the novel to a Broadway musical would need an author who could create dynamic, strong, believable female characters.[17] He chose Holzman, the writer behind the popular Clare Dane vehicle, *My So Called Life*—and serendipitously already interested in adapting *Wicked*—to write the musical's book. And they began work on the difficult task of translating Maguire's novel to the stage. Schwartz had already identified and published the story's *meaning*, now the trick was to figure out what to keep and what to throw out; to discover, as Holzman joked on the eve of the San Francisco premiere, the musical's narrative through-line. Holzman recalls, "I was gravitating right away to more of a love story," a plot that she certainly would have needed to wrest from Maguire's description of Fiyero's and Elphaba's tentative, secretive, and ultimately doomed affair.[18] However, Holzman continues, "the surprise came when it turned out that the love story was between two friends." This twist on a story that had been originally conceived as centered around Elphaba came, according to reports, relatively late in the game, when the chemistry between Kristin Chenowith and Stephanie Bloch during a reading transformed *Wicked* into a tale of two witches. "As we were refining the book," Holzman told Santa Rosa's *The Press Democrat*, "We found that this is really a story about the friendship of these two women. We start with them meeting in college and being forced to room together, the green girl and the blond girl, and we go from there."[19]

In going "from there," the musical riffs on the traditional Broadway romance plot while adhering to its central message. *Wicked* is, at its heart, a Golden Age Broadway musical, a celebration of an imagined community that brings its audience together within a constructed space to witness a tale that brings "seemingly incompatible peoples—or families, classes, races, ideas, ideologies, or whatever—into a stabilized partnership" and then sends that audience out into their communities with songs to be shared.[20] *Wicked* may tell a friend-meets-friend tale, but the relationship between Elphaba and Glinda still celebrates a union, still marks a moment of inclusion and diversity. By the end of the show, prior offenses are forgiven (if not forgotten); differences are resolved; and both parties are changed for good through having known each other. In their final scene together, Elphaba passes *The Grimmerie*, the central repository of Oz's power, to Glinda. As the two main characters sing "For Good," audiences bear witness to the power of female inclusiveness, as well as to the nascence of a morally grounded community capable of resisting the Wizard's repressive regime. The musical also controverts the traditional Broadway notion that a woman's path to fulfillment lies only through marriage (see, e.g., *Hello Dolly!*). Instead, *Wicked* places two powerful women on stage in a plot that emphatically passes the Bechdel Test.

Recasting the tale as she did enabled Holzman to provide consumers with an experience Maguire's tale could not, particularly with respect to Elphaba. Realizing that all her good intentions had come to naught, fully aware of her ineffectiveness in the split second between the flames and the water, Maguire's Elphaba dissolves into the arms of the Goddess of Gifts, still unable to decipher the words that may have given meaning to her life. By contrast, Holzman's Elphaba, fueled by female friendship, is empowered to defy gravity. And decipher most of *The Grimmerie*. While her defiant triumph is short-lived, she nevertheless enjoys a sunset-exile on the backside of Oz, knowing that she has both saved Fiyero and changed Galinda into Glinda the Good. These may represent Pyrrhic victories for the characters, but they hold as-yet untold riches for the show's creators. That's because while Maguire's novel appealed to baby boomers who had come to see the world without technicolored glasses, the show reached a new and much larger consumer segment: millennials. As Holzman may well have suspected, teenage girls would become the musical's first and most passionate fans.

"Popular! We're Gonna Make You Popular...."

Through multiple workshops and readings, an uneven preview run in San Francisco, including a nasty critique in *Variety* that sent the production into a two-month-long extensive rewrite, and an initial spate of dismal reviews, *Wicked*'s production team never faltered in their steadfast belief in the show. Beginning with *Variety*'s June 16, 2003, review of the San Francisco production, which declared "Ding, dong, the witch's prognosis is uncertain," and went on to lament the show's "crowd-pleasing ways," "heavy-handed parable," and "gluey, banal, sentiment, reach[ing] artery-choking levels," gatekeepers, for the most part, panned the show in its first months.[21] They didn't like "its politically indignant deconstruction of Oz" or "its topical transparency"; *New York Time*'s Ben Brantley scorned *Wicked* as a production that wore "its political heart as if it were a slogan button," and Michael Feingold of the *Village Voice* lamented its reduction of Baum's novel to a tale of "disaster and disillusion brought on by the White House's current infestation of unwinged monkeys."[22] At the same time, the gatekeepers complained, *Wicked* was "overproduced and overblown," "muddy," with "blandly synthetic pop-tunes" and cutesy dialogue written in the "language of the smurfs."[23] In the end, the major critics—mostly male—seemed to agree: *Wicked* was a production in search of a center, "a hokey stroll on the dark side," whose "political message [was] at war with its cupcake cuteness."[24] "*Wicked*, a hideous mess of a musical," Feingold concluded, "wants to be all things to all people, and rarely succeeds in being any of them. It wants to convey the childish pleasure of Baum's 'Wizard of Oz' myth, but it also wants to explain that myth, debunk it, draw morals from it, and occasionally ridicule it."[25] Feingold's response demonstrates exactly what *Wicked* was up against: the baby boomer critics' collective memories of Oz, colored by MGM and childhood nostalgia, and a deep-seated disdain for the megamusical, a genre they derided as based in simplistic, crowd-pleasing spectacle.

As both Oz and Broadway, the majority of the New York critics abhorred the *Wicked* experience; they also—like their predecessors who had panned Oz's original Broadway run—blamed its probable popularity on naïve consumers mindlessly attracted to "Oz," "the kind of tear-jerking ballads one can already hear tinkling in every piano bar," "girl power," and spectacle.[26] Michael Phillips of the *Chicago Tribune* observed, with some resignation, that "'Wicked' will probably run for a season or two on the virtue of its girl power witches" "Until we get a "Harry Potter Musical," he continued, "I suppose this one will do. And if teen-friendly mediocrities such as 'Aida' can run for years, this thing may do the same."[27] John Lahr, son of MGM's Cowardly Lion, was less charitable: "It is only fair to report that on the night I saw 'Wicked,' the spectators gave this fourteen-million dollar piece of folderol a standing ovation, a phenomenon that the musical inadvertently explains in… 'Dancing Through Life': 'Life is painless/For the brainless.'"[28]

Only a few gatekeepers "surrendered," as Ron Cohen of Back Stage termed it, to the Wicked experience. "Do we really need another Broadway musical deconstruction a beloved fantasy, especially 'The Wizard of Oz,' embedded in our collective consciousness with its own signature songs and technicolor special effects?" Cohen asked.[29] Whereas most of his fellow New York critics had answered that question with a resounding no, Cohen continued, "Bring what resistance you can to the Gershwin Theatre; I'll almost guarantee "Wicked" will eventually wear you down, overwhelm you, and generally impress you," with its breathtaking spectacle and clever integration of more modern popular texts, such as Harry Potter and Clueless.[30] If Cohen was won over by the production's spectacle, the critic for the Boston Herald succumbed to its emotional impact that "from the safe distance of a warts-and-all Oz…[left] room to have fun AND question if there is really no place like home."[31] And, in the most widely distributed of Wicked's positive reviews, USA Today's Elysa Gardner embraced the show as an "entrancing experience," "the most complete, and completely satisfying, new musical I have come across in a long time."[32]

Most of the show's initial audiences did succumb to the Wicked experience. From the San Francisco previews on, Wicked's word-of-mouth was strong. And, whereas Lahr snarkily dismissed the audience's standing ovation as a sign of their limited intelligence, the show's production team saw those ovations as proof that their adaptation offered consumers an Oz-and-Broadway experience that spoke to them. Wicked's press representative, Bob Fennel, reports that, as the curtain fell on the show's Broadway premiere, "My partner turned to me and said, 'This is going to be a hit. I've had shows in this theater before. I've never seen a reaction like this. The audience loves this show. They are going to leave tonight and tell their friends they have to see it.'"[33]

The challenge faced by Wicked then, as the show's marketing team recognized, was to find a way to bypass the gatekeepers and reach the consumers directly. Enter Nancy Coyne, who designed *Wicked*'s now-iconic poster: a stylized image of Glinda whispering a secret in Elphaba's ear, cast in a "yin/yang like curve of black and white" and punctuated by a scattering of flying monkeys.[34] Two taglines framed this image: on the top, "So much happened before Dorothy dropped in...." and, on the bottom, "Wicked: The untold story of the witches of Oz." Schwartz, reportedly, was unhappy with Coyne's poster, feeling that it didn't tell the story. Coyne retorted, "Look, I'm not trying to appeal to *you* with this poster. I'm trying to appeal to women who buy tickets, to tourists, and to mothers and their daughters. If the show's a flop, it doesn't matter what your poster is. If the show's a hit, and we can reach that market, it's the difference between running five and ten [or fifteen] years."[35] In other words, Coyne designed a poster for sustainability, seeking to reach the very consumers the New York critics disparaged. *Wicked*'s poster played on their previous experience of Oz, promising them "more," a secret about the tale they thought they knew so well; it focused not on Dorothy and her companions, but on the women and their unlikely friendship; and its lines were updated, sleek, hinting at a more modern Oz. Coyne's television promotion extended these themes. It begins with a close shot of the show's stylized map of Oz, focused on the Emerald City. "Long before Dorothy dropped in," the narrator relates, "two other girls met in the land of Oz." The camera switches to a shot of Elphaba and Glinda meeting at Shiz, followed by a brief clip from "Defying Gravity," and then back to a shot of the two witches embracing. "They became best friends," the narrator intones, "until they called one good and the other wicked." Over a series of shots that emphasize the show's grand spectacle, the narrator concludes, "the musical phenomenon, and the untold story of the witches of Oz...call now for tickets."[36]

Neither of Coyne's campaigns was aimed at gatekeepers or theater professionals; rather, they were targeted at everyday consumers, both naïve and knowing. "My first assignment," she observed, "is to reach the people who love to go to the theater...my second audience is teenage girls."[37] When Coyne reached those people, and got them through the door, the audiences' reactions to *Wicked* showed the producers that they had a potential hit on their hands, if only they could keep them coming through the door. Platt, with his Hollywood experience, and the marketing team kicked into full gear, launching a post-opening promotional campaign that has earned a place in marketing textbooks. Tickets were slashed 30%, which not only got first-time consumers into the theater, but also played into the post-home-video teenage desire for repeat-viewing and generated brisk intermission-sales as consumers lined up to see the musical again. They also deployed the internet, beefing up the show's website with feature articles and making sure *Wicked* made frequent appearances on multiple social media platforms. Stila developed a *Wicked*-line of makeup, and the show, in a precursor of the *Wicked* experiences we will discuss in Chapter 9, extended into the malls. Kristin Chenowith and Idina Menzel offered *Wicked* makeovers at Sephora and local malls hosted karaoke "auditions," awarding tickets to the show to budding Elphabas and Glindas.[38] All of these tactics served to reach the consumers where they browsed and shopped, generate buzz, and to sustain the show's word-of-mouth. As Coyne observed to *The Los Angeles Times*, "'Wicked' is a phenomenon because of teenage girls…At every matinee, you'll hear a girl saying, 'See? I told you you'd love it.' They're e-mailing their friends, and it's a powerful tool for sales."[39]

It worked. Soon tickets to *Wicked* were so impossible to come by that a cartoonist drew the famous companions begging for "a brain," "a heart," "courage," and "Wicked tickets." By the time the show went on tour in 2005, an article, which ran in several markets, told readers that while *Wicked*'s producers had made a TV commercial for the tour, they would not show it, because that would be "tantamount to the production thumbing its nose at the pitiably ticketless multitudes."[40] As of December 2005, the show that the critics panned, and that had been somewhat snubbed at the Tony's (winning lead actress for Menzel, costume, and design, but losing out to *Avenue Q* for the big awards), was raking in $1.3 million a week in New York City and was a "monster on tour."[41] It had earned its producers a quarter-billion dollars since its Broadway opening. As had happened with *The Wiz*, once the musical was a success, the critics mostly boarded the *Wicked* bandwagon; reviews of the touring production, on the whole, embraced the experience, as "a hit—a mix of Oz and Harry Potter- like fantasy and magic with zingy lines, a lush score, and a wildly talented cast."[42] Suddenly, the show's "cultural commentary" had been spun "into delightful entertainment [that] will make you laugh hard and think harder," and "comes together in a story so complex and relevant to our current world order that it makes 'Wicked' the most unforgettably moving musical comedy of the season."[43]

By the time *Wicked* hit the road, the musical had definitely provided Oz with another cultural touchpoint, a megahit that contributed to its sustainability by bringing the myth back into the public discourse, providing new experiences of Oz to new consumers, and making other Oz products marketable. Two instances from the early years of the *Wicked* phenomenon perfectly illustrate this synergy of sustainability. The first is Chicago's 2005 "Oz-explosion," explored by Web Behrens in the *Chicago Tribune*. "Ever since 'Wicked' arrived downtown in the spring, there's been a flurry of related art. Like flying monkeys descending upon the Winkie forest, our cultural sky is peppered with new [Oz] creations."[44] Consumers desiring more Oz could find it at no fewer than three productions (including a revival of a 2001 musical version of Ryman's *Was*, first workshopped at Lincoln Center), an exhibit on theater, focused on the 1902 stage *Wizard of Oz*, at the public library, the upcoming Ozmapolitan Convention and Chesterton Festival, and the Chicago Symphony. While the producers of these Ozes insisted that *Wicked* had nothing to do with their productions, with the exception of the convention and festivals, one suspects these producers are not being entirely transparent in their disavowal of influence. And one also suspects that the success of *Wicked* may well have increased Oz festival and convention attendance.

The second instance of Oz synergy loops back to Maguire and the novel that gave birth to the musical. *Wicked*, the musical, attracted new consumers to *Wicked*, the novel. Ten years after its publication, the novel hit the *New York Times* best seller list, where it remained for several weeks. And, like Baum before him, the musical's mega success led Maguire to satisfy consumers' desire for new Oz adventures, and one novel grew to a series, *The Wicked Years*. While not all of these new consumers really wanted Maguire's Oz—and Maguire himself was fully aware that his fantasy world was not suited to all of his new consumers, particularly the musical's younger fans—*Wicked*'s Broadway turn definitely extended the shelf life of Maguire's Oz narrative.

Also like Baum before him, Maguire moved from a skeptical distance from the work's adaptation to a full embrace of it—and he remains one of the musical's greatest fans. In a letter to the cast and production team, Maguire thanks them all for bringing his work to light and life through "the opportune magic of theater" "with all the power and magnificence of a big budget and a cabal of collaborators."[45] In a 2008 interview with

Broadway.com, having seen the production thirty-five times, he speculated on the musical *Wicked*'s lasting success:

> Forget the female-empowerment thing. Forget the identity-politics for any marginalized soul. Forget the way the story comments on current international tensions if you can. Forget even the clever and haunting presence of the original book and film of *The Wizard of Oz*, such a cultural touchstone in American childhoods. Forget the anthems and the costumes and the dazzling design of it all, the magic of the theater.

> The truth, I believe, is because while the story gratifies on a first viewing, the satisfaction intensifies on a second viewing....*Wicked* can be enjoyed over and over again because it isn't all about surprises. It is also about inevitabilities.[46]

> Which brings me to why I continue write about Oz when *Wicked* shows nightly in eight or nine theaters around the globe. Haven't I had enough?

> The question of the way we are imprisoned in our own skins—be they green or furry—continues to taunt me.

Maguire's musings on "the monstrous size" of *Wicked's* Broadway success dismisses the theories of marketers and cultural critics to meditate on narrative sustainability—what about a story makes us turn to it a second, a third, or even a thirty-fifth time? For Maguire, the satisfaction intensifies, the questions continue to taunt...and, not entirely coincidently, they produce, as he announces in this interview, volume three of *The Wicked Years, A Lion Among Men*, coming soon to a bookstore near you. Here, Maguire promises, consumers will find out what happened to the Cowardly Lion who makes such a brief appearance in Act I of the Broadway show, closing the loop between musical and novels, and the consumers' desire for more, with another Oz experience.

NOTES

1. Gregory Maguire, Liner Notes, Stephen Schwartz, *Wicked: Original Cast Recording Deluxe Edition*, Various Artists, Verve B00FL3Y06G, 2013, CD.
2. Peter Marks, "Season of the Witch: 'Wicked' Casts Quite a Spell," *The Washington Post*, December 18, 2005, N.01.
3. Carol Di Giere, *Defying Gravity: The Creative Career of Stephen Schwartz from Godspell to Wicked* (New York: Applause Books, 2008), 273.

4. David Cote, *Wicked: The Grimmerie, A Behind-the-Scenes Look at the Hit Broadway Musical* (New York: Hachette Books, 2005), 20.

5. Ibid., 20–21.

6. Di Giere, *Gravity*, 273.

7. Ibid., 321–322.

8. Ibid., 295.

9. Gregory M. Lamb, "Spin Cycle: A Musical Based on a Book, Based on Another Book That Was Turned Into Two Musicals—Is There Nothing New Under the Sun?," *Christian Science Monitor*, July 18, 2003, 13.

10. Maguire, liner notes.

11. Robert Hurwitt, "Every Witch Way—Spellbinding 'Wicked' a Charming Vision of Oz, but Is a Few Bricks Shy of a Road," *San Francisco Chronicle*, June 12, 2003, E1.

12. Michael Riedel, "Fix Witch Glitch—Oz-ish Musical Takes Time Pre-B'Way," *New York Post*, July 2, 2003, 045.

13. Di Giere, *Gravity*, 275.

14. Cote, *Grimmerie*, 35.

15. Ibid.

16. Di Giere, *Gravity*, 288.

17. Di Giere, *Gravity*, 321, 274.

18. Cote, *Grimmerie*, 35.

19. Debra D. Bass, "'Wicked' Asks Which Witch Is Which," *The Press Democrat*, May 18, 2003, Q12.

20. For further discussions of *Wicked* and the Broadway musical, see Paul Laird, *Wicked: A Musical Biography* (Maryland: Scarecrow Press, 2011), Raymond Knapp, *The American Musical and the Formation of National Identity* (Princeton: Princeton University Press, 2005) and *The American Musical and the Performance of Personal Identity* (Princeton: Princeton University Press, 2006), and Laurie Finke and Susan Aronstein, "Got Grail?: Monty Python and the Broadway Stage," *Theater Survey* 48 (2007): 289–311. Quote is from Knapp, *National Identity*, 8.

21. Harvey Dennis, "Ding, Dong, the Witch's Prognosis Is Uncertain at the Stage of 'Wicked'," *Variety*, June 16, 2003, 37.

22. Ben Brantley, "There's Trouble in the Emerald City," *New York Times*, October 31, 2003, 1; Peter Marks, "Kristen Chenowith, Good Luck Charm," *The Washington Post*, October 31, 2003, C.01; Michael Feingold, "Green Witch, Mean Time: Both On and Off-Broadway, New Musicals Suffer from Severe Multiple Personality Disorder," *Village Voice*, November 5, 2003, 77.

23. Linda Winer, "Bewitched and Bothered, Too/Bewildering 'Wicked' Tries to Be Both Dark and Cute; So Witch Is It?," *Newsday*, October 31, 2003, B02; Marks, "Charm;" Brantley, "Trouble."

24. Marks, "Charm;" Winer, "Bewitched."
25. Feingold, "Green Witch."
26. Daniel Handler, "Hey, Watch Who You're Calling Wicked," *New York Times*, June 29, 2003, 2.5.
27. Michael Phillips, "Brick Road Leads to Mediocre Musicals," *Chicago Tribune*, November 2, 2003, 17.
28. John Lahr, "Bitches and Witches: Ulterior Motives in 'Cat on a Hot Tin Roof' and 'Wicked,'" *New Yorker*, November 10, 2003, 126–127, 127.
29. Ron Cohen, "'Wicked,'" *Back Stage*, November 14, 2003, 48.
30. Ibid.
31. Terry Byrne, "Oz-Based Musical Is Spellbinding and 'Wicked' Fun," *Boston Herald*, October 31, 2003, E24.
32. Elysa Gardner, "Something 'Wicked' Comes to Broadway," *USA Today*, October 31, 2003, E.09.
33. Cote, *Grimmerie*, 181.
34. Di Giere, "*Gravity*," 374.
35. Ibid.
36. "Wicked on Broadway TV Commercial," YouTube video, 0:31, posted by Serino/Coyne, May 31, 2011, https://www.youtube.com/watch?v=E7z-EQk08Mo.
37. Dinah Eng, "Under the Moral's Spell; Teen Girls Are Entranced by 'Wicked,' The Latest Broadway Blockbuster with Issues that Speak to Them," *Los Angeles Times*, June 19, 2005, E.33.
38. Brooks Barnes, "How Wicked Cast Its Spell," *The Wall Street Journal*, October 22, 2005, https://www.wsj.com/articles/SB112994038461876413.
39. Eng, "Moral."
40. Marks, "Season."
41. Ibid.
42. Melissa Merli, "'Wicked' Puts Wonderful Spin on 'Oz' as Musical Prequel," *News Gazette*, July 24, 2005, E-7.
43. Lee Williams, "Totally Wicked; An Unforgettable Musical Breaks All the Rules," *Houston Press*, November 3, 2005.
44. Web Behrens, "OZ Is Everywhere Today, It Seems. So Much So that No One Would Blame You If You'd Started to Wonder if a Witch Had Cast a Spell on the Entire City," *Chicago Tribune*, November 6, 2005, 7.5.
45. Letter Maguire to Cast, Backstage at the Gershwin Theatre.
46. "Gregory Maguire Loving Wicked for the 35th Time," Broadway Buzz, October 15, 2008, https://www.broadway.com/buzz/6302/gregory-maguire-loving-wicked-for-the-35th-time/, accessed December 2, 2017.

CHAPTER 7

"My Entire Body Was Shaking": Consumers Respond to *Wicked*

Maguire's litany of commands that we dismiss all explanations for *Wicked*'s success except its "inevitabilities" solidifies his role as the knowing insider: the one who, in fashion as dramatic as the musical itself, cuts to the heart of the matter to explain $4 billion worth of revenue with a single sound byte. For consumer researchers, however, Maguire's opinion is precisely that: a single opinion, neither more nor less significant than the millions of opinions held by millions of other consumers who have seen *Wicked* over the past 15 years.

In fact, as we show in this chapter, the very explanations Maguire dismisses are the ones consumers express when asked to account for *Wicked*'s sustainability. While Maguire anticipates these, his own explanation is impactful only to the extent that other consumers share his view—which, in fact, they don't. In a case of who owns the text, consumer researchers, like reader-response critics, inevitably side with the audience. Of course, Maguire's opinion is useful in that it begs the question of what other consumers actually do think of *Wicked*: How they felt when they saw it, what sense they make of it upon reflection, and yes, what they believe accounts for its sustainability. The most obvious means of finding answers to such questions is to reach out to consumers directly. And that is exactly what we did.

Using a well-known research technique called depth interviewing, we conducted 75 interviews with consumers who had seen a live performance of *Wicked*, either in its pre-Broadway run in San Francisco, its extended (and ongoing) run on Broadway, or in one of its many

K. Drummond et al., *The Road to Wicked*,
https://doi.org/10.1007/978-3-319-93106-7_7

touring productions around the world.[1] We collected our sample of 75 respondents using a snowball sampling technique. We began by interviewing a handful of people whom we knew had seen a production of *Wicked*. These subjects knew others who had seen *Wicked*, so we interviewed those referrals. They in turn referred us to others who had seen the show, and so on—until we had collected 75 interviews. This number compares favorably to most Consumer Culture Theory-based research projects employing this technique.[2]

The reactions we cite here are deeply personal and wholly spontaneous.[3] We stressed to all our interviewees that it wasn't necessary that they liked the show; rather, we simply sought their general and specific impressions of *Wicked*, and what made the experience, for them, memorable or forgettable. We also emphasized that their responses, when quoted, would appear under pseudonyms. Here, we present and discuss the most significant findings.

WICKED ACTIVATES INTENSE EMOTIONS

Particularly for those consumers who have never been to a Broadway show, the impact of seeing and hearing a live performance of *Wicked* is simply overwhelming. Here is Carl, a dentist in his 30s, recalling his reaction:

> I have to tell you, I had no idea music could sound... this ... good. It exceeded my expectations by ... infinity! What is that song they sing right before intermission? I was so overcome by that song that my entire body was shaking during the break. My knees were like jelly – I could hardly walk [he imitates a wobbly walk, leaning onto the countertop in the dentist's office].

This reaction is all the more remarkable, given that Carl's recollection of it occurred more than 10 years after the event itself. Even though he could not recall the name of the number that sent him into the emotional stratosphere ("Defying Gravity"), for Carl, that wasn't the point; his emotional response to that song—and the physical imprint it left on him—was testament enough to *Wicked*'s impact.

Dan, an economics professor, part-time rugby coach, and self-confessed "tough guy," recalled the moment he took his daughter to see *Wicked*:

> I had taken my daughter to New York.... We visited my sister, and the three of us decided to go see *Wicked*. From the first notes, we were completely overcome by emotion. The tears streamed down my face and they wouldn't stop! I don't mind admitting that I cried through much of the show. The talent alone was overwhelming. But when you consider the people I saw it with – two very important women in my life – I was just not prepared for those emotions. I get choked up just thinking about it [starts tearing up].

Pamela, a twentysomething administrator at a business school, also recalls seeing *Wicked* for the first time:

> I never really understood what it meant to "see a Broadway show," until now. It's so much more than just a play! The sets, the costumes, the movement – everything is so tight and complex. The big scenery glided in and out, and I never heard a sound. And the singing – that's what really got me. I had no idea people could sing like that! The performers are simply amazing. Broadway musicals have a mystique about them. Now I know why.

Tara, a pharmacy student, concurs:

> I was impressed at how powerful each piece was and the emotion that was carried with it. I was especially impressed by the actors' singing – of course they are Broadway stars and obviously have great talent, but I had no idea that their singing would capture the audience in such a way that would give chills down my spine multiple times throughout the show.

In fact, "chills down my spine" was the phrase used by many to describe their overall reaction to *Wicked*. This was true regardless of our respondents' age, gender, or how long ago they had seen the show—which ranged from a few days prior to 13 years in the past. Other respondents used related phrases, many of them eloquent and poetic: "The show took me emotionally to a place of awe"; "When the first notes of the pit orchestra began to play, I was smiling so much that I was nearly crying"; "These people are like professional athletes. I could not believe how good they were"; "When the actors would sing, I would get chills throughout my body because it was all just so powerful"; "It was all just – you're so overcome, you know, the music and the scenery and everything – it just makes one big mesh of things." Note how this respondent said *mesh*, not mess, of things (we checked on the recording). What she experienced was an interconnected series of theatrical moments and related sensations that added up to more than just the sum of its parts. And this was true of so many respondents; for naïve consumers in particular, *Wicked* often packs a powerful emotional punch.

ELPHABA IS THE PORTAL

Time and again, respondents, unprompted, wanted to talk about Elphaba— specifically, how they connected to her character from the moment she stepped onstage: an outcast who was misunderstood, ostracized, and rejected. The number of respondents who voluntarily related to Elphaba—about two-thirds of our 75 respondents—was striking. Responses ranged from the abstract to the highly personal. For example, Louise, an office manager, notes: "You know, there's a lot of sympathy for Elphaba because of the way she was treated by her parents, her father, you know, her classmates. You know she was bullied, basically."

Louise's observation that Elphaba was "bullied" shows respondents' tendency to remove Elphaba from a fantasy world and recontextualize her in contemporary terms. It also presents a larger opportunity for consumer engagement not lost on *Wicked*'s promoters, as we will see in Chapter 8: "*Wicked* Experiences."

Other respondents identified with Elphaba more directly. Sheila, an executive assistant in her 40s, recalls: "As a teenager, I was always different. Intellectual, Artsy. Fantastical. I never watched TV. I felt like an outcast. Watching Elphaba deal with that onstage brought back so many memories of feeling out of place at school." And Karin, a telemarketer, explains: "I've definitely had periods in my life … where I felt awkward or unpopular, misunderstood. And so I could definitely relate to that and how it can–yeah, it just makes you have more compassion for her, for what she's going through." Carrie, a pre-med student, observes: "It struck close to home with me because I sympathized with Elphaba, the eager student who hoped the best of her mentors and in the end was manipulated and taken advantage of because she was young."

Elphaba's tale of rejection and isolation struck a nerve with dozens of our respondents. Interestingly—but perhaps not surprisingly—the vast majority of these were women. During our interviews, painful memories and their accompanying emotions frequently rose to the surface—sometimes 50 years after the events that gave rise to them. Reva, now in her mid-60s, recalls: "I was just really disliked as a kid. I mean, very, very much disliked as a kid. I think I probably only had two friends. I can tell you that there were two people that were my friends for the first 17 years of my life. [Starts crying]." At such moments, we would have to suspend the interview temporarily in order to comfort the respondent. We would then ask the respondent if he or she wished to continue—and the respondent always did.

Tory, a waitperson, reveals:

> Elphaba is incredibly strong! Nobody wants her, but she finds a way to rise above it all. That's my story. I was physically abused by my stepfather. He tried to break a two-by-four over my head once. I left home after that. I have been on my own ever since [Tory is 28]. Elphaba inspires me. No matter what happens, she keeps going.

In fact, we found Elphaba's character to be a lightning rod for deeply personal reactions such as Reva's and Tory's. Revelations about sexuality and other closely kept secrets poured out, in powerful ways we were simply not anticipating. Bryan, in his early 20s, is a case in point:

> Elphaba is different. During the course of the musical, she learns to embrace her individuality and her uniqueness, and this resonates well with me. As someone who grew up being sort of nerdy, not very popular in school, and a gay boy in Wyoming, I can relate to Elphaba when it comes to not fitting in socially. My political and social views tend to differ from the people of Wyoming – just like Elphaba's conflict with the Wizard's plan to domesticate all of the animals in Oz. Like Elphaba, I've managed to find places in the world where I belong.

Such was Bryan's identification with Elphaba that during this interview, he states on record that he is a gay man—one of the first times he had done so in a public setting.

Tom, a priest, is also drawn to Elphaba for deeply personal reasons:

> When I was in the seminary years ago, I was involved in a car accident. I had had too much to drink, and I was driving. The car overturned, and one of the passengers, a friend of mine, was killed. His parents decided not to press charges against me, but it is something I have lived with ever since. It may sound strange, but I do find strength in Elphaba's character with regards to this. She has a difficult path to follow; she knows she has to carry on. I take a lot of strength from her.

And Brittany, who miraculously survived a rare form of cancer, comments:

> When I was young I had cancer and the doctors didn't think I was going to make it. I did, but I've had a lot of complications since then. What I learned is that when you have cancer, a lot of people treat you like an outcast. Because you look really sick, they're afraid of you, like you're contagious or something. So I know what it means to be treated differently than everyone else. I think that's why Elphaba inspires a lot of people.

As seasoned consumer researchers, what struck us here was the propensity of many respondents to take Elphaba politically as well as personally. Not only did they identify with her at a private level; they made sense of her at a public level, as a responsible citizen shouldering struggles similar to their own. (Conversely, they thought Glinda would say whatever was necessary to get ahead.) Even when respondents didn't relate to Elphaba in deeply personal ways, they admired her for her depth of conviction and the lengths she was willing to go to defend her values. Elphaba's political convictions hold particular appeal for younger consumers. As Lindsay Vick, marketing director for the well-known fashion brand Fila, explains:

> Members of GenZ align their spending with their values. Their concerns center around climate change, gender equality – pressing issues of the day. So anything having to do with social or environmental issues will naturally attract the attention of Millennials.[4]

Elphaba's particular cause—protecting the rights and identities of the Animals of Oz—also resonated with many consumers. Peggy, a pre-vet student, says: "Obviously I'm drawn to animals or I wouldn't be in this profession. So when Elphaba takes a stand against the Wizard for basically enslaving the Animals, I admire her. She's standing up for what she believes in, and sometimes that's hard, particularly for a woman."

Some scenes reminded consumers of today's political landscape, and a handful of respondents were quick to draw links to current events. Sybil, now retired, notes:

> It was kind of expressed in that comment by the Wizard ... he said something about, 'Well, we just give the people what they want' or something like that. And I remember thinking, 'Oh, that sounds like Donald Trump!' And it's what Glinda was like, she's one of those who will give the people what they want. I think it's what's going on in the political world today. People don't want to think too deep.

Sybil also draws a link between *Wicked* and the much-publicized killing of an African lion by an American dentist:

> There are two extremely diverse groups in this country about nonhuman creatures and their worthwhileness, and what you can do to them. The dentist who went and hunted a lion. It was shot with a bow and arrow, and then the lion stayed alive for like 40 hours, and then they finally shot it ... The big issues now that's come out is: Why do you kill these things in the first place? What do you get out of it?

Reva, an accounting professor, sees a parallel with an ongoing chapter in American history:

> And the political angle here. The idea that an outsider came in and started making changes, and this may not be a good analogy, but I see that like the white people coming over and trying to regulate the American Indians. I mean Oz going into this land he knows absolutely nothing about and starting to make political changes. He doesn't know anything about the culture, and to him Animals are farm animals, but in Oz they were full citizens. And we came over and said these American Indians are savages and they need to be civilized, and we really didn't know what we were talking about.

Our interviewees indicated again and again that Elphaba is the portal through which they connected to *Wicked*. Regardless of their own circumstances, respondents connected broadly and deeply with her on a variety of levels. Consumers related immediately to her status as outcast, misunderstood, and vulnerable; they also connected with her in her role of a responsible citizen in a corrupt world. And, as the show progressed and Elphaba grew into her powers—and experienced the positive and negative consequences of that growth—consumers related to her even more intensely. Interestingly, these are exactly the qualities that attracted composer Stephen Schwartz to *Wicked* in the first place. As he has stated in numerous interviews, he was irresistibly drawn to her as the misunderstood outcast—a role he himself identified with all too well.[5]

WICKED PROVIDES A THERAPEUTIC NEW PERSPECTIVE ON THE WIZARD OF OZ

Our interviewees' connection to Elphaba often led to the phrase we heard more than any other when asking consumers about *Wicked*: "Everything you thought you knew gets turned on its head in *Wicked*." Naïve as well as knowing consumers repeatedly compared *Wicked* the musical to the 1939 movie, *The Wizard of Oz*, suggesting that for the vast majority of consumers, the movie is the Ur-text against which all other Oz texts are to be compared. For consumers over the age of 55— which made up approximately one-third of our sample—this is undoubtedly due to the fact that they grew up watching *The Wizard of Oz* on television in the annual, semi-ritualized viewing events we discussed in Chapter 4. Such events remain a formative part of that generation's childhood. Josie, in her early 60s, recalls:

> I just remember the family gathering and my mom would say, 'OK, this Sunday is when *The Wizard of Oz* is on,' and we'd all just sort of plan for it, and gosh, that's one of my earliest memories. Every year when it came on the whole family gathered and we'd watch the movie and sing along and do all of that. I don't remember if we had a color TV at first, but I remember my mom telling us that the first part would be in black and white, but then it would switch to color. And I remember how cool it was that you could watch things in color on a television!

Kate adds:

> It used to come on in October, right before Halloween, it was always on
> TV. So, um, we'd go over to Grandma's house and watch it on her TV –
> my sister, both brothers, my mom – it was a family event and we'd watch it
> with my grandmother ever year.

And June, now in her late 70s, recalls:

> I loved Billie Burke as the Good Witch and Margaret Hamilton as the Bad
> Witch, and she died not too many years ago, so she was very young when
> she played that part, and you didn't know it, the makeup was just fabulous.
> But there were so many things about it, you know. The chorus of small –
> little people, and the Yellow Brick Road was just so – it – that just stayed
> with me all my life, the Yellow Brick Road.

These accounts have several characteristics in common: the announcement, by an adult family member, of when the movie would be on;
the bundling up in pajamas of the younger family members (i.e., our
respondents) since the show would end well past their bedtimes; the
gathering of the family around a television set at the appointed time
(often in someone else's home, particularly if the family didn't own a
color television); the consumption of particular food snacks, ordinarily
forbidden (sodas, pop corn, candy); the singing of songs along with the
characters in the movie; and the recollection of being awestruck when
the picture changed from black-and-white to color.

The only thing missing from this list is perhaps the most important,
for the purposes of cultural consumption and sustainability: The absolute terror inspired by the Wicked Witch of the West. A full 95% of our
respondents admitted to being deeply frightened by the Witch—a fear
that seemed to jump out at them anew as they recalled it. Ron, a management professor in his late 50s, is a typical example. He recounts:

> I remember being quite scared by it through the years – the witch, you
> know, the Wicked Witch of the West. In the first scene in the tornado, when
> the woman on the bicycle turns into the witch? That's scary, you know, very
> scary. Then when the Munchkins are singin' a song and all of a sudden it
> explodes and the witch is there, that's pretty scary ... Oh, and I think the

other one was when Dorothy was looking in the ball – in the hourglass – because she saw Uncle Henry and Auntie Em, and then the witch appeared? That was pretty scary too. I remember bein' scared by the witch.

Note that Ron, a traditionally successful adult male approaching 60, uses some version of the word "scary" six times while recalling the Wicked Witch of the West. His memory of precisely when she appears in the film is also noteworthy, though by no means unique. Katherine, now a university president, recalls: "I used to be so afraid when the Wicked Witch of the West came on that I hid behind my father's chair! I asked him to tell me when she was gone so I could come out again. I was as bad as the Munchkins!"

Katherine's description is typical, in that her memory contains a physical response to seeing the Wicked Witch: hiding behind a chair. Similar reactions were true for so many others. Some recalled hiding their faces in their hands. Others hugged a parent or sibling. And still others hid under a blanket. If we extrapolate this reaction to an entire generation of baby boomers, then it is fair to say that the Wicked Witch of the West became an annualized object of terror, imprinted on their collective psyche for four decades, in some cases.

Yet in the hands of *Wicked*'s creators, the Wicked Witch of the West and the abjection she inspires present a rhetorical opportunity of which they take full advantage: to give the Wicked Witch a name and to portray her in a sympathetic light. While Maguire's novel did this to some extent, the Broadway musical, according to our respondents, goes full-bore in a way that inspires feelings of revelation, enlightenment, and even catharsis. So great is the relief among baby boomers that the Wicked Witch is not wicked after all that it creates a "slingshot effect" among over-40 consumers, who were calcified in their abject fear of her—until a retelling allowed them to identify with her. Rachel, a retired attorney in her mid-60s, explains:

> You realize as you watch *Wicked* that everything you've been taught up to now is wrong. The Wicked Witch of the West wasn't really wicked. The Good Witch wasn't really good. The Wizard is Elphaba's father, which is just weird. Everything we were taught as children is false! That's the real power of this show. You're forced to re-think everything you knew.

Sentiments such as these echoed throughout our responses, almost as though there had been a conspiracy. Daniel, a naval officer in his mid-50s, offers: "That was my biggest take-away, there's always two sides to the story, and we were only shown one, so we were manipulated down one path and there was one side, so you know, this just brought in another dimension, and that was so cool about *Wicked*."

Does the same hold true for subsequent generations? Many of our younger respondents, including Gen Xers and millennials, report being scared by the Wicked Witch of the West, though not with the same intensity as their older counterparts. Whether it's because they had access to technologies that would allow them to control their experience of the film, or because they were used to being scared by other cinematic characters and scenes (*Jaws, Nightmare on Elm Street*, and many others), respondents under the age of 40 tend to see the Wicked Witch as a character to be scared of, but not terrified by. Nevertheless, where the witch inspired feelings of antipathy and abjection, Elphaba now inspires empathy and familiarity across all demographics. Tara, in her mid-20s, observes:

> *Wicked* shows the other side of the Wicked Witch of the West. Elphaba is now revealed and sympathized. All that we had previously known about Elphaba is questioned. From the time that she was born, Elphaba was an outsider. Because of her green skin, she was feared or seen as less significant. However, *Wicked* proves that the one character we grew up to hate is the most genuine of all.

This backstory epiphany prompts many respondents to see Elphaba as a role model—a far cry from perceiving her as the one character they had to avoid. Bryan explains: "Elphaba shows me that even when the situation is tough, you can't lose sight of your goals. If someone treats me poorly, dislikes me, or tries to inhibit me in some way, I don't need them in my life. I can live happily, powerfully, and independently without having to lean on anyone." In short, *Wicked* questions all that consumers took for granted as children regarding this impactful narrative. It offers a new version of the Oz story and, in so doing, redeems one of the most reviled characters in cinematic history.

By providing this compelling narrative of how "*she*" came to be evil, *Wicked* provides the culture with an emotional release-valve, explaining away uncomfortable tensions harbored by some consumers for decades. Indeed, we were struck by the sense of relief many of our respondents expressed: relief that the Wicked Witch wasn't as wicked—hence, not as scary—as they had been led to believe. *Wicked* trades on the vast emotional undercurrent of *The Wizard of Oz*, snapping consumers' intense abjection into eager identification. This "slingshot effect" pays powerful dividends in the form of repeated viewings and positive word-of-mouth.

AND THE MORAL IS

If this effect were all *Wicked* accomplished, it would be impactful enough. However, our respondents take this revelation a step further, turning *Wicked* into a cautionary tale with a distinct moral lesson. Even as our respondents expressed their attachment to Elphaba, many were quick to point out that she remains misunderstood throughout the entire play. At the end of the story, the people of Oz assume she has been destroyed. This becomes the cause of their dissonant celebration at both the beginning and the end of the show, providing a frame within which the narrative is situated and related in flashback. This also occasions a moment of dramatic irony noticed by many of our respondents. Roxanne, a nursing student in her 20s, observes:

> It kind of annoyed me at the start of the show when the crowd was shouting in this very dissonant way. I thought, this is no way to start a musical! But then when Elphaba came on to sing 'The Wizard and I," it made more sense. There's a line in that song where she sings something like 'They're having a celebration, and it all has to do with me." And it really got to me, that the crowd was doing that at the start of the show. They were already celebrating her death!

Of course, unlike the movie or the novel, the witch doesn't die in the show; she gets to live with the man she loves. But as Roxanne further observes, it's a pyrrhic victory:

> The ending is definitely bittersweet. Elphaba and Fiyero get to escape, but they will have to live in exile for the rest of their lives. Even Glinda thinks Ephaba is dead. And Fiyero has basically become the Scarecrow, since Elphaba cast a spell on him earlier to save him. Unless she can find a way to change him back, he's stuck that way.

Seeing the heroine and her partner suffer this fate led many respondents to question how it could have been avoided—and more importantly, how it *can* be avoided in their own lives. This in turn occasions the moral and ethical dimensions of the show felt by many respondents. As Karin expresses:

> Sometimes the person you think is evil or bad has like ... maybe you need to give them a second chance and really try to understand from their perspective. Because, I mean, she did things that, if you see it from an outsider's point of view, is gonna look like, 'Oh, she's the bad guy, she's releasing those monkeys, or she's doing this or that.' But when you see it from the other side, she's actually just being defensive. I think that's something we can definitely apply to the real world, and that's what I liked about it. It teaches us something.

Pamela, a business school administrator in her 20s, agrees:

> What does it mean when others call you wicked? Is it because you don't conform? Is it because you're doing something they don't understand? Either way, this show is about acceptance – accepting people's differences, and accepting that sometimes being a true friend means allowing the other person to do what they need to do—not what you *want* them to do.

Josie observes:

> This is about judging people, you know? By the color of their skin or anything else. And maybe just being open-minded enough to change your point of view. If you've always believed this about a person or anything else and then started getting new information, to be open enough to let your opinion shift rather than saying 'Well, no, I've always believed that, so that's the way it has to be,' you know?

Rodney adds:

> I love how the show turns our preconceived notions about stereotypical characters such as the good and bad witches upside down and encourages the audience not to judge people, and that what society tells people they are is not actually who they are.

Paul says succinctly, "It's a great, like, moral to life. You know, not judging a book by its cover." In fact, the phrase most often used by respondents to encapsulate the moral takeaway of *Wicked* was "don't judge a book by its cover." This applied to Glinda as well as Elphaba. Bethany echoed what many respondents felt when she observed: "I think Glinda, technically, was the bad one, because she was, you know, very shallow and very kind of full of herself. She had a bad attitude. She would do whatever it took to get ahead, although it did not bring her happiness."

Other consumers—a distinct minority—were able to extend their empathy to Glinda. Karin, a telemarketer in her 30s, observes:

> You could see her both ways, too. You could see her as kind of a bad guy, like those mean girls in high school, but maybe they're not either. Maybe they have a reason for the way they behave too, and they kind of give you insight to see both sides of her, too. She has good and bad in her, because I think we all do, so it was nice that you got to see her like that.

And Pamela goes a step further, noting that Glinda may have changed more than Elphaba.

> I actually admire Glinda a bit more because of the distance she came, morally. In "Popular," which is a cute pop song, you have her basically doing this makeover on Elphaba. It's funny and everyone laughs, but that song makes me uncomfortable, because what she's doing is kind of immoral. She's forcing Elphaba to become someone she doesn't want to be. By the end of the show, she has come light years beyond that. She allows Elphaba to become the person she needs to be.

In fact, for some viewers, the whole notion of judging was extended to any type of evaluation by one group toward another. Jim, a sociologist who has worked with disadvantaged populations, observes: "Really, this show is about the dangers of prejudice, discrimination, and cruelty. I have a soft spot in my heart for underprivileged populations, and Elphaba clearly comes from one of those. How you treat people like that says a lot about you, and it says a lot about us as a society." Bryan ties these themes back to the millennial generation—a significant fan base of the show:

> Wicked's themes of empowerment, political activism, and individuality communicate very effectively to the millennial audience that is constantly growing to this day. The millennial generation is especially known for being entitled and wanting to feel "special." Wicked is incredibly effective in showing that no matter your interests, talents, the color of your skin, or who you are, you can do something impactful in this world "For Good."

Interestingly, a very few respondents failed to see any moral lesson pertinent to the discriminatory aspect of Elphaba's predicament. They focused instead on her ability to *rise above* her circumstances, rather than dwelling on those circumstances per se. Barry and Pat, a commercially successful couple in their early 60s, noted:

> Elphaba refused to see herself as an outcast. We really didn't see her that way either. She was always in control of her own fate. She pulled herself up by her own bootstraps. She developed her own magic powers, and people ultimately respected her for that.

Indeed, the theme of self-empowerment was seen by others as the moral theme of the show. Katherine observes: "I kept thinking as I was watching this show: Don't ever sell yourself short. Be who you are! That's the key to this show." Bill, a computer scientist, agrees:

> The real moment of truth for Elphaba is in "Defying Gravity." There, she's doing the right thing, standing up for what she believes in. And I think that's a huge message in the show: Will we do that as well? Will we have the courage when the time comes? That's why it's s cool when people get worked up in that moment.

Thus, although the takeaways vary, the critical point is that respondents seek—and find—a moral valence in *Wicked* not always present in a Broadway blockbuster. We see that consumers were not content to tell us that they could relate to Elphaba, or that they were relieved that she wasn't as wicked as they had remembered. Rather, they were eager to translate these reactions into a clear moral takeaway for daily living: don't judge a book by its cover. We heard repeatedly that in order to avoid the kind of discrimination and "bullying" Elphaba experienced in *Wicked*, people in real life need to be less superficially judgmental, more willing to consider a person's history, circumstances, and full range of actions before characterizing them as good or bad. Respondents felt that, like Glinda and Elphaba, people in real life are neither entirely good nor entirely bad. They felt that *Wicked* holds up a mirror to their own moral compromises, contradictions, and misperceptions.

Wicked also resonated with respondents along two sociopolitical fronts: the rights of women and the rights of animals. Many women in particular saw Elphaba's plight as resembling their own: ostracized for being different, feared for being talented, and resented for being success-ful, Elphaba becomes more misunderstood as her "career" in Oz pro-gresses. Nevertheless she persisted. Women of all ages could relate to this. Consumers also resonated with Professor Dillamond's metamorpho-sis from Animal to animal, as well as the frightened lion cub's evolution into the Cowardly Lion. In fact, many respondents wished this subplot had been developed further. In any case, consumers were quick to trans-late the lessons of *Wicked* into their own lives and relationships. While the show was seen as enjoyable, it was rarely seen as trivial.

Both Women and Men Enjoy a Story About Two Powerful Women

One of the most powerful meanings consumers found in *Wicked* cen-tered on its exploration of gender and female empowerment. When the show opened 2003, it was expected to appeal primarily to women—who represent almost 66% of the Broadway theater audience—due to its focus on the relationship between Glinda and Elphaba. And indeed, our find-ings resoundingly support this expectation.[6] In interview after interview, women were attracted to *Wicked* precisely *because* of the relationship between the two young women. This held true regardless of age. Cheryl, a successful dermatologist in her early 60s, exudes:

> *Wicked* is so different from all the other musicals I've seen! Look, it's a show about two powerful women in a relationship. How novel is that?! A lot of us have relationships like that in our own lives, but you never see them portrayed on the stage. This alone would be worth the price of admission. But when you see it done so truthfully … this *makes* the musi-cal, for me.

Katherine, a university president also in her 60s, concurs:

> I loved the *story*: these two very strong, very different young women start out as adversaries and end up as friends. They're enacting this deep emo-tional connection that so many of us have enjoyed in real life. Especially today, as more and more women climb to the top of the corporate lad-der, we need to learn how to navigate our relationships with other women. *Wicked* is the only show that even begins to do that.

Many of our younger female respondents felt the same way, perhaps more in principle than from direct personal experience—yet. Peggy, a veterinarian in her late 20s, states:

> Finding a purpose, betrayal, fitting in and weighing values against going with the flow – these are all pertinent in the lives of women as well as in *Wicked*. There are many pressures that a woman feels, and the show captures these pressures and offers some relief, with songs like "Defying Gravity." Defying gravity is an apt metaphor for what many women feel they have to do in order to succeed.

And Tara, a pharmacy student also in her 20s, observes:

> The theme throughout this musical will strike a chord for women in particular. Elphaba – who was seen as an underdog by all – proves to be an empowering and inspirational character to female viewers, who have also been deemed an underdog by our society. Against all odds, Elphaba turns out to be the most talented student in the class and gets to work with the Wizard, when everyone else was against her and didn't believe in her. *Wicked* shows women that they too can "defy gravity" and go after any dreams they wish to.

And June, 78, sees Elphaba's courage as an essential quality for women as they navigate the working world:

> I know women take less wages, but if they've got that enduring quality, they're gonna make it ... by having the strength and courage to keep going when everything's against you. You have to be courageous, like Elphaba was courageous. I left the theater, and I was ready to take on anyone! [Laughing].

Whether they are about to enter the workforce, are successful veterans within it, or are philosophical retirees from it, women eagerly relate to the Glinda–Elphaba story. Powerful reactions such as these help explain two different phenomena we observed over the years as we attended numerous performances of *Wicked*. One is a common backstage ritual that occurs when awestruck young girls approach the show's two stars and find it hard to speak. In order to break the ice, the actors pose the question, "Are you a Glinda, or an Elphaba?" This invariably draws a spontaneous response from the young fans. Mission accomplished. The other female-based occurrence involves the preponderance of women attending the show in large groups. In some instances, women come dressed in green or even wearing witches' hats; in others—especially "Hen Parties" in the UK and bachelorette parties in the USA—a group of women all dress the same, with one woman (the bride-to-be) wearing a veil or tiara.[7]

Clearly, female consumers relate closely to a show about a compelling friendship between two women. But one of the more striking findings to come out of our consumer interviews is that many men also enjoy watching a relationship unfold between two powerful women. Gary, a musician in his early 60s, offers this whimsical explanation:

> I've never had a problem watching women get along, or duke it out. I remember watching Diana Rigg in *The Avengers* when I was a boy. She was so badasss! I loved it when she would start doing martial arts on people. When she would fight another woman, I thought it was way cool. The classic cat-fight.

Bill, a software manager in his mid-50s, takes his examples from the present-day:

> Two strong women – what's the problem? I get so tired of seeing men act tough all the time. *Wicked* gives you the flip side. It's very refreshing. I like observing strong women in real life – Madonna, Hillary, Serena. Why can't we have women like that onstage? Women often have different ways of working things out.

Admiration, excitement, and novelty—these were some of the reactions male respondents shared with us. But one reaction kept surfacing that we hadn't anticipated: empathy. Men readily "felt with" Glinda and Elphaba as they went through challenges within the show. Jim, a sociologist and father of two daughters, explains: "When I hear either one of them sing 'I'm Not That Girl,' it really speaks to me. I think of all the times when 'I Wasn't That Guy.' It wouldn't matter if I were a man or a woman or a single guy or married, I would feel the same way at that moment. The feeling of rejection. We can all relate to that, can't we?"

In fact, rejection and isolation surfaced frequently as we asked men to elaborate on their reactions to certain moments in the show. Bill, who has seen *Wicked* seven times, observed:

To me, the most moving scene in the entire show is when Glinda gives Elphaba the witch's hat during the dance party. There she is in the middle of the dance floor, and people are ridiculing her and she doesn't even know it. Then Glinda realizes the cruelty of her ways. She goes up to Elphaba and begins dancing with her. That really gets me.

And Scott, a transportation manager in his 40s, volunteers:

I've seen *Wicked* three times, and I don't mind admitting that I've cried every time. Sometimes it's out of joy, or maybe defiance, like when she sings "Defying Gravity." And then it's with sadness, like in "For Good." I know it's against societal expectations for a man to react in this way, but I'm not going to apologize. This is how I felt.

Contrary to more traditional gender roles, then, we found that many men were quite capable of—and comfortable with—responding emotionally as the performance moved them, without feeling compromised in their masculinity. This phenomenon is critical in explaining how *Wicked* transcended the label of "a women's musical," enabling it to broaden its target market and capture more revenue as a result.

WICKED UNITES AUDIENCES AS WELL AS FAMILIES

Many men, of course, were not responding simply as men; they were also responding as fathers. Time and again, our consumer respondents told us that seeing *Wicked* became a family occasion, crossing generational boundaries, and in many cases, uniting them. Although no one described the show as a "family musical," they nevertheless treated it as one, including grandparents, children, siblings, and cousins in their parties. Such is not always the case when considering which Broadway show to attend with a family. Aside from Disney-based musicals such as *The Lion King* and *Beauty and the Beast*, viewers are often unable to discern what musicals are family-suitable, and which aren't. Gerri, a retired marketing professor, observed:

Recently I saw "Waitress," and while I liked the show well enough, I was taken aback by some of the things I was seeing onstage. There was an abusive marital relationship that went on for quite a while, then a highly suggestive scene between two married people in a gynecologist's office. I thought to myself, 'Gee, if I'd taken my twelve-year-old son or daughter to this, I would be so embarrassed!' You just don't know what you're going to get in a Broadway musical these days if it isn't Disney. If you take a family of four, you could easily spend $500 on something that you actually don't want your kids to see. What a mistake that would be!

What makes parents comfortable having both their parents and their children see *Wicked* in the same group? Respondents told us that while many of the characters and relationships portrayed in the show are dysfunctional, they are nevertheless shown realistically and palatably, in ways that all of us can recognize. Parents recognize these dynamics in their children, but the children (and their grandparents) recognize these patterns as well. Holly, who worked for years in international aid, elaborates:

> None of the characters in *Wicked* are perfect, and none of their relationships are perfect. But isn't that true in real life? The question is how you work out those relationships despite your imperfections. I saw *Wicked* when it first came out, and right then I knew I had to take my mother and sister to see it. We all went later, and it gave us *so* much to talk about afterwards!

Indeed, respondents told us that either Glinda or Elphaba translates easily into somebody's sister, daughter, or granddaughter, so that the show holds up a relational mirror to the families in attendance. Cheryl observes:

> If you're a mother and you have daughters, you'd better take them to see *Wicked*. It simply nails how siblings work through their relationship. You feel better as a mother knowing that you're not the only one to preside over that level of rivalry and conflict. If you're lucky, you will also get to preside over a similar resolution.

Even as mothers were automatically drawn to *Wicked* because of the female-to-female themes they so readily recognize, fathers were as well—due to the relationships they have with their daughters.

Jim, who earlier empathized with both female leads, also acknowledged that being a father of two daughters enabled him to easily relate to the story line:

I'm so proud of both my daughters and the amazing young women they've turned out to be. I've always supported them in sports, music – whatever they wanted to do. So naturally as I watch these two young women onstage, I can't help but feel paternal. I want to support them. I want them to succeed!

Finally, we found in some cases that the show went beyond an occasion to unite families; it provided a springboard to discuss sensitive family issues that the show itself portrayed. Katherine recalls:

After we saw *Wicked*, it was so clear that our older daughter was more like Elphaba, and our younger daughter was more like Glinda! The song "Popular" put it all into perspective. During that song, you can see the kind of pressure Glinda is putting on herself. She needs to be loved by everybody, to be good at everything, to appeal to the perfect guy. She appears to be happy, but if you look beneath the surface, you can see you insecure she is. I saw my daughter in a similar light, and I saw the toll it was taking on her. I sat down with her, and we actually used "Popular" as a way to discuss what she was going through. I think it helped us better understand what was going on, and how to deal with it.

Beyond familial ties, we were struck by the general awareness our respondents had of the people around them in the audience, and how their reactions helped shape their own. Repeatedly, we heard such reactions as these: "Seeing the enthusiasm on everyone in the theatre's faces, I don't think that it would make a difference whether I was seeing the show with my family or one other friend – everyone was experiencing the event as it it was the first time." "Some people started to shout during that song. I heard one woman say 'Amen!'" and "I heard a lot of sniffles around me. I knew that I was not the only crying."

Consumer behaviorists would argue that, in a world of increasingly isolated experiences, live theater brings people together both physically and emotionally. Marketing expert Lindsay Vick observes:

If you look around especially in big cities today, you see so much physical disconnection amid all the virtual connection. It's like we're all engaged in parallel play; that's how GenZ relates. But the fact is that people have not evolved *that* quickly. We still need each other. What *can't* you get online? Maybe it's hearing music live. Maybe it's seeing a famous performer. Maybe it's feeling the same emotion with lots of other people at the same time. Whatever those appeals are, that's what will get people out of their rooms and into a public space.[8]

That kind of peak experience, investigated by researchers such as Mihaly Csikszentmihalyi, is articulated beautifully by Hannah, a school secretary: "I just had the best time. I was with people that I loved, and we had a fabulous meal, and we were in a beautiful theater, and I loved the music, and I knew the story … everything about it was just a good experience."[9] To the extent that live musical theater can keep providing people with such "good experiences," its future is assured.

As our respondents show, *Wicked* connected with multiple market segments. But we also wanted to know if consumers had any sense of *Wicked*'s place in the broader cultural landscape. Their responses surprised us.

WICKED HAS REACHED A CULTURAL TIPPING POINT

In his best-selling book, *The Tipping Point*, author Malcolm Gladwell likens social trends to a single sick person starting a flu epidemic. Under the right circumstances, awareness of and interest in a phenomenon such as a fashion trend, a celebrity, or a particular social behavior reaches a critical mass and "boils over" into the culture at large.[10] After the tipping point is reached, it becomes difficult to find members of the culture who are *not* aware of the trend, celebrity, or behavior in question. Examples include the fashion trend that allows men to wear most of their shirts untucked, Justin Bieber, and the relatively recent (and rapid) acceptance of same-sex marriage by the majority of the US population. After 15 years of eight weekly performances on Broadway, in addition to almost constant tours across the USA, we wondered: has *Wicked* reached a tipping point of its own?

The answer is "yes," although it depends on the age of the respondents in question. Specifically, for our consumer respondents over the age of 40, *Wicked* exists primarily as a discreet entity whose major connection is to the 1939 film, *The Wizard of Oz*. "Isn't that the remake of the movie?" many of our older respondents would ask. Based on their formative, often traumatic experiences of watching *The Wizard of Oz* as children, they are drawn to the Broadway musical through their recollection of—and fondness for—the Hollywood movie. However, for respondents under 40—and especially for those under 30—*Wicked* is positioned within a complex web of social media outlets, mobile technologies, and performative events that enable younger consumers to become quite familiar with the show and its songs without ever having seen it. Barb, a psychology major in her 20s, relates: "I hadn't seen *Wicked* before, but I knew some of the songs from it because I streamed them on Pandora. I still to listen to them a lot while I work out. Then some of my friends saw the show in New York, and they posted photos of themselves on Instagram outside the Gershwin Theatre."

In this response alone, Barb captures several significant factors related to *Wicked*'s success, all having to do with technologies that we may take for granted today: a streaming service that would allow her to listen to the songs well in advance of having seen the show; a portable sound system that enables her to engage in other activities while listening to those songs; and a social media network that allows Barb's friends to show her photographs and videos of themselves attending the show. In this way, Barb can experience key elements of the show well in advance of having actually seen it first-hand. As media experts have noted, Barb lives in a world in which consumers "pull down" mediated artifacts when, where, and how it suits them, as opposed to traditional mediated programming in which such artifacts were "pushed out" to consumers at times and places controlled by producers. The convenience, the rapidity, and the immediacy with which consumers can experience phenomena previously unavailable to them have been the subject of countless studies on new media over the past several decades. Pertinent to our argument here is that new technologies, particularly streaming services and social media, have had a profound effect on consumers' ability to know, in some way, about *Wicked*.

The upshot is that younger consumers have been listening, moving, competing (in the case of auditions and talent shows), and socializing to songs from *Wicked* for many years now. As with any production that came of age after widespread use of the internet began (experts date this between 1993 and 1995), *Wicked* benefits from the thousands of internet entries having even the most tangential relationship to the musical itself. These include all "the making of" lectures and workshops, hundreds of renditions of songs such as "Defying Gravity" and "Popular" by singers of varying degrees of fame and talent, and elaborately produced homemade trailers heralding the much-anticipated arrival of the movie version of *Wicked*, scheduled to open in December of 2019. Add to this list the official websites of *Wicked* productions on Broadway and in London—continuously updated with new feature stories, cast changes, and links to videos of key performances—and it becomes difficult to find consumers who have *not* heard of *Wicked*. Indeed, of the more than 100 consumers we asked to interview for this project, only one had never heard of the novel or the show. A 99% level of brand awareness is something most marketers can only dream about. As far as is it possible to prove, almost everyone knows about *Wicked*—proof that a cultural tipping point has indeed been achieved. But does everyone like it?

Our findings reveal that, indeed, almost everyone finds a way to like *Wicked*. While some consumers may not enjoy every aspect of the show, they like it well enough to consider it a worthwhile expenditure of their time and money—and the vast majority of our respondents liked it much more than that. However, a distinct minority of our respondents truly disliked *Wicked*. How and why they did so is the subject of our next finding.

SOME PEOPLE GENUINELY DISLIKE *WICKED*

A small but vocal minority—about 15% of the consumer respondents we interviewed—took an unrelentingly dim view of *Wicked*, and they did so for a variety of reasons. They seemed to know they were in the minority, so we gave them ample time to articulate their disaffections. The reasons for their antipathy can be grouped into five semi-distinct clusters.

The first cluster centers around *Wicked*'s tendency to pander to the lowest common denominator. Jeannie, a teacher in her 50s, maintains: "The characters are so broadly drawn, and the humor is so low-level, that I'm shocked that this show has become a blockbuster. I just don't get it. There's so much build-up in many of the scenes, but they're all fluff, no substance. Maybe that's what people want." Cory, a marketing major in her 20s, concurs:

> I loved the time dragon, but I wish there had been a story line behind it. Why have something there if you're just going to show it off? It seems pretentious that you are just trying to amaze me with all of these tricks but not actually deliver a reason why. And Elphaba? I don't know how she furthered all the animal causes during that time. The ads showed me she was a rebel, but not much was used to enforce that idea in the play.

The themes of this show are supposed to be so important, but they set the wrong expectations for what the show actually delivers.

Laura, a writer, succinctly observes: "This play doesn't make the audience think too much. It just lets them relax and have a good time. It actually amazes me that this story line has made billions and billions of dollars!"

In a second, related cluster, some consumers saw *Wicked* as a cynical (and highly successful) attempt to take money from consumers without giving them much in return. For some, this was a sacrilege akin to allowing money changers in the temple. Cory observes: "From the moment I entered the theater, I kept running into merchandise, photo opportunities, and people. I felt like I was in a gift shop! Most people acted like they were going to get on a ride. I have seen many plays that were commercialized, but not like this." This quote bears striking resemblance to a quote from the following chapter, in which a composer likens writer Winnie Holzman's working style to construct a roller coaster. In that context, the remark is high complimentary, for it shows Holzman's innate ability to continually empathize with her audience. Here, the response is less flattering. Ben, a finance major, chose to look behind all of *Wicked*'s glitz and see a very large moneymaking machine—similar to discovering "that man behind the curtain" in *The Wizard of Oz*:

Make no mistake, *Wicked* is a major business venture with major business backing. It was produced by a conglomerate that took in $64 billion in 2013! This makes the "art" of the theatre look a lot less unique, and more like another profit stream for a multi-billion dollar conglomerate. Just think: this evening they made about a half-million dollars for two hours' work. Not bad!

While the accuracy of Ben's claim is difficult to substantiate, his perception is what matters: that *Wicked*'s real strength lies in turning a profit for its investors. Ben's complete emotional detachment from the show put him in the distinct minority.

The third cluster finds *Wicked*'s music and special effects entirely forgettable. Jeannie expressed her frustration at what many consumers found to be the most thrilling point in the show:

I first saw *Wicked* during its tryout run in San Francisco. When Elphaba started singing "Defying Gravity," I thought, 'This is it. She's going to fly!' Except that she never actually flew. She just waved her arms and shook her broomstick and *pretended* to fly. I was so annoyed by that! I was sure they'd find a way to make her fly by the time the show got to Broadway. But they didn't.

Gary, a professional musician who also saw the show in San Francisco, agreed: "They made Peter Pan fly, and they made Spider-Man fly. So they should have made Elphaba fly. All the lighting and sound effects in the world can't compensate for the fact that she never actually leaves the platform she's standing on. This is the 21st century. Surely they could've found a way."

If the special effects disappointed some consumers, so, too, did the music. Robin, a waiter in her 40s, echoed the opinion of many New York critics cited in the previous chapter when she complains: "I found the music completely forgettable. When I came out of the theater, I couldn't remember one melody from that show! It was *way* too pop oriented. If this is the direction Broadway is going, they can keep it. I would rather stay home and listen to my iPod." Of course, Robins' reaction runs counter to almost all of the consumers we interviewed. However, a few others agreed with her. They extended their opinion to assess *Wicked*'s place in the pantheon of Broadway musicals. Roxanne, a healthcare manager, submits: "I think that in the long run, this show doesn't qualify as one of the all-time greats. Sure, it's approachable, and you can take your kids to see it. But it's no *Phantom of the Opera*."

Interestingly, Roxanne's choice of comparators was not unique. Three respondents compared *Wicked* to *Phantom of the Opera* and found it lacking. Is that because some consumers don't see the songs of Stephen Schwartz on the same level as Andrew Lloyd Weber's? That was the opinion of George, an English publicist in his 70s: "I really don't see why they bothered making *Wicked*. It's all been done before, and better. I would much rather see something written by Lloyd Webber." We stress that these perspectives were held by only a handful of our respondents—and George, like Andrew Lloyd Webber, is British. After all, if even a sizable minority of consumers held these views, *Wicked* would not be the commercial success it has been over the years.

The fourth cluster maintains that *Wicked*'s long run at the Gershwin crowds out—literally and figuratively—promising new musicals that could bring in new audiences. Nick, a part-time actor, explains:

> I have nothing against *Wicked*'s success. It deserves that. But the problem comes when you try to bring something new to Broadway. There's *Wicked* at one theater, *Cats* in another, and *Phantom* in another. These things are dinosaurs! They sit there for years, and there's no room for something new. The trouble is that their composers are so rich, they can afford to take the hit when they're not selling out. That doesn't seem fair to the newer composers who are trying to break through.

Morgan, a painter, sees the same shortcoming from the consumer's point of view: "Most people have only so much money to spend on a Broadway show. If they can only see one, chances are they'll go with an old war horse rather than try something new. That's why everything looks the same on Broadway these days. We're not offering people that much to choose from." Morgan's claims are, in fact, false. There is tremendous variety in the range of musicals offered on Broadway and the West End in a given season. Furthermore, the workers advising theatergoers at half-priced ticket booths in New York and London are remarkably even-handed when suggesting which musicals consumers might see. We interviewed many of these employees, most of whom are trying to succeed in show business themselves. Even though they may have their well-considered personal favorites, they refrain from overtly steering buyers toward one musical over another, preferring instead to match shows with consumer preferences. Still, as marketers know, perception is all.

The fifth and final cluster, supported exclusively by much older consumers, holds that *Wicked* should never have been made in the first place. That's because *The Wizard of Oz* was, and remains, the last word on any story having to do with Dorothy and the land of Oz. Eve, who is 93 and enjoyed a successful career as an executive secretary, speaks eloquently to this point:

> You have to remember that I saw *The Wizard of Oz* when it was first released in movie theaters in 1939. That's when you could stay in the theater all day for 25 cents. It was hot in Tulsa, and the movies were the only place it was air-conditioned, so we would stay there most of the day. Judy Garland was only a few years older than I was. I thought she was

absolute perfection. The way she sang and acted – she was incredibly talented. But she was also innocent – she didn't know how talented she was. I adored her. We all did.

The high esteem in which Eve held Judy Garland also extended to her opinion of other stars in the show:

> Ray Bolger, Jack Haley, Bert Lahr, Billie Burke– these were well-known performers my parents and I enjoyed watching in other films before *The Wizard of Oz* came out. They were all trained in vaudeville – that's how far back we're talking. They could sing, dance, act – and they had perfect comedic timing. So if you put the four of them in those costumes and have them sing songs by Harold Arlen … you can't get any better than that.

Given the surfeit of talent on full display in *The Wizard of Oz*, Eve's reaction to *Wicked* is, at best, bewildered: "Really, I can't understand why they made it. What was the point? Did we learn anything new that we really needed to know? I don't think so. You can't improve on perfection. They should have left well enough alone and gone off in a completely different direction."

When pressed on her opinion of the performers in *Wicked*, Eve remained largely unmoved: "Well, I think they're very talented, but they shout too much. Judy Garland never shouted. She didn't have to. Is this the style of singing people want to hear now?" And as to the music of *Wicked*, Eve observes: "There are some catchy melodies. There are moments when I think it's quite beautiful [referring to 'I'm Not That Girl.']. But often it's too loud. I don't hear anything to compare with 'Over the Rainbow.'" When told that *Wicked* is one of the most successful musicals in recent history, Eve laughs: "Well, that goes to show I'm from a different era. I'm old – too old!"

These interviewee-responses show us that, although *Wicked* is a highly appealing theatrical experience for most consumers, some just don't "get" the show and wish they'd seen something else. Too commercialized, too pandering, too superficial, and too expensive—these were the major complaints about *Wicked*. For those who had read the novel first, the show was a distinct disappointment; for those who had seen the show first, the novel lacked energy and the happy ending they expected. Either way, "point of entry" played a powerful role in setting expectations and suggesting authenticity.

YOUR FIRST OZ MATTERS

As we interviewed dozens of respondents, we were struck time and again by their preference for one "version" of Oz over another. This most clearly applied to the two main iterations of *Wicked*—the novel and the musical. And the general rule became: whichever version the respondents encountered first was the version they preferred. This was especially true if consumers had seen the musical before they had read the novel. They usually liked the show a great deal and couldn't wait to read the novel. But when they did—or attempted to—they were invariably disappointed. Josie's response is typical: "Yes, my husband and I saw the musical and loved it. So we couldn't wait to read the book. We actually listened to it on tape as we drove across the country. It was like: when are we gonna get to the fun part? We just found the book so dark and heavy. We kept waiting for the play *Wicked*. When the tape was over, we said, 'Why did we do that?!'"

Indeed, for those who had seen the show first, the most common adjective used to describe the novel was "dark." Here is Gary, the musician, on reading the novel after seeing the show:

> I was just shocked at how that book became the basis for the musical! How did they get *that* from the book? The book is so dark. The scenes and images are stark. Most of the characters are unappealing. The Witch lives and dies shut off from everyone else. I felt like in the show, Elphaba has real moments of gratification – times when she really gets in touch with who she is. The audience revels in those moments with her. But I never felt that when I read the book. It's beautifully written, but it's desolate. I actually felt pretty lonely as I was reading it.

In sum, none of our respondents who saw *Wicked* the show first liked *Wicked* the novel when they read it. But the converse was also true: Those who had read the novel first simply did not like the musical. Jeannie's perspective was typical of our novel-first respondents:

> I was more than disappointed when I saw the show after I had read the novel. They took this wonderfully complex work of art and completely dumbed it down! They got a lot more people in the door, no doubt. But to me, it was one big missed opportunity. If they had tried to retain some of the darkness, it would have been a much better show.

Jeannie's sentiments echo those of many theater professionals, as we show in the next chapter. For them, *Wicked*'s musical adaptation was a calculated commercial move that ignored the more evocative aspects of the novel. They felt the adaptors could have "swung for the fences," but took the easy way out.

Thus, it appears that what respondents saw or read first matters, in terms of establishing their expectations—and in most cases, their preferences. This speaks to Hutcheon's concept of "point of entry": Consumers are always entering the stream of adaptation at differing points, so that what is old for one consumer (e.g., *Wicked* the novel) can be new for another. Although point of entry is largely beyond anyone's control, it powerfully affects how the next re-consumption is received.

Interestingly, while many of our older consumers preferred the film *The Wizard of Oz* to the newer musical *Wicked*—a point made in the previous section—a number of consumers of all ages preferred the opposite, maintaining that the musical is more complex and true-to-life than the movie. Paul, the security guard in his 40s, observes: "I feel like there's more of a family aspect to *The Wizard of Oz*. 'There's no place like home' type of thing. With *Wicked*, you get a more typical modern family where the dad is missing, there are jealous siblings, maybe less wholesome. It's a little more edgy, but I also think a little more relatable to this day and age than *The Wizard of Oz* is." Reva, in her 60s, agreed:

> I think that *The Wizard of Oz* is a kids' show, and I think it is a fairly simple message, you know: "Wherever you go, there you are" type of thing. I think that *Wicked* is more complex than that. It speaks to a lot of society and more deep personal conflict. The fact that you can be really good friends with somebody that you disagree with, for example.

In the future, it may well be that *The Wizard of Oz* will be seen as outdated and largely unrelatable by respondents, in ways similar to how Baum's original stories appear anachronistic to many respondents now. As that happens, *Wicked* may well emerge as the new Oz Ur-text.

WICKED CAN BE SOUL-STIRRING AND LIFE-CHANGING

Consumers are often moved by the artistic performances they have experienced; indeed, that would seem to be the point of attending almost any artistic performance. But in the case of *Wicked*, we were struck by the degree to which people were moved, as well as by the *range* of emotions the show elicited within a given respondent. When recalling the show or specific moments from it, voices cracked, hands shook, and tears flowed for over 10% of our respondents—an astonishing number, given that all our respondents were recalling the show at least one month after they had seen it. And some respondents became emotional *years* after they'd seen *Wicked*. What, we wanted to know, was the exact nature and direction of their emotional intensity?

For many, the fact that *Wicked* depended on music was enough to take them to a place of high emotions—a journey which, understandably, they found difficult to articulate. Josie relates: "A story that draws you in and makes you think, and of course, music that's either beautiful and happy, or the music that plays with your emotions a bit. They tend to stir your soul and make you think about things."

Karin expands on this notion:

> I think music definitely moves your emotions. That's why the great block-buster movies like *Star Wars* and *ET* have really great musical themes. The orchestral compositions – that's what moves people and our emotions. Music gives the story so much more emotional impact. When you're watching something and hearing the music tugging at your heartstrings, building excitement, sadness, joy, and all of those things … it stays with you.

For a subset of respondents, then, the music of *Wicked* is the gateway to the show's emotional intensity and impact. These consumers are able to recognize that the confluence of narrative and music can make a production "soul-stirring" in a way that either element, by itself, cannot. Callie observes: "People remember the songs and it keeps the story alive for them. It makes it stick in your mind longer than a play. *The Sound of Music*—why is it that 50 years later and we're still remembering it?" Loretta, an attorney in her early 60s, agreed: "The real takeaway from this show is: people should see more musicals! Watching beautiful young people use their talent to create a powerful moment—that is more important than the story itself!"

For others, the simple fact that they felt the full range of emotions— from elation to despair, from anticipation to dread, from hope to resignation—meant that *Wicked* had fulfilled its highest promise as a Broadway musical: to make them really feel something. To our surprise, these respondents reveled in feeling the entire spectrum of emotions, not just the "happy" ones. Kate captures this sentiment:

> Anytime that you can laugh or cry with the characters that you're watching, you feel happy, mad, and they can pull out those emotions, then yeah, it's been done right. I enjoy that; I want to feel something. Otherwise I don't connect with the play, I won't connect to the movie, I wouldn't connect to the book. Something has to pull me in. And if I can laugh and fall in love with the characters as I watch it, then that does it for me. And *Wicked* did. It did.

This desire to connect with the characters through the full range of emotions helps explain why most respondents are not disappointed by *Wicked*'s quiet "For Good" ending to Act II—as opposed to the death-defying "Defying Gravity" conclusion to Act I. Kelly explains:

> When I got to the intermission, I wondered how they were ever going to match that intensity again. But by the time Glinda and Elphaba held hands and started singing "For Good," I didn't care. I was totally in the moment. Even though I was crying, it was a beautiful sadness.

Finally, there was a distinct group of respondents whose lives were forever altered by *Wicked*, usually because of how it enabled them to celebrate a relationship. For Paul and Brittany, a promotional exhibit at a shopping mall—featuring *Wicked*—became an occasion to fall in love and eventually get married. Brittany recalls:

> I was staffing a promotional event in the mall called, "The World of *Wicked*." And Paul was a security guard at the mall. Part of his duty was to come through and make sure everything was in order. He'd stop by and make sure everything was going okay. Him and I just ended up striking up a friendship. And things sort of progressed from there. So we met because of the show. If *Wicked* hadn't come to town, the two of us probably wouldn't have met.

Paul, now Brittany's husband, continues:

> Yeah, *Wicked* is kind of 'our show.' We put "For Good" into our wedding ceremony. Every time I hear it, I think of how I first heard it with her, how she was crying when I looked over at her.

Others told us how the show encouraged them to value someone they already knew even more. For two sisters, the lyrics of "For Good" became a reason to get complementary tattoos as a symbol of their emotional connection. This was related to us quite spontaneously by their father, Jim, who was in the middle of recalling taking his daughters to see *Wicked* in Chicago when he suddenly remembered something they had done as a result of having seen the show. He explains:

> The girls saw *Wicked* at just the right age. It showed them that they could be these two beautiful, very powerful young women and still love each other not in spite of, but because of, their differences. And – oh my gosh, I just thought of something! They got tattoos that are related to each. One has a tattoo of a ship, and the other has a tattoo of a bird. Isn't that from one of the songs? "For Good," maybe?

Indeed, Jim's hunch is correct: Schwartz uses two similes to juxtapose these images in "For Good." Thus, in public displays filled with private meaning, consumers weave *Wicked* into their lives as points of commemoration, confirmation, and celebration of their long-term commitments to one another.

At its best, a Broadway musical can take viewers to emotional heights and depths they've never experienced, and *Wicked* accomplished this for many of our respondents. Interestingly, it was the range of emotions they felt gratified to experience. The old adage, "You'll laugh, you'll cry ..." rings true: Many respondents come to the theater for precisely that reason. To the extent a musical can deliver on that promise, it is deemed successful. Between the high-octane friendship that centers it, the diva-esque songs that enact it, and the revisionist history that frames it, *Wicked* sends some consumers into the emotional stratosphere. Trips of that type are forgotten neither quickly nor willingly. Rather, consumers commemorate them in ways that affirm their most meaningful relationships with others.

CONCLUSION

As our consumer interviews attest, *Wicked* succeeded in becoming a major cultural touchpoint—and thus a key player in Oz's cultural sustainability— for much the same reasons MGM's *The Wizard of Oz* did in 1939. As we can see in the following summation, which examines

Wicked within the framework we proposed at the end of Chapter 3, Schwartz' and Holzman's Broadway musical, like MGM's Technicolor film, offered consumers a re-consumption of Oz that was able to:

- **Tap into an unbroken chain of memory**: As did MGM's film and its television broadcast, *Wicked* premiered at a key point in Oz's history; the last mass-culture Oz event, *The Wiz*, had occurred nearly thirty years ago, and many consumers were too young to have participated in the television ritual. Yet, over and over, we heard consumers over the age of 40 recall their childhood-viewings of the annual *Wizard of Oz* broadcasts; a few of our older interviewees even remembered seeing the film in its original theatrical run. For all of these consumers, their memories of the film inflected their viewing of the musical. For some, *Wicked* compared positively, adding a new dimension to the tale—and indeed, some of their pleasure in the musical was the pleasure of recognition and delight in what Hutcheon calls "repetition with a difference." For many of these viewers, *Wicked* was a revelation—a delightful take on the story that gave it new relevance. Others found the experience of *Wicked* wanting, but even for these consumers, seeing the musical brought the film—and Oz—back into their consciousness, reviving more positive memories of early Oz experiences. Like it or hate it, *Wicked* brought Oz back into the conversation. Furthermore, *Wicked* gave older consumers a chance both to re-experience Oz and, as was indicated by our interviewees, to share that experience with their children and grandchildren, thus extending the cultural life of the narrative.
- **Reach a large pool of new consumers**: The diversification of viewing platforms and options in the 1980s lessened the impact of the MGM film. Additionally, other fantasy and science fiction narratives, such as *Harry Potter, The Hunger Games*, and *Lord of the Rings*, now competed with Oz for teen and tween consumers. Using new media and social networking platforms to aggressively market to this audience, *Wicked*, as we saw in Chapter 6 and in our response pool, drew a new generation to Oz, reaching a "cultural tipping point." And this generation played a critical role in introducing older consumers, raised on MGM, to the musical.
- **Go beyond repetition and imitation to offer something new**: As we saw with MGM's adaptation of Baum's book, an adaptation

needs to be "made suitable" to both new audiences and new media. *Wicked*'s remediation of Maguire's novel (and indirectly MGM's film and Baum's tale), as we saw in both our discussion of the adaptation process and consumer's responses to the musical, worked to make its originary text suitable for both the Broadway stage and a twenty-first-century audience. Consumers told us that the show's streamlined plot, emphasizing the relationship between Elphaba and Glinda and its (however qualified) happy ending met their Broadway expectations, at the same time as the musical's updated themes, particularly as they related to gender, resonated with audiences. Furthermore, our interviewees observed that the music heightened the emotions being played out onstage and gave them the emotional stimulation they expect from live musical theater.

- **Welcome new consumers, standing on its own merit**: While our established consumer-interviewees reveled in the pleasures of the knowing audience, recognizing allusions to previous Oz narratives, and reading this version of Oz in the context of MGM, new consumers were able to enjoy *Wicked* with limited previous exposure to the narrative. In fact, as we noted, the consumers who did not like the musical were those who refused to view it on its own merit, but insisted on comparing it to either Maguire or MGM. These consumers, on the whole, were unable to get past the point at which they had entered the chain of adaptations to look at the musical *as a Broadway musical*. Consumers who responded positively to *Wicked*, on the other hand, found it an exhilarating, soul-stirring *Broadway experience*. For many theatergoers, the true test of a Broadway musical is whether they leave the theater humming a tune from the show. Respondents told us that Schwartz's music passes this test many times over, imprinting the audience with a half-dozen memorable tunes. Between "The Wizard and I," "Popular," "I'm Not that Girl," "Defying Gravity," "No Good Deed," and "For Good," consumers were hard-pressed to choose a favorite song, although "Defying Gravity" was, by a clear margin, the bring-the-house-down number of the show.
- *Mean something* **beyond their re-presentation of the narrative but that something must be malleable**: As we have seen throughout our discussion, Oz has always had a moral and ethical valence, from Baum's meditations on a utopian society without evil or want, through MGM's celebration of home and hearth, to *Wicked*'s

examination of compassion and social justice. Like all good fairy tales and all culturally sustainable narratives, Oz teaches "simple" (or not so simple) truths, but exactly what those truths are is open to interpretation, even within a single text. In fact, while our interviewees all found meaning in *Wicked*, the moral they drew from it was inflected by their individual histories and circumstances. As the musical's co-producer David Stone, observes, *Wicked* "means different things to different people. I think that has helped it in all these years, in all these countries."[11]

- **Resonate emotionally with consumers**: As Freed observed in 1939, if MGM's adaptation of Baum was to succeed, it absolutely needed to connect consumers' emotions. Based on our interviews, *Wicked*'s ability to send many consumers into the emotional stratosphere may be the single most important factor in its unprecedented success. Years after having seen the musical, consumers still felt powerful emotions as they recounted their experience of *Wicked*.

Notes

1. This method is commonly used in CCT research, see Pauline Maclaran and Stephen Brown, "The Center Cannot Hold: Consuming the Utopian Marketplace," *Journal of Consumer Research* 32, no. 2 (2005): 311–323.
2. Craig Thompson and Diana Haytko, "Speaking of Fashion: Consumers' Uses of Fashion Discourses and the Appropriation of Countervailing Cultural Meanings," *Journal of Consumer Research* 24, no. 1 (1997): 15–42.
3. Craig Thompson, William Locander, and Howard Pollio (1989), "Putting Consumer Experience Back Into Consumer Research: The Philosophy and Method of Existential Phenomenology," *Journal of Consumer Research* 16, no. 2 (1989): 133–146.
4. Lindsay Vick, interview by Kent Drummond, August 18, 2017.
5. Carol Di Giere, *Defying Gravity: The Creative Career of Stephen Schwartz from Godspell to Wicked* (New York: Applause Books, 2008).
6. "The Demographics of the Broadway Audience, 2016-2017," *The Broadway League*, https://www.broadwayleague.com/research/research-reports.
7. Wolf's work on female fans anticipates this homosocial activity: Stacy Wolf, "Wicked Divas, Musical Theatre, and Internet Girl Fans," *Camera Obscura* 65 (2007): 351–376, and "Defying Gravity': Queer

Conventions in the Musical Wicked," *Theatre Journal* 60, no. 1 (2008): 1–21.

8. Vick, Interview.
9. Mihaly Csikszentmihalyi, *Flow: The Psychology of Peak Experiences* (New York: Harper Collins, 2008).
10. Malcolm Gladwell, *The Tipping Point: How Little Things Can Make a Big Difference* (New York: Back Bay Books, 2002).
11. David Stone, "The Women of 'Wicked Are Part of a Theatrical Movement," *Denver Post*, June 11, 2015, https://www.denverpost.com/2015/06/11/the-women-of-wicked-are-part-of-a-theatrical-movement/.

CHAPTER 8

"The Audience Unites in One Big 'Yes!'": Theater Professionals Reflect on *Wicked*

As we discussed in the previous chapter, consumers connected with *Wicked* the musical on a number of critical levels. Not only did they find the character of Elphaba endlessly fascinating, but they were intrigued by a central relationship that involved two powerful young women. The strong moral message they took away from the show meant that *Wicked* was suitable for families; some consumers even used scenes and characters from the play to address their own "family issues." First-time theatergoers in particular were emotionally overcome by *Wicked*; the combination of show-stopping songs delivered by powerhouse talent left many in tears. Consumers who genuinely disliked the show were in the distinct minority; most consumers saw *Wicked* as soul-stirring and life-changing, offering them watershed moments in which to experience the full range of emotions they had come to expect from a Broadway musical.

However, consumers, whether naïve or knowing, are but one class of respondents. Gatekeepers—the credentialed professionals such as critics and academics who tell consumers *what* and *how* to think about Broadway shows—are another. In the tradition of Howard Becker's *Art Worlds*, we described the complex role they played in the initial reception of *Wicked* the novel and *Wicked* the musical in Chapter 6.[1] One significant class of respondents remains: a group we call **theater professionals** (TPs)—those who make their living in the professions directly related to theatrical production. These would include actors and directors, dancers and choreographers, musicians and composers, writers, costume, lighting and set designers, producers, trainers and coaches, and promoters. We sought their reactions to *Wicked* in order help us understand the chasm between the gatekeepers' highly negative reception of the production and the consumers' enthusiastic embrace of it. How would industry insiders make sense of *Wicked*'s ability to sustain itself on the stage in spite of the overwhelmingly negative reviews? In other words, how do TPs assess the musical's value and impact 15 years after its debut?

Our sampling technique for collecting TP interviews resembled the snowball technique we used for collecting our consumer sample.[2] We began by interviewing people we knew who worked on Broadway and in London's West End; they in turn referred us to others within the industry, and so on, until we had collected 25 interviews of theater experts. Gathering these responses was both easier and more difficult than obtaining our consumer interviews. It was easier in the sense that everyone in the theater industry had seen *Wicked* at least once, and everyone wanted to weigh in on it—whether they liked the show or not. Yet it was more challenging in the sense that we sought to achieve balance and diversity in the specialty areas represented by these professionals. Our goal was to interview at least two experts in each specialty, i.e., two costume designers, two choreographers, two producers, and so on. As Exhibit 2 shows, we achieved that goal.

As with the consumer group, the TP group was asked a series of open-ended questions regarding *Wicked*. Beyond that, the interviews were unstructured. TPs love to talk about their industry, so prompting them to respond was not necessary. In every case, we met these professionals in their offices, squeezing in the interviews between the other commitments they had scheduled for the day. We recorded the interviews, then transcribed and analyzed them for over-arching themes and patterns. All respondents spoke with us on conditions of anonymity.

THE MUSICAL OVERSIMPLIFIES THE BOOK

Although our TPs grudgingly admitted that Holzman and Schwartz were ultimately savvy in focusing on the relationship between Glinda and Elphaba—a relationship largely marginal to the plot of the novel—they also felt this move oversimplified Maguire's dark, philosophical musings on the nature of good and evil. Including this omitted material would have made for a truly original, if difficult, musical experience, and the TPs felt the show's creators took the easy way out. One Broadway musician/composer noted:

> You could say that this musical dealt with only half of the book, and not the most interesting half at that. By focusing on the college years of Elphaba's life, Holzman keeps the musical at a more juvenile level. Later in the novel, Elphaba has become an underground renegade, a resistance fighter. Wouldn't *that* have made an interesting musical? That's the musical I wanted to see. But that's not the story *Wicked*'s writers wanted to tell.

However, in spite of their own lack of enthusiasm for the adaptation, the TPs recognized that the story *Wicked*'s creators wanted to tell resonated with consumers. Holzman's intuition that intense, emotional friendships between powerful women are "not something audiences see very often" rang true with consumers, as the previous chapter shows. But the TPs added color to this dynamic by recalling several early readings and incipient productions of *Wicked*.[3] Whenever the two women appeared in a scene together, audience reaction was highly positive. One Broadway performer who was a part of those early readings told us:

> The scene would be humming along and then BAM! Glinda and Elphaba would be in a scene together. You could *feel* the audience move to the edge of its seats. People were automatically drawn to these two opposites. It didn't matter if you were male or female, young or old, gay or straight. The audience's pulse just quickened when they did a scene together. You couldn't ignore it. And Winnie and Stephen didn't.

In that respect, *Wicked* was a consumer-driven musical from the beginning. This is not to say that *Wicked* was created by audience proxy—far from it—but "experiments" such as these early readings confirmed one thing above all else: the moments of Maguire's story that resonated most strongly with Holzman and Schwartz also resonated strongly with everyday consumers.

Yet this tight alignment may have as much to do with Holzman's working style as with consumer endorsement. Another composer who has worked with Holzman sheds light on her method:

> Winnie genuinely cares about the experience the audience is having. She knew the experience she wanted the audience to have, and she wrote the story toward that end. It's kind of like being a roller coaster designer. You're going to ask: What will this ride be like? Where are the highs, the lows, the pauses, the thrills? Winnie knows that adaptation is a collaborative process. But for her, the audience is the collaborative partner.

Holzman's sense of empathy enabled her to create a highly consumable story for millions of theatergoers around the world. Still, most of the TPs we interviewed hoped for a more substantive treatment of the novel. And some felt *Wicked* the musical relied too heavily on an earlier text: the 1939 film, *The Wizard of Oz*. One writer notes:

> I think *Wicked* the show has more to do with *The Wizard of Oz* than it does the novel. In the show, you see them retro-fitting so many of the story lines from the movie into their own plot, especially in the Second Act. Like how Fiyero (who dies in the novel) becomes the Scarecrow, how Boq becomes the Tin Man, or how the whimpering lion cub in the cage becomes the Cowardly Lion. If the Second Act feels more splintered than the First, that's why. Too many loose ends needed to be tied up in order to connect with the film.

However, there is one major difference between the film and the novel on the one hand, and the musical on the other. In the film and the novel, the Wicked Witch of the West (Elphaba) is melted by Dorothy. But in the Broadway show, Elphaba fakes her own death, then secretly escapes with Fiyero (now the Scarecrow) to live in permanent exile. This story turn, by itself, did not sit well with the TPs. One director remarked: "I couldn't believe they let Elphaba live! This is a Hollywood ending. But I guess they had to deliver that kind of outcome to a mainstream Broadway audience." Implicit in this comment is the wisdom that *Wicked*, like all adaptations, needs to be adapted in a manner suitable to its audience and genre. So, the TPs recognized, if Holzman can be faulted for oversimplification, she can also be praised (as she was by consumers) for her adroitness in making the story suitable to the audience she envisioned. But still many TPs—because they have a relatively sophisticated view of what their art can, and should, accomplish—had a different reaction. Therein lies the tension between commercial success and critical acclaim.

Yet a minority voice among our TPs felt that emphasizing the young women's relationship was an astute move after all—not simply for commercial reasons, but for relatability. An orchestra conductor summed up this perspective:

> The story of young people making their way in the world, whether it's navigating the boyfriend- girlfriend thing, or the BFF thing, are always relatable. They're learning how to do relationships. They feel conflicted much of the time. They also want to make a difference. That's why the Dr. Dillamond angle is very smart. Young people are idealistic. They want to do good in the world. And *Wicked* appeals to that impulse in a broad way.

As we heard from consumer respondents earlier, such issues clearly resonated with them. A marketing professional has additional insights here:

> What Holzman did to *Wicked* reminds me of what James Cameron did to *Titanic*. I remember hearing that Cameron was reading *Reviving Ophelia* when he wrote the script for *Titanic*. That film was very much targeted toward adolescent girls. It featured a very strong young lady who survived a horrific disaster, lost the love of her life, yet "went on" to live a full life without him. Girls don't often see a story like that in mainstream media. And look at the tremendous success it had at the box office. I see the same thing happening with *Wicked*. Like *Titanic*, you have female empowerment. But you also have a strong friendship between two very different young women. That's a powerful combination.

And a composer lauded the fact that the musical *Wicked* did not shy away from the ethical and moral issues so central to the novel *Wicked*:

> You think that the Witch is evil, but you find out that she's actually trying to do good – literally, make good – most of the time. On the other hand, you think Glinda is good, but you find out that her motivations are very self-centered. Her unquestioning belief in the Wizard also has harmful consequences. This story, even though it's a mainstream Broadway show, is not afraid to question the black-and-white assumptions we've held about good and evil since childhood. Does it do so with the complexity that Gregory Maguire did? Of course not. But it does raise these issues. And you can talk about them with your kids once the show is over.

Also drawing praise from TPs was Holzman's ability to pace events within the story relative to the audience's ability to grasp—or possibly even predict—them. Although it may sound obvious, these experts explained, the correct pacing greatly facilitates the audience's ability to grasp a story. Too quick, and not enough audience members can follow; too slow, and impatience and distraction may set in. One story writer who studied under Holzman appreciated the ways in which she paced her revelations, allowing the audience members just enough time to apply their prior knowledge of the story to the events at hand:

> In musicals especially, you only get one pass. That means you only get one chance to engage people. If you miss it, you've lost your audience. Holzman does something very clever in the Second Act. She offers up enough information for the audience to make a connection just before the plot itself does. So the audience figures out that Nessarose becomes the Wicked Witch of the East and gets a house dropped on her right before she actually does. It's the same with Boq becoming the Tin Man, and so on. It's an ingenious way of engaging the audience. As an audience member, you're slightly ahead of the plot, and you feel very satisfied with yourself.

Finally, several of the TP respondents, mostly those who didn't like the adaptation, couldn't help but wonder what *Wicked* might have sounded and looked like had a different creative team adapted it. One director speculated:

> If you had had Stephen Sondheim and Jame Lapine [the team who created shows such as *Into the Woods* and *Sunday in the Park with George*] adapting *Wicked*, it would have been a very different musical. It would have been much darker, more complex, and certainly more subtle. Sondheim and Lapine would have focused less on the Shiz years, and more on the resistance/exile years in the second half of the novel. And at the end, they would have let Elphaba die. Sondheim doesn't believe in happy endings!

And a vocal coach envisioned a different creative team:

> What if Andrew Lloyd Webber and Tim Rice had written *Wicked*? I think they would have emphasized the love triangle between Glinda, Fiyero, and Elphaba much more. Think *Phantom of the Opera*. We would have had lush, sweeping melodies and florid love songs. More love, more romance,

more regret. I think it would have been less appealing to young people for that reason. Instead of romance, you get female empowerment. That was a risk on Holzman's part, but it paid off.

While one can only imagine how *Wicked* would have looked and sounded had Stephen Sondheim and James Lapine—or Andrew Lloyd Webber and Tim Rice—adapted it from the novel, the point is this: they didn't. Winnie Holzman and Stephen Schwartz did. As such, *Wicked* bears the markings of the story they wanted to tell. Thus, while our professionals were often disappointed, even exasperated, that these creators developed the adaptation they did, it must be emphasized that in the end, Holzman and Schwartz made the show they wanted to make. On this subject, we give the last word to Winnie Holzman:

> We would have long conversations. And we were basically on a fishing expedition, where we're really kind of picking from the novel things that leaped out at us, things that we felt were going to want to be staged, that we wanted to see. I think we really talked out the whole show. And we tried to see: are you imagining what I'm imagining?[4]

STEPHEN SCHWARTZ IS A MUSICAL GENIUS

If TPs were mostly disappointed in what they saw as *Wicked*'s over-simplified adaptation, they were unanimously effusive about what they saw as Stephen Schwartz's uncanny ability to integrate music and lyrics with plot advancement, character development, and emotional engagement—an ability that stemmed from his and Holzman's organic, collaborative, and complementary adaptive process. And they were particularly struck by his ability to do so seamlessly, across a variety of musical styles. From "Popular" to "Defying Gravity" to "For Good," they agreed that Schwartz created songs that "rise to the emotional moment," pushing character, plot, and relationships forward in the process. This, they felt more than any other aspect of the production, makes *Wicked* impactful.

What made these professionals so enthusiastic about Schwartz's contribution to *Wicked*? There were several factors, but chief among them was his ability to deliver distinctive and engaging melodies at just the right moment, drawing on a variety of musical styles to do so. Time and again, TPs praised Schwartz's song-writing skills, even when they themselves didn't like his music. For example, one musical arranger acknowledges: "I must admit that I am not a big fan of Stephen Schwartz's music – it's too pop for me. But I also have to admit that I really do admire him. He has a knack for seizing the moment and giving the audience exactly the song it needs to hear right *now*. He is a genius at that." Another conductor notes the variety of music Schwartz is capable of generating:

> When you think of the variety of styles Schwartz used to create the music for *Wicked*, it's remarkable. You can hear strains of pop, jazz, Big Band, rock, acoustic, traditional musical theatre, symphonic, and operatic. All of these roots are present in the score he wrote for *Wicked*. It takes an amazing talent to do that.

A rehearsal pianist makes his point by sitting at the keyboard and playing "Twinkle, Twinkle Little Star."

> We all know what tune this is, right? Mozart mainly, but Liszt and Bach also used it. Now, if I took it and suddenly played it in a minor key [which he does] do you hear the difference? Do you even recognize the tune anymore? It's very evocative now, more haunting. That's the kind of thing Schwartz does – he takes something you think you know, and presents it in a new way. Critics don't like this because they feel it's too derivative. But everybody borrows. It's *how* you do it that counts.

As musicologist Paul Laird points out in his book, *Wicked: A Musical Biography*, Schwartz referenced many musical and lyrical materials to create *Wicked*: some of them his own, and some of them from earlier well-known musicals by other composers.[5] Our point here is not to identify points of musical and lyrical derivation (Laird accomplishes this deftly in his book, as does Carol de Giere in hers), but to highlight the consumability his work displays, which is to say his accessibility to both naïve and knowing consumers.[6]

Indeed, what makes Schwartz's songs so consumable, particularly in *Wicked*, our TPs observed, is that they pose a "triple threat." First, they advance the plot; second, they reveal something important about that state of a character or a relationship; and third, they hit the audience—the consumers—with a powerful emotional punch. According to the TPs we interviewed, almost every song from the *Wicked* meets these requirements. However, the three songs consistently lauded for these attributes were "Popular," "Defying Gravity," and "For Good." We therefore feature detailed discussions of them here.

In contrast to opening-night critics who dismissed "Popular" as pop fluff, our TPs thought it was a work of genius. One composer observes:

> "Popular" is very simple structurally, but remember what's happening onstage at the time. Glinda is fussing over Elphaba and wondering how she can make her more attractive. As a perfectionist, she's preening, proud and insecure – all at the same time. Will she make Elphaba attractive, and bring glory to herself and her ability to appeal to people superficially? But what if she makes Elphaba *too* attractive? She might compete with her – for friends, for Fiyero, for everything. And the song reveals all that. There's one moment in particular that kills me. It's when Glinda corrects herself at the end of a line, using the wrong pronunciation of 'popular' so that it will rhyme with 'are' from two lines before. Schwartz reveals Glinda's perfectionist personality by the way she rhymes words – as well as the tension she's feeling at that moment. That is an insanely clever bit of songwriting.

A dramatist also liked "Popular" because of how it advances the plot, what it portends for a budding friendship, and how it affects the audience emotionally.

> New friendships are very exciting – they can make you giddy. And "Popular" has that kind of effect. It reminds me of "Getting to Know You" from *The King and I*. Except that Elphaba is rolling her eyes the whole time, so there's this ironic commentary going on as well. It's also very intricate physically, in a slapstick kind of way. Frankly, the audience *needs* this lighter moment after the embarrassing moment at the school dance right before. Schwartz displays real emotional intelligence here. He gives you a new friendship, a reason to laugh, and a sense of hope after a moment of tension and possible despair. That's quite a lot to accomplish in one song.

If "Popular" was clever in the eyes of these respondents, then "Defying Gravity" was monumental. For almost every TP we interviewed, "Defying Gravity" represents the zenith of *Wicked*'s emotional engagement. Not only does the song occur at a pivotal moment in the story line—Elphaba decides to turn against the Wizard, and in so doing, learns to fly—but the music and lyrics perfectly match the moment of elevation. Like Elphaba, they soar. One veteran performer in West End musicals sums it up:

> I think it's impossible to watch "Defying Gravity" and not be moved. You want to stand up and cheer at the end of it. Elphaba is literally growing up as she sings this song. She's taking her own full measure. The music swells, the lyrics become more rebellious. There's a crowd gathered below her, and they start pointing and shouting, 'Look at her! She's wicked!' And Elphaba thrusts her arm into the air with her broomstick and defies the crowd to stop her. Then the curtain comes down. Theatrically speaking, it just doesn't get any better than that.

A stage manager at London's National Theater weighs in on the special effects (SFX) needed to execute such a moment:

> You have this tremendous elevation sequence, but it has to be look effortless. The actress playing Elphaba steps on a small hydraulic lift and it raises her up, while mounds of black material unfurl below her. Of course, she never actually flies, but the lighting suggests that she does. Intense flashes of light synchronize with the climactic notes in the song, so you have this multi-layered assault on your senses. It's the perfect synergy of light, sound, smell, and feel. The audience doesn't know what hit them. It's an amazing climax. But it's also incredibly choreographed.

All vocalists and vocal coaches we interviewed also stated an obvious, but important, point about "Defying Gravity": it requires that the singer "belt" at the climax in order for the song to achieve its full effect. One vocal coach elaborates:

> In a blockbuster musical, you've got to have a song when Ulla belts, to quote a line from *The Producers* [referencing the song "When You've Got It, Flaunt It"]. And "Defying Gravity" is that moment in *Wicked*. The song builds to this tremendous climax, and the vocalist just lets loose. She shouts, but she's still in control – barely. It's like a high-wire act for vocalists. Very risky, because your voice could crack at any moment, and the effect would be ruined. The audience tends to love these moments. And singers enjoy singing like this. All of my students want to learn how to belt! But it's dangerous to do too early in your career before your voice is ready. And if you do it long-term, it can harm the quality of your voice.

In other words, "Defying Gravity" is an iconic belting song, filled with vocal risks that coincide with the dramatic and logistical risks being taken onstage at that moment. So once again, Schwartz has created a song that advances plot, reveals personality, and engages the audiences to the point of supportive shrieks, exclamations, and fist-pumps. When done effectively, belting reflects an evolution of Elphaba's character, allowing the audience to see a side of her they hadn't seen before—a side that Elphaba herself didn't realize she had. A director observes:

> There's lots of dramatic tension on the stage at that moment. The guards are trying to break in. Glinda needs to make up her mind to join Elphaba in the resistance or stay and serve the Wizard. And Elphaba herself isn't sure she can pull this off. It's only as she sings "Defying Gravity" that she actually convinces herself she can. As her gown grows, so does her self-conviction. It's one of those moments in musical theatre when a character changes while she sings a song. Given the dramatic context, the song becomes the showstopper of the night.

Of course, the show actually does stop, because it's the end of Act I. The curtain falls, and intermission begins.

After the interval, as the curtain rises, *Wicked* faces a new challenge: how can the show exceed, or even match, the emotional heights it scaled in Act I? As we discussed earlier, most consumers don't even miss those heights because they are too enthralled by the benedictory spell of "For Good." But TPs take a harsher, more distanced view. For them, the heart-stopping climax at the end of Act I establishes high expectations for Act II that are not met. One choreographer noted:

> The first act of Wicked is clearly the stronger of the two. The through-lines get laid out, and you feel a real sense of dramatic purpose and momentum. And when the curtain falls after "Defying Gravity," you're in heaven. Musical theatre can't get any better than this. But the question becomes: what do you do in Act II? And the answer is that *Wicked* never really reaches those heights again. Act II is too fragmented. There are too many loose ends to tie up, and you lose the emotional focus.

Yet even as they expressed disappointment that *Wicked* failed to scale another emotional Everest, TPs agreed that "For Good" was the perfect ending to a musical already full of power ballads and high emotions.

A director who was disappointed in *Wicked*'s adaptation strategy lauded the choice of "For Good" to end the show:

> If what Holzman and Schwartz really wanted to emphasize was the female-to-female friendship of this story, they chose the perfect song to express it. After all the emotional highs and lows of the previous two hours, it really does boil down to Glinda and Elphaba, alone together onstage, holding each others' hands and singing their true feelings to one another. To choose to do this quietly was a master-stroke, in my opinion. You can't complete with "Defying Gravity," so don't even try. "For Good" stands out because it's quiet.

A vocal professor added her unexpectedly emotional reaction:

> There really are people in your life that change your life forever. And as you get older, you realize that you may never see them again to tell them that. When I think of people I've known that have truly changed me, it's sad to think I won't be able to see them again [starts to cry]. Sorry – I didn't know I would be so emotional about this! But if you had to sing a song to express that, you wouldn't be belting, would you? You would be quiet and heartfelt. You'd sing like no one else was listening. And that's what Glinda and Elphaba do.

The fact that a seasoned professional could be overcome with emotion as she recalls a song she heard several years prior speaks to the power "For Good" has for many producers. A Broadway composer explained this power by observing:

> Structurally, "For Good" is a perfectly written duet. In a song like this, you look for balance, harmony, and at the end, convergence. The two women have equal singing time. They both begin by stating what the friendship has meant to them. Then they each liken the friendship to several different metaphors, all involving natural forces. Elphaba starts the bridge, in which she asks for forgiveness for mistakes Glinda may still blame her for. Then Glinda notes that there's plenty of blame to share, and they agree that 'none of it seems to matter anymore.' Up to this point, they really haven't been singing together. But as the song builds to a contained climax, they sing in duet, with these beautiful harmonies intertwining with the lyrics. What I love here is that they each sing their respective metaphors, so the lyrics don't match. But their final metaphors both

happen to end with the word 'wood,' which of course rhymes with 'good.' So there's the convergence the audience was set up to feel. It's a very powerful moment.

Finally, a lyricist notes:

> The characters display a growth in awareness as the song develops. At the start, they seem unsure as to how they've been changed ('Who can say if I've been changed for the better?'). They only know that they've been changed for good – in the sense of being changed permanently. But as the song evolves, so does their realization they have been changed for Good – in the sense of being better people as a result of this friendship. It all depends on the pun contained in "for good," which Schwartz plays out beautifully.

In sum, TPs agreed that *Wicked*'s music and lyrics, more than any other theatrical element, captivates the audience with intense emotional appeals. One Broadway composer may have summed up Schwartz's achievement best when he noted: "You have to understand that *Wicked* is postmodern patriotism. Can we sympathize with the bad guy in a narrative we've loved since our youth? It's a big ask. Then the music hits, the story unfurls, and the audience unites in one big *Yes*."

Costumes, Sets, and Lighting Design Intensify Emotional Impact

Theater experts were in awe of the visual—and visceral—impact achieved by *Wicked*'s costume, set, and lighting designs. While costume designers in particular were astonished by the intricacy and subtlety of Elphaba's dresses, remarking on how they evolved as her character evolved, lighting experts noted how the lighting of the dresses heightened their dramatic effect in ways a naïve consumer might sense, but never detect. They found this to be particularly true in key moments of songs such as "Popular," "Defying Gravity," and "For Good." Furthermore, set designers lauded *Wicked*'s sets for their intricacy and spectacle.

Perhaps not surprisingly, given the Tony award Susan Hilferty won for her costume designs, TPs were stunned by *Wicked*'s costumes, and they were eager to tell us why. Several aspects caught their attention, including the color and quality of the materials. In addition, respondents remarked on the ways in which various features of the costumes illuminated the characters' personalities. They also noted how the costumes, like the characters, evolved as the musical unfolded. One costume designer had this to say about Elphaba's clothes:

> Elphaba's outfits are tight and self-contained. They are difficult to move in. And that matches her personality, initially. She hasn't learned to move, to be comfortable in her own skin. Even though she's always dressed in black, there is tremendous variation in the black dresses she wears. Each one uses many layers of dense material. Her dresses weigh a ton! But if you look closely, you'll see these iridescent shimmers of green running through them. These seem to intensify as Elphaba becomes more powerful. It's one of the most amazing displays of costuming I've ever seen.

While many of the respondents focused on Elphaba's costumes, others were similarly enthusiastic about Glinda's:

> Glinda comes off as a very superficial character, at least initially. And the surface she presents is very beautiful. Her dresses capture this perfectly. But as time goes on, you realize that there's a lot more to her than that. You want to get closer to her, but her costumes prevent introspection. By contrast, Elphaba's outfits invite introspection. She draws you in, like one of her spells. But Glinda keep you at a distance.

Indeed, the outfits of the two main characters drew most of the TPs' responses. But another respondent remarked on the Ozians' costumes featured in "One Short Day":

> Here, you have the people of Oz really cutting loose, showing their individuality, having fun with their eccentric sense of fashion. They're speaking a different language, not only in what they say, but in how they dress. That makes it tough for Glinda and Elphaba, who look and act a little out of place, even though they are enjoying themselves. They're tourists; they don't fit in with the cosmopolitan Ozians. It occurs to me that this might be how a lot of audience members feel, too. Many of them are also tourists, and here they are in New York City, which can be very intimidating. They're enjoying themselves, yes, but they still feel out of place.

No matter which character the TPs fixed their gaze upon, one thing was clear: the costumes were complex enough to stand up to repeated scrutiny. As one designer noted: "I was seeing this show for the third time, and I sat there amazed at how beautiful the costumes were. The way they catch the light – they take your breath away. There's something new to notice about them each time."

If *Wicked*'s costumes are complex, the lighting that sets them off appears simple. Yet that assessment would be an oversimplification. As Tony award-winning lighting designer Kenneth Posner explained in a telephone interview:

> What made this especially challenging was Elphaba's green skin. I've spent so much of my career making sure people don't look green. And now I had to use extra light to make sure she did! That was difficult because Elphaba's green skin absorbed the light. So I used special enhancers. I didn't pick my color palette until much later. The costumes were stunning, so I wanted to illuminate them. My goal was to look at these two beautiful characters in the best way possible. How could I enhance the experience of "looking" for the audience? I pulled out all the stops for the Emerald City production number. That for me was the highlight.[7]

Posner and other lighting designers often mention that their goal for lighting a production is not to be noticed by the audience; in other words, lighting should not get in the way of a production. And in that respect, *Wicked* succeeds. As Tony-nominated lighting designer Allen Hughes observed, "*Wicked*'s lighting does exactly what it's supposed to do: it reveals the characters' inner qualities, while not drawing too much attention to itself. If you come away from a show not commenting on the lighting, then the lighting director has succeeded."[8]

As for Wicked's scenic design, TPs were once again enthusiastic in their praise of Tony award winner Eugene Lee's sets and the role they played in the overall production. Remarked one set designer:

> The sets end up being effective, because they don't compete with the costumes or the characters. Aside from the giant set that frames the stage (the Clock of the Time Dragon) and the mechanically-controlled Wizard's Head (controlled by the Wizard himself, as an intimidating distraction to visitors) you're not going to remember the sets. But you will remember what happened on the sets.

By contrast, the related element of SFX tends to have a different goal in Broadway productions: to heighten the spectacle quotient, and to make the audience gasp in horror or delight. (The falling chandelier in *Phantom of the Opera* and the flying helicopter in *Miss Saigon* are famous examples). On that score, *Wicked* is off the charts, according to our respondents. They consistently expressed amazement for the creative minds that developed such effects, as well as admiration for the technicians who successfully implemented those effects eight times weekly. This was true whether they had seen the show on Broadway, or on tour. One scenic designer who has seen the show multiple times on Broadway summed it up this way:

> Glinda's bubble, the flying monkeys, Elphaba's elevation in "Defying Gravity" – *Wicked* is an SFX masterpiece. But logistically, it would be a nightmare to pull off. There are way too many moving parts. And that means opportunities for things to go wrong. These are all part of the spectacle, and they need to be done right. It's what audiences expect now. I've seen shows where they screwed up, but it's very difficult to tell unless you know what to look for.

In fact, the words "spectacle" and "expect" came up frequently, and often contiguously, from these experts. We probed them for more details here. Noted one Broadway veteran:

> The Gershwin is a big theater; it holds 1900 people for every performance. When they get seated, they're not expecting *Uncle Vanya*. They remember the falling chandelier from *Phantom*, and they want to see something on that scale. *Wicked* capitulates to their demands, but not to the point that it overpowers the show. With *Phantom*, people would ask "What did you think when the chandelier crashed down?" But with *Wicked*, they don't ask "What did you think when the witch flies?" Instead, they ask, "What did you think of *Defying Gravity*?" That tells me they got it right.

Former dance captain Alicia Allbright, who worked for many years on the Broadway production, elaborated on this point from a backstage perspective:

> *Wicked* is an extremely difficult show technically. All the special effects mean that there are dozens of wires, ropes, and pulleys going everywhere. Wires get crossed, literally. The costumes, wigs, and shoes are bulky and take up lots of space. For some scenes, the actors need to change in less than 60 seconds! What you see onstage is just the tip of the iceberg.

Backstage, it looks chaotic. But everyone knows what they're doing. And in the end, it's what the audience – all 1933 of them – want to see at every performance.

Indeed, a backstage tour taken by this book's first author shortly before the curtain went up on a recent Saturday matinee confirmed Allbright's summation. From field notes:

> The multi-level monolith that oversees every performance of *Wicked* felt more like a rabbit warren than a control center. It's filled with precarious perches and dark narrow passageways running in all directions. Although it was an hour before curtain time, most technicians were already at their stations, confirming that every element of the show's production – from batteries for the microphones to the levitation platform for "Defying Gravity" – was in good working order. Every technician backstage acted alert, confident, and totally in control. They recognized my presence more like a pleasant distraction than a nuisance. Then it was back to the game. In fact, this moment reminded me of the start of an important athletic event, like the first point at Wimbledon. Curtain up – it's show time!

If the technical challenges are daunting for the Broadway production, they can only be amplified when *Wicked* tours, which it continually does. A set designer who saw shows in Salt Lake City, Denver, and Omaha reacts:

> I would never want to take this show on the road! It's just too complicated. The frame around the stage, which is the Clock of the Time Dragon, is very complex. And anytime you have a bridge involved, you've got problems. The "Defying Gravity" scene speaks for itself. Since each venue is different, so every tech rehearsal in a new city is different. You travel with a skeleton crew and train the local union people there. That means everyone in the new city has to learn the ropes – literally. And there's not much time. I'm not sure how they pull this off.

Yet, the quality of the show does not seem to have suffered. From the same designer:

> I have to say, the quality of the production is amazing, no matter where you see it. In a smaller venue, such as Salt Lake City, the sets are modified, since there's not as much space to work with. But the auditorium is

smaller, so the feeling is more intimate. You don't lose anything. In fact, some people prefer this version over Broadway's.

Since *Wicked* has been touring the USA for over a decade—and has visited cities such as Boston and Denver five times—the learning curve for this technically demanding show must have flattened out by now. Regardless, consumers who see the show on tour remain dazzled by its spectacle—even on a smaller stage.

Only among our UK respondents was the reaction to *Wicked*'s production values less than enthusiastic. They critiqued the size of the London venue—the Apollo Victoria Theatre, which holds over 2300—for the poor sound quality and sight lines. One British director assesses:

> I know the producers want to make a lot of money with every performance, but the Apollo Victoria is just too damned big. It feels like a cavern! The girls were way over-mic'd. I stopped listening after the first number. You definitely reach a point where the size of the theatre can impact the quality of the performance.

A choreographer concurred. For her, the sight lines became an issue:

> Unless you've paid premium prices for premium seats, you're not going to be able to see that much. You can hear, sort of, because of the sound system, but you lose that sense of immediacy. You get the faintest sense of movement. We got half-price tickets at Leicester Square and sat near the back, and I didn't feel anything. It looked to me like they were mailing it in. I checked out mentally and emotionally as a result.

Nevertheless, the "experience" offered by *Wicked* (which we address in the next chapter) appears strong enough to compensate for such complaints, at least as far as most consumers are concerned.

Wicked's Promotional Poster is Brilliant

When addressing the promotional efforts surrounding *Wicked*, TPs wanted to discuss only the iconic poster of Glinda whispering a secret in Elphaba's ear. And their assessment can be summed up in one word: brilliant. One promoter explained:

That poster is brilliant, and you know why? It gets your attention, and it stays with you. Have you been to Broadway lately? The clutter there – it's unbelievable. You've got so many stimuli competing for your attention. Somehow, Nancy Coyne designed a poster so simple that it cuts right to the heart of things. From the contrast in colors, to the sweep of the shapes, to the smirk on Elphaba's face as she reacts to what Glinda has told her – these women are opposites, but together they form a whole.

This sentiment was echoed by another designer—a female—who stated:

Look at the images of the two women, and you see curve after curve. That in itself will appeal to women. And it's conspiratorial. The poster suggests that if you see the show, they might let you in on their secret. This is very appealing to the stereotypical view we have of women, which is that they like to gossip and share secrets with their best friends.

Finally, *Wicked*'s logo stands as an object lesson about what saved this much-hyped musical from failing. Conventional wisdom asserts that word-of-mouth turned *Wicked* it into a must-see event. One marketing expert explains:

After the New York reviews came out, which were merciless, *Wicked*'s fortunes were very uncertain. This was an expensive show to produce, $14 million. Ticket sales were not as strong as they'd hoped. It wasn't clear if they'd be able to recoup the initial investment. But then a curious thing happened: people started talking about this show. About how much they loved the show, how great the music was, how great these young stars were. And we all know that word-of-mouth is the most effective kind of publicity. A few months' later, *Wicked* is THE hottest ticket in town. So now when I look at that poster, it reminds me of the women who saved *Wicked* by talking it up.

In addition to the taxi tops and billboards still promoting *Wicked* within Broadway's purview, a more personal means of promotion has begun to occur: handing out leaflets to people on the street. One man, a former buyer at Bloomingdale's, was surprised at this technique.

I was walking past Columbus Circle the other night, and suddenly this guy walked up to me and handed me a pamphlet. I assumed it was for a strip joint or a comedy club. But no, it was for *Wicked*! And that surprised me.

Is the show in some kind of trouble? I doubt it. But it's been here so long, we tend to take it for granted. This reminds you that it's still here, and that maybe you should see it again. He certainly got my attention! I think it's pretty effective.

WICKED'S INFLUENCE EXTENDS FAR BEYOND THE GERSHWIN THEATRE

As the years roll on and *Wicked* continues to play to packed houses, TPs assessed the show's impact on other Broadway productions, as well its influence on other performances in other contexts. The ornate clock mechanism that frames *Wicked*'s stage is perfectly apt, notes one designer, because a Broadway smash, once established, "operates like clockwork. You flip the switch, set the wheels in motion, and the rest happens automatically." Scenic designer Eugene Lee might agree. In numerous interviews, he intended this massive frame around the stage— referencing the Clock of the Time Dragon in Maguire's novel—to expectorate an endless supply of mechanical pageants to a hungry, never-ending audience.

This is not to say that *Wicked*, or any other long-running musical, happens automatically, even after so many years. On the contrary, TPs stressed that the main challenge to a long-running show is maintaining its sense of freshness. "You can't let the production get stale," noted one performer in the Broadway production of *Wicked*. "That's why we have so many extra rehearsals. We never know when the original leadership team might show up. They want to see that the show still pops." And sustaining a "pageant that pops" resonates with key aspects of experiential marketing: immerse consumers in a multi-sensory, highly emotional experience that generates a sense of community, and the world will beat a path to your door. And in the case of *Wicked*, the world clearly has.

As we discuss in the next chapter, *Wicked*'s promoters have designed ingenious ways to experience the show well beyond the confines of its stage. But on Broadway, the show's impact is significant and sustained. For a start, it's two original stars—Kristen Chenoweth and Idina Menzel— have enjoyed successful careers far beyond their turns as Glinda and Elphaba. Both continue to star in other Broadway shows; both continue to enjoy extensive solo tours; and both have made multiple guest appearances on television shows such as *Glee*. One critic weighs in on the impact *Wicked* continues to have for these two performers:

> Both Kristen and Idina can't forget *Wicked*, nor do they want to. I've seen both of their solo tours, and they still sing their big songs from the show. Audiences demand it. Kristen does this hilarious version of "Popular" in which she sings it in seven different languages. But then she does a duet of "For Good" in which she pulls a performing arts student from the audience and sings it with her. These are available on YouTube and they are very moving. When I saw Idina appear onstage with the late, great Marvin Hamlisch, she had to sing "Defying Gravity," and it brought the house down. Earlier in the show, she sang "The Wizard and I."

Indeed, these songs have entered the popular lexicon of audition songs and karaoke performances. One marketing professor whose daughter is a professional singer explains:

> You have to realize that these songs, and the roles they represent, are highly operatic. There's a diva quality about them. You have to fill these songs with big voices and big personalities. If you nail a song like "Defying Gravity" or "The Wizard and I," you're showing the director you can be that very powerful young woman audiences want to see today. That's why these songs are now iconic audition pieces.

A vocal coach concurs, stating:

> I honestly hadn't heard of *Wicked* until all these young girls started asking for help with "Defying Gravity!" You have to belt at the end of that song, and they love doing that. Then pairs of girls wanted me to help them with "For Good." That's a safer song, because you have someone else to lean on. They also want to learn "The Wizard and I," but it's very risky.

Perhaps no better testament to the cultural impact of *Wicked*'s songs exists than this anecdote told to us by a dancer:

> I was sitting in the Apollo Victoria Theatre watching a production of *Wicked*, and it came time for Elphaba to sing "Defying Gravity." Although

it's a moment of high drama and there's a lot happening onstage, the young woman sitting next to me leaned over and whispered, 'Listen closely. This is the song of my generation.'

Indeed, it could be argued that *Wicked* has helped usher in new era of female-themed productions in the arts more generally, which in turn may reflect shifting values in production companies as well as in society. Television shows such as *High School Musical, Glee,* and *Rise* echo several of the plot lines established by *Wicked*. Movies such as *Frozen* (with its iconic song "Let It Go," written and performed by Menzel) and *Wonder Woman* (which recently became one of the top 20 highest-grossing movies of all time) center their narratives around action-oriented, yet highly accessible, young women. The recent Broadway show *War Paint* is based on the rivalry between cosmetic-industry titans Helena Rubenstein and Elizabeth Arden. *Wicked* itself will become a movie, set for release in December of 2019, the same month that *Wonder Woman 2* is scheduled to debut.

Finally, many TPs are well aware that *Wicked* was the first Broadway blockbuster to open after 9/11. That significance is expressed by a long-time Broadway tour guide, who witnessed the events of that day and frequently lectures to groups of young people on the subject:

> I was just a few blocks away when those towers went down. The ground was shaking, and I didn't know if I'd ever see my wife again. Thousands of people felt like that. For days afterward, the city was in a shambles. We didn't know if we would ever recover, and we didn't know if anyone would want to visit New York City again. But we knew that if we were ever going to come back, Broadway was key. We had to have a big hit. It took two years, but *Wicked* became that hit. Suddenly, people were talking about something besides 9/11. I don't think people will ever forget what *Wicked* did for New York City.

CONCLUSION

The TPs we interviewed echo gatekeeper and professional responses to the 1902 Broadway "extravaganza" and MGM's film. Like professional consumers of these earlier shows, they note the power of the spectacle to enrapture and transport the audience, and, while they may not entirely love *Wicked*'s adaptation of Maguire's novel, they recognize—as did

Baum—that "the people will have what pleases them," and they praise Schwartz's and Holzman's talent for connecting with the ticket-buying public. Similarly, while not all of them admire Schwarz's music, they all recognize that it connects—emotionally and powerfully—with audiences in the moment, and stays with them—tunes to whistle and songs to share—after they leave the theater. In this, *Wicked* takes a page from both the 1902 and the MGM songbooks, as the music sustains the show—culturally and economically—beyond its live performances. Thus, whatever they, as professionals, think of *Wicked*, TPs are able to astutely identify the qualities that account for the musical's unprecedented success and sustainability, and their analysis provides a professional framework for the consumers' more instinctual responses.

The TPs also recognize that *Wicked* is both good business and good for business. As was Baum, Nancy Coyne and Marc Platt are master-marketers, whose promotional campaigns attract consumers through the door and keep them coming back. If the early twentieth century saw repeat viewers packing the seats of America's theaters to demand encores and sing-along with their favorite songs, so the early twenty-first century sees viewers returning, again and again, to re-experience what the professionals affirm as *Wicked*'s high production values and compelling musical score—as well as the intense emotions those elements inspire. Furthermore, the TPs recognize that the show's success benefits Broadway and musical theater beyond *Wicked*'s stage, making the careers of its original stars (as the 1902's *Wizard of Oz* did for Fred Stone and David Montgomery, and the 1939 film for Judy Garland) and, also like these earlier productions, setting off a wave of other shows and products seeking to tap into the *Wicked* craze.

As the TPs affirm, *Wicked*'s success can be understood in the context of what Jessica Sternfeld terms the *megamusical*. Sternfeld analyzed Broadway's biggest blockbusters of the past 50 years (including *Jesus Christ Superstar*, *Evita*, *Cats*, *Les Miserables*, and *Phantom of the Opera*) and observed that they share several characteristics: they feature grand plots, preferably set in an exotic and non-modern locales; they trade on high emotions; they feature elaborate sets and stunning SFX; they are filled with music and singing throughout much of their run-times; and, while they are spectacularly popular with audiences, they are notoriously unpopular with critics. *Wicked* qualifies as a megamusical on all these counts. Megamusicals now form the "horizon of expectations" for Broadway's consumers, who today pay well over $100 per ticket for a show. Understandably, such consumers demand value for their money, which often translates into show-stopping production numbers inciting the full spectrum of emotions. *Wicked* is well-positioned to appeal to those costumers, and, TPs maintain, it does not disappoint—even after 15 years.

However, in order fully to understand *Wicked*'s success, we also need to consider what sets it apart from the other megamusicals, allowing it to surpass most of their box-office records. We would argue that the answer to this question is threefold. First, it is *Oz* itself, and the long cultural history of the narrative, which has the potential to endlessly offer consumers "more Oz," thus creating new and repeat consumers for *Wicked;* second, it is the prescience and ability of Stephen Schwartz and Winnie Holzman to speak to the *zeitgeist* of contemporary audiences, offering up the right product to the right people at the right time; and finally, it is the genius of *Wicked*'s marketing team that provides consumers with multiple *Wicked* experiences beyond the show itself. These experiences are the subject of our next chapter.

NOTES

1. Howard Becker, *Art Worlds* (Berkeley: University of California Press, 2008).
2. For a list of theater professionals, using pseudonyms, see Appendix B.
3. Winnie Holzman, "Behind the Emerald Curtain, Wicked: Book Writing," YouTube Video, 5:28, published by Wicked the Musical, October 1, 2013, https://www.youtube.com/watch?v=DTmeWxfT0uE.
4. Ibid.
5. Paul Laird, *Wicked: A Musical Biography* (Maryland: Scarecrow Press, 2011).
6. Ibid., Carol Di Giere, *Defying Gravity: The Creative Career of Stephen Schwartz from "Godspell" to "Wicked"* (New York: Applause Theatre and Cinema Books, 2008).
7. Kenneth Posner, Phone Interview by Kent Drummond, June 7, 2017.
8. Allen Hughes, Interview by Kent Drummond, October 20, 2016.

CHAPTER 9

Pulling Back the Curtain:
Wicked Experiences

Both the consumers and theater professionals we interviewed emphasized that, for them, *Wicked* was more than a show; it was a memorable *experience*. Indeed, this *experiential* quality may well account for the musical's success, and not just in the theater. As we noted in Chapter 6, Marc Platt recognized early on that, by extending the *Wicked* experience beyond the theater, he could both give consumers who had seen the musical a different experience of it and reach new consumers where they lived and shopped.[1] As the show took hold, Platt's experiential forays into suburban malls proved to be marketing gold—for *Wicked*, the consumers, and the malls themselves. Since more and more people were opting to shop online—a trend that continues to this day—Platt's promotional events gave consumers a reason to come back to the malls they had recently abandoned.

This new strategy could only delight brick-and-mortar retailers, discouraged as they were at declining foot traffic and anxious for a strategy beyond brick-and-click. Like their retailing forebears, who had welcomed the promotional plays and Oz Clubs of decades past, contemporary retailers welcomed *Wicked*'s extensive and repeated tours around the country. Its appearance in any city generated a "buzz quotient" all by itself, prompting consumers to leave their computer screens for at least an evening while they enjoyed dinner out and took in the show. Retailers and restaurateurs met them at the door (a trendy bar in Salt Lake City featured six Wicked-themed cocktails, including The Flying Monkey, Dr. Dillamond's Dram, and the Glinda-Licious, when *Wicked*

K. Drummond et al., *The Road to Wicked*,
https://doi.org/10.1007/978-3-319-93106-7_9

came to town), while *Wicked*'s marketing team continued to provide consumers with experiences beyond *Wicked* itself, encouraging them to enter into a long-term, interactive relationship with the musical while educating potential new consumers about the show. In this chapter, we will examine a limited selection of these many *Wicked* experiences, emphasizing how they offer consumers more points of entry into the narrative while serving as promotional touchpoints through which producers may control—and consumers may apprehend—the sensations, emotions, aesthetic vision, core values, and community that give the show its sustained power.

Here, as we did in our discussions of L. Frank Baum's and Reilly & Lee's similar attempts to extend the life of Oz in the early part of the twentieth century, we draw on the concept of experiential marketing—made famous by Joseph Pine, James Gilmore, and Bernd Schmitt—to examine the ways in which *Wicked*'s producers and marketers have sustained the show, keeping it profitable and in the public eye for 15 years.[2]

Baum, as we saw in Chapter 2, understood that *experiences*, more than goods and services, were the most important element in sustaining long-term customer relationships—and he did so nearly 100 years before Pine and Gilmore shocked the business world by asserting this was the only managerial principal that really mattered. Provide the consumer with a meaningful experience, they posited, and businesses would enjoy a loyal clientele for years to come. Experience-oriented companies such as Build-A-Bear Workshop, American Girl Place, Apple stores, Dave and Buster's, the Geek Squad, and, of course, Disneyland were held up by these authors as exemplars of the new (or not so new) experience economy.

Pine and Gilmore's perspective certainly struck a nerve in the corpus of American business at the end of the twentieth century. Not only did it sell 300,000 copies—a remarkable feat for a business-based book—but it penetrated to the level of everyday parlance. Particularly in advertising and promotion, the word "experience" is now tacked on to a vast array of goods and services: "Game of Thrones: The Live Concert Experience," "Spamalot: The VIP Experience," "NBC Olympics TV Experience," "the Sheraton Signature Sleep Experience," and "We hope you enjoyed your oil change experience" are just a few examples. Experiential marketing has also assumed a preeminent place in the boardrooms and marketing departments of American businesses large and small.

As we discussed in Chapter 1, experiential marketing prompts marketers to create memorable events and experiences for consumers, in order that those consumers might form a deep emotional connection with a given brand. This last point is key. It is one thing, as Sid Levy reminds us, to develop a definitive and recognizable brand identity in the marketplace; it is quite another to develop the desired *emotional* connection consumers feel *toward* that brand.[3] But when done effectively, experiential marketing enables marketers to elevate their brands above the competition—other Broadway shows, for example—compelling consumers to choose their brands due to the positive emotional connections they feel toward them.

In their quest to develop and sustain the *Wicked* brand, its producers faced a challenge similar to the one Baum had faced in the early twentieth century. How do you convince consumers to re-consume what is essentially the same product? Baum's answer to this question was to remediate and extend his original product, providing his consumers with multiple, connected Oz experiences; readers of *The Wonderful Wizard of Oz* could see the musical, read newspaper comics, purchase a different book, and attend the *Fairylogue and Radio Plays*. *Wicked*'s answer has been to provide multiple auxiliary experiences to the show itself, each designed both to keep the product in the public eye and to lead back to it: to entice both established and new consumers to a performance of the musical. That is why *Wicked*'s key promotional activities provide an especially good fit with experiential marketing's tenets—and go a long way toward explaining how the show maintains its blockbuster status years after its premiere.

As we explained in detail in Chapter 1, a successful consumption experience will: *create buzz*; *immerse* consumers in a sensory cocoon; *educate* them about the product; *facilitate synergy* of message across the brand; *foster an emotional connection* between people and product; and *encourage consumers to share* their experience. Bearing these key characteristics in mind, we describe each of these experiences in detail and then discuss the benefits that accrue to both producers and consumers as a result. We begin with a key experience available to consumers residing in or visiting New York City: the "Behind the Emerald Curtain" tour at the Gershwin Theatre.

"Behind the Emerald Curtain" Tour

"Behind the Emerald Curtain" is a behind-the-scenes tour solely aligned with *Wicked* and offered once or twice per month at the Gershwin Theatre in New York City. Costing $33 per person (as of March, 2018), the tours take place on Saturday mornings and last approximately 90 minutes.

"Behind the Emerald Curtain" is not a backstage tour—due to liability issues, that isn't possible—but it does feature a guided tour of the Gershwin's upstairs lobby, which, on tour days, is transformed into the Behind the Emerald Curtain Museum. There, a number of costumes, sets, and props are on display, and tour participants are free to wander around the exhibits before the formal tour begins. The tour then proceeds into the auditorium itself.

We visited the tour on a Saturday in April 2015. Approximately 300 participants joined us that morning, and the vast majority of them were groups of high school students interested in musical theater. They hailed from all around the country, and they would soon be seeing—or had just seen—*Wicked* itself. Those who weren't high school students tended to be families with teenaged girls, as well as middle-aged couples. Virtually no singles were in attendance.

Shortly after 10:00, one man and one woman, both in their early 30s, appeared in the middle of the lobby-museum and began speaking. They introduced themselves as Jerad Bortz and Alicia Albright and explained that they would be our tour guides. Both had strong connections to the show at that time: Jerad was a cast member in *Wicked*'s ensemble, while Alicia was a Dance Captain and an Understudy for, among other roles, the Witch's Mother. Both were friendly and engaging, bursting with high spirits and good humor. Dressed in loose-fitting black dance clothes, they looked as though they had just taken class or were on their way to an audition. Wearing small microphones that wrapped around their faces, Jerad and Alicia were clearly audible and highly mobile.

The two guides took a tag team approach to the tour. Alicia would discuss, for example, the complexities in constructing Elphaba's dress and then turn the floor over to Jerad, who would point out the importance of wigs and masks in the show. Since the mood was informal and relaxed, the tour was highly interactive.

The informational content of the tour ranged from the purely technical to the highly philosophical, sometimes in a single discussion point. Here is Jerad discussing how and why costumes, wigs, and masks are so meticulously constructed:

> Our costumes can cost up to $40,000! It takes about two months to put one together from start to finish. We also take face and hand casts so that

we can make masks. We use 26 masks every night. We're here to create a world. What we're going for is the willing suspension of disbelief.

Jerad's reference to Coleridge may have been lost on many—including Jerad himself—but the point was clear: plausibility is achieved through painstaking attention to detail, a point Disney learned decades ago, and that Broadway productions fully embrace today. Such a point would also resonate highly with the typical tour participant, since it was probably taught to him or her earlier in the semester.

Similarly, here is Alicia explaining why Elphaba's dress and hat look the way they do:

> Do you see those swatches of green underneath the layers of black crepe in her dress? You can barely see them now, but under the stage lights, they shimmer. This symbolizes Elphaba's character. She has powers that will be revealed as the show unfolds. And see how the swatches run diagonal, not straight up and down? That is consistent with everything in *Wicked*. It's just a little bit off.

Theater professionals, as we saw in our last chapter, immediately see costumes in symbolic terms, while everyday consumers have to be taught to see them that way. Alicia's description of Elphaba's costume performs this function, encouraging the audience to think symbolically by observing not only that the dress has layers of green, but that the green—and the direction it runs—means something. In other words, in a Broadway show costing $35 million (a figure quoted by the tour guides, although the actual figure is closer to $14 million), the smallest details communicate something. The secret lies in knowing what, how, and why the details communicate—questions the tour was designed to answer.

After 30 minutes in the lobby, the group moved into the auditorium. There, Jerad and Alicia climbed onstage, while tour participants sat in theater seats near the front of the stage. This configuration expanded Jerad and Alicia's performance space, and it allowed the tourists to become a Broadway audience, if only for a moment.

From the stage, Jerad and Alicia continued to discuss salient points about the production: How it was originally intended for a smaller theater, but that the elaborate frame around the stage (the Dragon Time Clock) helps shrink the space; how the show, on tour, requires 14 trailer-trucks to move the sets from one town to the next; and how the company manager hands out 300 checks per week, making payday "Actor Appreciation Day." The audience seemed to love these stories; it brought them as close as they could possibly be to witnessing—and even performing in—a live Broadway show.

A large projection screen then descended, and a video entitled "Wicked: The Creation" started playing. Lasting almost 20 minutes, the video was essentially a creation narrative, detailing the genesis of *Wicked* from book to (originally intended) movie to Broadway show. Producer Marc Platt, composer/lyricist Stephen Schwartz, and writer Winnie Holzman, among others, discussed their intentions in creating the show, telling the story we related in Chapter 6. After the video, the tour group filed out of the auditorium and into a side lobby. There, Alicia and Jerad answered questions, posed for photographs, and urged the crowd to look for their characters onstage at the next performance—which would be in several hours. The guides urged the crowd to "keep pursuing your dreams," then bid them farewell.

What does "Behind the Emerald Curtain" accomplish for both consumers and producers, and how may it support and enhance the overall experience of *Wicked*?

For producers, the tour provides an opportunity to convey technical accomplishment, as well as to reveal authorial intent. On the one hand were dozens of details about how the show gets put together, and on the other were bracketed moments, usually from the show's creators, that emphasized artistic vision. As we participated in the tour, we were reminded of the song, "Putting It Together," from Stephen Sondheim's *Sunday in the Park with George*. "Behind the Emerald Curtain" reveals how some of the most creative minds on Broadway put *Wicked* together, bit by bit. In 90 minutes, the tour articulates an aesthetic vision and demonstrates the means of production needed to achieve it.

In that sense, the tour is not just about *Wicked*; it's about all Broadway shows. As Jerad and Alicia pointed out, bringing any show to Broadway requires a vision, the ability to pitch that vision to interested investors, and the technical prowess needed to convince audiences that "this is really happening." Whether that show becomes a smash hit, such as *Wicked*, or a colossal flop, such as *Carrie: The Musical*, the process is the same. And so is the risk.

And because the tour is conducted by actors, the tour is also about *them*: their backgrounds, their personalities, and their all-in commitment to the shows in which they appear. Jerad left us with this "typical day" example:

> When I wake up, it's a ticking time bomb. I have to save up my energy. I try to get to the theatre about an hour before the show starts. The show ends at 11:00, and I get to bed at 1:00, maybe. Then I may have a workshop the next day. I miss out on many activities, such as family weddings.

Jerad's awareness of the price he pays for playing in a long-running Broadway show is exceeded only by his gratitude at being able to do so. Yet it was critical for him to convey that point to an audience of aspiring Broadway performers.

For consumers, the tour revealed a treasure trove of information that could enrich their appreciation of *Wicked*. This would hold true regardless of whether they had already seen the show or not. Like a guided tour of a Picasso exhibit, the product tends to mean more if one can understand the process behind its construction. As recipients of through-lines made explicit, consumers of the tour are inheritors of industrial secrets they may or may not choose to reveal to others.

In fact, by giving consumers an insider's knowledge of how *Wicked* works, the tour gives a group of consumers what Bourdieu terms cultural capital: a type of embodied knowledge that sets some consumers apart from others, which they can use to establish (or maintain) status and power across a variety of social contexts.[4] For example, at a dinner party, someone who had taken the tour could comfortably enter into a conversation about how much people enjoy *Wicked*—especially since most people do. But that particular person could one-up others in the conversation by explaining how and why *Wicked* works the way it does, based on information only they could have acquired from the tour. In such a moment, that consumer would be displaying cultural capital—as would the consumer who Snapchatted to hundreds of friends their attendance at the tour. Either way, the message is conveyed that these consumers put their bodies *there*, in that space, at that time, to gain a particular type of knowledge. That in turn displays something remarkable about their acquisition of taste and the social status they are allowed to occupy because of it.

Finally, the tour also conveyed the power consumers have in making any show a success. Jerad pulled no punches in saying that *Wicked* was not well-received by many critics. In that sense, "Behind the Emerald Curtain" encourages consumers to generally disregard critics and promote their own experience of an event, amplified by socially mediated word-of-mouth. Jerad threw down the gauntlet of public opinion to those present, challenging them to see *Wicked*, confident that it can measure up to their expectations. "People don't remember reviews," he said defiantly. "They remember their experience."

Judging by consumers' interest in seeing the show after having taken this tour, one would have to say that "Behind the Emerald Curtain" succeeded effectively as an experiential marketing tool. Those who hadn't seen the show were keen to get tickets, and those who had were looking forward to seeing the show "put back together."

For consumers unable or unwilling to visit New York City, touring shows of *Wicked* visit major metropolitan areas frequently. In fact, up until 2015, *Wicked* had two national tours traveling simultaneously. In 2015, the Emerald City Tour closed after 10 years of continuous touring. However, the Munchkinland Tour is still touring North America. Playing in somewhat smaller venues than the Emerald City Tour, the Munchkinland Tour show produces runs ranging from 12 days (Peoria, IL) to over one month (Denver, CO).

Concomitant with these tours is a combination of exhibits and events that help promote the show in the host city, such as an elaborate promotional display in a shopping mall or a live performance of songs from the show. We had the opportunity to experience these events the last time *Wicked* toured Denver, in the summer of 2015. They consisted of an exhibit of *Wicked* entitled "The World Of *Wicked*" in the upscale Cheery Creek Mall; "A Special Live Performance of *Wicked* Songs," which featured understudies for the roles of Glinda and Elphaba singing two popular songs from the show; and a cabaret-style evening of songs by performers from *Wicked* entitled "Witches' Night Off." We describe each of these events in detail and then discuss how they generate excitement among consumers, which in turn encourages them to see *Wicked*. We also discuss how these experiences establish expectations in consumers' minds for what the show will be about. Both aspects become critical ingredients for building consumer excitement—and ultimately, loyalty—toward the *Wicked* brand.

"The World of *Wicked*"

We visited "The World of *Wicked*" three times in May and June of 2015. Set in the middle of a large atrium inside the Cherry Creek Mall, the exhibit looked like a giant hot air balloon—perhaps referencing a memorable image from *The Wizard of Oz*. Its structure was made mostly of panes of transparent hard plastic. There was an opaque cover on top of the globe featuring the now-famous image of Glinda whispering to Elphaba, and the cover also featured the recognizable "Wicked" lettering printed in giant letters on either side. A winged monkey perched atop the globe, high enough to be on a level with shoppers on the second floor of the mall. Another winged monkey perched on the side of the globe, peering in at the consumers as they passed through the exhibit.

The entrance to the globe was literally framed by a version of the Time Clock prominent in the Broadway show and tour, complete with clock, gears, and the Time-Dragon perched atop the frame. As consumers passed through the arch, they entered "The World of *Wicked*" in a way similar to the way in which viewers enter the show of *Wicked* as the orchestra strikes its first chords. Here, consumers walk through the arch, literally placing their bodies in an alternative experience of *Wicked*.

Once inside the globe, shoppers encounter three costumes from the show, with designers' sketches next to them. Two of the costumes—Glinda's blue "petal dress" featured in the opening scene of the show, and Elphaba's black dress featured later in the show—are mounted on full mannequins whose countenances resemble their respective performers. A third costume is Glinda's bright pink dress from the dance party at Shiz. This is mounted on a headless mannequin, but a jeweled letter "G" is perched where the head would be. The mannequins are elevated so that as shoppers pass through the exhibit, the dresses are at eye level and arm's length. A video featuring key creators of the show plays continuously. Signs warn consumers not to touch the costumes.

In addition to these production features, at least one guide is manning the exhibit at all times to interact with visitors, explaining the costumes and the video, and encouraging them to participate in a contest that involves visiting selected stores within the mall. Our guide, we noted, had the ability to adapt her message to fit the needs and experiences of the visitor in front of her. If they had not heard of *Wicked*, she explained the essentials of the show to them. And if they were already familiar with it, she asked where and when they had seen a production and then struck up a conversation based on that. In either case, she reminded visitors that *Wicked* would be returning to Denver in the near future. She told them where they could purchase tickets—and advised them to purchase them soon, while good seats were still available. She then led them out of the globe toward two life-size cutouts of Glinda and Elphaba, where they posed with the characters and had their photographs taken by others in their party. Before sending them back into the mall, the guide encouraged them to post those photographs on social media. A typical visit took approximately 10 minutes.

What does "The World of *Wicked*" accomplish, and what makes it such an effective marketing experience for the touring show itself? First, it has the power to appeal to two groups of consumers: those who have already seen a live production of *Wicked*, and those who have not but may be persuaded to. In so doing, "The World of *Wicked*" captures the attention of all who pass by, creating buzz and urging action.

For those who have already seen *Wicked*, the exhibit is a chance to jog the memory and revisit the features that made the show so pleasantly memorable in the first place: the costumes, the sets, the music, the characters, and the central relationship between Glinda and Elphaba—displayed dynamically and emphatically at the end of the exhibit. For parents and their children who have already seen the show, this would certainly be the case. Then as these memories are jogged, the question becomes: Is it time to see the show again, especially now that it's coming around again soon, and we know where to purchase tickets, and good seats are going fast? The exhibit not only jogs the memory, it creates a sense of urgency in the minds of consumers: we had better act now if we want to relive those memories, and maybe this time bring along a younger sibling (with a friend) who was too young to see the show the last time it came through Denver.

For consumers who have never seen *Wicked*, the exhibit becomes an opportunity to incite their curiosity, whet their appetites, and persuade them that if they enjoy this small slice of the show, they would certainly like the whole pie. This exhibit, therefore, marks their initiation into the *Wicked* experience, overseen by an interactive guide who encourages them to cultivate this new-found relationship. In a best-case scenario, this could lead to multiple viewings of a live production of *Wicked*, resulting in hundreds of dollars in revenue. So particularly for consumers in this market segment, their first encounter with the show is critical. If they are repulsed, bored, or intimidated, it could result in a lost opportunity, as well as lost revenue. But if they are drawn in, engaged, and made to feel valued as an ongoing consumer of the show, the result could be long-term and lucrative. Regardless of whether or not visitors to this exhibit have seen *Wicked*, it still accomplishes a great deal of inter-action with consumers that facilitates an ongoing relationship with the show.

This is what marketers mean when they refer to Customer Lifetime Value or CLV.[5] How many dollars will the consumer spend over his/her lifetime as she/he interacts with our product? Cadillac makes such calcu-lations, knowing that some customers may purchase five to ten Cadillacs over the course of their lifetimes. Burger King makes such calculations as well, knowing that consumers will spend more money on fast food during certain phases of their life cycles (college years, young families) than others (young newlyweds, senior citizens). The producers of any Broadway show have made similar calculations, and they realize that first-time samplers of a show could easily become repeat patrons. An exhibit such as "The World of *Wicked*" plays a critical role in this eventuality.

"The World of *Wicked*" also provides an experiential consumption of *Wicked* apart from a performance of *Wicked* itself. It brings *Wicked* to the consumer, rather than waiting for the consumer to come to *Wicked*. This is an important and growing trend in arts consumption in which the col-lection, the performance, and the players come to the consumer, not vice versa. In so doing, potential barriers to entry for many consumers—be they price, inconvenience, or the intimidation and inadequacy many feel at the prospect of entering into a high-culture experience—are removed and replaced with a sense of immediacy and opportunity. Hence, a hand-ful of pieces from a permanent art collection takes to the streets in an artmobile; a small group of musicians from a larger symphony orchestra takes a road trip to rural communities in a sparsely populated state; and a handful of dancers from a world-class dance troupe performs in an inner-city classroom a subway ride away from Lincoln Center. "The World of *Wicked*" mirrors this trend by bringing the *Wicked* experience to the consumer. And the subtext is, of course, "You like this? Then come to a full-length performance of *Wicked*, and you will like it even better."

This exhibit also brings *Wicked* to consumers in a place where they are already doing other types of performance and consumption. It has suggestive power over consumers who are in a performative, acquisitive mood. The exhibit catches consumers in an experiential, even impulsive mood and beckons them to try something new: "You've bought this, and you've tried on that. Now why not try *this*?" Amplifying this impulsive state is the fact that the exhibit space is so accessible. Open on all sides, visible from both levels of the mall, and easily reachable by a glass elevator placed at its edge, the court is bounded by walkways but contains no barriers to entry. There is nothing to dissuade shoppers from entering this space other than the notion that other consumers may be watching. But given the nature of experiential marketing today, this would not be a deterrent for most consumers.

Furthermore, "The World of *Wicked*" is placed at a site where exhibits and performances traditionally take place: choir concerts, local celebrity interviews, extended exhibits (e.g., Black History Month), and most importantly, Santa's Village, all take place here. Consumers come to this space expecting something "different" to happen. As such, this area provides a respite from the First World problems of decision-making and spending money that accompany the shopping experience. Owners of the mall welcome any opportunity for consumers to spend more time there, since it increases the likelihood that they will eventually spend more money. If an event such as "The World of *Wicked*" gives shoppers a chance to collect themselves and prepare to shop once again, so much the better. In fact, the exhibit promotes shopping by providing visitors with a list of stores they "need" to visit. Participating stores give stamps of validation, and shoppers who have completed a list of stamped visits may place their names in a raffle. Prizes include a *Wicked* soundtrack, t-shirt, and other merchandise. Thus, the cycle of consumption continues, providing a win-win-win for mall tenants, mall owners, and producers of *Wicked*.

Most importantly, "The World of *Wicked*" is an immersive consumption experience. As with the "Behind the Emerald Curtain" tour in New York City, visitors to "The World of *Wicked*" see and smell authentic Broadway costumes at arm's length, hear the music, interviews, and consumer responses from the endless-loop video, and gain a sense of the props and themes of the musical, from the Time Clock entrance they walked through to the winged monkeys peering in at them. Once they leave, they are confronted with life-size cardboard cutouts of Glinda and Elphaba facing each other confrontationally. The figures are placed in front of a backdrop of an Oz set, complete with fallen house and corn stalks. Visitors are encouraged to don a witch's hat, a princess tiara, or a green feather boa and pose in front of the two characters. They are also encouraged to have their photographs taken, which they can then upload to *Wicked*'s Facebook site.

In this way, consumers are literally hailed into a mise-en-scene of the production of *Wicked* the musical. They are beckoned to take their place, even if only momentarily, within the boundaries of the musical itself, thus blurring the lines between fantasy and reality (something shopping malls encourage in the first place). And they are asked to embody one of the characters—both of whom are beautiful, magical, and mysterious—and enter into a confrontation with the other character. So not only do consumers choose a character, they enter into a relationship. And as we witnessed, many young girls imitate this relationship by imitating the disposition of the characters' bodies. To strike the pose is to inhabit the relationship. This lies at the heart of embodied consumption.

At this moment, visitors are taught that the relationship between Glinda and Elphaba is metonymic for the musical itself: to understand that relationship—to embody it—is to understand, and in some ways experience, the musical. This metonym is not something the show's author, Winnie Holzman, would disagree with. In an interview commemorating the show's 12th anniversary, she states:

> You know, friendship is a big part of women's lives, and you don't often see it depicted very interestingly... Elphaba and Glinda hate each other at first sight, but those feelings are a sign of how it's their destiny to be forever altered by their friendship. They're making each other better people and helping each other grow into the women they were meant to become.[6]

Thus, this portal into the *Wicked* experience is entirely consistent with authorial intent. A consistently sustained message for a product is what marketers call IMC or Integrated Marketing Communications.[7] In this instance, the emotions shoppers are asked to feel at an exhibit in a mall are consistent with the emotions they will be asked to feel during the musical itself. IMC asks marketers to establish a through-line from the original vision of a product to all the portals through which stakeholders can access that product. In the case of *Wicked*, as re-presented by The World of *Wicked*, the marketers have valiantly succeeded.

A SPECIAL LIVE PERFORMANCE OF *WICKED* SONGS

In early June of 2015, we returned to the Cherry Creek Mall's Grand Gallery to attend "A Special Live Performance of *Wicked* Songs," performed by two understudies for the lead roles of Glinda and Elphaba from the touring show. A full-length production of *Wicked* had already been playing in Denver for several days and would remain there for a month. This special performance, which had been advertised for several weeks on large posters throughout the mall, took place in front of "The World of *Wicked*" exhibit, discussed above.

The stage for this performance was quite simple: a 3-foot-high black rectangular platform had been placed directly in front of the exhibit. A small staircase, stage right, was the only way to access the stage. Two large black speakers were mounted on poles on either side of the stage. To the back of stage right was a table where a sound engineer monitored a portable console. There was a large open space in front of the stage for a crowd to gather.

Although the show started at 11:30, a crowd began to gather just after 10:00. There were only a few portable chairs, so most of the crowd sat on the floor. Early arrivals consisted almost entirely of young women between the ages of 5 and 18, many of whom wore green. Young mothers with strollers were also in attendance. As the crowd grew, people began standing at the rear of the gallery. Men and women aged 25–60 comprised the majority of this group. The crowd totaled approximately 250 by the time the show started.

Shortly after 11:30, the show began. A dark-suited executive from the mall cheerily welcomed the crowd. He then handed off the microphone to a twentysomething young lady as the strains of "The Wizard and I" began to play. Dressed in a dark smock with black leggings and spike-heeled boots, her dark red hair falling around her shoulders, this Elphaba understudy could easily have passed for a better-dressed version of many of the audience members seated in front of her. Yet she also happened to be a professionally trained vocalist. Powerful yet controlled, expressive but naturalistic, her performance captivated the audience all the more persuasively through her Everygal persona. Without the benefit of lighting, makeup, costume, props, or narrative, the performance took on the feel of an audition for *American Idol*—one that would culminate in a trip to Hollywood. And indeed, many audience members sang along in quiet acts of co-creation.

"The Wizard and I" was the perfect song choice for such a context. On one hand, it is song about youthful anticipation and the naivete that goes with it. Sung by the green-skinned Elphaba shortly after her arrival at Shiz University, the song looks forward to a time—undoubtedly in the near future—when she will meet the Wizard of Oz. Then, her true genius will be revealed, she sings, and the days of misunderstanding and ridicule will come to an end. At the same time, the song is also an exercise in dramatic irony. Elphaba does not realize how true her words will turn out to be when she sings that there will be a celebration in Oz having to do with her.

The celebration, of course, is over her own demise—a dissonant chorus-cry that opens and closes the show. Although Elphaba would have no way of knowing that yet, the audience may well have known it. Filled with ecstatic anticipation, she drives the song to an enthralling climax that showcases the performer's power and range. This is accomplished through the popular belting technique we discussed in Chapter 8. As is the case in the full-length show, this performance elicited emphatic "you-go-girl" shouts and whistles.

This euphoric mood was quickly dispelled by the onstage arrival of the second understudy, playing Glinda. Dressed in a soft pink cotton minidress and black espadrilles, her blonde hair pulled back in a bun, this character's gently revealing demeanor contrasted sharply with Elphaba's in-your-face attitude. She and Elphaba sang the famous closing duet from Wicked, "For Good." Whereas "The Wizard and I" is anticipatory, "For Good", as we saw in the last chapter, is benedictory. It quietly but profoundly marks the last time the two main characters appear onstage together. Despite misunderstandings, fights, and betrayals real or imagined, Glinda and Elphaba realize that they will not be seeing each other again. Heartfelt apologies are offered and accepted, and each character acknowledges the indelible effect the other has had on her.

"For Good" is a song about resolution, acceptance, and the recognition that some people change our lives forever, even though our face-to-face relationships with them may not last. In the context of a full-length, emotionally exhausting show, this song carries tremendous emotional impact: sniffles, handkerchiefs, and facial tissues abound. In the context of a noonday shopping mall, however, the effect was more superficial. The audience applauded appreciatively, almost relieved that such private emotion, displayed in the cold light of a vast retail space, was over. What had transpired between these two characters to inspire this song? Unless they had seen the musical, viewers would have no way of knowing. Yet even without the context, they could still appreciate the emotional intensity of the moment.

Once the applause had subsided, the dark-suited executive from the mall took to the stage once more. He brightly thanked everyone for coming and announced that the two performers would be signing autographs at a table behind the stage. About 50 people lined up for this, offering posters, programs, t-shirts, and CDs for the performers to sign. The performers went about their business cheerfully, asking brief questions and offering insights on what it was like to tour with the show as the fans slowly shuffled past. The songs took 10 minutes to perform, but the autographs took over an hour.

What did this performance of two songs from *Wicked* add to consumers' experience of the show itself? And how might it have motivated audiences to attend a full-length performance of the show, ensconced as it was in Denver's largest theater for a month-long run?

At the very least, the live performance of these songs enlivened the "World of *Wicked*" exhibit. Rather than watching an endless-loop video of producers talking *about* the show, consumers watched and listened as two vocalists performed songs *from* the show. For a brief moment, the cardboard cutouts that normally conclude the exhibit suddenly served as backdrop for their own enactment. Glinda and Elphaba came to life, coming and going as quickly as characters do in both *The Wizard of Oz* and *Wicked*.

Critically, however, the performers wore none of the costumes, or bore any of the props, that would mark them as Elphaba and Glinda to the unsuspecting viewer. No flowing gowns, no wands or broomsticks were in evidence here. Yet in the context of a shopping mall, the performance was all the more compelling because of this. The two understudies appeared as if pulled from the audience by chance—a fact that made them much more relatable than if they had been in full costume and makeup. Their status as understudies was celebrated rather than concealed. Thus, the performance took on a "they're-just-one-of-us" quality that motivated the audience to empathize with the performers and help them succeed.

And even though the songs were performed out of context, audience members got a taste of the tremendous emotional range and impact *Wicked* affords. From the euphoric expectancy of "The Wizard and I" to the resigned closure of "For Good," *Wicked* packs an emotional gut-punch in the finest tradition of Broadway musicals. Far from a liability, this you'll-laugh-you'll-cry quality is exactly what audiences expect from musical theater. And it became clear to the audience that morning—even from two songs—that *Wicked* will give it to them. In that sense, the choice of these two songs was enlightened. It maximized emotional contrast, hinting at what the full production would offer.

And if audience reaction was any indication, this brief performance appealed to those unfamiliar, as well as those familiar, with *Wicked* itself. People wearing *Wicked* t-shirts and carrying *Wicked* posters were obviously fans of the show already. Faithful converts, they knew when the "good parts" of each song were, and they responded appropriately at those moments. Those unfamiliar with the show hung back initially in their response, yet they too were swept along eventually—not only by the performers, but by their more seasoned seatmates. In that respect, this brief performance succeeded in whetting the audience's appetite for more *Wicked* scenes, songs, and sensations.

Finally, one should not overlook the importance of the dark-suited mall executive or the reason for his happiness. This brief performance of *Wicked* songs infused his property with a level of excitement he would not have had otherwise that morning. Foot traffic literally stopped for this event because it had to: shoppers on their way to somewhere else suddenly became audience members perforce. People on the upper level of the mall peered down fondly at the performers and the crowd. *Wicked* created an event in the mall that morning, and at its conclusion, 250 audience members became consumers once again. Happy and hungry, they dispersed into the mall like locusts.

WITCHES' NIGHT OFF

As with most shows on tour, *Wicked* plays eight times per week in the cities it visits. These include nightly performances from Tuesday through Friday, then matinee and evening performances on Saturdays and Sundays. Hence, as on Broadway, Monday is the only day with no scheduled performance.

However, in some larger cities, Monday becomes an opportunity for *Wicked*'s producers and consumers to participate in an entirely different event: "Witches' Night Off." This is a cabaret-style performance featuring *Wicked* cast members covering and dancing to their favorite Broadway and popular songs. Venues tend to be well-known bar/restaurant configurations such as Hard Rock Café. Tickets are sold (prices ranged from $20 to $40) with the bulk of the take going to a variety of charities. These evenings, announced shortly after *Wicked* settles in for a run in any given city, are extremely popular and usually sell out quickly.

Such was the case with "Witches' Night Off" in Denver, which took place at the Hard Rock Café shortly after *Wicked* opened there.

Although we had planned to attend this event, it quickly sold out, before we were able to purchase tickets. Here, we use photos and the direct observations given to us by our key informant for the touring *Wicked*, Bethany McClain, as the basis for our description.

The Hard Rock was completely taken over that night for this function alone; only *Wicked* fans, cast members, and their families and friends were there, totaling almost 200. The venue had a much more intimate, cabaret-style ambiance than either an ordinary night at Hard Rock, which seats 300, or at a typical performance of *Wicked* at Denver's Buell Theatre, which seats over 2800.

A small stage had been set up at one end of the restaurant, large enough only to hold a small band (drummer, bass player, keyboardist, and guitarist) and a small group of performers (three at most) at any given time. A shimmering red curtain served as backdrop, and in the middle of it was suspended an LED screen which read "Witches' Night Off." Guests were seated around small tables from which they could order drinks and small plates of food. The entire set was reminiscent, probably not accidentally, of the Kit Kat Club in *Cabaret*—although not quite as tawdry. An upstairs balcony ringed the room; only performers and special guests sat there, looking down over the proceedings and preparing for their turn on the stage.

From the start, the evening had a laid-back, *laissez-les-bon-temps-rouler* feel to it. There was no formal program to follow, no emcee to announce who would perform what song when, and no need for an intermission. Audience members came and went as they pleased. One goal was made clear, appropriately enough, by Carrie St. Louis (who would make her debut as Glinda on Broadway eight months later): proceeds from this evening would go to several charities, both local and national. Project Angel Heart and Rainbow Alley (local) and Broadway Cares/Equity Fights AIDS and Doctors Without Borders would be the recipients of the evening's gate.

The evening featured various configurations of performers singing mostly recognizable show tunes and popular songs. For example, a trio of female cast members sang "Up the Ladder to the Roof" (The Supremes), followed by a swing version of "I Will Survive" (Gloria Gaynor). Two men performed a poignant rendition of "Lily's Eyes" from *The Secret Garden*; the woman who played Madame Morrible sang a Garland-infused, slapstick version "The Trolley Song" (*Meet Me in St. Louis*). One vocalist sang "Meadowlark" (*The Baker's Wife*, another

Stephen Schwartz musical), while another female singer performed a rousing rendition of "Proud Mary" (Creedence Clearwater Revival). By turns parodic, heartfelt, rollicking, and camp, "Witches' Night Off" in Denver was a pastiche of kind-hearted frivolity that lasted three hours—and raised $12,000 for its designated non-profits.

Yet the benefits of this charity event reached far beyond the evening itself. Although its monetary impact on any given night is relatively modest, the cumulative effect of these functions nationwide is significant: *Wicked* has raised over $4 million for charitable causes.

At a macrolevel of marketing, this enables *Wicked* to claim not only immense profitability, but remarkable charitability. The show thereby engages in the kind of corporate social responsibility so valued by millennials in particular. Giving back helps *Wicked* solidify its long-term relationship to millennials, which is critical, given that female millennials and those born shortly after them are arguably its most important target market. And for their part, millennials can feel good about supporting a musical that has raised more money for Broadway Cares/Equity Fights AIDS than any other Broadway show in history.

However, at a microlevel of marketing, the impact of "Witches' Night Off" could be even greater, in several respects, including the new light in which a select general public gets to see *Wicked* cast members; the release it gives cast members for one evening; and the special ways cast members get to treat certain audience members.

"Witches' Night Off" allows audience members to see the *Wicked* cast out of character; it humanizes the players of a highly stylized show in ways inaccessible to a large audience at a formal performance. Under normal circumstances, the only way most audience members can see cast members out of character is to wait for them at the stage door after the show. Such moments tend to be mildly chaotic and potentially disappointing: performers are exhausted, hungry, and anxious to get away, while fans compete with each other for face time and autographs. Yet here, in the context of the cabaret format, fans spent three hours in relaxed performer–audience interaction. And interact they did: clapping, singing, guffawing, or hushing as the performances dictated. Many fans were old enough to be the performers' parents, and there was something parentally supportive about their encouragement of the actors, as though they were cheering on their own children at a talent show.

Additionally, the relaxed ambiance of "Witches' Night Off" may be as therapeutic for the performers as it is entertaining for the guests. *Wicked* is a relentlessly stylized show whose nightly demands take their toll on its performers ("It's like Mount Everest!" remarked one Elphaba understudy). Even the title of this one, "night off," suggests a sense of relief and release. Devoid of extreme physical transformation, the performers get to play themselves—and the effect is liberating. Without her tight blonde curls and sparkling pink gown, Carrie St. Louis (Glinda) looked like any other twentysomething one might pass in the mall. Stripped of her black hat and green skin, Alyssa Fox (Elphaba) could be an aspiring advertising executive.

Finally, "Witches' Night Off" enables the performers to form special bonds with certain guests. In Denver that night, Bethany brought along a friend: Molly Nash, the girl whose real-life story was the inspiration for the best-selling novel (and later, movie), *My Sister's Keeper*. Stricken with a rare disease as a child, a now mostly healthy Molly was about to turn twenty-one. Bethany bought Molly a *Wicked* apron as a birthday present at the small concession stand that evening. The two men who sold Molly the apron (they played two of the Flying Monkeys in the show) asked Molly if they could hang on to it for a short time. Bethany relates:

> And she was like, "Okay, whatever." So, they take the apron, come back twenty, thirty minutes later. They'd gotten the apron signed by the entire cast. And she ended up getting pictures with the Wizard, and Glinda, and with all – like, everybody. She was completely in her element, getting, you know spoiled as a little princess, as always! And everybody kept wishing her a happy birthday and giving her hugs, and she like –she was in heaven.

This story would be joyous enough had it only been witnessed by the performers and guests at the show that evening. But in this age of social media, the story continues:

> And then I get a picture from her that night after we dropped her off at home, and she's in bed and next to her on the bed is her signed apron. And she literally sleeps with it every single night. And she's like, "Oh my God, this is the best birthday present ever!" You know, it was really just a really special night.

Brenda went on to explain that Molly later posted these events on Facebook. Thus, *Wicked*'s mass-mediated message of empowerment gets re-enacted at the individual level during a cabaret performance. In turn, that image is captured and pushed through social media channels, then "liked" by a local celebrity's hundreds of followers. This ripple effect results in hundreds of positive impressions for *Wicked* based on a random and ordinarily unseen act of kindness.

Two additional *Wicked* experiences play an important role in endorsing the values *Wicked* stands for. Until relatively recently, Broadway shows weren't thought of in terms of the values they stood for—a blockbuster such as *Phantom of the Opera* comes to mind. While it is true that many shows like *Phantom* have been involved in charity work for years—particularly with Broadway Cares/Equity Fights AIDS—the opportunistic fit between the values a given show espouses and the appropriate philanthropic outlets it might support (termed *strategic philanthropy* in marketing circles) is not always obvious. But once it became clear that *Wicked* was in a position to sustain itself, producers of the show began to look for ways to sustain others. Spurred by the formation of *Wicked*'s philanthropic arm, "For Good," producer David Stone began to search for appropriate outlets. Ironically, narrative elements within the show itself pointed the way: on the one hand, the major character is literally green, which suggests an opportunity to promote environmental sustainability; on the other, *because* the major character is green, she is treated as an outcast, the perfect target for bullying, which suggests an opportunity to promote an anti-bullying campaign. We discuss these outreach projects below, emphasizing the goodwill *Wicked* generates as a result of supporting them. Our consumer responses show that audiences are sensitive to this fact, even using the term "bullying" to describe the way in which Elphaba is treated. This in turn speaks to an opportunity to promote social sustainability by supporting an anti-bullying campaign.

BROADWAY GREEN ALLIANCE

"And one day it sort of hit us like a thunderbolt," David Stone revealed in a 2013 interview, "that having a lead character who was green lent itself to focusing on green initiatives."[8] This in turn inspired *Wicked*'s cast and crew to organize a Broadway Town Hall meeting in 2008, attended by other members from many of Broadway's most successful shows. The result was the Broadway Green Alliance (BGA) which, in collaboration with the Natural Resources Defense Council, encourages sustainable business practices across the entire theater community.

How is such an initiative organized, and what changes have resulted from it? Each Broadway production appoints its own Green Captain, who can be anyone directly involved with the show, from actors to stage managers to musicians. Armed with welcome kits that instruct them how to keep their shows green, Captains communicate best practices to everyone in their respective shows; then, they ensure that those practices are being implemented. These can include everything from placing recycling bins in backstage areas, to replacing marquee lights and rooftop signs with energy-efficient lighting (this alone has saved 700 tons of carbon annually), to using rechargeable batteries in all of the microphones onstage. But these practices can also extend to "closing green," which affects shows that are about to close. Instead of throwing all of its sets and prop pieces in the dumpster, Green Captains make sure these items are repurposed and sent to off-Broadway and off-off-Broadway productions who need them, as well as to colleges and other not-for-profits. Similarly, the Binder Project collects and recycles the hundreds of ring binders amassed by Broadway shows from their readings and workshops. The binders are centralized into kind of lending library, accessible to any theater-related individual or organization who may need them.

These practices extend to fans of Broadway shows as well. The BGA's website encourages consumers to engage in best practices as they attend shows. Microlevel activities here include printing tickets at home on recycled paper, carpooling to the theater, and taking only one Playbill from the usher—all designed to sustain not only the environment, but also consumers' engagement with the theater.

As Broadway in general and *Wicked* in particular practice and promote green activities, they generate positive publicity and positive emotions for their efforts, particularly among millennials. Fans of *Wicked* can take pride in the fact that "their show" spearheaded these eco-friendly initiatives on Broadway; then, they themselves can emulate similar activities in their everyday lives—perhaps thinking of the show as they do so. This experience, while unconventional, carries the added advantage of contributing to the greater good.

THE "BULLYBUST" INITIATIVE

Consumer responses to *Wicked*, detailed in Chapter 7, reveal that audiences are sensitive to the fact that Elphaba is "bullied" in the show. In light of dozens of recent, highly publicized instances of bullying in recent years, the term has taken on a highly charged resonance throughout contemporary society. And in fictionalized accounts of bullying portrayed in such popular shows as *Glee* and *Rise*, it is clear that kids who "stick out," either through their appearance, their predilections, or their actions, are especially at risk of a being bullied.

Yet these circumstances became an opportunity for *Wicked* to partner with the National School Climate Center's "BullyBust" initiative, an anti-bullying program that encourages students and teachers to "call out" bullying when and where they see it.[9] Because the plot and characters of *Wicked* address this issue so directly, the show and the discussions it spurs have become central to the group's curriculum, activities, and overall campaign. This development has the added benefit of introducing *Wicked* and its recognizable characters into schools across the country. This type of partnership actually stemmed from a similar one in the UK. There, the London production of *Wicked* teamed up with an anti-bullying campaign, and the show featured the partnership on its website. Stone felt the program could be equally effective in America as well. Extending the reach of this cause, *Wicked* cast members have taken it upon themselves to speak to school groups independently of the formal program, either at the Gershwin or at the schools. The message conveyed is that *Wicked* supports any young person's right to feel protected and validated.

Taken together, these unconventional experiences extend the traditional notion of what an experience can be. Like "The World of *Wicked*" and "Witches' Night Off," participants will enjoy the experience, but they do so with the added satisfaction that their involvement is benefitting others, in ways that *Wicked* organically promotes in its own thematic content.

CONCLUSION

While these *Wicked* experiences represent but a few of the promotions that the marketers of the musical have devised to extend its cultural moment, they exemplify the experiential marketing strategies at the heart of *Wicked*'s continued success:

- **Wicked experiences are embodied experiences**: Each *Wicked* experience beckons the consumer to place his or her body in a particular space at a particular time—whether it be in the Gershwin Theatre in New York on a brisk April morning or in a shopping mall in Denver on a balmy June afternoon. Once consumers occupy these spaces, their visual, aural, tactile, and kinetic senses are stimulated in ways that connect them to *Wicked* powerfully and memorably. The effect—just as it did with 1939's *Wizard of Oz Tour,* where local children dressed up to lead the Oz parade—goes beyond immersive to embodied. Leading consumer researchers such as John Sherry and Annamma Joy and Jonathan Schroeder have illustrated the impact of this technique. And James Pine, co-author of *The Experience Economy,* notes that embodiment can produce a defining characteristic of all memorable experiences: *authenticity.*[10] Even though it is set in a fantasy world, *Wicked* "feels real," according to many consumers we interviewed. The *Wicked* experiences orbiting around the show continually validate this impression.

- **Wicked experiences offer consistency of message**: Each of the experiences we describe offers a consistent, oft-repeated message concerning *Wicked*'s meaning. According to the show's creator, Stephen Schwartz, *Wicked* is about "the untold story of the Witches of Oz." (During a 2013 discussion panel, Schwartz relates that the initial reactions to scenes in which both women were featured were so positive that he wrote a large note to himself which said, "It's the girls, stupid."). However reductionist this interpretation may be when compared with Maguire's—or Baum's—original intent, it is *the* through-line for this particular Oz-inspired revision. And this through-line is long: not only does it connect Schwartz to Winnie Holzman, the show's writer; it stretches to Alicia Albright, the show's dance Captain. Here is Holzman summing up the show: "This musical is about these two women finding each other as friends, and how they affect each other. It's unusual to have anything be about that. And luckily I think we were all picturing pretty much the same thing, which in itself is a miracle." And here is Albright discussing *Wicked,* 13 years and 5000 performances after its premiere: "This show is about this relationship between two very different women. The sparks really fly when they're onstage together. The contrast in how they look, sound, and move has to be emphasized for maximum effect." That this vision is still shared and repeated like a mantra so long after the show's debut is remarkable. It also becomes the focal point of all *Wicked* experiences, reminding consumers what the show is about.

- **Wicked experiences educate consumers**: Consistent with a key tenet of experiential marketing, *Wicked*'s producers take every opportunity to explain and demonstrate how the show is put together—from the behind-the-scenes tour to the live performance in the shopping mall. Contemporary consumers like to see how things get made—as the proliferation of food, automobile, and home improvement shows on television demonstrates. *Wicked* willingly complies with this trend. In so doing, the show's producers not only reinforce the prized quality of authenticity, but they show consumers that they, as producers, have nothing to hide. In the same way that Thomas Keller reveals to anyone who would watch precisely how his culinary creations are constructed (prompting Alice Waters to laud his creations for their transparency)—or for that matter, Baum divulged the technological secrets of his fairy films, so *Wicked* shows to anyone who would watch precisely how its magical world is achieved. This establishes a paradoxical trust bond between producers and consumers. On the one hand, producers show consumers how everything is done. On the other, consumers still offer the show their willing suspension of disbelief— despite their new-found knowledge. Thus, transparency seems to heighten, rather than diminish, consumer loyalty.

- **Wicked experiences serve as a platform for the expression and enactment of core social values**: If all *Wicked* did was communicate, for 15 years, a consistent message regarding female friendship, that would be achievement enough. But the show also espouses particular social values that are expressed and enacted beyond the confines of its own performance. Tolerance, inclusiveness, diversity, sensitivity, empowerment, ethics, and integrity are some of the core values expressed in the show, and our interviews with young consumers in particular show that these values are conveyed to them clearly and powerfully. These core values, in turn, become resources for positioning *Wicked* to hail a broad array of target markets, thus maximizing the show's appeal. In the same way that *The King's Speech* artfully positioned itself as a platform for all people with speech disabilities, so *Wicked* has become a forum for anyone who has felt ridiculed or ostracized for some aspect of their appearance, personality, or predilections. Such awareness and appeals on the part of *Wicked*'s producers are not disingenuous; rather, they show a masterful understanding of the range of consumers who may connect with the show. And they suggest ways in which fans can participate in real-world activities that promote its values, such

as anti-bullying campaigns, animal rights fundraisers, and green initiatives—often featured on the show's websites. *Wicked* experiences
are consistent with these values, encouraging participants to support local charities or become involved in community organizations.
Wicked therefore becomes not just another entertainment experience, but a call to do something "For Good." This call to (social)
arms is particularly important to millennials.

- **Wicked experiences provide a sense of community**: Because they
  bring together consumers—particularly young consumers—interested in the arts, *Wicked* experiences provide a sense of community
  for people who feel ostracized already. As episodes of *Glee* repeatedly show, kids in the arts get "shlushied" every day in school—
  literally and metaphorically. The *Wicked* experiences we discuss
  here proliferate moments in which they feel validated and celebrated, rather than ridiculed and rejected. The general exuberance
  we observed at these events reflects how valued they are by their
  participants. The tour, the gatherings at the mall, and the cabaret
  evenings become meaningful social events during which consumers
  are encouraged to express, in both interaction and appearance, their
  deep emotional connection to a Broadway show. In contrast to the
  athletic arena, for example, in which tailgates, pep rallies, and auto-
  graph sessions abound, moments such as these in the performing
  arts are rare. By providing occasions for community beyond a high-
  stakes, full-length performance of *Wicked*, *Wicked* experiences bond
  consumers in looser, more informal environments. In so doing, they
  enact the very core values the show itself espouses.

In all of these aspects, the strategies deployed by *Wicked*'s marketing
team are remarkably similar to those employed by L. Frank Baum nearly
a century earlier. Like Baum, *Wicked*'s marketers use experiential techniques to distinguish their product from other productions, while offering consumers multiple points of entry into the experience. Events like
the "Special Live Performance of Wicked Songs" and "Witch's Night
Off" provide a festive context for consumption and encourage the creation of an insider community. Each of the events we attended—most
of which were cost-free—emphasized an experiential rather than transactional relationship between ourselves and the musical. Finally, just as
Baum fashioned himself America's teller of fairy tales and the children's
friend, so *Wicked* endows itself with a compelling persona committed

to environmental sustainability, social justice, and a host of charitable causes. In this, *Wicked* raises the institutional marketing strategy deployed by corporate program sponsors in the 1950s to a high art, generating goodwill and transferring the symbolic values associated with these causes to the musical itself.

Although *Wicked*'s marketing team, like MGM's before it, was interested in sustaining their specific product rather than the Oz narrative, their remarkable success similarly made Oz newly marketable and consumable, inspiring producers to take a new look at the yellow brick road, leading to another wave of Oz activity, and extending the narrative into the twenty-first century.

NOTES

1. Brooks Barnes, "How Wicked Cast Its Spell," *The Wall Street Journal,* October 22, 2005, https://www.wsj.com/articles/SB112994038461876413.
2. Joseph Pine and James Gilmore, *The Experience Economy* (Boston: Harvard Business Review Press, Updated edition, 2011); Bernd H. Schmitt, *Experiential Marketing* (New York: Simon and Schuster, Freepress, 1999).
3. Burleigh B. Gardner and Sidney J. Levy, "The Product and the Brand," *Harvard Business Review* 33, no. 2 (1955): 33–40.
4. Pierre Bourdieu, "The Forms of Capital," in *Handbook of Theory and Research for the Sociology of Education*, ed. J. G. Richardson (New York: Greenwood, 1986), 241–258.
5. William Pride and O. C. Ferrell, *Marketing* (Boston: Cengage Learning, 2016).
6. Qtd in Kathy Henderson, "The Real Reason Audiences Adore Wicked," *Broadway Direct*, October 22, 2015, https://broadwaydirect.com/winnie-holzman-wicked/.
7. Don Schultz, Stanley Tannenbaum, and Robert Lauterborn, *Integrated Marketing Communications* (Chicago: NTC Business Books, 1993).
8. Josh Allendale, "For Good: A Blockbuster Gives Back," *Broadway Direct*, October 15, 2013, https://broadwaydirect.com/for-good-a-blockbuster-gives-back/, Accessed November 18, 2015.
9. Ibid.
10. Annamma Joy and John Sherry, "Speaking of Art as Embodied Imagination: A Multi-sensory Approach to Understanding Aesthetic Experience," *Journal of Consumer Research* 30, no. 2 (2003): 259–282; Jonathan Schroeder, *Visual Consumption* (London and New York: Routledge, 2002).

PART III

Beyond *Wicked*

CHAPTER 10

Whither Oz?: Stepping into the Twenty-First Century

Wicked premiered on the Broadway stage five years after the last of the annual broadcast showings of *The Wizard of Oz*, twenty-three years after the home-video release of the film had diminished the cultural impact of the annual event, and nearly thirty years after *The Wiz*, the last highly visible Oz event. Over these years, Oz's marketability had declined markedly. This is not to say that Oz faded from American culture and memory entirely; as John Fricke observes, there is always something Ozzy going on. But compared to the flurry of films, shows, and spin-offs that characterized the decades between 1960 and 1998, Oz production dwindled.[1] The years between 1998 and 2003 saw only a handful of new re-consumptions, none of which made a cultural impact. If not for *Wicked's* phenomenal success, Oz may well have become fossilized into a classic book and a classic film, passing into the hands of scholars and fans, a subject and a passion, moving it—at least temporarily—from the stream of cultural sustainability as a living, evolving narrative. The sold-out performances and cultural phenomena of *Wicked* averted this. *Wicked*, by making Oz culturally current once again, made the narrative newly marketable. The musical's large following of devoted fans, eager for new *Wicked* experiences, inspired producers who were more than willing to gamble on the chance that the consumers who had so eagerly embraced *Wicked's* tale behind the tale would also embrace other Oz experiences.

It's almost impossible to count the Oz re-consumptions brought to market between 2005 and today, not to mention the numerous projects (including the long-awaited *Wicked* film) still in production. A rough

© The Author(s) 2018
K. Drummond et al., *The Road to Wicked*,
https://doi.org/10.1007/978-3-319-93106-7_10

count of the most widely known products encompasses six young adult book series, four major stage productions, 2015's *The Wiz, Live!*, a concept album, twenty films, television specials and series, numerous cross-over series' episodes and commercials, and twenty video games. At least ten major film and television projects are in development. Not all of these re-consumptions have been well-received, and not all of them have brought the producers the profit they dreamed of. But enough of them have been embraced by consumers to keep Oz a marketable prospect and ensure the narrative's continued cultural sustainability. Successful post-*Wicked* Ozes, however, are not Baum's Oz or MGM's. Instead, like *Wicked*, both novel and musical, they are in dialogue with both, promising consumers the story behind the myth—Oz as they have never seen it before. Seeking to attract *Wicked's* consumer base, these new Ozes tend to focus on powerful women. Additionally, they adapt the narrative to other popular genres, making Oz new for the *Harry-Potter, Lord-of-the-Rings,* and *Game-of-Thrones* generation and tapping into the growing trend of "fairy tales with an edge" found in popular shows and films such as *Grimm, Once Upon a Time, Maleficent,* and *Snow White and the Huntsmen.*

NextGen Oz

The year 2007 saw the premiere of the first of these post-*Wicked* revisionist Ozes, the Sci-Fi channel's twenty-million-dollar miniseries, *Tin Man*.[2] Mark Stern, the channel's executive vice president for original programming, directly ties the series to *Wicked's* success. "I think *Wicked* is indicative of the fact that people want to revisit this stuff in a different way," he observed, "I certainly do. I think we're in that kind of nostalgia phase of 'Where's the next thing?' Probably *The Wiz* was for those people in that time.... I think for me, personally, as a parent of these kind of kids, and they're not really into *The Wizard of Oz*, I love it, I remember it, I grew up with it, and I really want to reintroduce it to them in a whole different way."[3] "The book," executive producer Robert Halmi added, "was written in 1900 and its story still lives."[4] Halmi's and Stern's observations encapsulate the conundrum of cultural sustainability—a story that still lives, the need for a line of transmission, the desire to remake the narrative for a new generation, and the driving force of an older generation's nostalgia. And the producers, as became evident in interview after interview, were fully aware of the monumental task they faced. In spite of being "huge fans of the original movie," and knowing that they "were attacking one of the greatest icons ever," they "came to the conclusion that it was better to take our chances and reinvent rather than redo."[5] "We feel collectively," CEO Dave Howe asserted, "that these classics deserve to be reimagined for a new generation."[6]

Tin Man's re-imagination of Oz set the tone for many of the narrative's major twenty-first-century manifestations. It "reintroduced" Oz to a generation "not really into *The Wizard of Oz*," enticing them, as the series' marketing tagline urged, to "follow a new yellow brick road." This yellow brick road led them through a world that was definitely not MGM's Oz. *Tin Man's* Oz is more *Lord of the Rings* than technicolor Emerald City—a vast wilderness punctuated by dark fortresses and urban landscapes, owing more to degenerate cyberpunk than Baum, in which wild forests displace cozy Munchkin villages, and threats of torture replace welcoming songs. Furthermore, while the series loosely retains *The Wizard of Oz's* basic quest-for-home-plot, as Dorothy moves from a sort of Munchkinland, meets up with versions of the Scarecrow, Tin Man, and Cowardly Lion and seeks the Wizard, this plot serves as a mere narrative convenience to carry along the series' dominant Harry Potter meets the Fisher King, with a heavy-dash of *Lord of the Rings*, storyline. *Tin Man's* Dorothy is an Ozian version of "the boy who lived," saved by a mother's love and hidden away—with no knowledge of her true destiny—until the time comes for her to save the world. There are prophecies, and fragments of old tales, and a young woman remembering her true past and regaining her power. There is an epic battle between good and evil for the future of Oz; there are redemption and restoration.

Appropriating the popular epic fantasy genre, full of special effects, elaborate sets, and sweeping camera work, *Tin Man* sought reinvent Oz at the same time that it offered established consumers the pleasures of recognition and the satisfaction of repetition with a difference. *Tin Man* provides knowing viewers with a veritable feast of allusions: iconic visuals (the farmhouse and windmill on the flat plains of Kansas, DG's pigtails, and blue-gingham waitress pinafore, the wizard's balloon); "Easter eggs" (DG's 1939 Kansas address and Glitch's repeated assertion that "there was a time when I was a fantastic dancer, I really cut a rug"); and re-contextualizing of the film's shots, angles, and cinematic sequences (notably, the scene where the flying monkeys capture the companions while they flee from the deserted royal palace). It also retains, within its epic frame, the ethics and lessons that many consumers agree are at the heart of the

Oz narrative: the value of home, of friends and family, and of self-knowledge. Just as in Baum and MGM, Dorothy and her companions do not need the all-powerful aid (here the "emerald of the eclipse") to defeat the witch and save Oz. They simply need to remember who they really are and then work together as a team to restore the land. In the end, we would argue that *Tin Man* is not so much a "dark Oz," as some reviewers and consumers argue, as a "postmodern Oz."

As such, *Tin Man* succeeded in making Oz suitable to a post-9/11 generation raised on Middle Earth and Hogwarts. Critical reviews may have been mixed, but the series itself was a hit, attracting the largest viewing audience the network had yet enjoyed, and *Tin Man's* success set the stage for a whole slew of post-*Wicked*, post-apocalyptic, adult destined-Dorothy-returns-to-save-Oz, but-first-must-remember-who-she-is narratives: 2011's miniseries and limited film-release *Dorothy and the Wizard of Oz*, two young adult series, *Shadow of Oz* (2012) and *Dorothy Must Die* (2014, although this time it's a different girl from Kansas), and, most recently, NBC's 2017 series, *Emerald City*.

These revisionist Ozes, however, are but one strand in the post-*Wicked* Oz revival. As they had during the broadcast years, several producers scrambled to provide consumers with new Oz products; some, like 2005's *The Muppet's Wizard of Oz* and Warner Brother's two straight-to-video *Tom and Jerry in Oz* adventures, merely exploit and repackage the MGM film. Others, such as 2011's *After the Wizard* and 2014's *Ozland*, offer meta-Ozes that explored the narrative's cultural impact. Most offered consumers a Baum and MGM-inspired Oz-of-continuing-adventures, aimed at the kiddie or family audience. While most of these many magical Ozes on offer between 2003 and the present are pretty forgettable, the three that we examine here illuminate how this branch of post-Wicked Oz contributes to Oz's overall cultural sustainability.

The first, and perhaps the most important—certainly the most expensive and profitable—of these, is Disney's second visit to Oz, 2013's *Oz the Great and Powerful*. If *Wicked* had not proved that Oz could bring in the box-office dollars, it is dubious that—after its economically disastrous *Return to Oz*—the studio would have green-lit another costly return to Oz. The studio did everything it could to make sure that its new Oz venture was marketable; it hired Sam Raimi, director of the popular *Spiderman* reboot, and cast bankable stars such as James Franco and Mila Kunis. And then it launched a 100-million-dollar marketing campaign, including a hot air balloon promotion that traveled from the

Disney lot in Burbank to Central Park, themed-shows at the Disney resorts, and special previews in the parks. Trailers, posters, and television spots supplemented the events, and by the time the film was given wide release, across multiple media platforms (including Disney Digital 3D and Imax 3D), on March 8, 2013, many consumers were, as the film's taglines promised, eager to, "find yourself in Oz" and experience "the land you know. The story you don't."

The studio excited consumers' interest with a trailer carefully crafted both to recall and replace the MGM film.[7] Beginning in a sepia-toned black and white Kansas, the camera focuses on the Disney logo etched into the wizard's wagon, and then transitions quickly into the iconic tornado before emerging into a technicolor dream of Oz, and concludes by teasing the audience with glimpses of the film's plot. It's a trailer that strives to reach as wide a market as possible, alternating echoes of MGM with eye-popping cinematography, moments of Shrek-style humor, and an epic battle between good and evil for the soul of Oz.

This appeal to a wide consumer base resulted in an Oz that balanced treats for the knowing consumer—the film's transition from a black and white Kansas, shot in academy square ratio, to a cinemascopic technicolor Oz, as many visual and shot allusions as the lawyers would allow, and a nearly identical quest plot in which the Wizard joins up with a set of unlikely companions and seeks to defeat a wicked witch—with nods to *Shrek, Enchanted,* and *Harry Potter.* Interestingly, in a period when Oz re-consumptions seemed to cater to female consumers, Disney used Oz as a way to branch out of its "princess brand." Producer Joe Roth observed, "During the years I spent running Walt Disney Studios, I learned how hard it was to find a fairy tale with a good strong male protagonist. You got your Sleeping Beauties, your Cinderellas, your Alices … but with the origin story of the Wizard of Oz, here was a tale with a natural male protagonist."[8]

Positioned as it was, *Oz the Great and Powerful* provided Disney with the opportunity to re-cast Oz into two of the studio's best-known plots: the story of the local boy, who—through his wit, imagination, and a little technological wizardry—makes good, and the tale that proves that, "with little more than luck and belief, we (can make) the impossible happen." From MGM, the film borrows a Kansas prologue to introduce Oscar Diggs, who wants more than Kansas offers: to be more than one of the many good men worn out by dirt and grime; more than Annie, the gingham-clad girl who loves him; and more than the friendship of

Frank, the man behind the curtain, who provides the special effects for Digg's two-bit carny magic shows. In Kansas, Diggs is a seducer and a trickster, a man without morals or heart, who cannot heal the wheel-chair-bound girl who expects a real miracle. Oz offers him a chance at what he thinks is his heart's desire: power, riches, and a bevy of beautiful witches.[9]

Again borrowing from the Oz tradition, many of the Kansas characters turn up in Ozian form: Annie as Glinda, Frank as the winged-monkey Oz saves, and the crippled girl as a broken china doll; in Oz, repeating (or foreshadowing) Dorothy's trip down the yellow brick road, the new Wizard is given a chance to correct his Kansas mistakes, to stay true to the girl, embrace the friend, and heal the child. At the same time, he and the viewers learn that "in Oz, nothing is as it seems." Or do they? *Oz the Great and Powerful* seeks to tap into *Wicked's* alternative narrative, but whereas the musical asked audiences to rethink what they thought they knew, the film mostly reconfirms their knowledge. Indeed, the Wicked Witch the companions seek to destroy is not wicked at all—as they know when she lowers her dark hood to reveal glowing blonde locks and a ball gown—in spite of the fact that they have found her in MGM's dark forest. The *real Wicked Witch of the West*, it turns out, looks just like Margaret Hamilton—or Elphaba. The only revisionist twist here is that Oz and his seducing ways are partly to blame; she becomes wicked because she foolishly accepts an apple from her truly wicked sister to take away the pain of her broken heart (has she never seen *Snow White* or *Enchanted*?). So, Glinda is good, green witches are bad, and Oz must be saved from wicked witchly plots. Enter the Wizard and technology; whereas Baum and MGM's wizards are "very good men" but "very bad wizards," in Disney's Oz, the wizard who becomes a great man, is also a great American wizard, a fitting heir to Thomas Edison, the Wizard of Menlo Park. Aided by the tinkers and farmers and sewers and bakers of Oz (who, by the way, live alongside a turreted, blue and white Disney princess castle), the man behind the curtain puts on a show that ultimately vanquishes the witches of Oz and establishes him as its Wizard. Judy Garland's Dorothy may have had to return to Kansas and embrace the idea of "there's no place like home," however gray it might be, but James Franco's Oz finds his family in the magical, technicolor land over the rainbow.

Oz the Great and Powerful offered consumers an old-fashioned, spectacular, optimistic Oz experience, one that celebrated the "man behind the curtain" and the technological magic of cinema, transformed its somewhat caddish hero into a good and great man, and taught clear lessons about friendship, responsibility, and belief. And many consumers embraced it; the film quickly made back its initial costs and garnered over 400 million dollars at the global box office, making it the highest grossing film of 2013, and positioning Disney to launch a new Oz franchise. The critical reaction to the film, however, illustrates the tug-of-war between gatekeepers and consumers that often occurs in the reception of re-consumed classic narratives. As with many Oz re-consumptions, the reviews were mixed—tilting toward negative; even positive reviews saw the film as, at best, secondary to the MGM classic; doggedly pro-Disney Leonard Matlin admitted, "no movie can, or will, replace 1939's *Wizard of Oz*." Matlin, being Matlin, went on to praise the film on its own merits—the fact that is was "played straight" with "sincerity" (for younger viewers) but not "overplayed so grownups can engage with it, too," its "sights of awe and wonder" and its ability to "rouse an audience." In the end, he leaves it to others to decide if "this is an Oz for the ages," but, he concludes, "it gives audiences of 2013 a satisfying big screen experience."[10]

Negative and positive, the reviews for *Oz the Great and Powerful* centered around the questions of ownership, canon, marketability, and sustainability. Just because it's marketable, is it a good idea? Which Oz is the definitive Oz? What new Oz is a worthy Oz? Can there be new Ozes at all? Liam Lacey from the *Globe and Mail* observed, "*Oz the Great and Powerful* has the cards stacked in its favour. There's global brand recognition, thanks to the still popular 1939 … film and the smash Broadway musical *Wicked* … this $200 million-special effects vehicle appears to have everything going for it."[11] Fully aware of Oz's marketability and its history, the cultural gatekeepers, on the whole, looked at *Oz the Great and Powerful* and found it wanting. David Edelston mused, "Say the words 'Oz the Great and Powerful' out loud, and I promise you'll smile. They conjure up so many wonderful, wizardly things. Judy Garland in pigtails … the madly cheerful munchkins; Toto too … and if you're old enough, the once-a-year Thanksgiving showings that spurred so many Americans to shell out finally for color sets. Make sure," he warned consumers, "to say those words before you see *Oz the Great and Powerful*, which will surely wipe the smile off your face."[12] For most critics, the film simply failed to live up to the MGM classic of their memories; nor, they felt, did it provide a satisfying new Oz experience for the next generation, opining the film "aims for nostalgia in older viewers who grew up on 'The Wizard of Oz,' while simultaneously enchanting a newer, younger audience. It never really accomplishes either."[13]

Marketable, they concluded, but not memorable, and, although the film, as we observed, did extremely well at the box office and certainly placed Oz squarely back in the public eye, whether or not it has an enduring effect on the Oz narrative remains to be seen. The announced sequel was already languishing in pre-production limbo before charges of sexual misconduct, perhaps temporarily, sidelined James Franco's career. *Oz the Great and Powerful* brought consumers in with the promise of a new Oz experience, but did it deliver on enough of its promise to keep them coming back? Or was it merely a bigger-budget version of countless other Oz continuations that have sought to ride on the coattails of Oz events, like the following spring's animated *Legends of Oz: Dorothy's Return?*

Unlike *Oz the Great and Powerful*, *Dorothy's Return* failed with both critics and consumers, in spite of an all-star cast that included Lea Michelle, then at the height of her *Glee* fame. Here again critics blame Oz's marketability, further fueled by the "hit success" of *Oz the Great and Powerful*, for the fact that the film was even made, let alone released on the wide-screen instead of going straight to video where it belonged. "Banking on audience affection for MGM's classic … while cooking up a relatively feeble set of adventures for Dorothy, Toto, and friends, this … outing … will likely melt away at the box office before finding a small ancillary pot of (video) gold."[14] The same could be said of many of the post-*Wicked* animated ventures. Marketability does not always lend itself to sustainability, and, for the most part, these continuing adventure films are one-offs, aimed at a limited pool of one-time consumers; as one reviewer opined of *Dorothy's Return*, "I am guessing toddlers who have yet to be exposed to *The Wizard of Oz* will be the only satisfied customers … This is one of those movies that parents will have to ask themselves if they love their child enough to sit through it."[15]

Marketability certainly played a part in the greenlighting of the final two filmed Oz re-consumptions we will discuss in this chapter: Amazon's Emmy-winning animated series, *Lost in Oz*, which premiered during the streaming-services pilot competition in 2015, dropped as a full season in 2017, and has been renewed for a second season, and *Emerald City*, NBC's expensive *Game-of-Thrones*-meets-Oz offering, which premiered in January of 2017, and was not renewed, in spite of strong fan support.

Unlike other animated series (the most recent of which is 2017's *Dorothy and the Wizard*), *Lost in Oz* offers consumers a completely reimagined Oz, with an updated technology (CGI), look (urban steampunk), and cast (very modern, smart-aleck teens). Even though the main storyline also entails a Dorothy following the "yellow-line" to get home to Kansas and perhaps to save Oz on the way, this is not the new-Dorothy-Gale's great-grandmother's Oz.[16] With its snappy dialogue, its tween-heroes, and its steampunk aesthetic, *Lost in Oz* targets a consumer group too old for the more traditional animated Oz series and too young for series like *Tin Man* and *Emerald City*. It successfully translates Oz into its magical more-urban descendent, offering an Oz experience that does not rely on viewers' nostalgia for—or even knowledge of—the MGM film; unlike many Oz products, in fact, the series cheerfully distances itself from the film and other "past Ozes." After all, it's the twenty-first century, and the generations, both in Oz and the real world, have moved on.

Not so with NBC's *Emerald City*, which offered consumers an expanded, revisionist Oz that, in the tradition of *Wicked*, asked its audiences to rethink what they thought they knew about the land over the rainbow. As such, the series is in constant dialogue with earlier Oz narratives, from MGM to *Wicked*. But the conditions that brought *Emerald City* to market, as many of the show's reviewers noted, encompassed more than Oz. NBC wanted its own *Game of Thrones*; Oz, with its long history and potential for epic re-imagining (as demonstrated in *Tin Man*), provided an open-access pool of characters and plots for a Westeros-style sweeping narrative. Print ads featured an iconic shot of Dorothy and Toto trudging down the yellow brick road toward the Emerald City, framed by a doorway straight out of Dorne; the epic cast of the series—a cast that would not be out of place on a poster for either *Game of Thrones* or *Lord of the Rings*—is grouped around this familiar shot. The predominant color is green. Throughout the series, *Emerald City* performs a similar feat of re-contextualization in which, as the trailer promised, "the legend becomes so much more." As did *Tin Man*, *Emerald City* offers knowing consumers the pleasures of recognition, from the rainbow sun-catcher that casts its colors over Dorothy's face as she tells her Aunt Em, "I wished that there was more," through repurposed visual imagery, such as the Scarecrow, to lines from the film ("Are you a good witch, or a bad witch?").[17]

In addition to capitalizing on the market trend in fantasy epics, *Emerald City* incorporates one of the narrative threads that made first

Wicked and, later, *Frozen*, so powerful: a female coming-of-age story that focuses on women coming into and embracing their power. Dorothy learns to wield the ruby gauntlets she inherited when she killed the Witch of the East; Mistress West emerges from the mists of poppies and despair; and young Ozma embraces the magic within her. All of these women learn, as West tells Ozma, to "do what we were born to do: we fly." This story of women coming into their power, of a female world of magic opposed to the Wizard's world of science as told through re-contextualized fragments of Oz, is put into the service of a very twenty-first-century tale, one in which there may well be no moral center, identities are uncertain, and friendship and loyalty have become commodities, for sale to the highest bidder.

Whether or not *Emerald City* would have emerged from this gray world of moral ambiguity to tell a more traditional epic saga of the return of the Queen and the restoration of the land is something that we will never know, as the series was not renewed for a second season. NBC gave no reason for its cancellation; *Emerald City*, however, was extremely expensive to produce, and its viewer percentage was mediocre at best (although in the era of fragmented viewing audiences and on-demand streaming, original viewing percentages may not be the best indicator of a show's performance). The show certainly had its fans, but, for the most part, not among the gatekeepers.

Indeed, *Emerald City* sparked a critical discussion about Oz's continued narrative sustainability—and what form future Ozes might take. The reviewers were "knowing consumers" of both Oz and pop culture who often began their reviews by running through the gamut of Oz history, from Baum to *Wicked*, stopping to pass judgment on the way, and ended with the ways in which NBC had re-envisioned Oz through other lenses. Like the rest of us, Verne Gay observes in *Newsday*, "the producers of *Emerald City* know their pop culture."[18] While they all agree that remaking Oz is not a bad thing, most gatekeepers insist that this Oz, this "gritty half-baked version of *Game of Thrones*," is an Oz-too-far, "the direct result," the *New York Observer's* Vinnie Mancuso opines, "of some evil thing hooking the cheerful technicolor classic *The Wizard of Oz* up to the death machine from *The Princess Bride* and sucking every ounce of life out of it …. If expertly dragging a beloved magical movie through a mile of blood and dirt and misery makes you a wiz, then (this show) is a wiz of a wiz if ever a wiz there was."[19]

This examination of the production, marketing, and consumption of Oz in the *Wicked* years illustrates Oz can be reimagined for a generation of consumers who—while they instantly recognize its lines and images—may well have never actually seen MGM's *Wizard of Oz* and are thus willing to embrace new Ozes. Entering into Oz through a different link in the chain of adaptation, such as *Wicked*, or *Tin Man*, or *Dorothy Must Die*, younger consumers have different expectations of Baum's magic land. Their Oz need not be the baby boomer Oz. Additionally, these consumers consume narratives differently than those who grew up with network television in a pre-home-video, pre-digital era. They are able to access media goods anytime across multiple devices, they are less likely to bow to the "expert" opinion of cultural gatekeepers, and much more likely to participate in the production of new media; they are participatory rather than passive consumers. And indeed, *Tin Man* may be over, *Oz the Great and Powerful 2* in production limbo, and *Emerald City* canceled, but consumers continue to produce new tales based on each of these Ozes in fanfiction forums, following their new yellow brick roads on decidedly non-MGM adventures.

THE WORK FANS DO ONLINE

The fans' continuation of canceled and suspended shows and films indicates that, just as the Oz story evolved in Baum's time with input from his "dear readers," Oz fans continue to be key to the narrative's cultural sustainability. Not only do they provide a ready-made pool of consumers for the various books, movies, videos, music, and live performances that promise new Oz experiences, but their involvement in Oz reaches far beyond passive consumption. Fandom is participatory and productive, and fans are very much part of the "convergence culture," defined by Henry Jenkins, that we discussed in Chapter 1. By actively participating in Oz across a variety of media, fans blur the line between the narrative's consumers and its producers, contributing as they do so to what Jenkins calls "collective intelligence," the sharing of knowledge and experience. Through this sharing, Oz fans gain the power and freedom to interact with and tailor their consumption of Oz. They take an active role in sustaining and embellishing tales of Oz. They collect, restore, and archive its artifacts. Finally, they produce events, places, and products—created by fans and for fans—that keep Oz in the public eye, offer established fans a community of like-minded Ozophiles, and provide opportunities for new consumers to encounter (or re-encounter) the narrative. In the second half of this chapter, we examine the remarkably varied work fans do as they contribute their time, talent, and treasures to keep Oz alive and moving forward.

As Jenkins notes, the rise of new media and digital spaces has changed the face of fandom, allowing virtual communities to form between people in dispersed geographical locations and facilitating communication in real time. The internet offers Oz fans seeking a digital Oz community a variety of interactive Oz experiences, produced by committed Ozzites. These range from the relatively traditional websites, such as that maintained by the International Wizard of Oz Club, through blogs, like the *Daily Ozmapolitan*, edited and monitored by long-time club member Blair Frodelius, to wikis and fanfiction sites.

The International Wizard of Oz Club is the least participatory of the digital spaces we will discuss here, but even so, it still provides a space for a virtual community of Oz fans.[20] To casual fans (or naïve consumers), the site offers "The World of Oz," which includes articles on Baum, the Oz books, and its films and adaptations, along with a detailed "Oz Timeline." To more knowing consumers, it provides information about the Club's publications, the *Baum Bugle*, a tri-annual journal of popular and scholarly articles on Oz and *Oziana*, an annual compilation of Oz stories written and illustrated by members. In addition to its educational and archival materials, the site promotes Oz conventions around the country, posts information on other Oz events, hosts a blog called Unknown Oz, and links to other sites for the Oz aficionado, including more blogs, fanfiction forums, and shopping opportunities for costumes, books, and collectibles. As such, the site supports the Club's historical mission to educate consumers about Oz and to provide a community in which like-minded individuals who are passionate about Oz can meet to share their passion, exchange ideas, and consume and produce Oz products.

While *The Daily Ozmapolitan* (a clear nod to the newspaper "founded" by Baum in 1904, and occasionally revived over the years) provides much of the same types of information as the Club's website, it is more current, more collective, and more interactive.[21] Rather than focusing on official events, performances, and publications, the blog features all manner of information about anything that relates to Oz ("L. Frank's Filing Cabinet") and interviews with Ozians—composers, biographers, historians, illustrators, authors and scriptwriters, game creators, and collectors ("The Wizard's Wireless"). The *Ozmapolitan*, however, goes beyond merely providing fans with useful information; most postings allow fans to participate in threaded discussions, providing ample opportunity for Ozophiles to engage with the information and with like-minded consumers who want to share their thoughts and feelings about all things Oz. This engagement, however, along with the site's content, is moderated and controlled by Frodelius. Fans who desire to engage in Oz without an editor or a moderator can do so on the Oz Wiki, where they can read and create material about Oz, participate community blogs and forums, and follow links to other Oz sites, including several fanfiction forums, where users both read and write new stories of Oz.[22]

A simple Google search will take fans to multiple Oz fanfiction sites. Some of the most prominent include FanFiction Archive, An Archive of Our Own, and Quotev, which all host Oz archives, as well as archives for *Wicked*, *Tin Man*, *Oz the Great and Powerful*, and *Emerald City*. All of these sites stem from the same desire that inspired hundreds of children to write to Baum, begging for more Oz. As John Fricke observes:

> Oz resonates due to its originality, astounding and appealing characters, and ceaseless ability to take one on 'the journey'–from page one of virtually any of the books ... From Chapter One, Page One, we all march right into the text and travel the route and adventures as they happen. And the sheer entertainment value of the stories... is well-nigh immeasurable.[23]

Whereas Baum's readers depended on Baum—with a little help from his readers—to keep the stories going, fans in a new-media convergence culture have been able to keep the story going themselves. Since fans, as many scholars of fandom have argued, care little about copyrights and property rights, Oz fanfiction includes stories based on Baum, and in the public domain, as well as tales extending copyright-protected adaptations, ranging from MGM to *Wicked* and the *Emerald City*.

Fanfiction travels Oz's open map, accepting the story's invitation to enter into its world and extend its narrative; it contributes to Oz's ever-expanding archive, from prequels and sequels, to alternate universes and mashups. "Mystic Man's Daughter" takes place in the *Emerald City's* Oz before Dorothy's return; "Breaking Through the Night" introduces Elphaba's and Glinda's daughters; "As Long as Your Mine" sends Oz to the vampires; and Dory, Mickey Mouse, and *Glee's* Mr. Shue are among the many well-known characters who visit Oz.[24]

Fanfiction, then, gives fans in the twenty-first century a chance to produce Oz stories at the same time that it provides other fans with new ways to experience Baum's land. While most fanfictions do not explicitly contribute to the narrative's cultural sustainability, the writing and reading of them keeps fans engaged with Oz, positioning them to consume other books, films, shows, and experiences. And these are just a click away on The International Wizard of Oz Club's site, or the *Daily Ozmapolitan*, or the Oz Wiki.

All of these virtual spaces provide consumers with easy access to a community-based, interactive experience of Oz that allows them to engage around and participate in a variety of Oz experiences. They can educate themselves, keep abreast of new developments and products, make contact with other fans, purchase books, films, and merchandise, contribute to the collective intelligence, and generate new narratives. As such, cyber-Oz attracts both established consumers and the Oz-curious and helps to satisfy and sustain interest in all things Ozian. But for many fans, virtual spaces are not enough, and many potential consumers are unlikely to seek out Oz on the internet; these consumers can visit Oz in towns and convention centers across American.

THE WORK FANS DO: CONVENTIONS, MATERIAL OBJECTS, AND FESTIVALS

For many members of the International Wizard of Oz Club, the annual regional and national Oz conventions the Club sponsors provide a space for the gathering together and renewal of a community centered around Oz. As we saw in Chapter 3, Oz Club members have proven to be masterful producers as well as consumers. While some members assiduously collect, display, and sell their extensive collections of Oz-related merchandise to like-minded enthusiasts, others revel in conducting archival work and debating the finer points of Oz's history in all its forms, and the Oz conventions provide them with an occasion to engage in all of these activities. For these participants—whom we view as consumers of an experience—OzCons serve three important functions. First, OzCons provide an intellectual forum for all things Oz. This occurs at a level far beyond what most consumers could simulate in their everyday lives. A regional Oz convention, such as the one we attended in Portland in the summer of 2017, has the feel of an academic conference in many respects: keynote speakers give plenary talks; sessions and workshops, often running concurrently, address topics of interest to Oz fans (e.g., "You be the Casting Director: Who Should be in the Movie of *Wicked?*"); and vendors and authors pitch their wares and sign books in spaces designated for those activities. In this way, state-of-the-art knowledge is disseminated, and the heritage of the organization is formally recalled and celebrated.

Second, OzCons allow consumers to "perform" Oz. Throughout the convention, ample opportunity is given for participants to engage in informal costume play (cosplay) on the one hand, or to perform, at a professional level, key scenes from Oz's history, such as the Jell-O radio show re-enactment discussed in Chapter 4. And participants take full advantage of these opportunities. Thus, a retired business executive becomes a giant frog; an accountant turns into a rainbow. These embodiments are performed with great flourish, and they are received with great fanfare by those who do not dress up. As cosplayers spontaneously appear in a hallway, spectators create spaces around them, allowing the performers to sweep, gesticulate, or strike their poses as required. Onlookers show their appreciation through exclamations of recognition, bursts of applause, and requests for photographs. Oz becomes physical reality in these moments, in direct contrast to the more cerebral engagement called for by the panels. Since most of the characters do not speak, they appear as living sculptures to be admired—even venerated and immortalized—by those surrounding them.

Third, OzCons enable consumers to socialize with other Oz fans. Consumers with particular hobbies or pastimes often seek out opportunities to share their passions with others of like mind. These "user communities" provide social stimulation for their participants, offering the possibility of longer-term relationships that extend beyond a shared interest. Convention organizers actively encourage this relationship building by providing ample time between sessions for catching up with old friends and making new ones. The result is that many consumers have "grown up together" over the course of many OzCons. In conversation with one another, they situate personal milestones (job changes, moves, marriages, births) by the OzCon year in which they took place. Some families have been attending OzCons for multiple generations; for them, an OzCon is a family reunion in the middle of a convention, observed and celebrated by all in attendance.

Finally, certain moments at OzCons combine all three of these functions: the intellectual, the performative, and the social come together spontaneously to produce unexpected high points. In Portland, one such moment began innocently enough. During a 10-minute interval between paper sessions, one of our authors asked John Fricke (55-year member of the Oz Club, and preeminent authority on Judy Garland and *The Wizard of Oz*) this question: "What is the future of the Oz Clubs and the OzCons?" John began to explain how attendance at the OzCons had fluctuated in recent years, and he listed some of the reasons that could account for this: shifting demographics, newer technologies, changing preferences for collecting over reading:

> In the last decade, social networking has both helped and hindered the Club. Because now, you can amass a huge collection of Oz memorabilia without ever leaving home. You can go to eBay, you can go to Amazon. You don't need to go to a convention to be convivial, since you can do that through Facebook and Twitter. You have all of that at your fingertips. So our younger members are asking, 'Why do I need a convention?' Well, the bottom line is that there is a delight in gathering.

No sooner had Fricke uttered these words when several people, overhearing him, came up and joined in the discussion. Before long, over 20 people had crowded around the two original conversationalists. The ensuing discussions were animated and impassioned, extending well beyond the scheduled break between sessions. As Fricke recalls:

> A lot of important things happened in that moment. You had older members recalling what OzCons were like in the '50s and '60s. We were so book-oriented in those days. Then middle-aged members recalled that by the 1960s, *The Wizard of Oz* film had become the dominant point of comparison. People began collecting more, and reading less. Finally, the youngest generation chimed in. They wanted to talk about *Wicked*, *Tin Man* and *Emerald City*–and how they have so many entertainment options besides going to OzCons! But that moment was critical in showing that OzCons mean different things to different people.

Indeed, the discussion ended with concern for the future of OzCons, as millennials and their children may be too busy with other activities to participate. As one thirtysomething member noted:

I know it sounds cliché, but we're a two-career family with two kids under ten. Between our work schedules and their soccer games, it becomes difficult to work in something like the OzCons. And I'm not sure our kids will find this as interesting as we do. We only hope they will, but we won't force it.

Taken together, these three functions have summative value for the cultural landscape they help shape. Active participants at OzCons, stimulated by the latest convention, become opinion leaders in their everyday lives in matters concerning popular culture in general and Oz in particular. How they convey the evolution of Oz to others, how they assess the quality of performances, where they place certain productions in the Oz canon—these become moments of both production and re-consumption in homes, offices, and grocery stores long after the convention has ended.

The future of the OzCons remains unclear. While changing demographics may deplete its numbers, new iterations of Oz may sustain it. Each new production has its adherents, and they want to hear about *that* version of Oz. These in turn result in new discussions, new collectibles, and new costumes—in short, new platforms in which to enact the three functions mentioned above. And through it all is a joy that may differentiate OzCons from their more popular counterparts. John Fricke concludes:

> You can compare OzCons, on a bland level, to every other fandom there is, like Star Wars, Star Trek, and so on. But because it's Oz, there's a joy that transcends everything else. You don't just like it; you *love* it. It can be intellectual, or analytical, but one thing it is above all else: it's emotional.

While OzCons provide fans with a *place* to share their joy in Oz, to experience together its emotional resonances, many Oz fans find similar joy in possession of a physical *object* associated with Oz—a souvenir, if you will, of their journeys there. Oz, as we saw in Chapter 2, has come with merchandising since *The Wizard of Oz* hit the stage in 1902, and each new adaptation or extension of the narrative has inspired its own merchandise. Add to these limited edition "collectibles," first editions of Baum's books, memorabilia associated with Baum and Oz producers and actors, and you get the incredible range of collectibles pictured in Fricke's *An Illustrated History of Oz*: books, drawings, DVDs, movie posters, photographs, dolls, toys, games, lunch boxes, stamps, figurines, Wogglebug buttons, clothes hangers, carved soaps, happy meal toys..... The list goes on.[25] Some collectors acquire anything and everything related to the Oz stories; others specialize in specific kinds of objects, such as books or dolls; still others base their collections on a single Oz product, such as *Wicked* or the *Return to Oz*.

Who consumes all of this merchandise? At the most basic level, *casual fans* pick up a mug or t-shirt at *Wicked*, a ruby slipper doorstop or an "I'd rather be in the Emerald City" apron at a museum gift shop, or a pair of Ozma-earrings or a handmade Dorothy puppet at a festival; for these consumers, the Oz product is a memento of their experience, one that allows them to visit that experience again by invoking the memory of it. At the next level, *super fans* collect and display large collections, using these items to "build" Oz around them. Melodie Foreman's collection in Independence, Missouri, for instance, fills her spare bedroom from floor to ceiling with Oz character Barbie dolls, Hallmark ornaments, souvenir plates, autographed Munchkin photographs, framed albums, Dorothy costumes, and replica hand-sequined ruby slippers. Finally, *major collectors* acquire, through purchase or inheritance, authentic historical items associated with either Baum or an Oz adaptation, such as the MGM film—often loaning or donating their collections to tourist sites or museums. For instance, the Aberdeen Public Library houses Baum's papers, donated by Maud Gage Baum; the Oz Museum in Wamego Kansas displays Joseph Cafiero's 25,000 piece collection, and Bob Evans Farm Homestead Museum in Rio Grande, Ohio, includes pieces from the collection of Jane Craddock.

Oz memorabilia and merchandising are both a symptom and a cause of the narrative's cultural sustainability. The fact that all of this stuff exists at all, and that it was and continues to be marketable attests to Oz's entrenched hold on our cultural imagination. However, as they circulate, these items also keep the narrative firmly in the public eye. Passing by a woman in a *Wicked* t-shirt or being handed coffee in a Toto mug, consumers are reminded of Oz (and perhaps inspired to purchase tickets, play the soundtrack, or stream the film). *Super fans* often attract media attention, and publicity surrounding their Oz collections places the narrative in current public discourses. And collections in museums not only tell the Oz story, but also provide relics for Oz fans to visit, as they conduct pilgrimages to Oz sites around the country.

Oz may be a faerie land, cut off from the world by shifting sands and Glinda's magic, but fans can still visit various heritage sites, museums, and tourist attractions—produced, maintained, and staffed by fans—offering Oz experiences that range from viewing historical artifacts and Oz relics to visiting reproductions of Oz places and re-enacting the film. Heritage sites, on the whole, cater to established consumers, many of whom visit these places historically associated with Baum as pilgrims. Chittenango's "Yellow Brick Road" tour guides visitors through the village where Baum was born and Aberdeen, South Dakota, offers them the chance to view Baum's papers in the Alexander Mitchell Library, his books in the museum, and the houses that the Baum and Gage family occupied. These sites promise fans an *authentic* experience in spaces Baum actually occupied and featuring historical artifacts. Even Chittenango's "All Things Oz" museum, which extends its collection past the Baum years, through the MGM years, and past *Wicked* to less well-known Oz films, such as *After the Wicked*, emphasizes their collection of rare articles, such as song sheets from 1902's *Wizard of Oz*, a Waddle Book, and a set of Oz hangers from the 1920s.

Wamego, Kansas' ties to Baum and Oz are certainly more tenuous, based on fiction rather than history, and bolstered by the Columbian Theatre's claim to a Beaux-Art architectural design *similar* the that of the Exhibition Halls in Chicago's White City, "which *may have* inspired the Emerald City"; the theater trades on this claim by exhibiting "rare paintings from the 1893 Chicago World's Fair."[26] Down the street, the Oz museum seeks to attract tourists with a collection of original Oz books and illustrations and exhibits devoted to Oz characters and adaptations, including a room in which the MGM film plays continuously. While Chittenango offers "real Oz" for Oz fans versed in Baum life and Oz history, Wamego offers a more popular exhibit, clearly labeled for and aimed at the naïve consumer and casual tourist who may not come seeking Oz but is perfectly to happy to spend an hour or two among familiar characters.

Liberal, Kansas also seeks to exploit their state's connection to Oz, by offering consumers two reproductions of Dorothy's witch-killing farmhouse; the first's connection to Oz is real: the model used in film's tornado scene; the second is a real house with no actual connection of Oz other that the man who donated it realized that his house had the same layout as the house in the movie. Now furnished with actual 1930s furniture and kitchen gadgets, this house provides consumers—35,000 of them a year—with the chance to visit a historically accurate replica of a replica of a fictional space. In other words, here consumers can both view and visit—if not Oz—at least the means of transportation there and trod down a yellow brick road emblazoned with donors names, including Liza Minelli, while they are there.

All of these sites, whether aimed at Ozites seeking to follow the yellow-brick road of Baum's life or at casual tourists looking to pass an afternoon off-the-road, contribute to the narrative's cultural sustainability; they both meet and provoke consumer's desire for all things Oz—and provide them with plenty of opportunities to purchase more Oz in large and well-stocked gift shops. Furthermore, both Chittenango and Wamego supplement their permanent exhibits with festivals, providing Ozophiles and families alike with an opportunity for embodied Oz consumption.

Wamego and Chittenango also hold two of the many Oz festivals that take place every summer and fall in consistent locations around the country: Wamego's October OztoberFest and Chittenango's June Oz-Stravaganza. Other annual celebrations of Oz include Grand Rapids' Wizard of Oz Festival in June and the Midwest Wizard of Oz Festival in August. Less focused than the Oz conventions, these heartland festivals are more generally accessible to the general consumer, with the feel of a county fair, featuring pancake breakfasts, petting zoos, theme-related shops (Auntie Em's Boutique, Tin Man's Garage), and parades.

This festive fair-atmosphere uses several techniques to offer consumers a unique experience of Oz—one not provided by page, stage, or screen. In the first instance, Oz festivals are multisensory. The sights, smells, sounds, tastes, and even textures of these events mean that consumers' senses are stimulated in controlled—and by and large, pleasant—ways. From food outlets to live animal encounters, from craft markets to parades, from ice cream trucks to singing contests, the festivals envelop consumers in sensory appeals usually unavailable to them in their everyday lives. And given the small towns in which they take place, the festivals tend to arouse the senses without assaulting them.

In the second instance, Oz festivals are immersive. Because they are themed, Oz festivals are bounded spaces; they tend to be circumscribed within several square blocks of a given town. Once inside this space, consumers are asked to enter a world resembling, most often, a rural tableau inspired by the 1939 film, *The Wizard of Oz*. Whether it be the Gale farm, the barnyard where the farmhands worked, the kitchen where Aunt Em would have spent most of her time, or the various merchants who would have supplied the goods to enable such a lifestyle—these become dramatistic touchpoints for present-day merchants seeking to market their own wares. And they do so by invoking nostalgic authenticity. Their appeal is to a bygone era when life was slower, simpler, and somehow more trusting.

Third, Oz festivals provide opportunities for embodiment. From costume and singing contests (requisite song for females: *Over the Rainbow*; for males: *If I Were King of the Forest*) to parades, to photo ops in front of Wizard of Oz cutouts or Oz-related celebrities such as Hamilton Meserve, the son of Margaret Hamilton—these festivals provide multiple opportunities for everyday consumers to place their bodies in heightened fantasy contexts: namely, in Oz scenes as Oz characters. In this way, passive onlookers actively "become" the characters they venerate or fear. The gingham dress, the witch's hat, and the lion's costume serve as portals through which consumers can channel their own inner Dorothy, Wicked Witch, or Cowardly Lion. Embodiment researchers posit that such activity powerfully imprints on the brain, affecting not only how the consumer is perceived by others, but how the consumer perceives him/herself.

Finally, Oz festivals appeal to multiple generations, often at the same time. Because they offer relatively safe, bounded spaces in which to experience a sanitized rural lifestyle, Oz festivals understandably attract families as their primary target market. Just as multiple generations crowded around the family television to watch *The Wizard of Oz* some 50 years ago, so now multiple generations stroll through the streets of the small towns that host the festivals. From infants to grandparents, each festival offers "something for everyone" in a low-stress, controlled atmosphere. Attending an Oz festival becomes one of those rare occasions when members of the same family congregate and enjoy an experience in roughly the same way at the same time.

But Oz festivals amount to more than just a theme-based county fair or pumpkin festival for those who attend them; they play a prominent role in sustaining Oz across the cultural landscape. Like their OzCon cousins, they often feature prominent guest speakers, panel presentations, and celebrity guests connected to Oz in some way—usually through the 1939 film. But unlike OzCons, they educate consumers who are not Oz fanatics. Oz festivals operate at a mainstream, populist level. They reaffirm wholesome heartland values, and many have been doing so for over 40 years.

And because they draw thousands of visitors to their respective small towns, Oz festivals infuse millions of dollars into local economies every year. As tens of thousands of visitors crowd into towns of only a few thousand, the economic effect is immediate and profound. Hotels, restaurants, and local businesses benefit monetarily from the influx, and the towns themselves benefit in a less tangible but no less important way, given the positive impression the festivals invariably generate.

What is the future of the Oz festivals? As the MGM film approaches its 80th birthday, this foundational reference for most festivals still holds up well, according to noted Oz authority John Fricke. He explains:

> By the time the 50th anniversary of the film came around, in 1989, all the stars of the film had died: Judy, Burt, Jack, Ray, Margaret–they were all gone. But even if they had been alive, can you imagine a 75-year-old Judy Garland riding on a float in a parade and singing "Over the Rainbow"? That would not have been convincing.[27]

What to do without the film's major stars? Hire the Munchkins, many of whom were still alive. Fricke continues:

> Only the Munchkins were left. And they became a real drawing card, the keynote to any festival. A town of 5,000 could draw 70,000 to their town across a three-day weekend, just by presenting the surviving little people from the movie. You see, they hadn't aged that much, they were still small, so people could still relate to them. Some even wore replicas of their costumes and carried a prop, like a lollipop. They could take you back. Not only did the kids at the parade love them, but the parent and grandparents who had seen them on television also did!

Now, the last of the Munchkins has passed on. But Oz Festivals can draw from other re-consumptions of Oz, as recent gatherings attest. Shanice Williams, who played Dorothy in the live televised version of *The Wiz* in late 2015, appeared at the Wamego festival in the fall of 2017. Thus, cross-fertilization occurs between Oz festivals and Oz re-consumptions. Stars of Oz re-consumptions enliven Oz gatherings, breathing new life into the festivals while extending the shelf-lives of their own re-consumptions and careers. In short, Oz festivals continue to function effectively because of their ability to provide an authentic Oz experience to the mainstream public. They become predictable occasions in which "all things Oz" are infused once again into the cultural consciousness.

CONCLUSION

In the title to this chapter, we posed a question: whither Oz? And, as we have seen in our discussion of consumer and gatekeeper reactions to the reimagined Ozes of the post-*Wicked* years, and in Oz's multiple fandoms, not everyone agrees as to where Oz is or should be going. But one thing is clear: from two-hundred-million-dollar blockbuster films to homespun small-town festivals, on TV, online, on stage, Oz is very much alive in 2018. And, in 2019, we will see *Wicked* on the big screen; in 2020, we will celebrate *The Wonderful Wizard of Oz's* 120th birthday. The yellow brick road seems set to lead well into the twenty-first century and beyond.

NOTES

1. John Fricke, Interview by Kent Drummond, February 2, 2018.
2. *Tin Man*, Directed by Nick Willing et al., Imagiquest Entertainment et al., 2007, Amazon Video, Streaming.
3. Interview with Mark Stern, *SciFiWire*, 2007, www.scifi.com, accessed January 12, 2018.
4. Kinney Littlefield, "There's No Place Like Postmodern 'Oz,'" *Seattle Times*, December 2, 2007, http://old.seattletimes.com/html/television/2004041481_tinman02.html.
5. Judith S. Gillies, "An Update That's All Heart," *Washington Post*, December 2, 2007, http://www.washingtonpost.com/wp-dyn/content/article/2007/11/27/AR2007112702124.html.
6. Gary Levin, "Sci-Fi Channel Takes Its Own Trip Down the Yellow Brick Road," *USA Today*, November 28, 2007, https://usatoday30.usatoday.com/life/televisionnews/2007-11-28-tin-man_N.html.
7. "Oz the Great and Powerful Trailer," YouTube Video, 1:49, posted by Disney Movie Trailers, July 13, 2012, https://www.youtube.com/watch?v=_1NGnVLDPog.
8. Jim Hill, "Joe Roth Reflects on Oz the Great and Powerful," *Huffington Post*, March 4, 2013, https://www.huffingtonpost.com/jim-hill/joe-roth-reflects-on-oz-t_b_2806542.html.

9. *Oz the Great and Powerful*, Directed by Sam Raimi (2013: Disney Studios), Amazon Video, Streaming.
10. Leonard Matlin, "Oz the Great and Powerful," *IndieWire*, March 8, 2007, http://www.indiewire.com/2013/03/oz-the-great-and-powerful-180408/, accessed January 11, 2018.
11. Liam Lacey, "Oz the Great and Powerful: The Very Opposite of Big Budget Movie Magic," *The Globe and Mail*, March 8, 2013, https://www.theglobeandmail.com/arts/film/film-reviews/oz-the-great-and-powerful-a-big-budget-misfire-thats-the-very-opposite-of-magic/article9479230/.
12. David Edelstein, "Oz the Great and Powerful Is Peculiarly Joyless," *Vulture*, March 8, 2013, http://www.vulture.com/2013/03/movie-review-oz-the-great-and-powerful.html.
13. Christy Lemire, "'Oz the Great and Powerful Is Neither," *Mass Live*, March 7, 2013, http://www.masslive.com/entertainment/index.ssf/2013/03/movie_review_oz_the_great_and.html.
14. Justin Chang, "Legends of Oz: Dorothy's Return," *Variety*, May 7, 2014, http://variety.com/2014/film/reviews/film-review-legends-of-oz-dorothys-return-1201174414/.
15. Susan Wloszczyna, "Legends of Oz: Dorothy's Return," *Roger Ebert.com*, May 9, 2014, https://www.rogerebert.com/reviews/legends-of-oz dorothys-return-2014, accessed January 14, 2018.
16. *Lost in Oz* (2015, 2017: Amazon Studios) Amazon, Streaming.
17. *Emerald City*, Created by Matthew Arnold and Josh Friedman (2017: Shaun Cassidy Productions), Amazon, Streaming.
18. Verne Gay, "'Emerald City' Review: Grim Series Doesn't Compare to Book, Film," *Newsday*, January 4, 2017, https://www.newsday.com/entertainment/tv/emerald-city-review-grim-series-doesn-t-compare-to-book-film-1.12863840.
19. Vinnie Mancuso, "We Should Probably Discuss NBC's 'Emerald City'," *Observer*, January 11, 2017, http://observer.com/2017/01/emerald-city-nbc-review-vincent-donofrio-wizard/.
20. "The International Wizard of Oz Club," ozclub.org, accessed December 10, 2017.
21. *Daily Ozmapolitan*, ozmapolitan.wordpress.com, accessed January 30, 2018.
22. "Oz Wiki," ppc.wikia.com/wiki/The_Wizard_of_Oz, accessed February 1, 2018.
23. John Fricke, "Interview with Blair Frodelius," *The Wizard's Wireless*, *The Daily Ozmapolitan*. http://www.frodelius.com/wirelesstelegraph/fricke.html. accessed February 20, 2018.

24. Phoenix 144, "Mystic Man's Daughter," February 3, 2010, https://
www.fanfiction.net/s/4707412/1/The-Mystic-Man-s-Daughter,
accessed February 15, 2018; Pink-Saber-Girl, "Breaking Through the
Night," October 7, 2005, https://www.fanfiction.net/s/2279487/1/
Breaking-Through-the-Night, accessed February 15, 2018; PrincessTin,
"As Long as Your Mine," March 17, 2008, https://www.fanfiction.
net/s/4136384/1/Az-Long-As-Your-Mine, accessed February 15, 2018.
25. John Fricke, *The Wonderful World of Oz: An Illustrated History of the
American Classic* (USA: Down East Books, 2013).
26. Exhibit Note, Columbian Theatre Museum and Arts Center.
27. Fricke, Interview.

CHAPTER 11

At the Gates of the Emerald City: Toward a New Theory of Cultural Sustainability

At the outset of this book, we sought to investigate how a complex inter-action of forces has enabled Oz to sustain itself for over a century. How, we asked, does Oz keep reinventing itself, such that it becomes newly relevant to new segments of consumers, while still offering products that resonate with an already established consumer base? Drawing on the fields of consumer behavior, literary and cultural studies, and theories of adaptation and remediation, we brought an interdisciplinary approach to the socio-history of Oz that allowed us to examine that history as an ongoing dialogue between producers and consumers, marketing and consumption, the culture at large and a collection of cultural artifacts. Like all ongoing dialogues, these pairings are, in fact, symbiotic relation-ships. Accordingly, our examination has taken place at the meso-level, midway between micro and macro perspectives, for only from this van-tage point could we appropriately collect and analyze data that reveal the richness and complexity of those relationships.

Now, having described those relationships in detail, we offer a foun-dational framework that builds toward a new theory of cultural sustain-ability. We establish that framework in three ways: first, expanding on the taxonomy we developed at the conclusion of Chapter 5, we code over 500 instances of Oz from the past 117 years along the dimensions of Kind, Function, Mode of Access, Distribution Level, and Target Audience. Second, we use Disant Reading, a method developed by lit-erary critic Franco Moretti to render the resulting data in a series of graphs and offer findings based on them.[1] And third, we generalize our

© The Author(s) 2018
K. Drummond et al., *The Road to Wicked*,
https://doi.org/10.1007/978-3-319-93106-7_11

289

observations to a set of explanatory conditions under which any artistic experience might achieve cultural sustainability. Working as we are in the research tradition of analytic induction we attempt here to "read the world in a grain of sand."[2] Having captured the rich interplay of marketplace forces that resulted in one exemplary instance of cultural sustainability, we suggest sufficient, if not necessary, conditions for other instances to do the same.

How to Do Things with Oz

As we saw at the conclusion of Chapter 5, the massive splintering of Oz in the 1960s significantly changed our task as present-day researchers. Instead of one monolithic Oz that could be referred to as such, it became necessary to ask a series of questions that could determine "which Oz" was being offered to consumers at any given moment. In response to this realization, we developed a taxonomy that would allow us to locate each re-consumption of Oz at an intersection of chosen dimensions, regardless of when that re-consumption entered the marketplace.

The taxonomy we offered in Chapter 5 (and briefly review here) focuses on Oz as a *narrative*; in order to understand how Oz has achieved cultural sustainability, however, we need also to consider Oz as a *product*, so we add here three new dimensions addressing medium, availability, and market, to propose a taxonomy consisting of five major dimensions, each containing a series of sub-categories:

Dimension One: What *kind* of Oz is offered? Not all Ozes are created equal, and not all of them are equally interested in Oz. Some are very close to Baum's vision, while others turn that vision on its head. We identify seven kinds of Ozes on offer:

- **Magical Oz**: This is the Oz closest to Baum's vision, a "fairyland" rife with magic, talking animals, Witches, and Wizards. Right and wrong, good and evil are clearly delineated, and good always wins in the end. Although people from our world may—and usually do—find themselves there, Oz exists in its own right; it has a history and a purpose apart from what Baum calls the "civilized" world.

- **Translated Oz**: These Ozes take Baum's characters and/or plot and translate them into another context. Characters from Oz find themselves in another imagined universe or a different genre and then play out the narrative in that landscape.
- **Allegorical Oz**: Allegorical Oz does not exist in its own right, nor do its characters. Instead, Oz characters stand-in for abstract concepts, existing solely to teach a moral.
- **Revisionist Oz**: Often referred to as "Dark Oz," Revisionist Oz deconstructs Magical Oz. Here, Oz is deeply political. Shades of gray (literally as well as metaphorically) blur the lines between good and evil. Happy endings are not guaranteed.
- **Parodic Oz**: Here, Oz exists as a site of parody or of ironic revisitation. This is Oz as an inside joke, to be enjoyed with an ironic wink. It invites the kind of laughter that dismisses or undermines the values, styles, and tastes of previous Ozes—most often the MGM film—as old-fashioned, quaint, and out-of-touch with the modern world.
- **Opportunistic Oz**: Oz is merely a pretext for providing producers with an opportunity to lure consumers in, but the experience provided has little or nothing to do with Oz. Examples include educational games, television and print advertisement, and peanut butter jars.
- **Archival Oz**: Oz is a *subject* for preservation, study, exhibition, and analysis. Archival Oz ranges from museums, exhibitions, and conventions, through studies of Baum and his works, through reproductions of first-editions, restorations of early films, and special viewings of rare footage.

Dimension Two: How does Oz *function*? In this dimension, we ask: What is the intended purpose of Oz in this work? What values does it teach, and what is the consumer meant to take away from an encounter with it?

- **As a conveyor of ethics and values**: Oz narratives often uphold values-based ethical behavior, emphasizing the role of the individual in the community. The narrative valorizes friendship, compassion, bravery, intelligence, self-reliance, and commitment—heart, courage, and brains—as the center of Oz's utopian vision.

- **As a model of self-discovery**: The main character, almost always Dorothy or another visitor from the "real" world, begins the tale in a state of lack, not certain of who they are or where they belong in the community. Their time in Oz teaches them who they are and where they belong. In Oz, they learn to become their "best self."
- **As a site of lost truth**: Oz has been forgotten, and with it essential truths and values; in these versions of Oz, both Oz and the real world have become a wasteland and the beloved characters are in crisis. Only by remembering Oz can both worlds be restored and the characters be healed.
- **As a commentary on our world**: Oz, as either a utopia or a dystopia, serves as a foil to the contemporary world. Lessons learned in Oz are meant to be applied to real-world situations. Here, individual adventures take a back seat to Ozian political and social structures.
- **As a marketing device**: Oz does not exist in its own right, but rather as a way to sell a product, idea, or experience. The crossover appropriation of Oz into established storylines, such as *Passions* and *Spongebob*, where Oz is used merely to advance the plot and themes is also an example of Oz as a marketing device.

Dimension Three: Through which medium do consumers *access* Oz? From Baum on, Oz-experiences have crossed media platforms to provide consumers with multiple ways of encountering the narrative.

- **Traditional media**: Oz can be experienced in print, on stage, on the large and small screen, and in digital spaces.
- **Material object**: Consumers can purchase a piece of Oz, from first-editions, through collectibles and merchandising, to cookbooks and costumes.
- **Event**: Oz can be experienced as an event such as a conference, a festival, or a parade.
- **Place**: Consumers can visit Oz in a dedicated space, such as a museum, playground, or theme park. Unlike Oz events, which are transitory, Oz places are intended to be permanent.

Dimension Four: How available is the Oz item to American consumers? Is it readily available, requiring a minimal amount of time and effort to obtain it, or is it difficult to obtain, requiring much thought, planning, and effort? While the availability of a product changes over time and with new technologies, the database codes for availability at the time of initial release.

- **Exclusive**: It can only be obtained in one place, such as a Broadway production or a rare piece of memorabilia.
- **Limited**: It can be obtained somewhat more broadly, such as a touring show or less-than-rare but still unusual piece of memorabilia.
- **Wide**: The product or experience is broadly available, though some effort is still required to obtain it, such as a group viewing of Oz in one's home.
- **Mass**: The product or service is available virtually anytime, anywhere the consumer wants to experience it, such as the *Wicked* soundtrack.

Dimension Five: Whom does the Oz item target? Who is the intended audience?

- **General**: Products such as the 1939 film intended everyone, families, children, and "children of all ages."
- **Market Segment**: Products aimed at particular demographic, whether based on age (juvenile and young adult), readers of a particular genre (science fiction, fantasy, comics, and literary fiction), the audience for the crossover show (*Once Upon A Time; Suite Life*), art film viewers, or the followers of a director or artist.
- **Specialized**: Products produced for Oz specialists, fans, and experts. These products range from the publications of specialized Oz groups and presses (the International Wizard of Oz Club, Books of Wonder, Hungry Tiger, and Emerald City Presses), through works written by members of the Baum family, to critical and academic studies.

Of course, in order to be consistent, we could not apply this taxonomy to only those re-consumptions occurring after 1960; we had to apply it to all re-consumptions since the creation of the Oz archive in 1900. And so we did, coding over 500 instances (all that we could find, but we suspect there are others), beginning with Baum's 1902 Broadway extravaganza and ending with Cartoon Network's 2018 animated short,

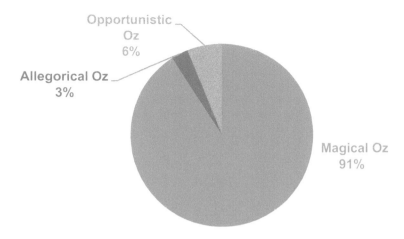

Graph 11.1   Kinds of Oz: Era I

"The Patchwork Girl of Oz." We then clustered them over time, first by decade, and then, by what we identify as the five major eras of Oz: Era I refers to the Baum years (1900–1919); Era II is the period from Baum's death through MGM's *Wizard of Oz* (1920–1939); Era III references the period between MGM's theatrical release and CBS's first television showing (1939–1956); Era IV is the Broadcast years, up to but not including *Wicked*'s premier on Broadway (1957–2003); and Era V begins with *Wicked*'s opening and ends in the present day (2003–2018). As we tracked these codings, first by each dimension on its own, then by various combinations of dimensions, we found a variety of revealing trends that inform our theoretical framework. For the purposes of illustration, we focus here on a single dimension: Kinds of Oz.

As we see from Graph 11.1, "Kinds of Oz: Era I," the overwhelming majority of Oz re-consumptions here are of the Magical Oz type. That's because the original version of Oz, *The Wonderful Wizard of Oz*, was released in 1900. From that time until Baum's death, the re-consumptions entering the marketplace were under his strict control. While it is true that there are remediations (stage adaptations, *Fairylogues and Radio Plays*, etc.), they are still Magical Oz; they simply provide multiple points of access to Baum's Oz, ensuring synergy across his brand.

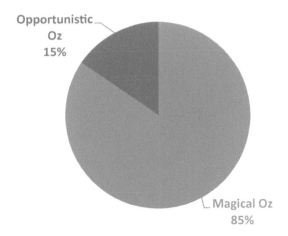

Graph 11.2 Kinds of Oz: Era II

Opportunistic Oz comprises 6% of the re-consumptions during this time, as producers bait consumers with promises of Oz, such as the Oz attraction at Chutes Amusement Park, yet nothing substantive is offered. Note that Allegorical Oz comprises only 3% of releases. This consisted of two political cartoons intentionally presented as allegory. During this time, broadly speaking, Oz's first cultural moment is achieved, and the Oz brand is set.

Graph 11.2, "Kinds of Oz: Era II," shows that in the years between Baum's death but before the release of *The Wizard of Oz*, the landscape of Oz changes, though not appreciably. These are basically the Reilly & Lee years, in which the instances of Magical Oz decrease from 91% in Era I to 85% here. That residual is absorbed by Opportunistic Oz, which increases from 6% in Era I to 15% now. Reilly & Lee are basically "cranking out" new books, but the publishers seem to be uninterested in expanding their juvenile market. Similarly, the vast majority of adaptations and remediations, such as the Jell-O radio broadcast, target this market segment. The percentage increase in Opportunistic Oz is accounted for by the fact that Reilly & Lee offered experiences such as the Ozmite Club and *A Day in Oz* that were not really a new point of entry, or a new experience of Oz; they were book-selling promotions.

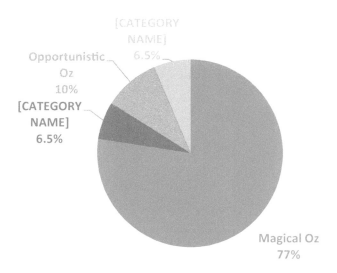

Graph 11.3 Kinds of Oz: Era III

In Graph 11.3, "Kinds of Oz: Era III," we see Magical Oz's share of the pie beginning to shrink, and two new kinds of Oz, Archival Oz and Translated Oz, make their first appearance, accounting for 13% of the Ozes on offer. Three factors, we believe, play a role in this diversification of Oz. The first is Oz's longevity: towards the end of this period, it reaches the half-century mark; second, the original Oz generation has grown up and grown nostalgic. Taken together, these two factors account for the beginning of Archival Oz. Finally, this era begins with the release of the MGM film which was the first major Oz event since the 1902 Broadway extravaganza. It remediated Oz to a new media and offered consumers a new experience. Furthermore, it was highly promoted, bringing Oz to the attention of a larger market. MGM diversified Oz's market and kept it in the public eye, which, along with the fact that Oz's original consumers had now become adults (and potential producers), offers an explanation for the appearance of Translated Oz. Producers can play with the narrative and reliably expect that their consumers will be able to play along.

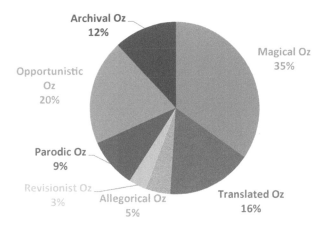

Graph 11.4 Kinds of Oz: Era IV

Graph 11.4, "Kinds of Oz: Era IV," reveals that between 1957 and 2003, occurrences of Magical Oz decreased by more than 50% from Era II. Translated Oz's share has more than doubled, Opportunistic Oz's has, and Archival Oz's nearly so. And three new Ozes, Parodic Oz (9%), Allegorical Oz (5%), and Revisionist Oz (3%) have made their first appearance. As with Era III, three factors account for these shifts. First, in 1960, Oz begins to pass into the public domain, making it available of all sorts of "off-brand" uses. Second, the annual television broadcasts have so embedded Oz into the cultural imaginary that producers can rely on it as a hook for marketing, a shorthand for allegory, and a readily understood allusion for parody and translation. These broadcasts also piqued interest in Oz and Baum, which accounts for the increase in Archival Oz. Finally, the cultural shifts of the late 1960s and 1970s led authors who had grown up on MGMs Oz to produce Revisionist Ozes.

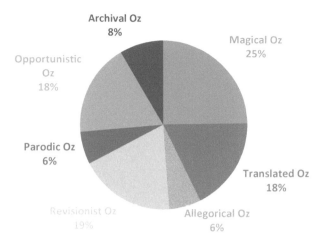

Graph 11.5   Kinds of Oz: Era V

In Graph 11.5, "Kinds of Oz: Era V," we find that instances of Magical Oz continue to decrease, now down to a mere 25% of Ozes produced, while Revisionist Oz has increased from 3 to 19%. Translated Oz and Opportunistic Oz each decrease 2%, while Allegorical Oz gets a slight 1% bump. Parodic Oz and Archival Oz are both down by one-third (9 to 6% and 12 to 8%, respectively). The increase in Revisionist Oz may well account for the decrease in Magical, Translated, and Parodic Ozes as, Post-*Wicked*, Revisionist Oz becomes both the expected mode for Oz and the most popular mode for re-consuming it. The popularity of Revisionist Oz may also explain the decrease in Archival Oz, as consumers are drawn to new Ozes rather than focused on the recovery of old ones.

What can be said about the Kind of Oz on offer when we compare these graphs over the five Eras they represent? Broadly speaking, we see that Oz has become increasingly diverse over time. In the first two Eras, Oz was limited to Baum's Magical Oz and a small percentage of Opportunistic and Allegorical Ozes that tapped into its popularity. Then, in the third, its persistence and visibility in the culture gave rise to Archival Oz and Translated Oz. In the fourth Era, when Oz is both highly visible and in the public domain, it is able to diversify its "brand,"

and, thus its markets, becoming available to assortments. Finally, in the fifth Era, Baum's kind of Oz, Magical Oz, loses its dominance, with Revisionist Oz closing in on its market share.

What might this mean? In order to answer this question, we turn again to our database to examine patterns of Oz occurrences over time. Here, we discover that as Oz diversifies, it proliferates. The Baum years averaged 1.7 per year, a rate that increased slightly to 2.2 in the years between his death and the MGM film (an increase accounted for by both Reilly & Lee's rapid production of new books and the promotional activities surrounding the film), and then dipped to 1.6 in the period between the film's initial release and its television broadcasts as the hoopla surrounding MGM's film faded. When Oz diversifies in the wake of becoming both a television ritual and a public domain text, instances of Oz increase 250% to 5.6 a year, and as that diversification increases, and as traditional Magical Oz loosens its stranglehold on the narrative in the post-*Wicked* years, instances jump again by nearly 100% to 10.6 a year. While other factors may also account for these increases—for instance, new platforms for remediating Oz and new technologies making it easier to produce, deliver, consume, and track Oz products—it remains clear that Oz's availability for re-consumption and the fact that it has been re-consumed in multiple ways to attract diverse assortments of consumers play key roles in its cultural sustainability.

KEY CHARACTERISTICS OF CULTURAL SUSTAINABILITY

As with most studies that proceed inductively, ours is concerned not so much with answering *why*, but *how*. In other words, we didn't ask the question, why has Oz sustained itself for over a century? but rather, how has Oz sustained itself for over a century? And we have answered that question by examining the complex interaction of forces, including those of production and marketing, that have enabled that sustainability to occur. Drawing on the additive conclusions from previous chapters—and paying particular attention to the trends revealed by our coded cases, an example of which is discussed in the previous section—we build on earlier work on narrative vitality, remediation, and transmedia storytelling, adding the insights of experiential marketing and consumer culture theory to offer the following key characteristics of cultural sustainability[3]:

- **In order to keep moving, a narrative must be an "open" text, extending beyond its original owners.** A closed, wholly-owned narrative is, by definition, fixed; it is unavailable to play, adaptation, or convergence. It becomes a closed system, and closed systems perish. To attain sustainability, a narrative needs to be open and accessible to authors beyond its original creator(s), who in turn can reach new audiences with new media, creating new experiences. For example, the Oz archive enjoyed a "boost" in sustainability when its original stories began to enter the public domain.

- **A narrative must be adaptable to multiple market segments.** Particularly in today's niche-driven world, a re-consumption will usually target a specific market segment. (Indeed, marketing students are taught never to think of their new products as appealing to everyone). Until *The Wiz*, broadcast-era Oz re-consumptions mostly targeted the young children and family market. While such targeting of a continually repopulating pool of consumers ensures that the product offered will always find a market, it risks sidelining the narrative to a small niche market. Multiple Ozes mean multiple audiences, and by the end of the broadcast era, Oz experiences were offered across a range of markets, from young children to adult, from popular to literary, from reader to tourist.

- **A narrative claims what are perceived to be "universal" truths.** Oz may have splintered between 1956 and the present, but each Oz claims to be the site of universal truths, whether it is MGM's famous "there's no place like home" or *Was*'s meditation on the power of art. Marketing for *The Wiz*, which began by targeting "blacks, young whites, chic whites, people who listen to top 40 radio," as a hip black musical, and ended by appealing to mainstream family audiences as a universal fairy tale, provides an excellent example of the ways in which the narrative's "universality" extends it beyond its original market segment.

- **Periodically, a narrative needs to reach a galvanizing cultural moment.** Over the course of Oz's 117-year lifespan, we have identified four such moments: the initial publication of Baum's *The Wonderful Wizard of Oz* in 1900; MGM's *The Wizard of Oz* in 1939; *The Wiz* in 1975; and *Wicked* the musical in 2003. In these centralizing moments, the consumer gaze is focused collectively on a single re-consumption of the Oz archive, as potentially millions of viewers, listeners, or participants regard it, experience it, and assess it. It has to be collectively available so that it can be taken in a variety of directions. These moments can extend—at least in the case of Oz—for over a decade, and sometimes two. And our research shows that the re-consumptions that follow such moments are usually in alignment with, or repudiations of it, as consumers-turned-producers say, "Wait a minute! This isn't the Last Word after all." Subsequent re-consumptions must engage in the prior moment—or multiple prior moments—in some way, in order to be recognizable as belonging to that discourse, that narrative archive. Some re-consumptions do this quite successfully, and they, too become cultural moments (e.g., *The Wizard of Oz*, *The Wiz*, and *Wicked*). Others fail miserably (e.g., *Return to Oz*).

- **It needs be available experientially, meaning immersively, multi-sensorily, immediately, and collectively.** Following the tenets of experiential marketing in general, and recalling consumers' reactions to *Wicked* experiences in particular, we note that the Oz narrative lends itself to a multitude of experiences capable of immersing the consumer in multi-sensory ways. From Baum's awe-inspiring *Fairylogue and Radio Play*, through the festive tree-lined streets of The Land of Oz, to the party-hearty ambiance of "Witches' Night Off," successful re-consumptions of Oz enable consumers to lose themselves in the moment. In almost all cases, particularly among consumers under 40, these are collective moments, immediately experienced and immediately shared.

- **The successful narrative—and the most successful re-consumptions within it—arouse the full range of emotions.** Time and again, as we listened to consumers' responses to *Wicked* (see Chapter 7) we were struck by the extent to which consumers wanted to feel—expected to feel—a full spectrum of emotions, from joy to sadness, from self-assurance to self-doubt, from vindication to humiliation. In fact, they judged the ultimate worth of *Wicked* by the degree to which it did just that ("soul-stirring" was the profound descriptor used by several). We heard the same thing as we listened to consumers' recollections of watching *The Wizard of Oz* in their homes as children. The bright gaiety inspired by the Munchkins, the abject terror inspired by the Wicked Witch, the reassuring comfort inspired by Dorothy's return to her own bedroom—these, too, constitute a spectrum of emotions that have subsisted in consumers' psyches for decades. Similar accounts from the

Baum and MGM years indicate that Oz, from its soothing effect on sick children to the tears in the eyes of usually blasé critics, has always invoked a deeply felt emotional response in consumers.

- **The narrative is adaptable—then actually adapted—to new technologies**. Oz began in written form, but over time, new technologies emerged that enabled Baum to first envision, then realize, new re-consumptions of his Oz tale. Not only was he aware of these new technologies and the new possibilities they occasioned, but he learned how to use them—and when he didn't or couldn't, he sought out those who could. Similarly, MGM relied on its own talent pool to realize a new Technicolor vision of Oz that amounted to a new experience of it, which CBS translated to the emerging medium of television. In more recent years, Oz has been remediated to digital platforms, ranging from fan forums and Facebook to YouTube and video games.

- **Narratives and their re-consumptions attract the gaze of cultural gatekeepers**. Certain re-consumptions—and the larger archive of which they are a part—must attract the attention of people who assess, critique, and pass judgment on cultural artifacts for a living. The artifact in question must "matter" enough for professional critics and academics to find it worthy of their engagement, commentary, appraisal, or scholarly gaze. This may mean that such arbiters are truly, deeply, and dramatically elated or offended by the re-consumption under examination (such extreme reactions tend to be good for business), but either way, the artifact achieves greater notoriety and impact as a result. All of Oz's cultural moments attracted the attention of cultural gatekeepers and, as such, were widely reviewed and discussed. In 1939, the critics almost functioned as part of MGM's marketing team; in 1975, reviews first lambasted and then sold *The Wiz*; and, in 2003, the critical establishment repeatedly returned to *Wicked*.

- **Overtime, the narrative archive must generate a sufficient number of assortments to satisfy a sufficient number of consumers**. As we illustrated graphically, recent decades have seen a proliferation of the Kinds of Oz available now available to consumers. On the one hand, this proliferation can be seen in a negative light, suggesting a fragmentation or splintering of Oz products and Oz markets. But on the other, this proliferation can be seen in a positive light, suggesting that a variety of assortments—in this case, re-consumptions of the Oz narrative—fulfills a something-for-every-one condition. To the extent that consumers are drawn to and hailed by the particular assortment(s) that fulfill(s) their needs, value is achieved. To name a few: There are Oz assortments for the female YA market (*Dorothy Must Die, Bewitched in Oz*), for the twenty- and thirty-something "geek" demographic (*Tin Man, Emerald City*) and for the tween audience (*Lost in Oz*).

- **The "key of keys" to cultural sustainability may lie in the cyclical alternation of cultural moments with proliferations of assortments.** As we examine the arc of Oz's own cultural sustainability, we suggest that its four cultural moments provide the rallying points necessary to collect consumers, gatekeepers, pro-sumers, and producers in a profoundly new artifactual event. Those moments hold sway for an extended period, temporarily fixing the narrative in a particular time and space. Then, it's as though, having regarded such moments for an extended period, these systemic par-ticipants retreat and disperse—to their own lived experiences, their own meaning-makings, and their own communities of consumption and, perhaps, means of production. Armed with new visions and new technologies, the new experiences of Oz they create can both respond to and extend the moments that gave rise to them. And in rare instances, a re-consumption will itself become a cultural moment, and the process begins again. As we suggest at the end of Chapter 10, the future of Oz—its near-term sustainability, at least—looks bright. Oz appears to be in an assortment proliferation phase, for the time being. But if our intuition is correct, it will "need" a cultural moment that unifies the collective gaze once again. That moment could presumably come as early as 2019, if the *Wicked* movie speaks deeply to consumers, or it could arrive in years hence, in a re-consumption yet unknown and unimagined.

FURTHER DOWN THE ROAD

As with any study, limitations abound, and this study is no exception. At present, we cluster its limitations into three categories, all of which present promising opportunities for future research.

First, with the exception of some theater professionals and *Wicked* performances in London's West End, our study was limited to American consumers seeing American productions arising from American culture.

The same is true of the Oz products we studied. As such, the claims we make regarding Oz's cultural sustainability are, perforce, limited to America's shores. But Oz itself has been a global as well as American phenomenon from the early twentieth century on; *Wicked*, for instance, has toured successfully in such far-flung countries as Australia, Germany, and Japan. The natural antidote to this limitation is to extend our study globally; possible directions include analyzing Oz adapted for consumers behind the Iron Curtain, or asking how consumers, gatekeepers, and prosumers in cultures that may or may not know *The Wizard of Oz* made sense of *Wicked*.

Second, although our sample of 75 consumer respondents encompassed an impressive diversity in age—from 16 to 93—it was not as diverse along other dimensions. Partly because of the snowball sampling technique we employed, and partly because of the types of consumers who can afford to attend a Broadway show today, the preponderance of our respondents was white, relatively affluent, and relatively well-educated. It would be extremely useful to know how consumers from different ethnic groups, educational backgrounds, and income levels would make sense of *Wicked*. Would they notice the same things, respond to the same moments, take away the same lessons as members of our current sample did? For example, would they respond to the Otherness of Elphaba at an equally personal level? Would they also disclose their own vulnerabilities?

Finally, our taxonomy itself is not fixed, but will evolve as we ask new questions. For instance, the dimensions we have identified thus far are based on the product as opposed to the consumer's experience of or interaction with it—or gatekeepers appraisal of it. This limitation can be resolved by adding consumer and gatekeeper-based dimensions to our taxonomy. This, is turn, suggests further research in which we conduct interviews, similar to those we did for *Wicked*, with consumers about other Oz experiences.

Apart from these limitation-driven opportunities for future research lie a host of other new research possibilities. Chief among these are studies that test what we identify as key characteristics of cultural sustainability against the production, marketing, and consumption of other narrative or artistic archives. Here, we could bring a marketing and consumption focus to existing historical studies of the adaptation and remediation of texts and authors (e.g., Shakespeare, Austen, and fairy tales), and extend those studies in new directions and to other art-forms.[4] We could also look at the ways in which cultural sustainability contributes to the sustainability of cultural institutions. *The Nutcracker*, for instance, has been in existence eight years longer than the Oz narrative. It may have entered the culture as a story, but its cultural sustainability stems from its status as a canonical dance piece and symphonic artifact—one that has undergone significant variations in its lifetime, and one whose annual production serves to sustain dance and performing arts companies[5] worldwide. The dimensions we would use to code and track new archives might differ from those we used for Oz. But would our findings remain the same? Similarly, would the paintings of Caravaggio, whose archive is over 400 years old and whose blockbuster showings often comprise cultural moments in themselves, exhibit a profile similar to that of Oz?[6] What about the music of the Beatles? Its archive is much younger than any of the others, yet it was so carefully controlled, curated, and confounded by its founding members. Would we draw the same conclusions about its sustainability as we have for Oz? The opportunities presented by different archives, originating in different periods, media, and accessibility, are limited only by the time we have to study them.

Notes

1. Franco Moretti, *Distant Reading* (UK: Verso, 2013).
2. As developed by Florian Znaniecki, see "Analytic Induction," in *International Encyclopedia of the Social and Behavioral Sciences*, ed. Neil Smelse and Paul Baltes, vol. 20 (UK: Elsevier Science Ltd., 2001), 480–484.
3. See Henry Jenkins, *Convergence Culture: Where Old and New Media Collide* (New York: New York University Press, 2006); David Bolter and Richard Grusin, *Remediation: Understanding New Media* (Boston: MIT Press, Reprint Edition, 2008). For recent examples of studies on transmedia storytelling see: Kelly McErlean, *Interactive Narratives and Transmedia Storytelling* (New York: Routledge, 2018); Matthew Freeman, *Historicizing Transmedia Storytelling: Early Twentieth Century Transmedia Story Worlds* (New York: Routledge, 2016).
4. There have been many studies on the adaptation of Shakespeare, Austen and fairy tales. Examples include Maurizio Calbi, *Spectral Shakespeares: Media Adaptations in the Twenty-First Century* (New York: Palgrave Macmillan, 2013); Douglas Lanier, *Shakespeare and Modern Popular Culture* (Oxford: Oxford University Press, 2002); Susan Aronstein and Peter Parolin, "'The Play's the Thing:' The Cinematic Fortunes

of Chaucer and Shakespeare," in *Chaucer on Screen: Absence, Presence and Adapting the Canterbury Tales*, ed. Kathleen Kelly and Tison Pugh (Ohio State University Press, 2016), 33–44; Suzanne R. Pucci and James Thompson, *Jane Austen and Co.: Remaking the Past in Contemporary Culture* (New York: State University of New York Press, 2003); and the works of Jack Zipes, including *The Irresistible Fairy Tale: The Cultural and Social History of a Genre* (Princeton: Princeton University Press, 2012).

5. See Kent Drummond, "The Queering of Swan Lake: A New Male Gaze for the Performance of Sexual Desire," *The Journal of Homosexuality* 45, no. 2/3/4 (2003): 235–255.

6. See Kent Drummond, "The Migration of Art from Museum to Market: Consuming Caravaggio," *Marketing Theory* 6, no. 1 (2006): 85–105.

Appendix A: List of Consumers Interviewed

Pseudonym	Age	Occupation
Roxanne	20	Student
Ali	18	Student
Bri	21	Student
Cory	20	Student
Tessa	19	Student
Rudy	19	Student
Barbara	21	Student
Tara	18	Student
Misty	20	Student
Carrie	18	Student
Bryan	21	Student
Laura	19	Student
Peggy	20	Student
Anna	21	Student
Ben	19	Student
Liz	13	Student
Dale	14	Student
Natalie	16	Student
Lizzie	21	Student
Becca	19	Student
Skye	16	Student
Craig	22	Student
Greg	26	Law Student
Dan	38	Economics Professor

© The Editor(s) (if applicable) and The Author(s) 2018   307
K. Drummond et al., *The Road to Wicked*,
https://doi.org/10.1007/978-3-319-93106-7

Pseudonym	Age	Occupation
Carl	40	Dentist
Katherine	62	University Administrator
Jim	56	Sociologist
Cheryl	60	Dermatologist
Eve	93	Retired Executive Secretary
Loretta	62	Retired Attorney
Rachel	63	Attorney
Scott	47	Transportation Manager
Barry	65	Energy Executive
Pat	62	Project Manager
Sheila	46	Office Manager
Ron	58	Management Professor
Tom	39	Priest
Tory	28	Waitperson
Diana	35	Artist
June	78	Retired
Reva	63	Accountant
Sybil	70	Retired
Louise	58	Office Manager
Paul	41	Security Guard
Brittany	39	Tour Guide
Kate	45	Custodian
Callie	58	Administrative Assistant
Daniel	55	Naval Officer
Hannah	54	School Secretary
Josie	61	Artist
Karin	35	Telemarketer
Bill	55	Software Manager
Russ	32	College Recruiter
Pamela	30	Program Manager
Carisa	36	Lecturer
Luke	33	Graduate Student
Madison	31	Homemaker
Gary	60	Musician
Gerri	63	Marketing Professor Emerita
Tyra	34	Foreign Aid Worker
Alan	77	Publicist
Dee	55	Hospitality Manager
John	27	Computer Game Designer
Kevin	62	Administrator
Sydney	49	Homemaker

Pseudonym	Age	Occupation
Doug	56	Librarian
Rae	60	Travel Agent
Randi	25	Marketer
Jay	60	English Professor
Trish	34	Office Administrator
Ryan	25	Teacher
Molly	30	Engineer
Tina	42	Physician's Assistant
William	63	Computer Engineer
Connie	55	Teacher

Appendix B: List of Theater Professionals Interviewed

Pseudonym	Age	Profession
Vivien	58	Actor
Terry	57	Actor
Sean	56	Producer
David	55	Critic
Alicia	35	Dance Captain
Jerad	32	Wicked Cast Member
Tim	23	Dancer
Steve	38	Vocalist
Ken	57	Lighting Designer
Stu	56	Costume Designer
Barry	60	Vocal Coach
Mark	59	Conductor
Lindsay	30	Marketer
John	64	Author and critic
Lisa	58	Choreographer
Karl	57	Director
Fran	29	Director
Renee	43	Vocal Coach
Don	41	Composer
Richard	63	Marketing Consultant
Brian	78	Publicist
Sherry	63	Vocalist
Lynn	58	Literary Scholar
Brent	60	Marketer
Sheila	29	Producer

A Brief Glossary of Key Terms

Narrative: The "Cauldron of Story" as coined by Tolkien. To build on his metaphor, the narrative refers to the all-encompassing, ever-growing pot of soup from which samples are taken, changed in some way, and then returned to the pot. In our case, it's the entire corpus of Oz-related products, services, and experiences that have entered the marketplace since Baum's first book was published over a century ago. **Narrative archive** and **corpus** are equivalents.

The original version: The original story that started it all. In the case of the Oz narrative, the original version is *The Wonderful Wizard of Oz*, written by L. Frank Baum and published in 1900. To extend Tolkien's metaphor, it is the bone that Baum put in the pot to make the soup in the first place. Baum adds a variety of other ingredients to this soup before leaving the kitchen in 1919.

Re-consumption: A single iteration of a product, service, or experience that occurs after the original version enters the marketplace. It represents a single serving of soup prepared by a cook who took something from the cauldron, altered it in some way, and offered it to consumers before putting it back in the pot. Every re-consumption is also a reproduction, but following Hutcheon's adage that producers are consumers before they are producers, we choose the former term to emphasize the consumptive nature of the reproduction. Also referred to as an **iteration**, **single instance**, or **artifact**, re-consumptions are the building blocks of the narrative archive. In researching

© The Editor(s) (if applicable) and The Author(s) 2018
K. Drummond et al., *The Road to Wicked*,
https://doi.org/10.1007/978-3-319-93106-7

the Oz narrative, we identified over 500 re-consumptions, and there are certainly more.

Assortment: A single re-consumption, or cluster of re-consumptions, that suits the needs of a particular consumer or cluster of consumers. An assortment corresponds to a cup of soup that tastes "just right" to one or more consumers. According to Wroe Alderson, who developed the concept, the process by which assortments and consumers match up is called sorting. We find that assortments play a critical role in sustaining the Oz narrative.

Cultural moment: A re-consumption that grows in cultural significance until it collects the consumer gaze for an extended period of time. It corresponds to a particularly memorable and seemingly long-lasting cup of soup drawn from the cauldron; it staste affects other cups of soup consumers try after it. A cultural moment is rare in the Oz narrative; we have identified only three besides the original version.

Naïve consumer: A consumer who has little or no experience with this particular cauldron of soup. As it applies to our research, the naïve consumer can be someone who has never encountered a version of the Oz narrative, or one who has not previously attended a performance on Broadway and may feel intimidated at the prospect.

Knowing consumer: A consumer who is familiar with other instances of the Oz narrative, or one who has attended at least one performance on Broadway and has also seen other professional productions (or both). The knowing Broadway consumer tends to be more knowledgeable about and less intimidated by artistic experiences than a naïve consumer.

Gatekeeper: A professional arbiter of quality, worth, or significance. In the soup metaphor, gatekeepers are professional tasters who try out each new offering of soup and respond with a proclamation: "This is great – you've got to try this!" or an explanation: "This bowl reminds me of one I had several years ago." Gatekeepers tend to be credentialed by some institutional authority, which gives them the power to pass judgment on the re-consumption or archive in question. In the case of Oz, gatekeepers tend to be critics, reviewers, and academics who follow or research any performance or subject related to Oz. Since they often experience a re-consumption in advance of everyday consumers, gatekeepers are pre-consumers who often wield significant influence on the opinions of others.

Prosumer: Standing midway between a consumer and a producer, a prosumer displays elements of both. Having experienced one or more re-consumptions of a narrative, a prosumer eagerly produces his or her own, often hoping that large numbers of consumers and producers will notice. In the Oz narrative, the performer Todrick Hall is a highly successful prosumer. His self-produced, self-promoted fantasia on Oz themes recently landed him a role in Broadway's *Kinky Boots*.

Producer: A producer has the ability, the power, and the authority to actually create a re-consumption and get paid for doing so. When it comes to the Oz archive, almost all producers operate in some version of a collaborative team. For example, the musical *Wicked*'s production team would certainly include composer and lyricist Stephen Schwartz and writer Winnie Holzman, but it would also extend to veteran producer Marc Platt, director Joe Montello, and many others.

Meso-level perspective: The location of this study, situated as it is between the micro- and macro-levels of analysis. Taking a meso-level perspective enabled us to examine not only the artifact-level of re-consumption (micro) but also the cultural-level forces (macro) that produce and absorb those re-consumptions.

Cultural sustainability: Our view of cultural sustainability differs from more traditional perspectives. For us, cultural sustainability is the result of a long-term interplay between a series of artifacts and the culture that produced them, re-absorbed them, and renewed them. What is the interplay of forces such that most Americans have heard of Oz more than 100 years after its inception? What enables them to eagerly consume contemporary re-consumptions of Oz, such as *Wicked* and *Oz the Great and Powerful*? How has Oz stayed relevant after all these years? What role does Oz play in sustaining cultural, national and personal identities? In our view, cultural sustainability doesn't just happen; it is an achievement.

Analytic induction: The system of logic by and through which this study functions. AI is a common method of analyzing qualitative data in particular. Having established that Oz has achieved cultural sustainability, we examine and describe the rich interplay of forces that characterize this achievement. We then generalize that description, building toward a new model of sustainability against which other cases may be tested.

BIBLIOGRAPHY

Aims, Walter. "A New Generation to See 'Wizard of Oz' Tonight." *Los Angeles Times*, November 3, 1956.

Alderson, Wroe. *Dynamic Marketing Behavior.* Homewood, IL: Richard D. Irwin Press, 1965.

Alexander, Ron. "A Celebration to Touch the Heart of a Tin Man." *New York Times*, August 20, 1989.

Allendale, Josh, "For Good: A Blockbuster Gives Back." Broadway Direct, October 15, 2013. https://broadwaydirect.com/for-good-a-blockbuster-gives-back/. Accessed November 18, 2015.

Arnould, Eric J., and Craig J. Thompson. "Consumer Culture Theory (CCT): Twenty Years of Research." *Journal of Consumer Research* 31, no. 4 (March 2005): 868–882.

Auster, Al. "The Wiz." *Cineaste* 9, no. 2 (Winter 1978): 41–42.

Bailey, Peter. "The Wiz." *Black Enterprise*, January 1976.

Baltake, Joe. "Return to Oz." *Philadelphia Daily News*, June 21, 1985. ProQuest.

Barnes, Brooks. "How Wicked Cast Its Spell." *The Wall Street Journal*, October 22, 2005. https://www.wsj.com/articles/SB112994038461876413.

Barnes, Clive. "'The Wiz, (of Oz)." *New York Times*, January 6, 1975.

Bass, Debra D. "'Wicked' Asks Which Witch is Which." *The Press Democrat*, May 18, 2003.

Baugham, Roland. *L. Frank Baum: The Wonderful Wizard of Oz, an Exhibition of His Published Writings in Commemoration of the Centenary of His Birth.* New York: Columbia University Libraries, 1956.

© The Editor(s) (if applicable) and The Author(s) 2018   317
K. Drummond et al., *The Road to Wicked*,
https://doi.org/10.1007/978-3-319-93106-7

Baum Bugle, 76 (Spring 1983). Reproduced on PJFarmer.com. http://www. pjfarmer.com/WRITTEN-ABOUT-reviews.html#barnstormer.   Accessed November 1, 2017.

Baum, Frank Joslyn, and Russell MacFall. *To Please a Child: A Biography of L. Frank Baum, Royal Historian of Oz*. Chicago: Reilly & Lee, 1961.

Baum, L. Frank Papers. Syracuse University Libraries Special Collections Research Center. Syracuse University Library.

Baum, L. Frank. *The Wonderful Wizard of Oz*. Chicago: George M. Hill, 1900. Kindle.

———. *The Marvelous Land of Oz*. Chicago: Reilly & Britton, 1904. Kindle.

———. *Ozma of Oz*. Chicago: Reilly & Britton, 1907. Kindle.

———. *Dorothy and the Wizard in Oz*. Chicago: Reilly & Britton, 1908. Kindle.

———. *The Road to Oz*. Chicago: Reilly & Britton, 1909. Kindle.

———. *The Emerald City of Oz*. Chicago: Reilly & Britton, 1910. Kindle.

———. *Tik Tok of Oz*. Chicago: Reilly & Britton, 1914. Kindle.

———. *The Scarecrow of Oz*. Chicago: Reilly & Britton, 1915. Kindle.

———. *Glinda of Oz*. Chicago: Reilly & Lee, 1920. Kindle.

———. *The Annotated Wizard of Oz*. Edited by Michael Patrick Hearn. New York: W. W. Norton, 1973.

Baum, L. Frank, and Ruth Plumly Thompson. *The Royal Book of Oz*. Chicago: Reilly & Lee, 1921. Kindle.

"Baum's Castorine." Hagley Digital Archives. http://digital.hagley.org/islandora/object/islandora:2307008#page/1/mode/1up. Accessed October 20, 2017.

Becker, Howard. *Art Worlds*. Berkeley: University of California Press, 2008.

Behrens, Web. "OZ is Everywhere Today, It Seems. So Much so that No One Would Blame You if You'd Started to Wonder if a Witch Had Cast a Spell on the Entire City." *Chicago Tribune*, November 6, 2005.

Belk, Russell W. "The Role of the Odyssey in Consumer Behavior and Consumer Research." *Advances in Consumer Research* 14 (1987): 357–361.

Bolter, David, and Richard Grusin. *Remediation: Understanding New Media*. Boston: MIT Press, Reprint edition, 2008.

Boyar, Jay. "Return Trip to Land of Oz Is Grim Going." *Orlando Sentinel*, June 22, 1985, ProQuest.

Bradbury, Ray. "Foreword." In L. Frank Baum, *The Wonderful Wizard of Oz: The Kansas Centennial Edition*. Lawrence, KS: University of Kansas Press, 1999, Xiii–xvii.

Brantley, Ben. "There's Trouble in the Emerald City." *New York Times*, October 31, 2003.

Britton, Andrew. "Blissing Out: The Politics of Reaganite Entertainment." In *Britton on Film: The Complete Film Criticism of Andrew Britton*. Edited by Barry Grant. Ann Arbor: Wayne State Press, 2009, 97–154.

Brown, Sally Joy. "A Good Letter Is Passport to 'Wizard of Oz.'" *Chicago Daily Tribune*, August 22, 1939.

Burger, Allissa. *The Wizard of Oz as American Myth*. Jefferson, NC: McFarland, 2012.

Busse, Kristina, and Karen Hellekson. "Introduction: Work in Progress." In *Fan Fiction and Fan Communities in the Age of the Internet*, edited by Kristina Busse and Karen Hellekson. Jefferson, NC: McFarland, 2006. Kindle.

Byrne, Terry. "Oz-based Musical Is Spellbinding and 'Wicked' Fun." *Boston Herald*, October 31, 2003.

Carr, Jay. "Summer Movies; The Winners and Losers." *Boston Globe*, August 29, 1985, ProQuest.

Chabon, Michael. *Maps and Legends: Reading and Writing Along the Borderlands*. New York: Harper Collins, 2008.

Chandler, Melanie. "Wicked Puts Witch in a Kinder, Gentler Light." *The Vancouver Sun*, December 2 1995, ProQuest.

Chang, Justin. "Legends of Oz: Dorothy's Return." *Variety*, May 7, 2014. http://variety.com/2014/film/reviews/film-review-legends-of-oz-dorothys-return-1201174414/.

Childs, C. "THE WIZ." *Chicago Tribune*, October 26, 1975, ProQuest.

"Closing Credits for *Ford Star Jubilee* (1956)." YouTube video, 2:01. Posted by MattTheSaiyan, August 3, 2016. https://www.youtube.com/results?search_query=ford+star+jubilee+closing+credits.

Cohen, Ron. "*Wicked*'. *Back Stage*, November 14, 2003.

Colbert, Francois. *Marketing Culture and the Arts*. Montreal: HEC, 2007.

Cote, David. *Wicked: The Grimmerie, A Behind-the-Scenes Look at the Hit Broadway Musical*. New York: Hatchette Books, 2005.

Cox, Gordon. "'Wicked Hits $1 Billion on BROADWAY FASTER than Any Other Show." *Variety*, March 15, 2016. http://variety.com/2016/legit/news/wicked-broadway-sales-1-billion.

Crowley, John. "The Road to Hell Is Paved with Yellow Bricks." *New York Times*, July 5, 1992, ProQuest.

Csikszentmihalyi, Mihaly. *Flow: The Psychology of Peak Experiences*. New York: Harper Collins, 2008.

Daily Ozmapolitan. ozmapolitan.wordpress.com. Accessed January 30, 2018.

"Death Valley Days S18 E14 the Wizard of Aberdeen." YouTube Video, 25:41. Posted by This Is Invader, February 20, 2017. https://www.youtube.com/watch?v=2RJZjkAK1xg.

Dennis, Harvey. "Ding, Dong, the Witch's Prognosis Is Uncertain at the Stage of 'Wicked'." *Variety*, June 16, 2003.

Derecho, Abigail. "Archontic Literature: A Definition, A History, and Several Theories of Fan Fiction." In *Fan Fiction and Fan Communities in the Age of the Internet*, edited by Kristina Busse and Karen Hellekson. Jefferson, NC: McFarland, 2006. Kindle.

Desmond, Ryan. "Sadly, Few Choose To 'Return To Oz'. "*Philadelphia Inquirer*, July 16, 1985, ProQuest.

Dighe, Ranjit, ed. *The Historian's Wizard of Oz: Reading L. Frank Baum's Classic as a Political and Monetary Allegory*. New York: Praeger, 2002.

Di Giere, Carol. *Defying Gravity: The Creative Career of Stephen Schwartz from Godspell to Wicked*. New York: Applause Books, 2008.

Dorothy Meets Ozma of Oz. Directed by Myrna Bushman et al. 1987: Kushner-Locke Company. YouTube video, 28:21. Posted by Connor Hicks, May 14, 2916. https://www.youtube.com/watch?v=IbH5QsCK9sk.

"Dorothy the Librarian." *Life Magazine*, February 16, 1949.

Drummond, Kent. "The Queering of Swan Lake: A New Male Gaze for the Performance of Sexual Desire." *The Journal of Homosexuality* 45, no. 2/3/4 (2003): 235–255.

Drummond, Kent. "The Migration of Art from Museum to Market: Consuming Caravaggio." *Marketing Theory* 6, no. 1 (2006): 85–105.

Edelstein, David. "Oz the Great and Powerful Is Peculiarly Joyless." *Vulture*, March 8, 2013. http://www.vulture.com/2013/03/movie-review-oz-the-great-and-powerful.html.

"Eight-Year-Old Previews Wizard of Oz." *Washington Post*, August 20, 1939.

Emerald City. Created by Matthew Arnold and Josh Friedman. 2017: Shaun Cassidy Productions. Amazon Video. Streaming.

Eng, Dinah. "Under the Moral's Spell; Teen Girls Are Entranced by 'Wicked', the Latest Broadway Blockbuster with Issues that Speak to Them." *Los Angeles Times,* June 19, 2005.

Farmer, Phillip Jose. *A Barnstormer in Oz*. New York: Berkley Press, 1982.

Feingold, Michael. "Dorothy Plays the Palace." *Village Voice*, 1975. http://www.thewizthemusical.com/productions/original-broadway-production-1975/press-and-reviews/article/1004.

———. "Green Witch, Mean Time: Both on and Off-Broadway, New Musicals Suffer from Severe Multiple Personality Disorder." *Village Voice*, November 5, 2003.

"Film Wiz Drops a Great Yellow Brick." *The Globe and Mail*, October 28, 1978.

Finke, Laurie A., and Susan Aronstein. "Got Grail?: Monty Python and the Broadway Stage." *Theater Survey* 48 (2007): 289–311.

Freeman, Matthew. *Historicizing Transmedia Storytelling*. New York: Routledge, 2017.

Fricke, John. *The Wonderful World of Oz: An Illustrated History of the American Classic*. Camden, ME: Down East Books, 2013.

———. "Timeless Appeal: The "Wizard of Oz' Comes to Television Sixty Years Ago." *Baum Bugle* 60, no. 2 (August 2016): 8–15.

———. "History of the Oz Club." Paper Presented at Oz-Con, Portland, OR, June 2017.

———. Interview by Kent Drummond. August 17, 2017.

———. Interview by Kent Drummond. February 2, 2018.

———. "Interview with Blair Frodelius." *The Wizard's Wireless, The Daily Ozmapolitan.* http://www.frodelius.com/wirelesstelegraph/fricke.html. Accessed February 20, 2018.

———, Jay Scarfone, and William Stillman. *The Wizard of Oz: The Official 50th Anniversary Pictorial History.* New York: Warner Books, 1989.

Gardner, Burleigh B., and Sidney J. Levy, "The Product and the Brand." *Harvard Business Review* 33, no. 2 (1955): 33–40.

Gardner, Elysa. "Something 'Wicked' Comes to Broadway." *USA Today,* October 31, 2003.

Gay, Verne. "'Emerald City' Review: Grim Series Doesn't Compare to Book, Film." *Newsday,* January 4, 2017. https://www.newsday.com/entertainment/tv/emerald-city-review-grim-series-doesn-t-compare-to-book-film-1.12863840.

Gillies, Judith S. "An Update that's All Heart." *Washington Post,* December 2, 2007. http://www.washingtonpost.com/wp-dyn/content/article/2007/11/27/AR2007112702124.html.

Gladwell, Malcolm. *The Tipping Point: How Little Things Can Make a Big Difference.* New York: Back Bay Books, 2002.

"Glenn Beck Ties the Wizard of Oz to Today's Problems." YouTube video, 10:07. Posted by TheBlaze, November 7, 2013. https://www.youtube.com/watch?v=iPXYWhZlj0g.

Gould, Jack. "Program Crisis." *New York Times,* November 11, 1956.

Gray, Tim. "The Wiz: How TV Turned a Troubled Stage Show into a Smash." *Variety,* December 2, 2015. http://variety.com/2015/tv/news/the-wiz-broadway-tv-1201651417/.

"Gregory Maguire Loving Wicked for the 35th Time." *Broadway Buzz,* October 15, 2008. https://www.broadway.com/buzz/6302/gregory-maguire-loving-wicked-for-the-35th-time/. Accessed December 2, 2017.

Hainer, Cathy. "Somewhere over the Rainbow Lies a 'Wicked' Fable.'" *USA Today,* October 23, 1995.

Hall, Jane. "The Wizard of Oz," *Good Housekeeping,* August 1939.

Handler, Daniel. "Hey, Watch Who You're Calling Wicked." *New York Times,* June 29, 2003.

Harmetz, Aljean. "'A Wizard of Oz': A TV Success Story." *New York Times,* March 16, 1983.

Harris, Mary. "'Wizard of Oz Begins Second Palace Week." *Washington Post,* September 9, 1939.

———. "After 46 Years, Hollywood Revisits Oz. "*New York Times,* June 16, 1985, ProQuest.

Hawkes, Jon. *The Fourth Pillar of Sustainability: Culture's Essential Role in Public Planning.* Melbourne: Common Ground Publishing Pty Ltd., 2001.

Hill, Jim. "Joe Roth Reflects on Oz the Great and Powerful." *Huffington Post,* March 4, 2013. https://www.huffingtonpost.com/jim-hill/joe-roth-reflects-on-oz-t_b_2806542.html.

"History in the Making." *Land of Oz,* 2017. https://www.landofoznc.com/history. Accessed December 15, 2017.

Holbrook, Morris B., and Elizabeth C. Hirschman. "The Experiential Aspects of Consumption: Consumer Fantasies, Feeling and Fun." *Journal of Consumer Research* 9 (September 1982): 132–140.

Holzman, Winnie. "Behind the Emerald Curtain, Wicked: Book Writing." YouTube video, 5:28. Posted by Wicked the Musical, October 1, 2013. https://www.youtube.com/watch?v=DTmeWxfTouE&index-2&list=PLFD7E32F6E398FD1B.

Hughes, Allen. Interview by Kent Drummond. October 20, 2016.

Hurwitt, Robert. "Every Witch Way—Spellbinding 'Wicked' a Charming Vision of Oz, but Is a Few Bricks Shy of a Road." *San Francisco Chronicle,* June 12, 2003.

Hutcheon, Linda. *A Theory of Adaptation.* New York: Routledge, 2012.

Jackson, Shirley. "The Lost Kingdom of Oz." *The Reporter,* December 10, 1959.

Jauss, Hans Robert. *Towards an Aesthetic of Reception.* Translated by Timothy Bahti. Minnesota: University of Minnesota Press, 1982.

Jenkins, Henry. *Convergence Culture: Where Old and New Media Collide.* New York: New York University Press, 2006.

Jezer, Mary. *The Dark Ages: Life in the United States, 1945–1965.* Cambridge: South End Press, 1982.

Jones, Rachel. "The Real Oz Is a Slice of Life." *Chicago Tribune,* August 11, 1985, ProQuest.

Journey Back to Oz. Directed by Hal Sutherland. 1972, 1974: Filmation Associates. YouTube video. Posted by darthraner83, December 14, 2011. https://www.youtube.com/watch?v=FwQCfCSjOns.

Joy, Annamma, and John Sherry. "Speaking of Art as Embodied Imagination: A Multi-Sensory Approach to Understanding Aesthetic Experience." *Journal of Consumer Research* 30, no. 2 (2003): 259–282.

"Jumping Jivernacular." *Time,* January 20, 1975. http://www.thewizthemusical.com/productions/original-broadway-production-1975/press-and-reviews/article/1022.

Kakutani, Michiko. "Books of the Times; Using the Reality of Oz as the Basis for Fantasy." *New York Times,* June 9, 1992, ProQuest.

———. "Let's Get This Straight: Glinda Was the Bad One." *New York Times,* October 24, 1995, ProQuest.

Kelleter, Frank. "Toto, I Think We're in Oz Again" (And Again and Again): Remakes and Popular Seriality." In *Film Remakes: Adaptations and Fan Productions*, edited by Kathleen Loock and Constantine Verevis. New York: Palgrave Macmillan, 2012. 19–44.

Knapp, Raymond. *The American Musical and the Formation of National Identity*. Princeton: Princeton University Press, 2005.

———. *The American Musical and the Performance of Personal Identity*. Princeton: Princeton University Press, 2006.

Kroll, Jack. "Oz with Soul." *Newsweek*, 1975. http://www.thewizthemusical. com/productions/original-broadway-production-1975/press-and-reviews/ article/1009.

Lacey, Liam. "Oz the Great and Powerful: The Very Opposite of Big Budget Movie Magic." *The Globe and Mail*, March 8, 2013. https:// www.theglobeandmail.com/arts/film/film-reviews/oz-the-great-and-powerful-a-big-budget-misfire-thats-the-very-opposite-of-magic/ article9479230/.

Lahr, John. "Bitches and Witches: Ulterior Motives in 'Cat on a Hot Tin Roof' and 'Wicked.' *New Yorker*, November 10, 2003.

Laird, Paul. *Wicked: A Musical Biography*. Maryland: Scarecrow Press, 2011.

Lamb, Gregory M. "Spin Cycle: A Musical Based on a Book, Based on Another Book that Was Turned into Two Musicals—Is There Nothing New Under the Sun?" *Christian Science Monitor*, July 18, 2003.

Lanier, Clinton, and C. Scott Rader. "Consumption Experience: An Expanded View." *Marketing Theory* 14, no. 4 (2015): 487–508.

Larson, Susan. "Off to See the Wizard in a Whole New Light." *Times-Picayune*, October 29, 1995.

Layton, Roger A., and Zhirong Duan. "Diversity and Marketing System Assortments." *The Journal of Macromarketing* 35, no. 3 (2015): 320–333.

Lears, Jackson. *Fables of Abundance: A Cultural History of Advertising in America*. New York: Hatchette Book Group, 1995.

———. *Rebirth of a Nation: The Making of Modern America, 1877–1921*. New York: Harper Perrenial, 2010.

Lemire, Christy. "'Oz the Great and Powerful is Neither." *Mass Live*, March 7, 2013. http://www.masslive.com/entertainment/index.ssf/2013/03/ movie_review_oz_the_great_and.html.

"Letters to the Editor: Judy Lacked Punch." *Wall Street Journal*, July 12, 1985, ProQuest.

Levin, Gary. "Sci-Fi Channel Takes Its Own Trip Down the Yellow Brick Road." *USA Today*, November 28, 2007. https://usatoday30.usatoday.com/life/tel-evisionnews/2007-11-28-tin-man_N.html.

Lewis, Ruth. "'The Wizard of Oz.'" *Austin American*, August 27, 1939.

Littlefield, Henry M. "The Wizard of Oz: Parable on Populism." *American Quarterly* 16, no. 1 (1964): 47–58.

Littlefield, Kenny. "There's No Place Like Postmodern 'Oz.'" *Seattle Times*, December 2, 2007. http://old.seattletimes.com/html/television/2004041481_tinman02.html.

"Liza Minelli, and Burt Lahr debut of THE WIZARD OF OZ." YouTube video, 2:29. Posted by Buzz Stephens, November 2, 2015. https://www.youtube.com/watch?v=BwubJJgRLRI.

Lost in Oz. Amazon Studios, 2015, 2017. Amazon Video. Streaming.

Maclaran, Pauline, and Stephen Brown. "The Center Cannot Hold: Consuming the Utopian Marketplace." *Journal of Consumer Research* 32, no. 2 (2005): 311–323.

Maguire, Gregory. *Wicked: The Life and Times of the Wicked Witch of the West*. New York: Harper Collins, 1995.

———. "Foreword: Oz and Ourselves." In *Oz Reimagined: New Tales from the Emerald City and Beyond*, edited by John Adams and Douglas Cohen. Las Vegas: 47 North, 2013. 1–5.

———. Letter to *Wicked* Cast. Gershwin Theatre.

Mancuso, Vinnie. "We Should Probably Discuss NBC's 'Emerald City.'" *Observer*, January 11, 2017. http://observer.com/2017/01/emerald-city-nbc-review-vincent-donofrio-wizard/.

Mannix, Daniel P. "The Father of *The Wizard of Oz*." *American Heritage*, December 1964.

Marks, Peter. "Kristen Chenowith, Good Luck Charm." *The Washington Post*, October 31, 2003.

———. "Season of the Witch: 'Wicked' Casts Quite a Spell." *The Washington Post*, December 18, 2005.

Matlin, Leonard. "Oz the Great and Powerful." *IndieWire*, March 8, 2007. Online http://www.indiewire.com/2013/03/oz-the-great-and-powerful-180408/. Accessed January 11, 2018.

McCall's Magazine, May 1954.

McCarthy, Anna. *The Citizen Machine: Governing by Television in 1950s America*. New York: New Press, 2010.

McCracken, Grant. "Culture and Consumption: A Theoretical Account of the Structure and Movement of the Cultural Meaning of Consumer Goods." *Journal of Consumer Research* 13 (June 1986): 71–84.

McLeod, Erin. "FROM OZ TO AIDS." *The Whig-Standard*, August 29, 1992, ProQuest.

Merli, Melissa. "'Wicked' Puts Wonderful Spin on 'Oz' as Musical Prequel." *News Gazette*, July 24, 2005.

Mickey Mouse Club. Season 3, Episode 1. September 30, 1957. "Walt Disney's Wizard of Oz." YouTube video, 10:21. Posted by freedogshampoo, August 4, 2007. https://www.youtube.com/watch?v=kJjhqBb3qGI.

Moretti, Franco. *Distant Reading.* London: Verso, 2013.

Nadel, Alan. *Television in Black and White America: Race and National Identity.* Lawrence, KS: University Press of Kansas, 2005.

"New Films: State and Orpheum." *Daily Boston Globe*, August 18, 1939.

Nye Russel, and Martin Gardner, eds. *The Wizard of Oz and Who He Was.* East Lansing: Michigan State Press, 1957, 1994.

"Oil in the Land of Oz." Energy Education Resources. https://aoghs.org/energy-education-resources/oil-in-the-land-of-oz/. Accessed October 20, 2017.

"Original Journey Back to Oz Trailer 1." YouTube video, 3:20. Posted by VIdeoSam16, December 7, 2009. https://www.youtube.com/watch?v=IuY-Psc2n_0.

"Oz Advertisement." *Ladies' Home Journal*, September 1939.

"Oz Dress Prize Awarded to Children." *Atlanta Constitution*, August 19, 1939.

Oz the Great and Powerful. Directed by Sam Raimi. 2013: Disney Studios. Amazon Video. Streaming.

"Oz the Great and Powerful Trailer." YouTube video, 1:49. Posted by Disney Movie Trailers, July 13, 2012. https://www.youtube.com/watch?v=_1NGnVLDPog.

"Oz Wiki." ppc.wikia.com/wiki/The_Wizard_of_Oz. Accessed February 1, 2018.

Paulson, Michael, and David Gelles. "'Hamilton Inc': The Path to a Billion-Dollar Broadway Show." *New York Times*, June 8, 2016. https://www.nytimes.com/2016/06/12/theater/hamilton-inc-the-path-to-a-billion-dollar-show.html.

Phillips, Michael. "Brick Road Leads to Mediocre Musicals." *Chicago Tribune*, November 2, 2003.

Pine, Joseph, and James Gilmore. *The Experience Economy.* Cambridge: Harvard Business Review Press, Updated edition, 2011.

Posner, Kenneth. Phone Interview by Kent Drummond. June 7, 2017.

Price, Linda. "Round Table Discussion of the Future of CCT." Consumer Culture Theory Consortium. Anaheim, CA, July 2017.

Pride, William, and O. C. Ferrell. *Marketing.* Boston: Cengage Learning, 2016.

Pugh, Sheenagh. *The Democratic Genre: Fan Fiction in a Literary Context.* Bridgend, Wales: Seren, 2006.

Pugh, Tison. "'Are We Cannibals, Let Me Ask? Or Are We Faithful Friends?': Food, Interspecies Cannibalism, and the Limits of Utopia in L. Frank Baum's Oz Books." *Lion & The Unicorn* 32, no. 3 (September 2008): 324–343.

———. "There Lived in the Land of Oz Two Queerly Made Men": Queer Utopianism and Antisocial Eroticism in L. Frank Baum's Oz Series." *Marvels and Tales*, 22, no. 2 (2008): 217–239.

"Radio-Television: The Weekend Trendex." *Variety*, November 7, 1956.

Reed, Rex. "The Wiz." *New York Daily News*, January 6, 1975. http://www.thewizthemusical.com/productions/original-broadway-production-1975/press-and-reviews/article/1015.

Return to Oz. Directed by Walter Murch. 1985: Disney Studios. Amazon Video. Streaming.

"Return to Oz (1985) Original Trailer." YouTube video, 1:36. Posted by SKYTV, August 1, 2011, https://www.youtube.com/watch?v=CklyKCKFtwE.

Return to Oz. Directed by F. R. Crawley et al. 1964: Rankin/Bass Productions.

"Return to Oz Intro." YouTube video, 5:05. Posted by Martin Boyce, January 30, 2012. https://www.youtube.com/watch?v=2LHjhae98tQ.

Riedel, Michael. "Fix Witch Glitch—Oz-ish Musical Takes Time Pre-B'Way." *New York Post*, July 2, 2003.

Riley, Michael O. *Oz and Beyond: The Fantasy Worlds of L. Frank Baum*. Lawrence, KS: University of Kansas Press, 1997.

Rodi, Robert. "It's Not Easy Being Green: An Alternate History of the Wicked Witch of the West." *Los Angeles Times*, October 29, 1995, ProQuest.

Rogers, Katherine M. *L. Frank Baum: Creator of Oz*. New York: St. Martins Press, 2007.

"Round Table on the Commonalities Between Macromarketing and Consumer Culture Theory." The Consumer Culture Theory Consortium, Anaheim, CA, July 2017.

Rushdie, Salman. "Out of Kansas." *New Yorker*, May 11, 1992, https://www.newyorker.com/magazine/1992/05/11/out-of-kansas.

R.W.D. "'Wizard of Oz' Opens Today." *New York Herald Tribune*, August 17 1939.

Ryman, Geoff. *Was*. Easthampton, MA: Small Beer Press, 1989, 2013.

Scaraboto, Daiane, and Eileen Fischer. "Frustrated Fatshoinistas: An Institutional Theory Perspective on Consumer Quests for Greater Choice in Mainstream Markets." *Journal of Consumer Research* 39 (April 2013): 1234–1257.

Scarfone, Jay, and William Stillman. *The Wizardry of Oz: The Artistry and Magic of the 1939 MGM Classic*. New York: Applause Books, 2004.

Schallert, Edwin. "'Wizard of Oz' Epochal as Fantasy." *Los Angeles Times*, August 10, 1939.

Scheuer, Philip. "A Town Called Hollywood." *Los Angeles Times*, November 25, 1956.

Schmitt, Bernd H. *Experiential Marketing*. New York: Simon and Schuster, Free Press, 1999.

Schroeder, Jonathan. *Visual Consumption*. London and New York: Routledge, 2002.

Schultz, Don, Stanley Tannenbaum, and Robert Lauterborn. *Integrated Marketing Communications*. Chicago: NTC Business Books, 1993.

Schwartz, Evan L. *Finding Oz: How L. Frank Baum Discovered the Great American Story*. New York: Houghton Mifflin, 2009.

Schwartz, Stephen. *Wicked: Original Cast Recording Deluxe Edition*. Various Artists. Verve B00FL3Y06G. 2013. CD.

Scott, Jay. "Tripping Out in Oz." *The Globe and Mail*, February 1, 1978.

Shirley Temple's Story Book Hour, "The Land of Oz." Season 2, Episode 1, September 18, 1969. YouTube Video, 51:22. Posted by Gerald Hine, June 3, 2015, https://www.youtube.com/watch?v=H8mD5L7QQig.

Silverman, Jeff. "One Man's Dream Brings a Different Sort of 'Oz' Story Onto the Screen." *Chicago Tribune*, June 30, 1985, ProQuest.

Starrett, Vincent. "'The Wizard of Oz.'" *Chicago Sunday Tribune Magazine*, May 2, 1954.

Stasio, Marilyn. "Witty Wiz." *Cue Magazine*, 1975. http://www.thewizthemusical.com/productions/original-broadway-production-1975/press-and-reviews/article/1026.

Stern, Mark. Interview. *SciFiWire*, 2007. www.scifi.com. Accessed January 12, 2018.

Sternfield, Jessica. *The Megamusical*. Bloomington, IN: Indiana University Press, 2006.

Stone, David. "The Women of 'Wicked Are Part of a Theatrical Movement." *Denver Post*, June 11, 2015. https://www.denverpost.com/2015/06/11/the-women-of-wicked-are-part-of-a-theatrical-movement/.

Sullivan, D. "Stage Review." *Los Angeles Times*, June 20, 1977. Proquest.

Swartz, Mark. *Oz Before the Rainbow: L. Frank Baum's The Wonderful Wizard of Oz on Stage and Screen to 1939*. New York: Johns Hopkins Press, 2000.

Tales of the Wizard of Oz. 1961–1964: Rankin Bass. "Rankin/Bass's Tales of the Wizard of Oz." YouTube video, 10:20. Posted by robby4000, December 20, 2006. https://www.youtube.com/watch?v=KS-K02xqV6w&list=PLy0m-RMkCOQbPlBpVFemGyJl50T4TkWMWj.

"Thanksgiving in Oz." Directed by Charles Swensen et al. 1980: Mueller-Rosen Productions. YouTube video, 23:46. Posted by OTAKUMEDIATV, December 4, 2015. https://www.youtube.com/watch?v=pMDDqTvJIrI&list=PL0R_avcBGqm6IbeQ9J5UNs_R3QfO-z2EJ.

The Dreamer of Oz. Directed by Jack Bender. 1990: Bedrock Productions. YouTube video, 131:15, posted by Steve Klimetti, January 29, 2018. https://www.youtube.com/watch?v=TlwveL698Ig.

"The International Wizard of Oz Club." ozclub.org. Accessed December 10, 2017.

"The Oz Bowl Game." *Time*, January 1965.

The Ozmapolitan. San Diego: Hungry Tiger Press. http://www.hungrytiger-press.com/tigertreats/ozmapolitan_1904.pdf. Accessed September 2, 2017.

"The Weirdest Wizard of Oz Adaptations Even Made." YouTube video, 6:54. Posted by Matt Blume. August 21, 2015. https://www.youtube.com/watch?v=ELTcxcPso3I.

Thielman, Sam. "Wicked Writer Explores Phenomenon." *Variety*, October 24, 2008. http://variety.com/2008/legit/news/wicked-writer-explores-phenomenon-1117994631/.

Thompson, Craig J., and Diana Haytko, "Speaking of Fashion: Consumers' Uses of Fashion Discourses and the Appropriation of Countervailing Cultural Meanings." *Journal of Consumer Research*, 24, no. 1 (1997): 15–42.

Thompson, Craig J., Locander, William, and Howard Pollio. "Putting Consumer Experience Back into Consumer Research: The Philosophy and Method of Existential Phenomenology." *Journal of Consumer Research* 16, no. 2 (1989): 133–146.

Thompson, Craig J., and Tuba Ustuner. "Women Skating on the Edge: Marketplace Performances as Ideological Edgework." *Journal of Consumer Research* 42 (2015): 235–265.

Thompson, Ruth Plumly. *Kabumbo in Oz*. Chicago: Reilly & Lee, 1922. Kindle.

Tin Man. Directed by Nick Willing et al. 2007: Imagiquest Entertainment et al. Amazon. Streaming.

"Tin Man," *Entertainment Weekly*. November 26, 2007. http://ew.com/article/2007/11/26/tin-man/.

Tolkien, J. R. R. "On Faerie Stories." In *Tree and Leaf*. New York, Houghton Mifflin, 1964. 3–73.

———. "Forward." *The Fellowship of the Rings*. New York: Houghton Mifflin, 1965.

TV Guide, 1956. Image reproduced on Ozmuseum.com. https://ozmuseum.com/blogs/news/15727188-is-this-the-road-to-iconic. Accessed November 2, 2017.

Vick, Lindsay. Interview by Kent Drummond. August 18, 2017.

Vidal, Gore. "On Rereading the Oz Books." *The New York Review of Books*. October 3, 1977, ProQuest.

Wade, Tony. "The 'Wizard of Oz' Used to be an Annual Television Event." *Daily Republic*, November 26, 2015. http://www.dailyrepublic.com/solano-news/local-features/local-lifestyle-columns/the-wizard-of-oz-used-to-be-an-annual-television-event/. Accessed October 20, 2017.

Watts, Douglas. "Fine Cast and Splendid Look in Wiz." *New York Daily Review*, 1975. http://www.thewizthemusical.com/productions/original-broadway-production-1975/press-and-reviews/article/1024.

Weingarten, P. "People." *Chicago Tribune*, December 24, 1976, ProQuest.

"Wicked Author Gregory Maguire Is Headed Out of Oz." *Wired*, February 20, 2013. Online. https://www.wired.com/2013/02/geeks-guide-gregory-maguire/. Accessed February 10, 2018.

Wicked on Broadway TV Commericial," YouTube video, 0:31. Posted by Serino/Coyne, May 31, 2011. https://www.youtube.com/watch?v=E7z-EQk08Mo.

Williams, Lee. "Totally Wicked; An Unforgettable Musical Breaks All the Rules." *Houston Press*, November 3, 2005.

Winer, Linda. "Tempo the Arts." *Chicago Tribune*, November 13, 1976, Proquest.

———. "Bewitched and Bothered, Too/Bewildering 'Wicked' Tries to Be Both Dark and Cute; so Witch Is It?" *Newsday*, October 31, 2003.

Witchel, Alex. "Mr. Wicked." *New York Times Magazine*, March 11, 2007. http://www.nytimes.com/2007/03/11/magazine/11maguire.t.html.

Witkowski, Terry. "The Commonalities Between Macromarketing and Consumer Culture Theory." Paper Presented the Consumer Culture Theory Consortium, Anaheim, CA, July 2017.

The Wiz. Directed by Sidney Lumet. 1978: Universal; Amazon. Streaming.

The Wizard of Oz. Directed by Larry Semon. 1925: Chadwick Pictures Corporation. YouTube, 124:56. Posted May 24, 2015. https://www.youtube.com/watch?v=uDiXIgfQSu0.

The Wizard of Oz. Directed by Ted Eshbaugh. 1933: Ted Eshbaugh Studios. YouTube, 7:45. Posted on January 15, 2014. https://www.youtube.com/watch?v=QlcivMXxXPk.

The Wizard of Oz. Directed by Victor Fleming. 1939: MGM; Warner Home Video, 2013. DVD.

"'The Wizard of Oz.'" *Hartford Courant*, August 25, 1939.

"The Wizard of Oz—Early Edition." *Christian Science Monitor*, October 23, 1939.

"The Wizard of Oz Original Trailer" [1939]. YouTube video, 2:11. Posted November 26, 2013. https://www.youtube.com/watch?v=_AtOEMlOahg.

The Wonderful Wizard of Oz. Directed by Otis Turner. 1910: Selig Polyscope Company. YouTube, 13:30. Posted January 18, 2011. https://www.youtube.com/watch?v=jpV29YZ7Ksw.

"Wizard of Oz Commercials." YouTube Playlist. Digital DG.

"'Wizard of Oz,' Review." *Variety*, August 16, 1939.

"'Wizard of Oz' Smash Hit." *Los Angeles Times*, August 29, 1939.

"'Wizard of Oz, Special Section'." *Modern Screen*, August 1939.

"'Wizard of Oz' Is Well Done." *Chicago Daily Tribune*, August 26, 1939.

Wizard of Oz on Ice. Directed by Paul Miller. 1996: CBS. YouTube video. Posted by WizardofOzfan39, August 20, 2008. https://www.youtube.com/watch?v=5gm55VXGZY4.

Wloszczyna, Susan. "Legends of Oz: Dorothy's Return." *Roger Ebert.com*. May 9, 2014. https://www.rogerebert.com/reviews/legends-of-oz-dorothys-return-2014. Accessed January 14, 2018.

Wolf, Stacy. "Wicked Divas, Musical Theatre, and Internet Girl Fans." *Camera Obscura* 65 (2007): 351–376.

————. "'Defying Gravity': Queer Conventions in the Musical Wicked." *Theatre Journal* 60, no. 1 (2008): 1–21.

"Youngsters Do Own 'Wizard of Oz.'" *The Christian Science Monitor,* August 18, 1939.

Zeiger, Scott. "Keynote Address on the Consumer Experience in Arts and Culture." Leadership Nouveau Conference, New York, 2016.

INDEX

© The Editor(s) (if applicable) and The Author(s) 2018
K. Drummond et al., *The Road to Wicked*,
https://doi.org/10.1007/978-3-319-93106-7

Beck, Glenn, 4
Becker, Howard, 4, 209
"Behind the Emerald Curtain" tour,
     235, 236, 238, 240, 244
Bolger, Roy, 84, 86, 99, 198
Bolter, David, 8, 15
Bradbury, Ray, 6, 7, 115, 142
Britton, Andrew, 138
Broadcast years, 22, 106, 121, 130,
     132–134, 142, 147, 266, 294
Broadway Green Alliance (BGA), 253
"BullyBust" Initiative, 254, 255
Busse, Kristine, 13

C
Chabon, Michael, 13
Chenowith, Kristen, 160, 165
Chittenango, Oz Industry, 119, 131,
     281, 282
Collins, James, 37, 38, 44
Consumer culture, 15, 21, 34, 39
Consumer Culture Theory (CCT), 5,
     16, 17, 299
Consumption experiences, 3, 18, 35,
     62, 235, 244
Convergence culture, 5, 14, 57, 273,
     275
Cosgrove, Rachel, 118
Cote, David, 25
Cowardly Lion, 7, 54, 57, 63, 86, 95,
     96, 110, 120, 127, 141, 163,
     167, 186, 212, 265, 283
Coyne, Nancy, 164, 165, 227, 231
Cultural sustainability, 3, 4, 9, 10, 13–
     15, 17, 18, 21, 24, 26, 34, 67,
     80–82, 98–100, 105, 111–113,
     115–119, 130, 132, 135, 140,
     142, 143, 147, 150, 203, 263,
     264, 266, 273, 276, 280, 282,
     289, 290, 299, 303–305
Customer Lifetime Value (CLV), 243

D
Daily Ozmapolitan, 274, 276
Day in Oz, promotion play, 77, 295
"Defying Gravity", 25, 164, 172, 185,
     187, 189, 193, 196, 202, 205,
     215, 217–221, 224, 225, 229
Denslow, William, 44, 46, 47, 86
Department stores, 90
Depth interviews, 23, 171
Derecho, Abigail, 13
Di Giere, Carol, 25, 157
Disney Studios, 138, 139, 267
     Oz the Great and Powerful, 3, 24,
          266–270, 273, 275
     Rainbow Road to Oz, 127, 128, 138
     Return to Oz, 23, 129, 138–141,
          144, 266, 280
     Snow White, 82, 85, 264, 268
Dodd, Dorothy, 114
Dorothy, 4, 8, 12, 35, 54, 55, 57, 58,
     64, 76, 85, 89, 94–97, 110, 114,
     120, 122, 127–129, 132, 137,
     139–141, 143, 146, 164, 197,
     265, 268, 270–272, 280, 281,
     284, 301
Dorothy Meets Ozma of Oz, animated
     short, 128
Dreamer of Oz, The, 33, 45, 55, 62,
     119–122

E
Elphaba, 158–161, 164, 165, 174–
     176, 178, 180–185, 187–191,
     196, 202, 205, 209, 211,
     212, 214, 217–224, 226, 228,
     236, 237, 240–242, 244–248,
     252–254, 268, 304
Embodied consumption, 245
Emerald City, 3, 6, 7, 9, 24, 34,
     48, 50, 58, 65, 129, 132, 133,
     136, 141, 145, 164, 265, 266,
     270–273, 275, 278, 303

experiential marketing (EM), 5, 16,
    18, 20, 26, 49, 234, 235, 240,
    244, 256, 299, 301

F
Fairylogue and Radio Plays, 53–55,
    77, 82, 87, 235
Fanfiction
    Oz fanfiction, 275
    theory, 14
Farmer, Phillip Jose, 23, 142–144
Ferrell, O.C., 259
"For Good", 161, 184, 189, 202,
    203, 205, 215, 217, 219–221,
    229, 247, 248, 253, 258
Ford Star Jubilee, 105, 108, 109
Freed, Arthur, 95–97, 100, 147
Fricke, John, 17, 24, 90, 111, 117,
    118, 263, 275, 278–280, 284

G
Game of Thrones, 234, 271, 272
Garland, Judy, 86, 88, 89, 91, 97, 99,
    108–111, 129, 135, 139, 143,
    197, 198, 231, 268, 269, 278,
    284
Gershwin Theatre, 228, 255
Gilmore, David, 18
Gladwell, Malcolm, *Tipping Point*, 192
Glinda, 64, 129, 131, 143, 145, 161,
    164, 165, 177, 183–189, 191,
    202, 210, 211, 213, 214, 217,
    220, 222, 224, 227, 240–242,
    245, 247, 250, 252, 268, 281
Grusin, Richard, 8, 15

H
Haley, Jack, 86, 99, 198
Hamilton, Margaret, 8, 84, 129, 145,
    146, 179, 268, 283

Harper, Ken, 134, 135, 137
Harry Potter, 3, 9, 10, 15, 58, 163,
    165, 204, 265, 267
Hawkes, Jon, 4
Hearn, Michael Patrick, 24, 118
Hedonic consumption, 35, 65
Hellekson, Karen, 13
Holder, Geoffrey, 136
Holzman, Winnie, 21, 23, 147,
    157–161, 195, 210–212, 214,
    215, 232, 238, 245, 256
Hutcheon, Linda, 9–12, 16, 200, 204

I
Integrated Marketing
    Communications (IMC), 50, 245
International Wizard of Oz Club, 122,
    274, 276, 293

J
Jackson, Shirley, 115
Jauss, Hans Robert, 132
Jenkins, Henry, 9, 14, 15, 273, 274
Journey Back to Oz, 129, 130

K
Kabumpo in Oz, 76

L
Lahr, Burt, 86, 96, 99, 109, 117, 163,
    198
Laird, Paul, 25, 216
Land of Oz, theme park, 131
Lanier, Clinton, 18
Lears, Jackson, 34, 35
Legends of Oz: Dorothy's Return, 270
LeRoy, Mervyn, 84, 85, 94, 95, 134,
    138
Lord of the Rings, 13, 204, 265, 271

CPSIA information can be obtained
at www.ICGtesting.com
Printed in the USA
LVHW071654180419
614692LV00012B/330/P